The DevOps 2.0 Toolkit

Automating the Continuous Deployment Pipeline with
Containerized Microservices

Viktor Farcic

The DevOps 2.0 Toolkit

Automating the Continuous Deployment Pipeline with Containerized Microservices

Viktor Farcic

ISBN 978-1523917440

Tweet This Book!

Please help Viktor Farcic by spreading the word about this book on Twitter!

The suggested tweet for this book is:

I just bought The DevOps 2.0 Toolkit by @vfarcic

The suggested hashtag for this book is #devops2book.

Find out what other people are saying about the book by clicking on this link to search for this hashtag on Twitter:

https://twitter.com/search?q=#devops2book

Contents

Preface

I started my career as a developer. During those early days, all I knew (and thought I should know) was to write code. I believed that a great software designer is a person that is proficient in writing code and that the path to the mastery of the craft was to know everything about a single programming language of choice. Later on, that changed and I started taking an interest in different programming languages. I switched from Pascal to Basic and then ASP. When Java and, later on, .Net came into existence, I learned benefits of object oriented programming. Python, Perl, Bash, HTML, JavaScript, Scala... Each programming language brought something new and taught me how to think differently and how to pick the right tool for the task at hand. With each new language I learned, I felt like I was closer to being an expert. All I wanted was to become a senior programmer. That desire changed with time. I learned that if I was to do my job well, I had to become a *software craftsman*. I had to learn much more than to type code. Testing became my obsession for some time, and now I consider it an integral part of development. Except in very special cases, each line of code I write is done with *test-driven development (TDD)*. It became an indispensable part of my tool-belt. I also learned that I had to be close to the customer and work with him side by side while defining what should be done. All that and many other things led me to *software architecture*. Understanding the "big picture" and trying to fit different pieces into one big system was the challenge that I learned to like.

Throughout all the years I've been working in the software industry, there was no single tool, framework or practice that I admired more than *continuous integration (CI)* and, later on, *continuous delivery (CD)*. The real meaning of that statement hides behind the scope of what CI/CD envelops. In the beginning, I thought that CI/CD means that I knew *Jenkins* and was able to write scripts. As the time passed I got more and more involved and learned that CI/CD relates to almost every aspect of software development. That knowledge came at a cost. I failed (more than once) to create a successful CI pipeline with applications I worked with at the time. Even though others considered the result a success, now I know that it was a failure because the approach I took was wrong. CI/CD cannot be done without making architectural decisions. Similar can be said for tests, configurations, environments, fail-over, and so on. To create a successful implementation of CI/CD, we need to make a lot of changes that, on the first look, do not seem to be directly related. We need to apply some patterns and practices from the very beginning. We have to think about architecture, testing, coupling, packaging, fault tolerance, and many other things. CI/CD requires us to influence almost every aspect of software development. That diversity is what made me fall in love with it. By practicing CI/CD we are influencing and improving almost every aspect of the software development life cycle.

To be truly proficient with CI/CD, we need to be much more than experts in operations. The DevOps movement was a significant improvement that combined traditional operations with advantages that development could bring. I think that is not enough. We need to know and influence architecture, testing, development, operations and even customer negotiations if we want to gain all the benefits that CI/CD can bring. Even the name DevOps as the driving force behind the CI/CD is not suitable since it's not only about development and operations but everything related to software development. It should also include architects, testers, and even managers. DevOps was a vast improvement when compared to the traditional operations by combining them with development. The movement understood that manually running operations is not an option given current business demands and that there is no automation without development. I think that the time came to redefine DevOps by extending its scope. Since the name *DevOpsArchTestManageAndEverythingElse* is too cumbersome to remember and close to impossible to pronounce, I opt for **DevOps 2.0**. It's the next generation that should drop the heavy do-it-all products for smaller tools designed to do very specific tasks. It's the switch that should go back to the beginning and not only make sure that operations are automated but that the whole system is designed in a way that it can be automated, fast, scalable, fault-tolerant, with zero-downtime, easy to monitor, and so on. We cannot accomplish this by simply automating manual procedures and employing a single do-it-all tool. We need to go much deeper than that and start refactoring the whole system both on the technological as well as the procedural level.

Overview

This book is about different techniques that help us architect software in a better and more efficient way with *microservices* packed as *immutable containers*, *tested* and *deployed continuously* to servers that are *automatically provisioned* with *configuration management* tools. It's about fast, reliable and continuous deployments with *zero-downtime* and ability to *roll-back*. It's about *scaling* to any number of servers, design of *self-healing systems* capable of recuperation from both hardware and software failures and about *centralized logging and monitoring* of the cluster.

In other words, this book envelops the whole *microservices development and deployment lifecycle* using some of the latest and greatest practices and tools. We'll use *Docker, Kubernetes, Ansible, Ubuntu, Docker Swarm and Docker Compose, Consul, etcd, Registrator, confd, Jenkins*, and so on. We'll go through many practices and, even more, tools.

Finally, while there will be a lot of theory, this is a hands-on book. You won't be able to complete it by reading it in a metro on a way to work. You'll have to read this book while in front of a computer getting your hands dirty. Eventually, you might get stuck and in need of help. Or you might want to write a review or comment on the book's content. Please post your thoughts on the The DevOps 2.0 Toolkit channel in Disqus[1]. If you prefer one-on-one discussion, feel free to send me an email to *viktor@farcic.com*, or to contact me on HangOuts, and I'll give my best to help you out.

---

[1]https://disqus.com/home/channel/thedevops20toolkit/

Audience

This book is for professionals interested in the full microservices lifecycle combined with continuous deployment and containers. Due to the very broad scope, target audience could be *architects* who want to know how to design their systems around microservices. It could be *DevOps* wanting to know how to apply modern configuration management practices and continuously deploy applications packed in containers. It is for *developers* who would like to take the process back into their hands as well as for *managers* who would like to gain a better understanding of the process used to deliver software from the beginning to the end. We'll speak about scaling and monitoring systems. We'll even work on the design (and implementation) of self-healing systems capable of recuperation from failures (be it of hardware or software nature). We'll deploy our applications continuously directly to production without any downtime and with the ability to rollback at any time.

This book is for *everyone wanting to know more about the software development lifecycle* starting from requirements and design, through development and testing all the way until deployment and post-deployment phases. We'll create the processes taking into account best practices developed by and for some of the biggest companies.

About the Author

Viktor Farcic is a Senior Consultant at CloudBees[2].

He coded using a plethora of languages starting with Pascal (yes, he is old), Basic (before it got Visual prefix), ASP (before it got .Net suffix), C, C++, Perl, Python, ASP.Net, Visual Basic, C#, JavaScript, etc. He never worked with Fortran. His current favorites are **Scala** and **JavaScript** even though most of his office hours he spends with **Java**.

His big passions are Microservices, Continuous Deployment and Test-Driven Development (TDD).

He often speaks at community gatherings and conferences.

He wrote Test-Driven Java Development[3].

---

[2]https://www.cloudbees.com/

[3]https://www.packtpub.com/application-development/test-driven-java-development

The DevOps Ideal

Working on small greenfield projects is great. The last one I was involved with was during the summer of 2015 and, even though it had its share of problems, it was a real pleasure. Working with a small and relatively new set of products allowed us to choose technologies, practices, and frameworks we liked. Shall we use microservices? Yes, why not. Shall we try Polymer and GoLang? Sure! Not having baggage that holds you down is a wonderful feeling. A wrong decision would put us back for a week, but it would not put in danger years of work someone else did before us. Simply put, there was no legacy system to think about and be afraid of.

Most of my career was not like that. I had the opportunity, or a curse, to work on big inherited systems. I worked for companies that existed long before I joined them and, for better or worse, already had their systems in place. I had to balance the need for innovation and improvement with obvious requirement that existing business must continue operating uninterrupted. During all those years I was continuously trying to discover new ways to improve those systems. It pains me to admit, but many of those attempts were failures.

We'll explore those failures in order to understand better the motivations that lead to the advancements we'll discuss throughout this books.

Continuous Integration, Delivery, and Deployment

Discovering CI and, later on, CD, was one of the crucial points in my career. It all made perfect sense. The integration phase back in those days could last anything from days to weeks or even months. It was the period we all dreaded. After months of work performed by different teams working on different services or applications, the first day of the integration phase was the definition of hell on earth. If I didn't know better, I'd say that Dante was a developer and wrote Infierno during the integration phase.

On the dreaded first day of the integration phase, we would all come to the office with grim faces. Only whispers could be heard while the integration engineer would announce that the whole system was set up, and the "game" could begin. He would turn it on and, sometimes, the result would be a blank screen. Months of work in isolation would prove, one more time, to be a disaster. Services and applications could not be integrated, and the long process of fixing problems would begin. In some cases, we would need to redo weeks of work. Requirements defined in advance were, as always, subject to different interpretations and those differences are nowhere more noticeable than in the integration phase.

Then *eXtreme Programming (XP)* practices came into existence and, with them, *continuous integration (CI)*. The idea that integration should be done continuously today sounds like something obvious. Duh! Of course, you should not wait until the last moment to integrate! Back then, in the waterfall era, such a thing was not so obvious as today. We implemented a continuous integration pipeline and started checking out every commit, running static analysis, unit and functional tests, packaging, deploying and running integration tests. If any of those phases failed, we would abandon what we were doing and made fixing the problem detected by the pipeline our priority. The pipeline itself was fast. Minutes after someone would make a commit to the repository we would get a notification if something failed. Later on, *continuous delivery (CD)* started to take ground, and we would have confidence that every commit that passed the whole pipeline could be deployed to production. We could do even better and not only attest that each build is production ready, but apply *continuous deployment* and deploy every build without waiting for (manual) confirmation from anyone. And the best part of all that was that everything was fully automated.

It was a dream come true. Literally! It was a dream. It wasn't something we managed to turn into reality. Why was that? We made mistakes. We thought that CI/CD is a task for the operations department (today we'd call them *DevOPS*). We thought that we could create a process that wraps around applications and services. We thought that CI tools and frameworks are ready. We thought that architecture, testing, business negotiations and other tasks were the job for someone else. We were wrong. I was wrong.

Today I know that successful CI/CD means that no stone can be left unturned. We need to influence everything; from architecture through testing, development and operations all the way until management and business expectations. But let us go back again. What went wrong in those failures of mine?

Architecture

Trying to fit a monolithic application developed by many people throughout the years, without tests, with tight coupling and outdated technology is like an attempt to make an eighty-year-old lady look young again. We can improve her looks, but the best we can do is make her look a bit less old, not young. Some systems are, simply put, too old to be worth the "modernization" effort. I tried it, many times, and the result was never as expected. Sometimes, the effort in making it "young again" is not cost effective. On the other hand, I could not go to the client of, let's say, a bank, and say "we're going to rewrite your whole system." Risks are too big to rewrite everything and, be it as it might, due to its tight coupling, age, and outdated technology, changing parts of it is not worth the effort. The commonly taken option was to start building the new system and, in parallel, maintain the old one until everything was done. That was always a disaster. It can take years to finish such a project, and we all know what happens with things planned for such a long term. That's not even the waterfall approach. That's like standing at the bottom of Niagara Falls wondering why you get wet. Even doing trivial things like updating the JDK was quite a feat. And those were the cases when I would consider myself lucky. What would you do with, for example, codebase done in Fortran or Cobol?

Then I heard about microservices. It was like music to my ears. The idea that we can build many small independent services that can be maintained by small teams, have codebase that can be understood in no time, being able to change framework, programming language or a database without affecting the rest of the system and being able to deploy it independently from the rest of the system was too good to be true. We could, finally, start taking parts of the monolithic application out without putting the whole system at (significant) risk. It sounded too good to be true. And it was. Benefits came with downsides. Deploying and maintaining a vast number of services turned out to be a heavy burden. We had to compromise and start standardizing services (killing innovation), we created shared libraries (coupling again), we were deploying them in groups (slowing everything), and so on. In other words, we had to remove the benefits microservices were supposed to bring. And let's not even speak of configurations and the mess they created inside servers. Those were the times I try to forget. We had enough problems like that with monoliths. Microservices only multiplied them. It was a failure. However, I was not yet ready to give up. Call me a masochist.

I had to face problems one at a time, and one of the crucial ones was deployments.

Deployments

You know the process. Assemble some artifacts (JAR, WAR, DLL, or whatever is the result of your programming language), deploy it to the server that is already polluted with... I cannot even finish the sentence because, in many cases, we did not even know what was on the servers. With enough time, any server maintained manually becomes full of "things". Libraries, executables, configurations, gremlins and trolls. It would start to develop its own personality. Old and grumpy, fast but unreliable, demanding, and so on. The only thing all the servers had in common was that they were all different, and no one could be sure that software tested in, let's say, pre-production environment would behave the same when deployed to production. It was a lottery. You might get lucky, but most likely you won't. Hope dies last.

You might, rightfully, wonder why we didn't use virtual machines in those days. Well, there are two answers to that question, and they depend on the definition of "those days". One answer is that in "those days" we didn't have virtual machines, or they were so new that management was too scared to approve their usage. The other answer is that later on we did use VMs, and that was the real improvement. We could copy production environment and use it as, let's say testing environment. Except that there was still a lot of work to update configurations, networking, and so on. Besides, we still did not know what was accumulated on those machines throughout the years. We just knew how to duplicate them. That still did not solve the problem that configurations were different from one VM to another as well as that a copy is the same as the original only for a short period. Do the deployment, change some configuration, bada bing, bada boom, you go back to the problem of testing something that is not the same as it will be in production. Differences accumulate with time unless you have a repeatable and reliable automated process instead of manual human interventions. If such a thing would exist, we could create immutable servers. Instead of deploying applications to existing servers and go down the path of accumulating differences, we could create a new VM as part of the CI/CD pipeline. So, instead of creating JARs, WAR, DLLs, and so on, we started creating VMs. Every time there was a new release it would come as a complete server built from scratch. That way we would know that what was tested is what goes into production. Create new VM with software deployed, test it and switch your production router to point from the old to the new one.

It was awesome, except that it was slow and resource demanding. Having a separate VM for each service is overkill. Still, armed with patience, immutable servers were a good idea, but the way we used that approach and the tools required to support it were not good enough.

Orchestration

The orchestration was the key. *Puppet* and *Chef* proved to be a big help. Programming everything related to servers setup and deployment was a huge improvement. Not only that the time needed to setup servers and deploy software dropped drastically, but we could, finally, accomplish a more reliable process. Having humans (read operations department) manually running those types of tasks was a recipe for disaster. Finally a story with a happy ending? Not really. You probably started noticing a pattern. As soon as one improvement was accomplished, it turned out that it, often, comes with a high price. Given enough time, Puppet and Chef scripts and configurations turn into an enormous pile of **** (I was told not to use certain words so please fill in the blanks with your imagination). Maintaining them tends to become a nightmare in itself. Still, with orchestration tools, we could drastically reduce the time it took to create immutable VMs. Something is better than nothing.

The Light at the End of the Deployment Pipeline

I could go on and on describing problems we faced. Don't take me wrong. All those initiatives were improvements and have their place in software history. But history is the past, and we live in the present trying to look into the future. Many, if not all of the problems we had before are now solved. *Ansible* proved that orchestration does not need to be complicated to set up nor hard to maintain. With the appearance of *Docker*, containers are slowly replacing VMs as the preferable way to create immutable deployments. New operating systems are emerging and fully embracing containers as first class citizens. Tools for service discovery are showing us new horizons. *Swarm, Kubernetes and Mesos/DCOS* are opening doors into areas that were hard to imagine only a few years ago.

Microservices are slowly becoming the preferred way to build big, easy to maintain and highly scalable systems thanks to tools like *Docker, CoreOS, etcd, Consul, Fleet, Mesos, Rocket*, and others. The idea was always great, but we did not have the tools to make it work properly. Now we do! That does not mean that all our problems are gone. It means that when we solve one problem, the bar moves higher up, and new issues emerge.

I started by complaining about the past. That will not happen again. This book is for readers who do not want to live in the past but present. This book is about preparations for the future. This book is about stepping through the looking glass, about venturing into new areas and about looking at things from a new angle.

This is your last chance. After this, there is no turning back. You take the blue pill - the story ends, you wake up in your bed and believe whatever you want to believe. You take the red pill - you stay in Wonderland and I show you how deep the rabbit-hole goes.

– Morpheus (Matrix)

If you took the blue pill, I hope that you didn't buy this book and got this far by reading the free sample. There are no hard feelings. We all have different aspirations and goals. If, on the other hand, you chose the red one, you are in for a ride. It will be like a roller coaster, and we are yet to discover what awaits us at the end of the ride.

The Implementation Breakthrough: Continuous Deployment, Microservices, and Containers

On the first look *continuous deployment (CD)*, *microservices (MS)* and *containers* might seem like three unrelated subjects. After all, *DevOps* movement does not stipulate that microservices are necessary for continuous deployment, nor microservices need to be packaged into containers. However, when those three are combined, new doors open waiting for us to step through. Recent developments in the area of containers and the concept of immutable deployments enable us to overcome many of the problems microservices had before. They, on the other hand, allow us to gain flexibility and speed without which CD is not possible or cost effective.

Before we move forward with this line of thinking, we'll try to define correctly each of those terms.

Continuous Integration

To understand *continuous deployment* we should first define its predecessors; *continuous integration* and *continuous delivery*.

Integration phase of a project development tended to be one of the most painful stages in software development life-cycle. We would spend weeks, months or even years working in separate teams dedicated to separate applications and services. Each of those teams would have their set of requirements and tried their best to meet them. While it wasn't hard to periodically verify each of those applications and services in isolation, we all dreaded the moment when team leads would decide that the time has come to integrate them into a unique delivery. Armed with the experience from previous projects, we knew that integration will be problematic. We knew that we will discover problems, unmet dependencies, interfaces that do not communicate with each others correctly and that managers will get disappointed, frustrated, and nervous. It was not uncommon to spend weeks or even months in this phase. The worse part of all that was that a bug found during the integration phase could mean going back and redoing days or weeks worth of work. If someone asked me how a feel about integration I'd say that it was closest I could get to becoming permanently depressed. Those were different times. We thought that was the "right" way to develop applications.

A lot changed since then. *Extreme Programming (XP)* and other agile methodologies become familiar, automated testing become frequent, and continuous integration started to take ground. Today we know that the way we developed software back then was wrong. The industry moved a long way since then.

Continuous integration (CI) usually refers to integrating, building, and testing code within the development environment. It requires developers to integrate code into a shared repository often. How often is often can be interpreted in many ways and it depends on the size of the team, the size of the project and the number of hours we dedicate to coding. In most cases it means that coders either push directly to the shared repository or merge their code with it. No matter whether we're pushing or merging, those actions should, in most cases, be done at least a couple of times a day. Getting code to the shared repository is not enough and we need to have a pipeline that, as a minimum, checks out the code and runs all the tests related, directly or indirectly, to the code corresponding to the repository. The result of the execution of the pipeline can be either *red* or *green*. Something failed, or everything was run without any problems. In the former case, minimum action would be to notify the person who committed the code.

The continuous integration pipeline should run on every commit or push. Unlike continuous delivery, continuous integration does not have a clearly defined goal of that pipeline. Saying that one application integrates with others does not tell us a lot about its production readiness. We do not know how much more work is required to get to the stage when the code can be delivered to production. All we are truly striving for is the knowledge that a commit did not break any of the existing tests. Never the less, CI is a huge improvement when done right. In many cases, it is a very hard practice to implement, but once everyone is comfortable with it, the results are often very impressive.

Integration tests need to be committed together with the implementation code, if not before. To gain maximum benefits, we should write tests in *test-driven development (TDD)* fashion. That way, not only that tests are ready for commit together with implementation, but we know that they are not faulty and would not pass no matter what we do. There are many other benefits TDD brings to the table and, if you haven't already, I strongly recommend to adopt it. You might want to consult the Test-Driven Development[4] section of the Technology Conversations[5] blog.

Tests are not the only CI prerequisite. One of the most important rules is that when the pipeline fails, fixing the problem has higher priority than any other task. If this action is postponed, next executions of the pipeline will fail as well. People will start ignoring the failure notifications and, slowly, CI process will begin losing its purpose. The sooner we fix the problem discovered during the execution of the CI pipeline, the better we are. If corrective action is taken immediately, knowledge about the potential cause of the problem is still fresh (after all, it's been only a few minutes between the commit and the failure notification) and fixing it should be trivial.

So how does it work? Details depend on tools, programming language, project, and many other factors. The most common flow is the following.

- Pushing to the code repository
- Static analysis
- Pre-deployment testing

---

[4] http://technologyconversations.com/category/test-driven-development/

[5] http://technologyconversations.com/

- Packaging and deployment to the test environment
- Post-deployment testing

Pushing to the Code Repository

Developers work on features in separate branches. Once they feel comfortable that their work is stable, the branch they've been working on is merged with the mainline (or trunk). More advanced teams may skip feature branches altogether and commit directly to the mainline. The crucial point is that the mainline branch (or trunk) needs to receive commits often (either through merges or direct pushes). If days or weeks pass, changes accumulate and benefits of using continuous integration diminish. In that case, there is no fast feedback since the integration with other people's code is postponed. On the other hand, CI tools (we'll talk about them later) are monitoring the code repository, and whenever a commit is detected, the code is checked out (or cloned) and the CI pipeline is run. The pipeline itself consists of a set of automated tasks run in parallel or sequentially. The result of the pipeline is either a failure in one of its steps or a promotion. As a minimum, failure should result in some form of a notification sent to the developer that pushed the commit that resulted in a failed pipeline. It should be his responsibility to fix the problem (after all, he knows best how to fix a problem created by him only minutes ago) and do another commit to the repository that, in turn, will trigger another execution of the pipeline. This developer should consider fixing the problem his highest priority task so that the pipeline continues being "green" and avoid failures that would be produced by commits from other developers. Try to keep a number of people who receive the failure notification to a minimum. The whole process from detecting a problem until it is fixed should be as fast as possible. The more people are involved, the more administrative work tends to happen and the more time is spent until the fix is committed. If, on the other hand, the pipeline runs successfully throughout all its tasks, the package produced throughout the process is promoted to the next stage and, in most cases, given to testers for manual verifications. Due to the difference in speed between the pipeline (minutes) and manual testing (hours or days), not every pipeline execution is taken by QAs.

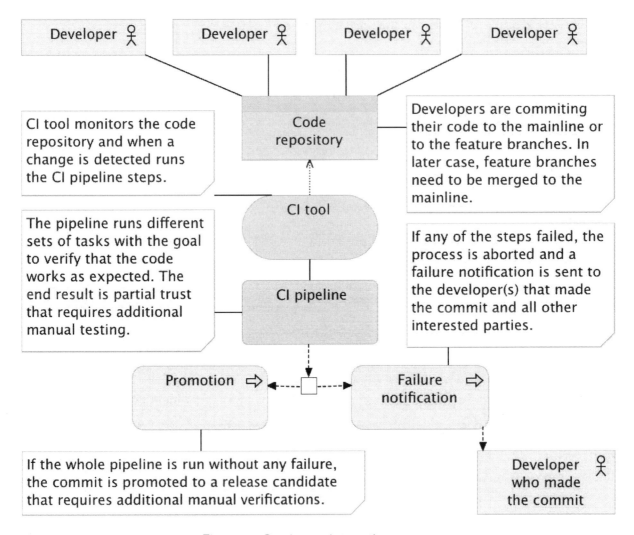

Figure 2-1: Continuous integration process

The first step in the continuous integration pipeline is often static analysis.

Static Analysis

Static analysis is the analysis of computer software that is performed without actually executing programs. Like its opposite, the analysis performed while executing programs is known as *dynamic analysis.*

The *static analysis* goals vary from highlighting possible coding errors to making sure that agreed formatting is followed. While benefits of using static analysis are questionable, the effort required to implement it is so small that there is no real reason not to use it.

I won't provide a comprehensive list of tools since they vary from one programming language to another. CheckStyle[6] and FindBugs[7] for Java, JSLint[8] and JSHint[9] for JavaScript, and PMD[10] for a variety of languages, are only a few examples.

Static analysis is often the first step in the pipeline for the simple reason that its execution tends to be very fast and in most cases faster than any other step we have in the pipeline. All we have to do is choose the tools and often spend a little up-front time in setting up the rules we want them to use. From there on, the cost of the maintenance effort is close to nothing. Since it should not take more than few seconds to run this step, the cost in time is also negligible.

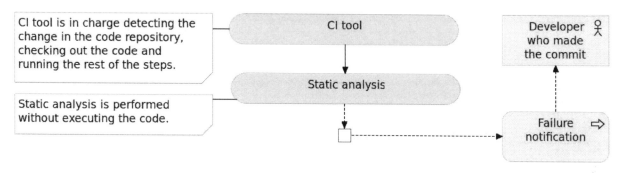

Figure 2-2: Continuous integration pipeline: static analysis

With the static analysis set up, our pipeline just started, and we can move to pre-deployment testing.

Pre-Deployment Testing

Unlike (optional) static analysis, *pre-deployment* tests should be mandatory. I intentionally avoided more specific name for those tests because it depends on the architecture, programming language, and frameworks. As a rule of thumb, all types of tests that do not require code to be deployed to a server should be run in this phase. *Unit tests* always fall into this category and with few others that might be run as well. If, for example, you can execute *functional tests* without deploying the code, run them now.

Pre-deployment testing is probably the most critical phase in *continuous integration pipeline*. While it does not provide all the certainty that we need, and it does not substitute *post-deployment testing*, tests run in this phase are relatively easy to write, should be very fast to execute and they tend to provide much bigger code coverage than other types of tests (for example integration and performance).

---

[6]http://checkstyle.sourceforge.net/

[7]http://findbugs.sourceforge.net/

[8]http://www.jslint.com/

[9]http://jshint.com/

[10]https://pmd.github.io/

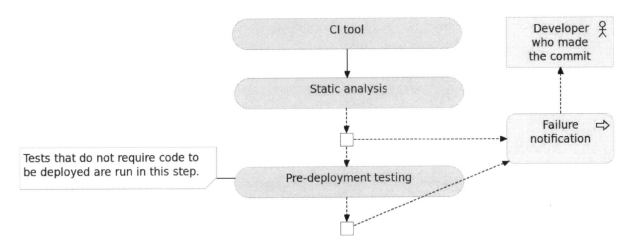

Figure 2-3: Continuous integration pipeline: pre-deployment testing

Packaging and Deployment to the Test Environment

Once we did all types of verifications that could be done without actually deploying the application, it is time to package it. The method to do it would depend on framework and programming language. In the Java world we would create JAR or WAR files, for JavaScript we would minimize the code and maybe send it to the CDN server, and so on and so forth. Some programming languages do not require us to do anything in this phase except possibly compress all the files into a ZIP or TAR a file for easier transfer to servers. An optional, but in the case of this book mandatory, step is to create a container that contains not only the package but also all other dependencies our application might need like libraries, runtime environment, application server, and so on.

Once the deployment package is created, we can proceed to deploy it to a test environment. Depending on the capacity of the servers you might need to deploy to multiple boxes with, for example, one being dedicated to performance testing and the other for all the rest of tests that require deployment.

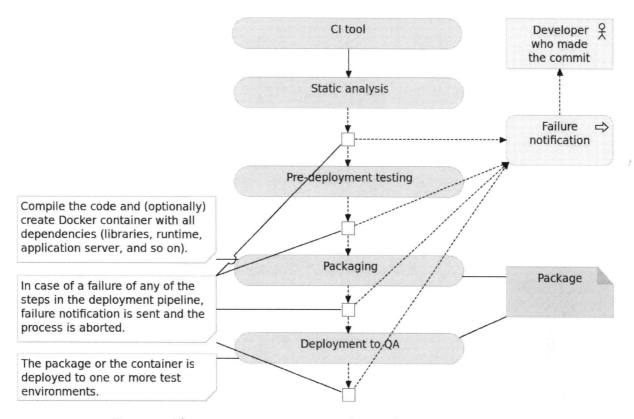

Figure 2-4: The continuous integration pipeline: packaging and deployment

Post-Deployment Testing

Once deployed to a test environment, we can execute the rest of the tests; those that could not be run without deploying the application or a service as well as those that prove that the integration was successful. Again, types of tests that can be run in this phase depend on frameworks and programming language but, as a general rule, they include functional, integration and performance tests.

Exact tools and technologies used to write and run those tests will depend on many aspects. My personal preference is to use *behavior-driven development* for all functional tests that, at the same time, act as acceptance criteria and Gatling[11] for performance tests.

Once the execution of post-deployment tests is finished successfully, the continuous integration pipeline is typically completed as well. Packages or artifacts we generated during the *packaging* and *deployment to test environment* are waiting for further, usually manual, verifications. Later on, one of the builds of the pipeline will be elected to be deployed to production. Means and details of additional checks and deployment to production are not part of continuous integration. Every build that passed the whole pipeline is considered integrated and ready for whatever comes next.

---

[11]http://gatling.io/

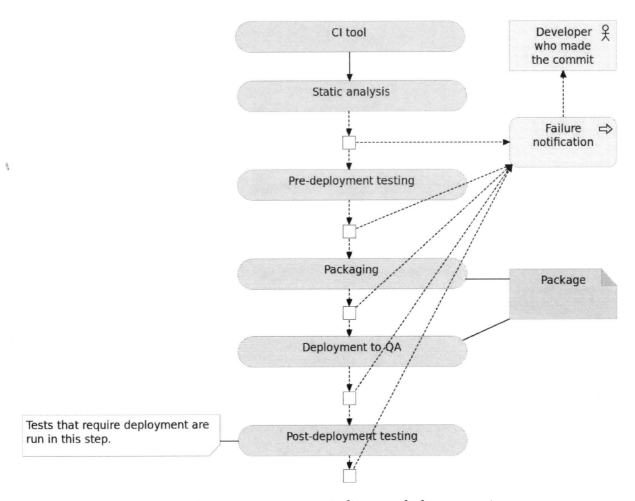

Figure 2-5: Continuous integration pipeline: post-deployment testing

Many other things could be done in the pipeline. The pipeline presented here is a very general one and often varies from case to case. For example, you might choose to measure code coverage and fail when a certain percentage is not reached.

We're not going into details right now but trying to get a general overview of the process so let us move into continuous delivery and deployment.

Continuous Delivery and Deployment

The *continuous delivery* pipeline is in most cases the same as the one we would use for CI. The major difference is in the confidence we have in the process and lack of actions to be taken after the execution of the pipeline. While CI assumes that there are (mostly manual) validations to be performed afterward, successful implementation of the CD pipeline results in packages or artifacts being ready to be deployed to production. In other words, every successful run of the pipeline *can be deployed to production,* no questions asked. Whether it will be deployed or not depends more on political than technical decisions. The marketing department might want to wait until a certain date, or they might want to go live with a group of features deployed together. No matter the decision which build to deploy and when, from the technical perspective, the code of every successful build is fully finished. The only difference between the continuous integration and continuous delivery processes is that the latter does not have the manual testing phase that is performed after the package is promoted through the pipeline. Simply put, the pipeline itself provides enough confidence that there is no need for manual actions. With it, we are technically capable of deploying every promoted build. Which one of those will be deployed to production is a decision often based on business or marketing criteria where the company decides the right time to release a set of features.

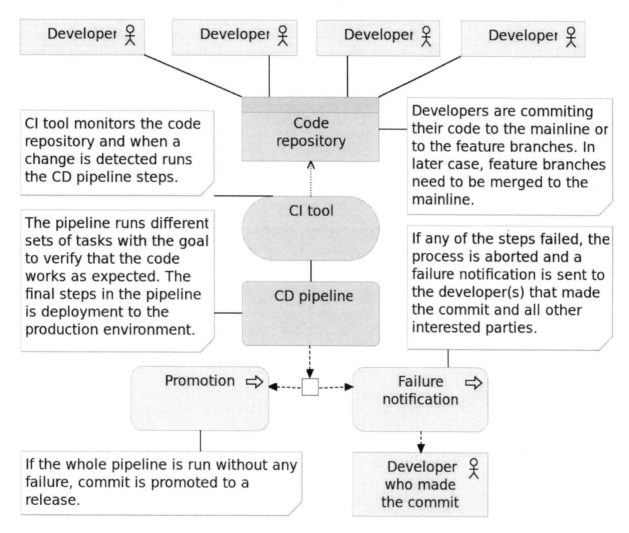

Figure 2-6: Continuous delivery process

Keep in mind that we continued using *CI tool* in the continuous delivery process diagram. The reason for this is a lack of any substantial difference between CI and CD tools. This does not mean that there are no products being marketed as CD tools - there are many. However, in my experience, this is more of a marketing stunt as both processes are almost the same assuming that processes rely on a high level of automation.

Regarding the pipeline process, there is also no substantial difference between continuous integration and continuous delivery. Both go through the same phases. The real difference is in the confidence we have in the process. As a result, the continuous delivery process does not have the manual QA phase. It's up to us to make a decision which one of the promoted packages will be deployed to production.

The *Continuous deployment* pipeline goes a step further and automatically deploys every build that passed all verifications. It is a fully automated process that starts with a commit to the code repository and ends with the application or the service being *deployed to production*. There is no human intervention, nothing to decide and nothing to do but to start coding the next feature while results of your work are finding their way to the users. In cases when packages are deployed to QA server before being deployed to production, post-deployment testing is done twice (or as many times are the number of servers we deploy to). In such a case, we might choose to run different subsets of post-deployment tests. For example, we might run all of them on the software deployed to QA server and only integration tests after deploying to production. Depending on the result of post-deployment tests, we might choose to roll-back or enable the release to the general public. When a proxy service is used to make a new release visible to the public, there is usually no need to roll-back since the newly released application was not made visible before the problem was detected.

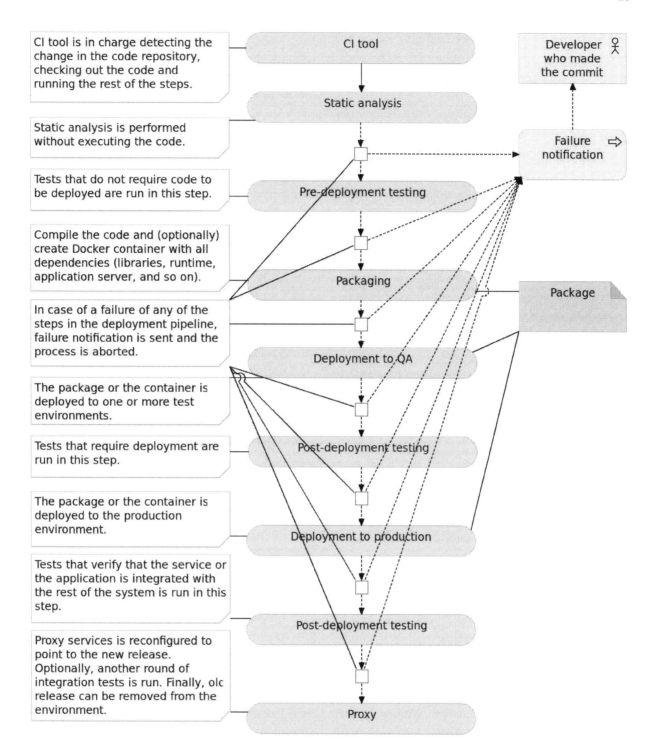

CI tool is in charge detecting the change in the code repository, checking out the code and running the rest of the steps.

Static analysis is performed without executing the code.

Tests that do not require code to be deployed are run in this step.

Compile the code and (optionally) create Docker container with all dependencies (libraries, runtime, application server, and so on).

In case of a failure of any of the steps in the deployment pipeline, failure notification is sent and the process is aborted.

The package or the container is deployed to one or more test environments.

Tests that require deployment are run in this step.

The package or the container is deployed to the production environment.

Tests that verify that the service or the application is integrated with the rest of the system is run in this step.

Proxy services is reconfigured to point to the new release. Optionally, another round of integration tests is run. Finally, old release can be removed from the environment.

CI tool

Static analysis

Pre-deployment testing

Packaging

Deployment to QA

Post-deployment testing

Deployment to production

Post-deployment testing

Proxy

Developer who made the commit

Failure notification

Package

Figure 2-7: Continuous deployment pipeline

We need to pay particular attention to databases (especially when they are relational) and ensure that changes we are making from one release to another are backward compatible and can work with both releases (at least for some time).

While continuous integration welcomes, but does not necessarily require, deployed software to be tested in production, continuous delivery and deployment have production (mostly integration) testing as an absolute necessity and, in the case of continuous deployment, part of the fully automated pipeline. Since there are no manual verifications, we need to be as sure as possible that whatever was deployed to production is working as expected. That does not mean that all the automated tests need to be repeated. It means that we need to run tests that prove that the deployed software is integrated with the rest of the system. The fact that we run, possibly same, integration tests in other environments does not mean that due to some differences, software deployed to production continues to "play nicely" with the rest of the system.

Another very useful technique in the context of continuous deployment is *feature toggles*. Since every build is deployed to production, we can use them to disable some features temporarily. For example, we might have the login screen fully developed but without the registration. It would not make sense to let the visitors know about a feature that requires another still not deployed feature. Continuous delivery solves that problem by manually approving which build is deployed to production and would choose to wait. Since, in the case of continuous deployment that decision-making it not available, feature toggles are a must or we would need to delay merging with the mainline until all related features are finished. However, we already discussed the importance of constant merging with the mainline and such delays are against the logic behind CI/CD. While there are other ways to solve this problem, I find feature toggles to be indispensable to all those who choose to apply continuous deployment. We won't go into feature toggles details. For those interested obtaining more info, please visit the Feature Toggles (Feature Switches or Feature Flags) vs Feature Branches[12] article.

Most teams start with continuous integration and slowly move towards delivery and deployment since former are prerequisites for later. In this book, we'll practice continuous deployment. Don't be scared. Everything we'll do can be easily modified so that there are pauses and manual interventions. For example, we will be deploying containers directly to production (actually to VMs that imitate production) without passing through test environments. When applying techniques from this book, you can easily choose to add a testing environment in between.

The important thing to note is that the pipeline phases that we discussed are performed in particular order. That order is not only logical (for example, we cannot deploy before compiling) but also in order of the execution time. Things that take less to run are run first. For example, as a general rule, pre-deployment tests tend to run much faster than those we'll run as post-deployment. The same rule should be followed within each phase. If, for example, you have different types of tests within the pre-deployment phase, run those that are faster first. The reason for this quest for speed is time until we get feedback. The sooner we find out that there is something wrong with the commit, the better. Ideally, we should get that feedback before we move to the next development task. Do the commit, have a quick coffee, check your inbox and if there is no angry email stating that something failed, move to the next task.

Later on, throughout this book, you'll see that some of the phases and details of the presented pipeline are a bit different due to advantages brought by microservices and containers. For example,

---

[12]http://technologyconversations.com/2014/08/26/feature-toggles-feature-switches-or-feature-flags-vs-feature-branches/

packaging will finish with immutable (unchangeable) containers, deployment to a test environment might not be required at all, we might choose to perform testing directly to the production environment using the blue/green technique, and so on. However, I am ahead of myself. Everything will come in due time.

With CI/CD out of the way (for now), it is time to discuss microservices.

Microservices

We already spoke about speed in the context of continuous deployment. This speed refers to the time from conception of the idea for new functionality until it is fully operational and deployed to production. We want to be able to move fast and provide the shortest possible time to market. If a new functionality can be delivered in a matter of hours or days, business will start seeing benefits much faster than if it takes weeks or months.

Speed can be accomplished in multiple ways. For example, we want the pipeline to be as fast as possible both in order to provide quick feedback in case of a failure as well as to liberate resources for other queued jobs. We should aim at spending minutes instead of hours from checking out the code to having it deployed to production. Microservices can help accomplishing this timing. Running the whole pipeline for a huge monolithic application is often slow. Same applies to testing, packaging, and deployment. On the other hand, microservices are much faster for the simple reason that they are far smaller. There is less code to test, less code to package and less code to deploy.

We would not be switching to microservices if that were be the only reason. Later on, there will be a whole chapter dedicated to a much deeper examination of microservices. For now, the important thing to note is that due to the goals today's competition sets in front of us (flexibility, speed, and so on), microservices are probably the best type of architecture we can apply.

Containers

Before containers became common, microservices were painful to deploy. In comparison, monolithic applications are relatively simple to handle. We would, for example, create a single artifact (JAR, WAR, DLL, and so on), deploy it to the server and make sure that all required executables and libraries (for example JDKs) are present. This process was most of the time standardized, and had relatively few things to think about. One microservice is equally simple, but when their number multiplies with ten, hundred or even thousand, things start getting complicated. They might use different versions of dependencies, different frameworks, various application servers, and so on. The number of stuff we have to think about starts rising exponentially. After all, one of the reasons behind microservices is the ability to choose the best tool for the job. One might be better off if it's written in GoLang while the other would be a better fit for NodeJS. One could use JDK 7, while the other might need JDK 8. Installing and maintaining all that might quickly turn servers into garbage cans and make people in charge of them go crazy. The most common solution applied back then was standardizing as much as possible. Everyone must use only JDK 7 for the back-end. All front-end has to be done with JSP. The common code should be placed in shared libraries. In other words, people tried to solve problems related to microservices deployment applying the same logic they learned during years of development, maintenance, and deployment of monolithic applications. Kill the innovation for the sake of standardization. And we could not blame them. The only alternative were immutable VMs and that only changed one set of problems for another. That is, until containers become popular and, more importantly, accessible to masses.

Docker[13] made it possible to work with containers without suffering in the process. They made containers accessible and easy to use to everyone.

What are containers? The definition of the word container is "an object for holding or transporting something". Most people associate containers with *shipping containers*. They should have strength suitable to withstand shipment, storage, and handling. You can see them being transported in a variety of ways, most common one of them being by ship. In big shipyards, you can find hundreds or even thousands of them stacked one besides the other and one on top of the other. Almost all merchandise is shipped through containers for a reason. They are standardized, easy to stack and hard to damage. Most involved with shipping do not know what's inside them. Nobody cares (except customs) because what is inside is irrelevant. The only important thing is to know where to pick them and where to deliver them. It is a clear separation of concerns. We know how to handle them from outside while their content is known only to those who packed them in the first place.

The idea behind "software" containers is similar. They are *isolated* and *immutable* images that provide designed functionality in most cases accessible only through their APIs. They are a solution to make our software run reliably and on (almost) any environment. No matter where they are running (developer's laptop, testing or production server, data center, and so on), the result should always be the same. Finally, we can avoid conversations like the following.

QA: There is a problem with the login screen.

Developer: It works on my computer!

The reason such a conversation is obsolete with containers is that they behave in the same way no matter the environment they're running on.

The way for containers to accomplish this feat is through *self-sufficiency* and *immutability*. Traditional deployments would put an artifact into an existing node expecting that everything else is in place; the application server, configuration files, dependencies, and so on. Containers, on the other hand, contain everything our software needs. The result is a set of images stacked into a container that contains everything from binaries, application server and configurations all the way down to runtime dependencies and OS packages. This description leads to the question about differences between a container and a VM. After all, all that we described by now is equally valid for both.

For example, a physical server running five virtual machines would have five operating systems in addition to a *hypervisor* that is more resource demanding than *lxc*. Five containers, on the other hand, share the operating system of the physical server and, where appropriate, binaries and libraries. As a result, containers are much more lightweight than VMs. With monolithic applications this is not

---

[13]https://www.docker.com/

so big of a difference, especially in cases when a single one would occupy the whole server. With microservices however, this gain in resource utilization is critical considering that we might have tens or hundreds of them on a single physical server. Put in other words, a single physical server can host more containers than virtual machines.

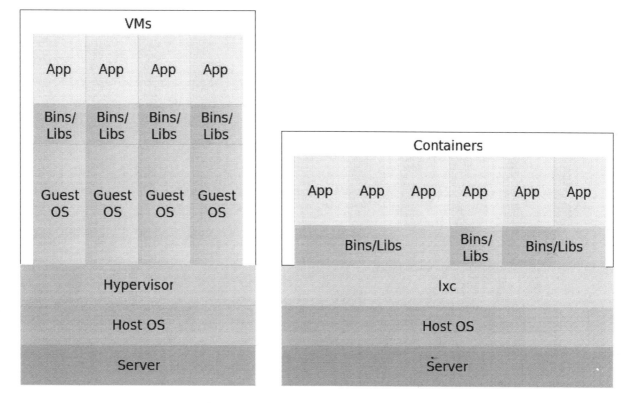

Figure 2-8: Virtual machines and containers resources utilization comparison

The Three Musketeers: Synergy of Continuous Deployment, Microservices, and Containers

Continuous deployment, microservices, and containers are a match made in heaven. They are like the three musketeers, each capable of great deeds but when joined, capable of so much more.

With continuous deployment, we can provide continuous and automatic feedback of our applications readiness and deployment to production, thus increasing the quality of what we deliver and decreasing the time to reach the market.

Microservices provide us with more freedom to make better decisions, faster development and, as we'll see very soon, easier scaling of our services.

Finally, containers provide the solution to many of deployment problems; in general and especially when working with microservices. They also increase reliability due to their immutability.

Together, they can combine all that and do so much more. Throughout this book, we'll be on a quest to *deploy often and fast, be fully automatic, accomplish zero-downtime, have the ability to rollback, provide constant reliability across environments, be able to scale effortlessly, and create self-healing systems able to recuperate from failures.* Any of those goals is worth a lot. Can we accomplish all of them? Yes! Practices and tools we have at our disposal can provide all that, and we just need to combine them correctly. The journey ahead is long but exciting. There are a lot of things to cover and explore and we need to start from the beginning; we'll discuss the architecture of the system we are about to start building.

> *Knowing is not enough; we must apply. Willing is not enough; we must do.*
>
> – Johann Wolfgang von Goethe

System Architecture

From here on, the whole book will be one big project. We'll go through all the stages starting from development all the way until production deployment and monitoring. Each phase will begin with a discussion about different paths we can take to accomplish the goal. We'll choose the best given our needs and implement it. The objective is to learn techniques that you can apply to your projects so please feel free to adapt instructions to fit your needs.

As most other projects, this one will start with high-level requirements. Our goal is to create an online shop. The complete plan is still not available, but we do know that selling books has priority. We should design services and a Web application in a way that it can easily be extended. We do not have the whole set of requirements in front of us, so we need to be prepared for the unknown. Besides books, we'll be selling other types of goods, and there will be other kinds of functionality like a shopping cart, registration and login, and so on. Our job is to develop bookstore and be able to respond to the future requirements in a fast manner. Since it is a new endeavor, not much traffic is expected at the beginning, but we should be prepared to scale easily and quickly if the service becomes successful. We want to ship new features as fast as possible without any downtime and to be able to recuperate from failures.

Let us start working on the architecture. It is clear that requirements are very general and do not provide many details. That means that we should be prepared for very likely changes in the future as well as requests for new features. At the same time, business requires us to build something small but be prepared to grow. How should we solve the problems given to us?

The first thing we should decide is how to define the architecture of the application we're about to build. Which approach will allow us possible changes of the direction, additional (but at this moment unknown) requirements and the need to be ready to scale? We should start by examining two most common approaches to applications architecture; monoliths and microservices.

Monolithic Applications

Monolithic applications are developed and deployed as a single unit. In the case of Java, the result is often a single WAR or JAR file. Similar statement is true for C++, .Net, Scala and many other programming languages.

Most of the short history of software development is marked by a continuous increment in size of the applications we are developing. As time passes, we're adding more and more to our applications continuously increasing their complexity and size and decreasing our development, testing and deployment speed.

We started dividing our applications into layers: presentation layer, business layer, data access layer, and so on. This separation is more logical than physical, and each of those layers tends to be in charge of one particular type of operations. This kind of architecture often provided immediate benefits since it made clear the responsibility of each layer. We got separation of concerns on a high level. Life was good. Productivity increased, time-to-market decreased and overall clarity of the code base was better. Everybody seemed to be happy, for a while.

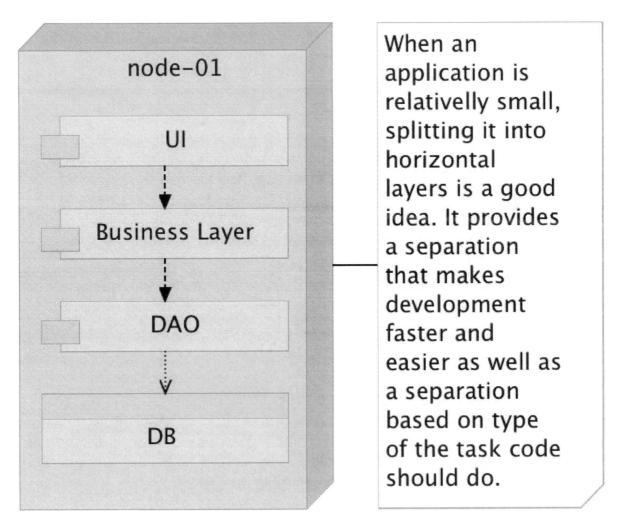

When an application is relativelly small, splitting it into horizontal layers is a good idea. It provides a separation that makes development faster and easier as well as a separation based on type of the task code should do.

Figure 3-1: Monolithic application

With time, the number of features our application was required to support was increasing and with that comes increased complexity. One feature on UI level would need to speak with multiple business rules that in turn require multiple DAO classes that access many different database tables. No matter how hard we try, the sub-division within each layer and communication between them gets ever more complicated and, given enough time, developers start straying from the initial path. After all, a design made initially often does not pass the test of time. As a result, modifications to any given sub-section of a layer tends to be more complicated, time demanding and risky since they might affect many different parts of the system with often unforeseen effects.

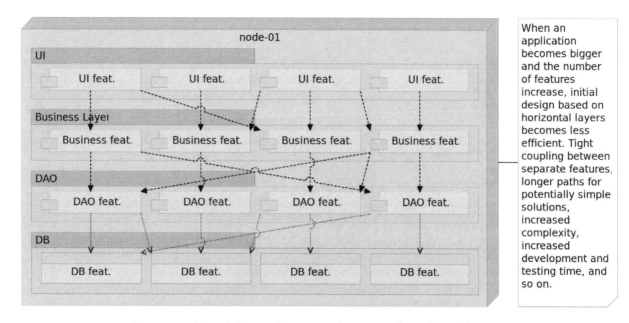

When an application becomes bigger and the number of features increase, initial design based on horizontal layers becomes less efficient. Tight coupling between separate features, longer paths for potentially simple solutions, increased complexity, increased development and testing time, and so on.

Figure 3-2: Monolithic application with increased number of features

As time passes, things start getting worse. In many cases, the number of layers increases. We might decide to add a layer with a rules engine, API layer, and so on. As things usually go, the flow between layers is in many cases mandatory. That results in situations where we might need to develop a simple feature that under different circumstances would require only a few lines of code but, due to the architecture we have, those few lines turn up to be hundreds or even thousands because all layers need to be passed through.

The development was not the only area that suffered from monolithic architecture. We still needed to test and deploy everything every time there was a change or a release. It is not uncommon in enterprise environments to have applications that take hours to test, build and deploy. Testing, especially regression, tends to be a nightmare that in some cases last for months. As time passes, our ability to make changes that affect only one module is decreasing. The primary objective of layers is to make them in a way that they can be easily replaced or upgraded. That promise is almost never actually fulfilled. Replacing something in big monolithic applications is hardly ever easy and without risks.

Scaling monoliths often mean scaling the entire application thus producing very unbalanced utilization of resources. If we need more resources, we are forced to duplicate everything on a new server even if a bottleneck is one module. In that case, we often end up with a monolith replicated across multiple nodes with a load balancer on top. This setup is sub-optimum at best.

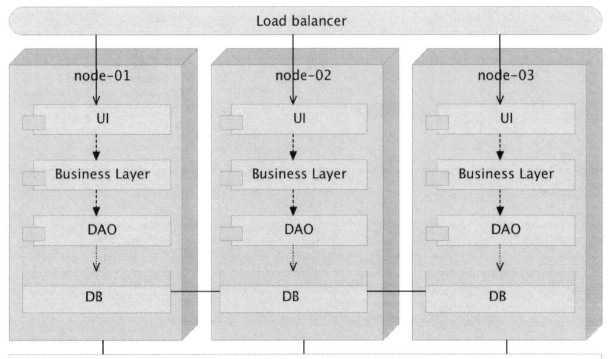

Figure 3-3: Scaling monolithic application

Services Split Horizontally

Service-oriented architecture (SOA) was created as a way to solve problems created by, often tightly coupled, monolithic applications. The approach is based on four main concepts we should implement.

- Boundaries are explicit
- Services are autonomous
- Services share schema and contract but not class
- Services compatibility is based on policy

SOA was such a big hit that many software providers jumped right in and created products that should help us in the transition. The most used type born out of SOA movement is *Enterprise Service Bus (ESB)*. At the same time, companies that experienced problems with monolithic applications and big systems jumped into the train and started the SOA transition with ESB as the locomotive. However, the common problem with this move is the way we are used working that often resulted in an intention to artificially apply SOA architecture into the existing model.

We continued having the same layers as we had before, but this time physically separated from each other. There is an apparent benefit from this approach in that we can, at least, develop and deploy each layer independently from others. Another improvement is scaling. With the physical separation between what used to be layers, we are allowed to scale better. That approach was often combined with acquisitions of one of the enterprise service bus (ESB) products. In between services we would put ESB that would be in charge of transformation and redirection of requests from one service to another. ESB and similar products are beasts of their own and we often end up with another monolithic application that is as big or even bigger than the one we tried to split. What we needed was to *break services by bounded contexts* and separate them physically with each running in their own process and with clearly defined communication between them. Thus, microservices were born.

Microservices

Microservices are an approach to architecture and development of a single application composed of small services. The key to understanding microservices is their independence. Each is developed, tested and deployed separately from each other. Each service runs as a separate process. The only relation between different microservices is data exchange accomplished through APIs they are exposing. They inherit, in a way, the idea of small programs and pipes used in Unix/Linux. Most Linux programs are small and produce some output. That output can be passed as input to other programs. When chained, those programs can perform very complex operations. It is complexity born from a combination of many simple units.

In a way, microservices use the concepts defined by SOA. Then why are they called differently? SOA implementations went astray. That is especially true with the emergence of ESB products that themselves become big and complex enterprise applications. In many cases, after adopting one of the ESB products, the business went as usual with one more layer sitting on top of what we had before. Microservices movement is, in a way, reaction to misinterpretation of SOA and the intention to go back to where it all started. The main difference between SOA and microservices is that the latter should be self-sufficient and deployable independently of each other while SOA tends to be implemented as a monolith.

Let's see what Gartner has to say about microservices. While I'm not a big fan of their predictions, they do strike the important aspect of the market by appealing to big enterprise environments. Their evaluations of market tendencies usually mean that we passed the adoption by greenfield projects, and the technology is ready for the big enterprises. Here's what Gary Olliffe said about microservices at the beginning of 2015.

Microservice architectures promise to deliver flexibility and scalability to the development and deployment of service-based applications. But how is that promise delivered? In short, by adopting an architecture that allows individual services to be built and deployed independently and dynamically; an architecture that embraces DevOps practices.

Microservices are simpler, developers get more productive and systems can be scaled quickly and precisely, rather than in large monolithic globs. And I haven't even mentioned the potential for polyglot coding and data persistence.

Key aspects of microservices are as follows.

- They do one thing or are responsible for one functionality.
- Each microservice can be built by any set of tools or languages since each is independent of others.
- They are truly loosely coupled since each microservice is physically separated from others.
- Relative independence between different teams developing different microservices (assuming that APIs they expose are defined in advance).
- Easier testing and continuous delivery or deployment.

One of the problems with microservices is the decision when to use them. In the beginning, while the application is still small, problems that microservices are trying to solve do not exist. However, once the application grows and the case for microservices can be made, the cost of switching to a different architecture style might be too big. Experienced teams tend to use microservices from the very start knowing that technical debt they might have to pay later will be more expensive than working with microservices from the very beginning. Often, as it was the case with Netflix, eBay, and Amazon, monolithic applications start evolving towards microservices gradually. New modules are developed as microservices and integrated with the rest of the system. Once they prove their worth, parts of the existing monolithic application gets refactored into microservices as well.

One of the things that often gets most critique from developers of enterprise applications is decentralization of data storage. While microservices can work (with few adjustments) using centralized data storage, the option to decentralize that part as well should, at least, be explored. The option to store data related to some service in a separate (decentralized) storage and pack it together into the same container or as a separate one and link them together is something that in many cases could be a better option than storing that data in a centralized database. I am not proposing always to use decentralized storage but to have that option in account when designing microservices.

Finally, we often employ some kind of a lightweight proxy server that is in charge of the orchestration of all requests no matter whether they come from outside or from one microservice to another.

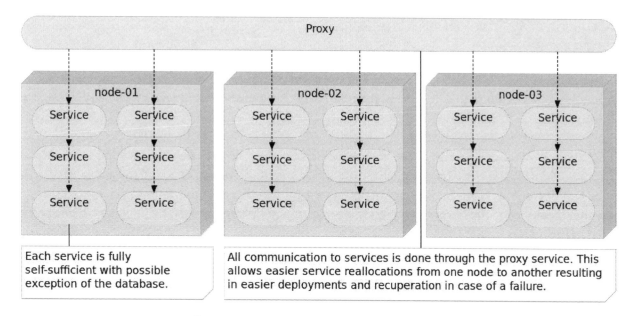

Figure 3-4: Microservices with a proxy service

Armed with a basic knowledge about monoliths and microservices, let us compare the two and evaluate their strengths and weaknesses.

Monolithic Applications and Microservices Compared

From what we learned by now, seems that microservices are a better option than monoliths. Indeed, in many (but far from all) cases they are. However, there is no such thing as a free lunch. Microservices have their set of disadvantages with *increased operational and deployment complexity*, and *remote process calls* being the most common.

Operational and Deployment Complexity

The primary argument against microservices is *increased operational and deployment complexity*. This argument is correct, but thanks to relatively new tools it can be mitigated. *Configuration Management (CM)* tools can handle environment setups and deployments with relative ease. Utilization of *containers with Docker* significantly reduces deployment pains that microservices can cause. CM tools together with containers allow us to deploy and scale microservices quickly.

In my opinion, increased deployment complexity argument usually does not take into account advances we saw during last years and is greatly exaggerated. That does not mean that part of the work is not shifted from development to DevOps. It is. However, benefits are in many cases bigger than the inconvenience that change produces.

Remote Process Calls

Another argument for monolithic applications is *reduced performance* produced by microservices' *remote process calls*. Internal calls through classes and methods are faster and this problem cannot be removed. How much that loss of performance affects a system depends on case to case basis. The important factor is how we split our system. If we take it towards the extreme with very small microservices (some propose that they should not have more than 10-100 lines of code), this impact might be considerable. I like to create microservices organized around bounded contexts or functionality like users, shopping cart, products, and so on. That reduces the number of remote process calls but still keep services organization within healthy boundaries. Also, it's important to note that if calls from one microservice to another are going through a fast internal LAN, the negative impact is relatively small.

So, what are the advantages microservices have over monoliths? The following list is by no means final nor it represents advantages only available with microservices. While many of them are valid for other types of architecture, they are more prominent with microservices.

Scaling

Scaling microservices is much easier than monolithic applications. With monoliths, we duplicate the whole application into a new machine. On the other hand, with microservices, we duplicate only those that need scaling. Not only that *we can scale what needs to be scaled* but we can distribute things better. We can, for example, put a service that has heavy utilization of CPU together with another one that uses a lot of RAM while moving the other CPU demanding service to a different hardware.

Innovation

Monolithic applications, once the initial architecture is made, do not leave much space for innovation. I'd go even further and claim that *monoliths are innovation killers*. Due to their nature, changing things takes time, and experimentation is perilous since it potentially affects everything. One cannot, for example, change Apache Tomcat for NodeJS just because it would better suit one particular module.

I'm not suggesting that we should change programming language, server, persistence, and other architecture aspects for each module. However, monolithic servers tend to go to an opposite extreme where changes are risky if not unwelcome. With microservices, we can choose what we think is the best solution for each service separately. One might use Apache Tomcat while the other could use NodeJS. One can be written in Java and the other in Scala. I'm not advocating that each service is different from the rest but that each can be made in a way we think is best suited for the goal at hand. On top of that, changes and experiments are much easier to do. After all, whatever we do affects only one out of many microservices and not the system as a whole as long as the API is respected.

Size

Since *microservices are small*, they are much easier to understand. There is much less code to go through to see what one microservice is doing. That in itself greatly simplifies development, especially when newcomers join the project. On top of that, everything else tends to be much faster. IDEs work faster with a small project when compared to big ones used in monolithic applications. They start faster since there are no huge servers nor an enormous number of libraries to load.

Deployment, Rollback and Fault Isolation

Deployment is much faster and easier with microservices. Deploying something small is always quicker (if not easier) than deploying something big. In case we realized that there is a problem, that problem has potentially limited effect and can be rolled back much easier. Until we roll back, the fault is isolated to a small part of the system. Continuous delivery or deployment can be done with speed and frequencies that would not be possible with big applications.

Commitment Term

One of the common problems with monolithic applications is commitment. We are often forced to choose from the start the architecture and the technologies that will last for a long time. After all, we're building something big that should last for a long time. With microservices that *need for a long-term commitment is much smaller.* Change the programming language in one microservice and if it turns out to be a good choice, apply it to others. If the experiment failed or is not the optimum, there's only one small part of the system that needs to be redone. Same applies to frameworks, libraries, servers, and so on. We can even use different databases. If some lightweight NoSQL seems like the best fit for a particular microservice, why not use it and pack it into the container?

Let us go one step back and look at this subject from the prism of deployment. How do those two architectural approaches differ when the time comes to deploy our applications.

Deployment Strategies

We already discussed that continuous delivery and deployment strategies require us to rethink all aspects of the application lifecycle. That is nowhere more noticeable than at the very beginning when we are faced with architectural choices. We won't go into details of every possible deployment strategy we could face but limit the scope to two major decisions that we should make. First one is architecturally related to the choice between monolithic applications and microservices. The second one is related to how we package the artifacts that should be deployed. More precisely, whether we should perform mutable or immutable deployments.

Mutable Monster Server

Today, the most common way to build and deploy applications is as a *mutable monster server*. We create a web server that has the whole application and update it every time there is a new release. Changes can be in *configuration* (properties file, XMLs, DB tables, and so on), *code artifacts* (JARs, WARs, DLLs, static files, and so on) and *database schemas and data*. Since we are changing it on every release, it is mutable.

With mutable servers, we cannot know for sure that development, test, and production environments are the same. Even different nodes in the production might have undesirable differences. Code, configuration or static files might not have been updated in all instances.

It is a *monster server* since it contains everything we need as a single instance. Back-end, front-end, APIs, and so on. Moreover, it grows over time. It is not uncommon that after some time no one is sure what is the exact configuration of all pieces in production and the only way to accurately reproduce it somewhere else (new production node, test environment, and so on) is to copy the VM where it resides and start fiddling with configurations (IPs, host file, DB connections, and so on). We just keep adding to it until we lose the track of what it has. Given enough time, your "perfect" design and impressive architecture will become something different. New layers will be added, the code will be coupled, patches on top of patches will be created and people will start losing themselves in the maze the code start looking like. Your beautiful little project will become a big monster. The pride you have will become a subject people talk about on coffee breaks. People will start saying that the best thing they could do is to throw it to trash and start over. But, the monster is already too big to start over. Too much is invested. Too much time would be needed to rewrite it. Too much is at stake. Our monolith might continue existing for a long time.

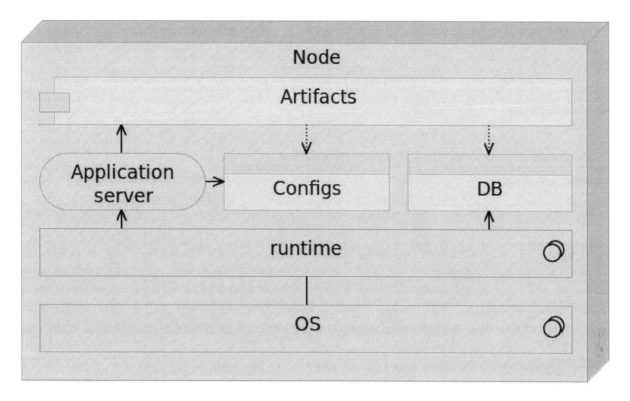

Figure 3-5: Mutable application server as initially designed

Mutable deployments might look simple, but they are usually not. By coupling everything into one place, we are hiding complexity thus increasing the chance of discrepancies between different instances.

Time to restart such a server when it receives a new release can be considerable. During that time server is usually not operational. Downtime that the new release provokes is a loss of money and trust. Today's business expects us to operate 24/7 without any downtime, and it is not uncommon that a release to production means night work of the team during which our services are not available. Given such a situation, applying continuous deployment is a dream out of the reach. It is a dream that can not become a reality.

Testing is also a problem. No matter how much we tested the release on development and test environments, the first time it will be tried in production is when we deploy it and make it available not only to our testers but also to all our users.

Moreover, fast rollback of such a server is close to impossible. Since it is mutable, there is no "photo" of the previous version unless we create a snapshot of a whole virtual machine that brings up a whole new set of problems.

By having architecture like this, we cannot fulfill all, if any, of the requirements described earlier. We cannot deploy often, due to inability to produce zero-downtime and easily rollback. Full automation is risky due to mutable nature of its architecture thus preventing us to be fast.

By not deploying often we are accumulating changes that will be released and, in that way, we are increasing the probability of a failure.

To solve those problems, deployments should be immutable and composed of small, independent, and self-sufficient applications. Remember, our goals are to deploy often, have zero-downtime, be able to rollback any release, be automated and be fast. Moreover, we should be able to test the release on production environment before users see it.

Immutable Server and Reverse Proxy

Each "traditional" deployment introduces a risk tied with changes that need to be performed on the server. If we change our architecture to immutable deployments, we gain immediate benefits. Provisioning of environments becomes much simpler since there is no need to think about applications (they are unchangeable). Whenever we deploy an image or a container to the production server, we know that it is precisely the same as the one we built and tested. Immutable deployments reduce the risk tied to unknown. We know that each deployed instance is exactly the same as the other. Unlike mutable deployment, when a package is immutable and contains everything (application server, configurations, and artifacts) we stop caring about all those things. They were packaged for us throughout the deployment pipeline and all we have to do is make sure that the immutable package is sent to the destination server. It is the same package as the one we already tested in other environments and inconsistencies that could be introduced by mutable deployments are gone.

A reverse proxy can be used to accomplish zero-downtime. Immutable servers together with a reverse proxy in a simplified form can be as follows.

First we start with a reverse proxy that points to our fully self-sufficient immutable application package. This package could be a virtual machine or a container. We'll refer to this application as application image to establish a clear distinction from mutable applications. On top of the application is a proxy service that routes all the traffic towards the final destination instead of exposing the server directly.

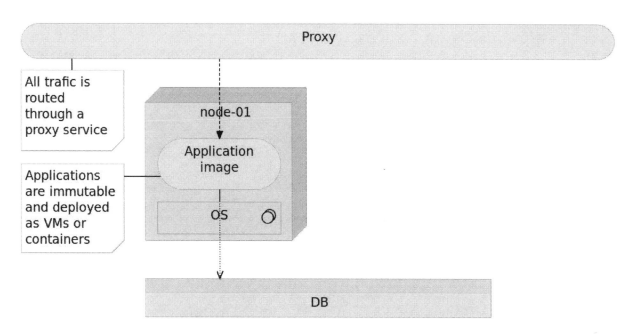

Figure 3-6: Immutable application server deployed as an image (a virtual machine or a container)

Once we decide to deploy a new version, we do it by deploying a separate image to a separate server. While in some cases we could deploy this image to the same server, more often than not, monolithic applications are very resource demanding and we cannot have both on the same node without affecting the performance. At this moment, we have two instances. One old (previous release) and one new (latest release). All traffic still goes to the old server through the reverse proxy so users of our application still do not notice any change. For them, we're still running the old and proven software. This is the right moment to execute the final set of tests. Preferably those tests are automatic and part of the deployment process but manual verification is not excluded. For example, if changes were done to front-end, we might want to do the final round of user experience tests. No matter what types of tests are performed, they should all "attack" the new release bypassing the reverse proxy. The good thing about those tests is that we are working with the future production version of the software that resides on production hardware. We are testing production software and hardware without affecting our users (they are still being redirected to the old version). We could even enable our new release only to a limited number of users in the form of A/B testing.

To summarize, at this stage we have two instances of the server, one (the previous release) used by our users and the other (the latest release) used for testing.

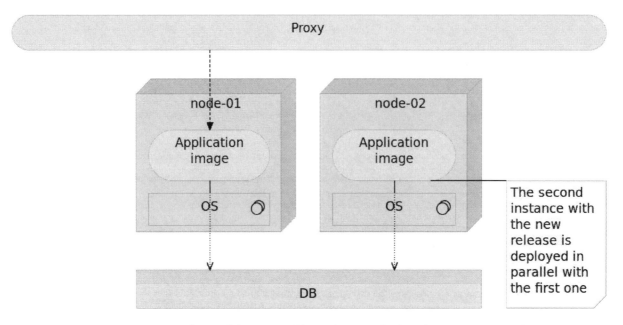

Figure 3-7: New release of the immutable application deployed to a separate node

Once we are finished with tests and are confident that the new release works as expected, all we have to do is change the reverse proxy to point to the new release. The old one can stay for a while in case we need to rollback the changes. However, for our users, it does not exist. All traffic is routed to the new release. Since the latest release was up-and-running before we changed the routing, the switch itself will not interrupt our service (unlike, for example, if we would need to restart the server in case of mutable deployments). When the route is changed we need to reload our reverse proxy. As an example, *nginx* maintains old connections until all of them are switched to the new route.

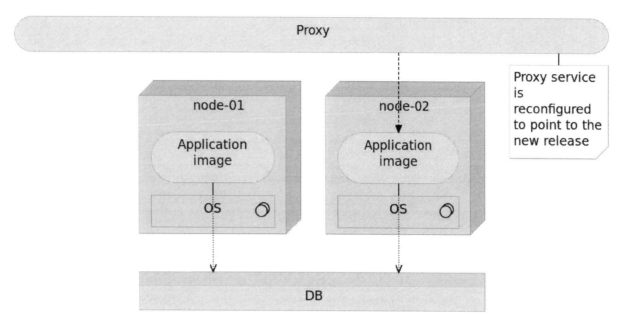

Figure 3-8: Poxy is rerouted to point to the new release

Finally, when we do not need the old version, we can remove it. Even better, we can let the next release remove it for us. In the latter case, when the time comes, release process will remove the older release and start the process all over again.

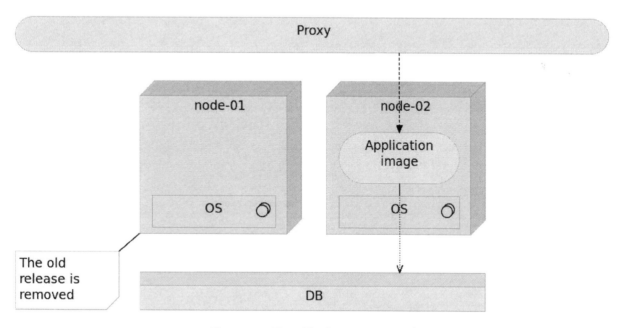

Figure 3-9: The old release is removed

The technique described above is called blue-green deployment and has been in use for a long time. We'll be practicing it later on when we reach the Docker packaging and deployment examples.

Immutable Microservices

We can do even better than this. With immutable deployments, we can easily accomplish automatism of the process. Reverse proxy gives us zero-downtime and, having two releases up and running allows us to rollback easily. However, since we're still dealing with one big application, deployment and tests might take a long time to run. That in itself might prevent us from being fast and thus from deploying as often as needed. Moreover, having everything as one big server increases development, testing and deployment complexity. If things could be split into smaller pieces, we might divide complexity into easily manageable chunks. As a bonus, having small independent services would allow us to scale more easily. They can be deployed to the same machine, scaled out across the network or multiplied if the performance of one of them becomes the bottleneck. Microservices to the rescue!

With "monster" applications we tend to have decoupled layers. Front-end code should be separated from the back-end, business layer from data access layer, and so on. With microservices, we should start thinking in a different direction. Instead of having the business layer separated from the data access layer, we would separate services. For example, users management could be split from the sales service. Another difference is physical. While traditional architecture separates on a level of packages and classes but still deploys everything together, microservices are split physically; they might not even reside on the same physical machine.

Deployment of microservices follows the same pattern as previously described.

We deploy our microservice immutable image as any other software.

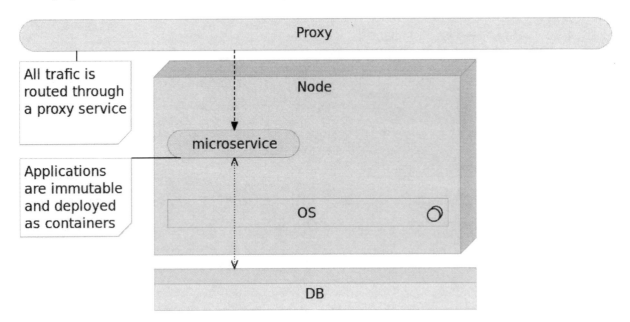

Figure 3-10: Immutable microservice deployed as an image (a virtual machine or a container)

When the time comes to release a new version of some microservice we deploy it alongside the older version.

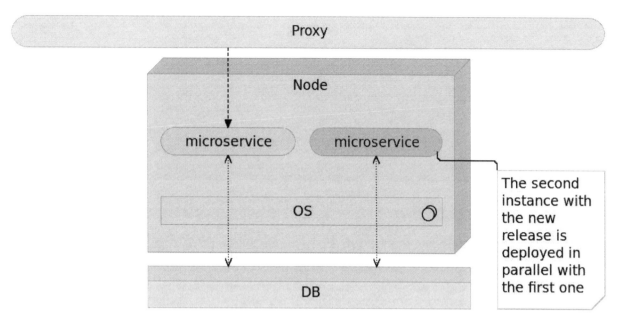

Figure 3-11: New release of the immutable microservice deployed alongside the old release

When that microservice release is properly tested we change the proxy route.

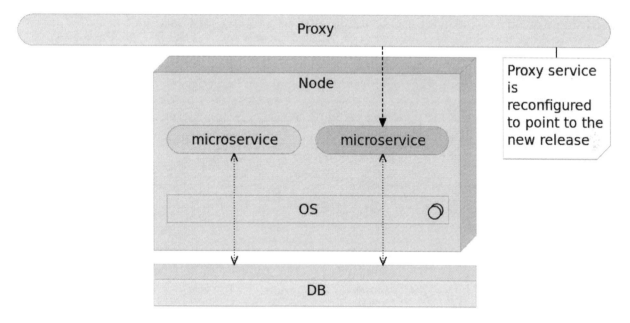

Figure 3-12: Poxy is re-configured to point to the new release

Finally, we remove the older version of the microservice.

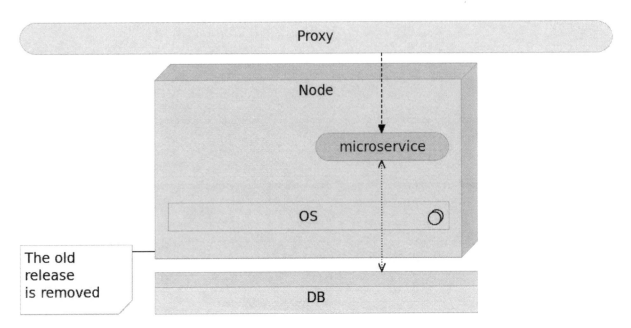

Figure 3-13: The old release is removed

The only significant difference is that due to the size of microservices, we often do not need a separate server to deploy the new release in parallel with the old one. Now we can truly deploy often automatically, be fast with zero-downtime and rollback in case something goes wrong.

Technologically, this architecture might pose particular problems that will be the subject of the next chapters. For now, let's just say that those problems are easy to solve with the tools and processes we have at our disposal.

Given our requirements that are poor at best and the advantages microservices bring over monoliths, the choice is clear. We will be building our application using immutable microservices approach. That decision calls for a discussion about the best practices we should follow.

Microservices Best Practices

Most of the following best practices can be applied to services oriented architecture in general. However, with microservices, they become even more significant or beneficial. Following is a very brief description that will be extended later on throughout the book when the time comes to apply them.

Containers

Dealing with many microservices can quickly become a very complex endeavor. Each can be written in a different programming language, can require a different (hopefully light) application server or can use a different set of libraries. If each service is packed as a container, most of those problems will go away. All we have to do is run the container with, for example, Docker and trust that everything needed is inside it.

Containers are self-sufficient bundles that contain everything we need (with the exception of the kernel), run in an isolated process and are immutable. Being self-sufficient means that a container commonly has the following components.

- Runtime libraries (JDK, Python, or any other library required for the application to run)
- Application server (Tomcat, nginx, and so on)
- Database (preferably lightweight)
- Artifact (JAR, WAR, static files, and so on)

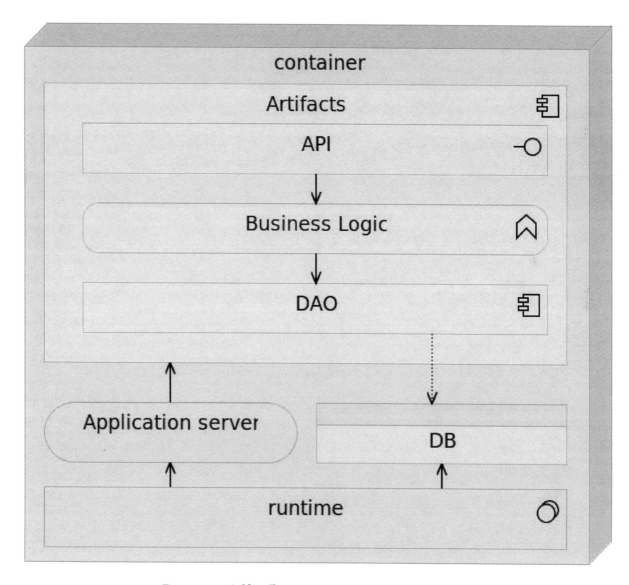

Figure 3-14: Self-sufficient microservice inside a container

Fully self-sufficient containers are the easiest way to deploy services but pose a few problems with scaling. If we'd like to scale such a container on multiple nodes in a cluster, we'd need to make sure that databases embedded into those containers are synchronized or that their data volumes are located on a shared drive. The first option often introduces unnecessary complexity while shared volumes might have a negative impact on performance. Alternative is to make containers almost self-sufficient by externalizing database into a separate container. In such a setting there would be two different containers per each service. One for the application and the other for the database. They would be linked (preferably through a proxy service). While such a combination slightly increases deployment complexity, it provides greater freedom when scaling. We can deploy multiple instances of the application container or several instances of the database depending performance testing results or increase in traffic. Finally, nothing prevents us to scale both if such a need arises.

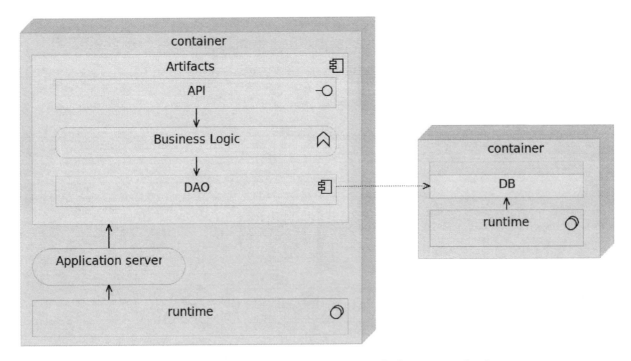

Figure 3-15: **Microservice inside a container with the separate database**

Being self-sufficient and immutable allows us to move containers across different environments (development, testing, production, and so on) and always expect the same results. Those same characteristics combined with microservices approach of building small applications allows us to deploy and scale containers with very little effort and much lower risk than other methods would allow us.

However, there is a third commonly used combination when dealing with legacy systems. Even though we might decide to gradually move from monolithic applications towards microservices, databases tend to be the last parts of the system to be approved for refactoring. While this is far from the optimal way to perform the transition, the reality, especially in big enterprises is that data is the most valuable asset. Rewriting an application poses much lower risk than the one we'd be facing if we decide to restructure data. It's often understandable that management is very skeptical of such proposals. In such a case we might opt for a shared database (probably without containers). While such a decision would be partly against what we're trying to accomplish with microservices, the pattern that works best is to share the database but make sure that each schema or a group of tables is exclusively accessed by a single service. The other services that would require that data would need to go through the API of the service assigned to it. While in such a combination we do not accomplish clear separation (after all, there is no clearer more apparent than physical), we can at least control who accesses the data subset and have a clear relation between them and the data. Actually, that is very similar to what is commonly the idea behind horizontal layers. In practice, as the monolithic application grows (and with it the number of layers) this approach tends to get abused and ignored. Vertical separation (even if a database is shared), helps us keep much clearer bounded context each service is in charge of.

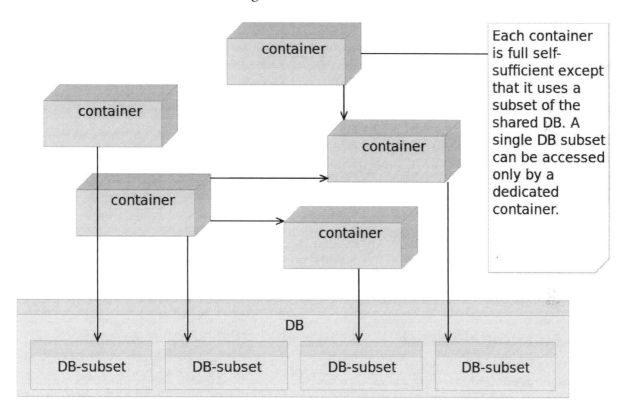

Figure 3-16: Microservices inside containers accessing the shared database

Proxy Microservices or API Gateway

Big enterprise front-ends might need to invoke tens or even hundreds of HTTP requests (as is the case with Amazon.com). Requests often take more time to be invoked than to receive response data. Proxy microservices might help in that case. Their goal is to invoke different microservices and return an aggregated service. They should not contain any logic but only group several responses together and respond with aggregated data to the consumer.

Reverse Proxy

Never expose microservice API directly. If there isn't some orchestration, the dependency between the consumer and the microservices becomes so big that it might remove freedom that microservices are supposed to give us. Lightweight servers like *nginx*, *Apache Tomcat*, and *HAProxy* are excellent at performing reverse proxy tasks and can easily be employed with very little overhead.

Minimalist Approach

Microservices should contain only packages, libraries, and frameworks that they truly need. The smaller they are, the better. That is quite in contrast to the approach used with monolithic applications. While previously we might have used JEE servers like JBoss that packed all the tools that we might or might not need, microservices work best with much more minimalistic solutions. Having hundreds of microservices with each of them having a full JBoss server becomes overkill. *Apache Tomcat*, for example, is a much better option. I tend to go for even smaller solutions with, for instance, *Spray* as a very lightweight RESTful API server. Don't pack what you don't need.

The same approach should be applied to OS level as well. If we're deploying microservices as *Docker* containers, *CoreOS* might be a better solution than, for example, *Red Hat* or *Ubuntu*. It's free from things we do not need allowing us to obtain better utilization of resources. However, as we'll see later, choosing OS is not always that simple.

Configuration Management

As the number of microservices grows, the need for *Configuration Management (CM)* increases. Deploying many microservices without tools like *Puppet*, *Chef* or *Ansible* (just to name few) quickly becomes a nightmare. Actually, not using CM tools for any but simplest solutions is a waste, with or without microservices.

Cross-Functional Teams

While no rule dictates what kinds of teams are utilized, microservices are done best when the team working on one is multifunctional. A single team should be responsible for it from the start (design) until the finish (deployment and maintenance). They are too small to be handled from one team to another (architecture/design, development, testing, deployment and maintenance teams). Preference is to have a team that is in charge of the full lifecycle of a microservice. In many cases, one team might be in charge of multiple microservices, but multiple teams should not be in charge of one.

API Versioning

Versioning should be applied to any API, and this holds true for microservices as well. If some change breaks the API format, it should be released as a separate version. In the case of public APIs as well as those used by other internal services, we cannot be sure who is using them and, therefore, must maintain backward compatibility or, at least, give consumers enough time to adapt.

Final Thoughts

Microservices as a concept existed for a long time. Take a look at the following example:

```
1   ps aux | grep jav[a] | awk '{print $2}' | xargs kill
```

The command listed above is an example of the usage of *pipes* in Unix/Linux. It consists of four programs. Each of them is expecting an input (*stdin*) and/or an output (*stdout*). Each of them is highly specialized and performs one or very few functions. While simple by themselves, when combined those programs are capable performing some very complex operations. Same holds true for most of the programs found in today's Unix/Linux distributions. In this particular case, we're running ps aux that retrieves the list of all running processes and passing the output to the next in line. That output is used by grep jav[a] to limit the results to only Java processes. Again, the output is passed to whoever needs it. In this particular example, next in line is awk '{print $2}' that does, even more, filtering and returns only the second column that happens to be the process ID. Finally, xargs kill takes the output of *awk* as input and kills all processes that match IDs we retrieved previously.

Those not used to Unix/Linux might think that the command we just examined is an overkill. However, after a bit of practice, those working with Linux commands find this approach very flexible and useful. Instead of having "big" programs that need to contemplate all possible use cases, we have a lot of small programs that can be combined to fulfill almost any task we might need. It is a power born out of utmost simplicity. Each program is small and created to achieve a very specific objective. More importantly, they all accept clearly defined input and produce well-documented output.

Unix is, as far as I know, the oldest example of microservices still in use. A lot of small, specific, easy to reason with services with well-defined interfaces.

Even though microservices exist for a long time, it is not a chance that they become popular only recently. Many things needed to mature and be available for microservices to be useful to all but selected few. Some of the concepts that made microservices widely used are *domain-driven design, continuous delivery, containers, small autonomous teams, scalable systems*, and so on. Only when all those are combined into a single framework microservices start to shine truly.

Microservices are used to create complex systems composed of small and autonomous services that exchange data through their APIs and limit their scope to a very specific bounded context. From a certain point of view, microservices are what object-oriented programming was initially designed to be. When you read thoughts of some of the leaders of our industry and, especially, object-oriented programming, their descriptions of best practices when absorbed for their logic and not the way authors implemented them initially, are the reminiscence of what microservices are today. The following quotes correctly describe some of the aspects of microservices.

The big idea is 'messaging'. The key in making great and growable systems is much more to design how its modules communicate rather than what their internal properties and behaviors should be.

– Alan Kay

Gather together those things that change for the same reason, and separate those things that change for different reasons - Robert C. Martin

When implementing microservices, we tend to organize them to do only one thing or perform only one function. This allows us to pick the best tools for each of the jobs. For example, we can code them in a language that best suits the objective. Microservices are truly loosely coupled due to their physical separation and provide a great level of independence between different teams as long as APIs are clearly defined in advance. On top of that, with microservices, we have much faster and easier testing and continuous delivery or deployment due to their decentralized nature. When concepts we discussed are combined with the emergence of new tools, especially *Docker*, we can see microservices in a new light and remove part of the problems their development and deployment was creating earlier.

Still, do not take bits of advice from this book as something that should be applied to all cases. Microservices are not an answer to all our problems. Nothing is. They are not the way all applications should be created and no single solution fits all cases. With microservices, we are trying to solve very specific problems and not to change the way all applications are designed.

Armed with the decision to develop our application around microservices, it is time to do something practical. There is no coding without development environment so that will be our first goal. We'll create a development environment for our "fancy" books store service.

We had enough theory and the time is ripe to put this book in front of a computer. From now on, most of the book will be a hands-on experience.

Setting Up the Development Environment With Vagrant and Docker

The development environment is often the first thing newcomers to the project need to face. While each project is different, is it not uncommon for them to spend a whole day setting up the environment, and many more days trying to understand how the application works.

How much time it takes to, for example, install JDK, setup local instance of JBoss server, do all the configuration and all other, often complicated, things required for the back-end part of the application. On top of that, add the time to do the same for the front-end when it is separated from the back-end. How much time does it take to, for example, understand inner workings of some monolithic application that has thousands, tens of thousands or even millions of lines of code split into layers upon layers of what was initially thought as a good idea but with time ended up as something that adds more complexity than benefits?

Development environment setup and simplicity are some of the areas where *containers* and *microservices* can help a lot. Microservices are, by definition, small. How much time does it take to understand a thousand (or less) lines of code? Even if you never programmed in the language used in the microservice in front of you, it should not take a lot of time to understand what it does. Containers, on the other hand, especially when combined with Vagrant, can make the development environment setup feel like a breeze. Not only that the setup process can be painless and fast, but the result can be as close as one can get to the production environment. Actually, with the exception of hardware, it can be the same.

Before we start working on such an environment, let us discuss the technology behind the service we are building.

Please note that the code that will be used throughout this book might change and, therefore, might not fully reflect snippets from this book. While this might create occasional confusion, I thought you might benefit from bug fixes (every code has them) and well as updates. Technology stack we'll use is so new that changes and improvements are coming on a daily basis, and I'll try to include them in the code even after this book has been released.

Combining Microservice Architecture and Container Technology

The *books* microservice (*books-ms*) that we'll use throughout this book was created in a bit different way than most microservices proponents tend to recommend.

Apart from things we already discussed the need for a service to be small, limited to a well-defined bounded context, and so on, it is important to notice that most microservices are created only for the back-end part of the system. Microservices proponents would split monolithic back-end into a lot of small microservices but would often leave the front-end untouched. The result in those cases is an overall architecture with monolithic front-end and back-end split into microservices. Why is that? I think that the answer lies in technologies we're using. The way we are developing front-end is not designed to be split into smaller pieces.

Server-side rendering is becoming history. While enterprise might not agree with that statement and continues pushing for server-side frameworks that "magically" transform, for example, Java objects to HTML and JavaScript, client-side frameworks will continue to increase in popularity slowly sending the server-side page rendering into oblivion. That leaves us with client-side frameworks. Single-page applications are what we tend to use today. AngularJS, React, ExtJS, ember.js and others proved to be the next step in the evolution of front-end development. However, single-page applications or not, most of them are promoting the monolithic approach to front-end architecture.

With back-end being split into microservices and front-end being monolithic, services we are building do not truly adhere to the idea that each should provide a full functionality. We are supposed to apply vertical decomposition and create small loosely coupled applications. However, in most cases we're missing visual aspect inside those services.

All front-end functionality (authentication, inventory, shopping cart, and so on) is part of a single application and communicates with back-end (most of the time through HTTP) that is split into microservices. This approach is a big advancement when compared with a single monolithic application. By keeping back-end services small, loosely coupled, designed for a single purpose and easy to scale, some of the problems we had with monoliths become mitigated. While nothing is ideal, and microservices have their set of problems, finding production bugs, testing, understanding the code, changing framework or even language, isolation, responsibility and other things became easier to handle. The price we had to pay was deployment, but that was significantly improved with containers (Docker) and the concept of immutable servers.

If we see the benefits microservices are providing with the back-end, wouldn't it be a step forward if we could apply those benefits to the front-end as well and design microservices to be complete with not only back-end logic but also visible parts of our applications? Wouldn't it be beneficial if a developer or a team could fully develop a feature and let someone else just import it into the application? If we could do business in that way, front-end (SPA or not) would be reduced to a scaffold that is in charge only of routing and deciding which services to import.

I'm not trying to say that no one is developing microservices in such a way that both front-end and back-end are part of it. I know that there are projects that do just that. However, I was not convinced that benefits of splitting the front-end into parts and packing them together with back-end outweigh downsides of such an approach. That is, until web components came into being.

I won't go into details how web components work since one of the goals of this book is to be language-agnostic (as much as that is possible). If you're interested to know more about the subject, please visit the Including Front-End Web Components Into Microservices/[14] article.

For now, the important thing to note is that the *books-ms* that we are about to start using has both the front-end web components and the back-end API packed into a single microservice. That allows us to keep the full functionality in one place and use it as we see fit. Someone might invoke the service API while someone else might decide to import web components into their Web site. As the authors of the service, we should not care much who is using it but only that it provides all the functionality potential users might require.

The service itself is coded using Scala[15] with Spray[16] that serves API requests and static front-end files. Web components are done with Polymer[17]. Everything is coded using test-driven development[18] approach that produced both unit and functional/integration tests. The source code is located in the vfarcic/books-ms[19] GitHub repository.

Don't worry if you never worked with Scala or Polymer. We won't be going into more details nor are we going to develop this application further. We'll use it to demonstrate concepts and to practice. For now, we'll use this service to setup the development environment. Before we do that, let us briefly go through the tools we'll use for this task.

Vagrant and Docker

We'll set up our development environment using Vagrant[20] and Docker[21].

Vagrant is a command-line tool for creating and managing virtual machines through a hypervisor like VirtualBox[22] or VMWare[23]. Vagrant isn't a hypervisor, just a driver that provides a consistent interface. With a single *Vagrantfile*, we can specify everything Vagrant needs to know to create, through VirtualBox or VMWare, as many VMs as needed. Since all it needs is a single configuration file, it can be kept in the repository together with the application code. It is very lightweight and portable and allows us to create reproducible environments no matter the underlying OS. While containers make the usage of VMs partly obsolete, Vagrant shines when we need a development environment. It's been used, and battle tested, for years.

> Please make sure that your Vagrant version is at least 1.8. Some of the readers experienced problems on older versions.

---

[14]http://technologyconversations.com/2015/08/09/including-front-end-web-components-into-microservices/

[15]http://www.scala-lang.org/

[16]http://spray.io/

[17]https://www.polymer-project.org

[18]http://technologyconversations.com/2014/09/30/test-driven-development-tdd/

[19]https://github.com/vfarcic/books-ms

[20]https://www.vagrantup.com/

[21]https://www.docker.com/

[22]https://www.virtualbox.org/

[23]http://www.vmware.com/

Please note that containers do not always replace VMs. Virtual machines provide an additional layer of isolation (security). They, also, allow more permutations than containers. With VMs, you could run Android if you wanted to. VMs are complimentary to containers. As Kelsey Hightower (formerly CoreOS, now Google) says *"If you replace all your VMs with containers, I look forward to seeing how your site was hacked on the front page of HackerNews."* That being said, containers reduce the usage of VMs. While it is still debatable whether we should run containers on "bare metal" or inside VMs, there is no need anymore to waste resources by creating one VM per application or service.

Docker containers allow us to wrap up some software in a complete filesystem. They can contain everything that software needs to run with complete autonomy; code, runtime libraries, database, application server, and so on. Since everything is packed together, containers will run the same no matter the environment. Containers share the kernel of the host OS making them more lightweight than virtual machines since they require a fully operational operating system. One single server can host many more containers than VMs. Another noticeable feature is that they provide process isolation. That isolation is not as solid as the one offered by virtual machines. However, VMs are much heavier than containers, and it would be very inefficient to pack each microservice into a separate VM. Containers, on the other hand, are a perfect fit for that task. We can pack each service into a separate container, deploy them directly on top of OS (without VMs in between) and still maintain the isolation between them. Apart from the kernel, nothing is shared (unless we choose to) and each container is a world in itself. At the same time, unlike VMs, containers are immutable. Each is a set of unchangeable images, and the only way to deploy a new release is to build a new container and replace the running instance of the old release. Later on, we'll discuss strategies for blue-green deployment that will run both releases in parallel, but that is the subject of one of the next chapters. As you will soon discover, containers can have a much broader usage than running production software.

Just like Vagrantfile that defines everything needed for Vagrant to create a virtual machine, Docker has *Dockerfile* that contains instructions how to build a container.

At this point, you might be asking why do we need Vagrant if Docker does the same and more? We'll use it to bring up a virtual machine with Ubuntu OS[24]. I could not be sure which operating system you are using. You might be a Windows user or an OS X fan. You might prefer one of Linux distributions. This book, for example, is written on Ubuntu as it is my OS of choice. The decision was made to use VMs to ensure that all the commands and tools throughout this book work on your computer no matter the underlying OS. Right now we are about to start one as an example of setting up the development environment. Later on, we'll create many more. They will simulate testing, staging, production, and other types of environments. We'll use Ubuntu[25] and a few more operating systems. That does not mean that you should use Vagrant VMs as presented in this book when you try to apply what you learned. While they are useful for development scenarios and for trying new things, you should reconsider deploying containers directly on top an of OS installed on "bare metal" or to a production ready VM.

The time has come to stop talking and move towards more practical parts. Throughout the rest of this

---

[24]http://www.ubuntu.com/

[25]http://www.ubuntu.com/

book, I will assume that Git[26] and Vagrant[27] are installed on your computer. There will be no other requirement. Everything else you might need will be provided through instructions and scripts.

If you are using Windows, please make sure that Git is configured to use "Checkout as-is". That can be accomplished during the setup by selecting the second or third options from the screen depicted in the Figure 4-1. Also, if you do not have SSH installed, please make sure that [PATH_TO_GIT]\bin is added to your PATH.

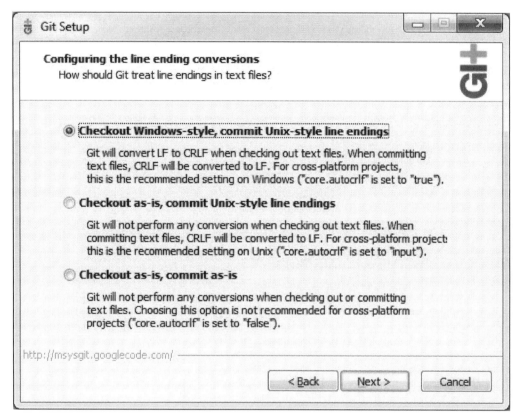

Figure 4-1: On Windows, "Checkout as-is" option should be selected during the Git setup

Development Environment Setup

Let us start by cloning the code from the books-ms[28] GitHub repository.

```
1  git clone https://github.com/vfarcic/books-ms.git
2
3  cd books-ms
```

With the code downloaded we can proceed and create the development environment.

---

[26]https://git-scm.com/

[27]https://www.vagrantup.com/downloads.html

[28]https://github.com/vfarcic/books-ms

Vagrant

Creating a Vagrant virtual machine is easy.

```
1  vagrant plugin install vagrant-cachier
2
3  vagrant up dev
```

The first command is not mandatory, but it will help speeding up the creation of new VMs. It caches all packages that are being used so that the next time we need them, they are obtained from the local HD instead being downloaded. The second command does the "real" work. It brings up the VM called *dev*. The first attempt might take some time since everything, starting with the base box, needs to be downloaded. Bringing up this VM will be much faster each consecutive time. Bringing up any other Vagrant VM based on the same box (in this case *ubuntu/trusty64*) will be fast.

Please note that some of the commands we'll be executing throughout the book might require a substantial time to finish. As a general rule, feel free to continue reading while commands are running (at least until you are asked to run a new command). Let us use the time needed to bring up the VM to go through the Vagrantfile[29] located in the root of the code we just cloned. It contains all the information Vagrant needs to create the development environment VM. The contents are as follows.

```
1  Vagrant.configure(VAGRANTFILE_API_VERSION) do |config|
2    config.vm.box = "ubuntu/trusty64"
3    config.vm.synced_folder ".", "/vagrant"
4    config.vm.provider "virtualbox" do |v|
5      v.memory = 2048
6    end
7    config.vm.define :dev do |dev|
8      dev.vm.network "private_network", ip: "10.100.199.200"
9      dev.vm.provision :shell, path: "bootstrap.sh"
10     dev.vm.provision :shell,
11       inline: 'PYTHONUNBUFFERED=1 ansible-playbook \
12         /vagrant/ansible/dev.yml -c local'
13   end
14   if Vagrant.has_plugin?("vagrant-cachier")
15     config.cache.scope = :box
16   end
17 end
```

---

[29]https://github.com/vfarcic/books-ms/blob/master/Vagrantfile

For those unfamiliar with Ruby, the syntax might look a bit cryptic but after a very short practice, you'll notice that it is very easy and straightforward to define one or more VMs with Vagrant. In our case, we started by specifying the box to be *ubuntu/trusty64.*

 Vagrant boxes are the package format for Vagrant environments. Anyone can use a box, on any platform supported by Vagrant, to bring up an identical working environment.

In other words, the box is (a kind of) a VM on top of which we can add things we require. You can browse available boxes from Atlas[30] or create your own[31].

After the box, comes the specification that *local directory* should be synced with VM. In our case, we set that the current directory (.) should be synced with the */vagrant* directory inside the VM. This way, all the files from the current directory will be freely available within the virtual machine.

Moving on, we specified that the VM should have *2 GB of RAM* and defined one VM called *dev.* Further on, throughout the book, we'll see how we can specify multiple virtual machines within the same *Vagrantfile.*

Inside the definition of the *dev* VM, we set the IP that Vagrant will expose and that it should run the Ansible playbook *dev.yml.* We won't go into more details regarding Ansible since that is reserved for one of the next chapters. Suffice to say that Ansible will make sure that *Docker* and *Docker Compose* are up and running.

We'll use *Vagrant* on many occasions throughout this book so you'll have plenty of opportunities to learn more about it. However, this book does not provide detailed guidelines and documentation. For more information and the complete documentation, please visit the Vagrant's official site[32].

Hopefully, you have a fast internet connection and by this time, execution of vagrant up probably finished. If not, grab a coffee and have a short break.

Let us enter the VM we just created and take a look what's inside.

```
1   vagrant ssh dev
2
3   ansible --version
4
5   docker --version
6
7   docker-compose --version
8
9   cd /vagrant
10
11  11
```

---

[30]https://atlas.hashicorp.com/boxes/search
[31]http://docs.vagrantup.com/v2/boxes/base.html
[32]https://www.vagrantup.com/

The first command allows us to enter inside the *dev* VM. You will be greeted with Ubuntu's welcome message. The next three are just demonstrations that *Ansible*, *Docker* and *Docker Compose* are installed. Finally, we're entering the */vagrant* directory and listing its content. You'll notice that it is the same as the host directory where we cloned the GitHub repository. Both of them are synchronized.

Now that we have the VM with all the software up and running, let us take a look at our second star of this chapter.

Docker

We already had a short discussion about Docker and containers in general. Never the less, we might want to explore the subject a bit more. There were very few technologies that experienced such a fast adoption. What makes Docker so popular?

VM hypervisors are all based on emulating virtual hardware. A huge percentage of resources VMs use is spent on that emulation. The exact percentage depends on specific configurations of each VM, but it is not uncommon to spend 50% or more of hardware resources on hardware virtualization. What that means in practical terms is that they are very demanding on resources.

Docker, on the other hand, uses shared OS. That feature alone makes it much more efficient. With well-defined containers, we can easily have 5 times more applications running than when they are deployed to separate virtual machines. By using the host kernel, containers manage to maintain almost the same separation between processes without the hardware virtualization. Even if Docker does not bring anything else to the table, that would be enough for many to start using it.

Curious thing is that many think that containers are something new that came into being with Docker. The reality is that they've been in use at least from the year 2000. Oracle Solaris Zones[33], LXC[34] and OpenVZ[35] are few of the examples. Google is one of the companies that started using containers long time before Docker emerged. The question you might ask is what makes Docker so special if containers existed long before its first release. Docker made it easy for us to use containers and is built on top of LXC. It made useful technology simple to use and built a very powerful ecosystem around it.

Docker company quickly become the partner with almost all software industry leaders (Canonical, RedHat, Google, Microsoft, and so on) and managed to standardize containers. This partnership also brought containers to almost all operating systems. At the time of this writing, Windows Server 2016 technical preview was released featuring Docker engine running natively.

Developers and DevOps love it since it provides them with a very easy and reliable way to pack, ship and run self-sufficient applications that can be deployed virtually anywhere. Another important Docker tool is the Hub[36] that contains official, unofficial and private containers. Whatever you need,

---

[33]http://www.oracle.com/technetwork/server-storage/solaris11/technologies/virtualization-306056.html

[34]https://linuxcontainers.org/

[35]http://openvz.org/Main_Page

[36]https://hub.docker.com/

be it an application, server, database or anything in between, chances are you will be able to find it in the Docker Hub and have it up and running with a single command in a matter of minutes.

There's much more to Docker (and containers in general) than what we discussed and you'll see throughout this book many different usages and test cases. For now, let's see how we can utilize Docker to help us with the development environment.

Development Environment Usage

At this moment, we won't go into details how to write *Dockerfile*, build containers, and push them to the public or a private registry. Those will be the subjects of following chapters. At the moment, we'll focus on running pre-made containers. In particular, vfarcic/books-ms-tests[37] container. It contains everything developers might need in order to work with the *books-ms* service that we cloned.

The container itself contains MongoDB, NodeJS, NPM, Git, Java, Scala, SBT, FireFox, Chrome and Gulp. It has all the Java and JavaScript libraries required by the project, configurations properly set, and so on. If you happen to work with all those languages and frameworks, you probably already have them installed on your computer. However, the chances are that you work only with some of them and lack the others. Even if you have everything already installed, you'd need to download Scala and JavaScript dependencies, fiddle with some configurations, run your instance of MongoDB, and so on. Instructions for this single microservice could be imposing. Now, multiply that with tens, hundreds or even thousands of microservices your enterprise might need. Even if you work only on one or very few of them, you would probably need to run some done by others. For example, your service might need to communicate with services done by some other team. While I am a strong believer that those cases should be solved with well-defined mocks, sooner or later you'll run into a situation when mocks are just not good enough.

There are different types of development tasks that we might need to perform with the *books-ms* service. Remember, it contains both the back-end (Scala with Spray) and front-end (JavaScript/HTML/CSS with PolymerJS).

We can, for example, execute Gulp[38] watcher that will run all front-end tests every time there is any change in client's source code. Getting continuous feedback of the correctness of your code is especially useful if you are practicing test-driven development. For more information regarding the way front-end was developed, please consult the Developing Front-End Microservices With Polymer Web Components and Test-Driven Development[39] article series.

The following command runs the watcher.

---

[37]https://hub.docker.com/r/vfarcic/books-ms-tests/

[38]http://gulpjs.com/

[39]http://technologyconversations.com/2015/08/09/developing-front-end-microservices-with-polymer-web-components-and-test-driven-development-part-15-the-first-component/

```
1   sudo docker run -it --rm \
2       -v $PWD/client/components:/source/client/components \
3       -v $PWD/client/test:/source/client/test \
4       -v $PWD/src:/source/src \
5       -v $PWD/target:/source/target \
6       -p 8080:8080 \
7       --env TEST_TYPE=watch-front \
8       vfarcic/books-ms-tests
```

A couple of readers commented that in rare occasions, the tests fail (probably due to concurrency). Also, NPM tends to get broken fairly often recently. To avoid problems, tests have been, temporarily, disabled. Instead the expected result you'll see a message "NPM is broken (again) so front-end tests are temporarily disabled."

A lot of layers need to be downloaded before this container is run. The container occupies around 2.5GB of virtual space (the actual physical size is much smaller). Unlike production containers that should be as small as possible, those used in development tend to be much bigger. For example, only NodeJS modules occupy almost 500MB, and those are just the front-end development dependencies. Add Scala libraries, runtime executables, browsers, and so on. Things sum up pretty quickly. Hopefully, you have a fast internet connection, and it won't take long until all the layers are pulled. Feel free to continue reading until the download is done or until you reach the instruction to run another command.

Parts of the output should be as follows (timestamps are removed for brevity).

```
1   ...
2   MongoDB starting : pid=6 port=27017 dbpath=/data/db/ 64-bit host=072ec2400bf0
3   ...
4   allocating new datafile /data/db/local.ns, filling with zeroes...
5   creating directory /data/db/_tmp
6   done allocating datafile /data/db/local.ns, size: 16MB,  took 0 secs
7   allocating new datafile /data/db/local.0, filling with zeroes...
8   done allocating datafile /data/db/local.0, size: 64MB,  took 0 secs
9   waiting for connections on port 27017
10  ...
11  firefox 43               Tests passed
12  Test run ended with great success
13
14  firefox 43 (93/0/0)
15  ...
16  connection accepted from 127.0.0.1:46599 #1 (1 connection now open)
17  [akka://routingSystem/user/IO-HTTP/listener-0] Bound to /0.0.0.0:8080
18  ...
```

We just run *93 tests* using Firefox, run the MongoDB and started the Web server with Scala and Spray. All Java and JavaScript dependencies, runtime executables, browser, MongoDB, JDK, Scala, sbt, npm, bower, gulp and everything else we might need are inside this container. All that was accomplished with a single command. Go ahead and change the client source code located in the *client/components* directory or tests in the *client/test*. You'll see that as soon as you save changes, tests will run again. Personally, I tend to keep my screen split in two. The first half with the code and the other half with the terminal when those tests are running in. We got a continuous feedback with a single command and no installations or setup of any kind.

As mentioned above, it's not only front-end tests that we are running with this command but also the Web server and MongoDB. With those two we can see the result of our work by opening the http://10.100.199.200:8080/components/tc-books/demo/index.html[40] in your favorite browser. What you see is a demo of Web components that we are going to use later on.

We won't go into details of what each argument in the command we just run means. That is reserved for one of the next chapters when we'll explore Docker CLI in more depth. The important thing to notice is that we run the container that was downloaded from the Docker Hub. Later on, we'll install our own registry where we'll store our containers. Another important thing is that a few local directories are mounted as container volumes allowing us to change the source code files locally and use them inside the container.

The major problem with the command above is its length. I, for one, am not capable remembering such a long command, and we cannot expect all developers to know it either. While what we did by now is by far easier than alternative methods for setting up the development environment, this command in itself clashes with the simplicity we're trying to accomplish. Much better way to run Docker commands is through Docker Compose[41]. Again, we'll reserve deeper explanation for one of the next chapter. For now, let us just get a taste of it. Please stop the container that is currently running by pressing *CTRL+c* and run the following command.

```
1   sudo docker-compose -f docker-compose-dev.yml run feTestsLocal
```

As you can see the result is the same but the command is this time much shorter. All the arguments needed for this container to run are stored in the docker-compose-dev.yml[42] file under the target *feTestsLocal*. The configuration file is using *YAML* (Yet Another Markup Language) format that is very easy to write and read for those who are familiar with Docker.

That was only one of many usages of this container. Another one, out of many more, is to run all tests once (both back-end and front-end), compile Scala code and minify and prepare JavaScript and HTML files for the distribution.

Before proceeding, please stop the container that is currently running by pressing *CTRL+c* and run the following.

---

[40]http://10.100.199.200:8080/components/tc-books/demo/index.html

[41]https://docs.docker.com/compose/

[42]https://github.com/vfarcic/books-ms/blob/master/docker-compose-dev.yml

```
1  sudo docker-compose -f docker-compose-dev.yml run testsLocal
```

This time, we did even more. We started MongoDB, run back-end functional and unit tests, stopped the DB, run all front-end tests and, finally, created the JAR file that will be used later on to create the distribution that will, ultimately, be deployed to the production (or, in our case, imitation of the production) node. Later on, we'll use the same container when we start working on our continuous deployment pipeline.

We won't need the development environment anymore, so let's stop the VM.

```
1  exit
2
3  vagrant halt dev
```

That was another one of the advantages of Vagrant. VMs can be started, stopped or destroyed with a single command. However, even if you choose the latter option, a new one can be as easily recreated from scratch. Right now, the VM is stopped. We might need it later and next time it won't take that long to start it. With the vagrant up dev, it will be up and running in a matter of seconds.

This chapter served two purposes. First one was to show you that, with Vagrant and Docker, we can setup development environment in a much easier and faster way than with the more traditional approaches. The second purpose was to give you a taste of what is to come. Soon we'll explore *Docker* and *Docker Compose* in more depth and start building, testing and running containers. Our goal will be to start working on the deployment pipeline. We'll begin by running commands manually. Next chapter with deal with basics and from there on we'll slowly progress towards more advanced techniques.

Implementation of the Deployment Pipeline: Initial Stages

Let us start with some basic (and minimum) steps of the continuous deployment pipeline. We'll check out the code, run pre-deployment tests and, if they are successful, build a container and push it to the Docker registry. With the container safely available in the registry, we'll switch to a different VM that will serve as an imitation of a production server, run the container and perform post-deployment tests to ensure that everything works as expected.

Those steps will cover the most basic flow of what could be considered the continuous deployment process. Later on, in the next chapters, once we are comfortable with the process we did so far, we'll go ever further. We'll explore all the steps required for our microservice to safely and reliably reach the production servers with zero-downtime, in a way that allows us to scale easily, with the ability to rollback, and so on.

Spinning Up the Continuous Deployment Virtual Machine

We'll start by creating the continuous delivery server. We'll do that by creating a VM with Vagrant. While using VMs is useful as a mean to perform easy to follow exercises, in the "real world" scenario you should skip VM altogether and install everything directly on the server. Remember, containers are in many cases a better substitute for some of the things we are used to doing with VMs and using both, as we'll do throughout this book, is in most case only a waste of resources. With that being said, let us create the *cd* and *prod* VMs. We'll use the first one as a continuous deployment server and the second as an imitation of the production environment.

```
1  cd ..
2
3  git clone https://github.com/vfarcic/ms-lifecycle.git
4
5  cd ms-lifecycle
6
7  vagrant up cd
8
9  vagrant ssh cd
```

We cloned the GitHub repository, brought up the *cd* virtual machine and entered it.

There are a few basic Vagrant operations you might need to know to follow this book. Specifically, how to stop and run the VM again. You never know when you might be left with an empty battery on your laptop or have a need to free your resources for some other tasks. I wouldn't like you to get into a situation where you are not able to follow the rest of the book just because you shut down your laptop and was not able to get back to the same situation you were before. Therefore, let's go through two basic operations; stopping the VM and bringing it up again with the provisioners.

If you want to stop this VM, all you have to do is run the vagrant halt command.

```
1  exit
2
3  vagrant halt
```

After this, VM will be stopped and your resources free for other things. Later on, you can start the VMs again with the vagrant up.

```
1  vagrant up cd --provision
2
3  vagrant ssh cd
```

The --provision flag will, among other things, make sure that all the containers we need are indeed up and running.

> Please note that Vagrant, by default, runs provisioning scripts only if VM is not created (when running vagrant up for the first time). If a VM is stopped (*halt*) and then started again (*up*), --provision argument needs to be added for provisioning scripts to run again.

Deployment Pipeline Steps

With the VM up and running (or soon to be), let us quickly go through the process. We should perform the following steps.

1. Check out the code
2. Run pre-deployment tests
3. Compile and/or package the code
4. Build the container
5. Push the container to the registry
6. Deploy the container to the production server
7. Integrate the container

8. Run post-integration tests
9. Push the tests container to the registry

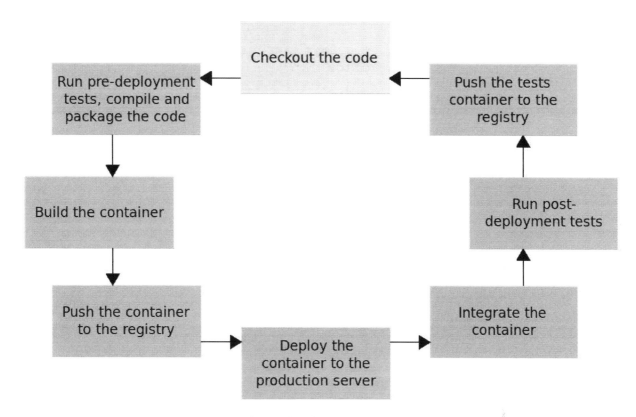

Figure 5-1: The Docker deployment pipeline process

At the moment we'll limit ourselves to manual execution and once we're comfortable with the way things work we'll transfer our knowledge to one of the CI/CD tools.

Checking Out the Code

Checking out the code is easy, and we already did it a couple of times.

> Please make sure that you are inside the *cd* VM before running the commands that follow.

```
1  git clone https://github.com/vfarcic/books-ms.git
2
3  cd books-ms
```

Running Pre-Deployment Tests, Compiling, and Packaging the Code

With the code checked out, we should run all the tests that do not require the service to be deployed. We already did the procedure when we tried different things we could do in the development environment.

```
1  docker build \
2      -f Dockerfile.test \
3      -t 10.100.198.200:5000/books-ms-tests \
4      .
5
6  docker-compose \
7      -f docker-compose-dev.yml \
8      run --rm tests
9
10 ll target/scala-2.10/
```

First we built the tests container defined in the Dockerfile.test file and tagged it with the -t argument. The name (or tag) of the container is *10.100.198.200:5000/books-ms-tests*. That is the special syntax with the first part being the address of the local registry and the second part the actual name of the container. We'll discuss and use the Registry later on. For now, it's important to know that we use it to store and retrieve containers we're building.

The second command run all the pre-deployment tests and compiled the Scala code into a JAR file ready for the distribution. The third command is only for demonstration purposes so that you can confirm that the JAR file is indeed created and resides in the *scala-2.10* directory.

Keep in mind that the reason for such a long time it took to build the container is because of a lot of things had to be downloaded for the first time. Each consecutive build will be much faster.

All we did up to now was running different commands without trying to understand what is behind them. Please note that commands to build Docker containers can be repeated in case of a failure. For example, you might lose your internet connection and, in such a case, building container would fail. If you repeat the build command, Docker will continue from the images that failed.

I wanted you to get a feeling of how Docker works from the perspective of those who just use pre-made containers or Dockerfile definitions created by others. Let us change this rhythm and dive into Dockerfile that is used to define containers.

Building Docker Containers

With all the tests passed and the JAR file created, we can build the container that we'll deploy to production later on. Before we do that, let us examine the Dockerfile[43] that contains all the

---

[43]https://github.com/vfarcic/books-ms/blob/master/Dockerfile

information Docker needs for building the container. Contents of the Dockerfile are as follows.

```
1   FROM debian:jessie
2   MAINTAINER Viktor Farcic "viktor@farcic.com"
3
4   RUN apt-get update && \
5       apt-get install -y --force-yes --no-install-recommends openjdk-7-jdk && \
6       apt-get clean && \
7       rm -rf /var/lib/apt/lists/*
8
9   ENV DB_DBNAME books
10  ENV DB_COLLECTION books
11
12  COPY run.sh /run.sh
13  RUN chmod +x /run.sh
14
15  COPY target/scala-2.10/books-ms-assembly-1.0.jar /bs.jar
16  COPY client/components /client/components
17
18  CMD ["/run.sh"]
19
20  EXPOSE 8080
```

You can find the *Dockerfile* file together with the rest of the *books-ms*[44] GitHub repository.

Let us go through it line by line.

```
1   FROM debian:jessie
```

The first line specifies which image should be used as the base of the container we're building. In our case, we are using *Debian* (version *Jessie*). That means that we should have most of the functionality we would get with Debian OS. However, that is not to say that the whole OS is downloaded when we pull this container. Remember, Docker is using host kernel so when we specify that container should use, for example, Debian as its base, we are only downloading image that has things specific to the OS we specified, like, for instance, packaging mechanism (*apt* in the case of Debian). What are the differences between various base images? Why did we choose the *debian* image to part from?

In most cases the best choice for a base image is one of the official Docker images[45]. Since Docker itself maintains those, they tend to be better controlled than those created by the community. The

---

[44]https://github.com/vfarcic/books-ms.git

[45]https://hub.docker.com/explore/

choice of the exact image one should use depends on the needs. Debian[46] is my preference in many cases. Besides my liking of Debian-based Linux distributions, it is relatively small (~125 MB) and still a full distribution with everything you might need from a Debian OS. On the other hand, you might be familiar with RPM packaging and prefer, for example, CentOS[47]. Its size is around 175 MB (approximately 50 % bigger than Debian). There are, however, some other cases when size is of utmost importance. That is especially true for images that would serve as utilities that are run once in a while to perform some specific actions. In such cases, Alpine[48] might be a good start. Its size is 5 MB making it minuscule. However, bear in mind that, due to its minimalistic approach, this image might be hard to reason with when more complicated commands are run on top of it. Finally, in many cases, you might want to use more specific images as a base of your containers. For example, if you need a container with MongoDB but have few specific actions to perform on its initialization, you should use the mongo[49] image.

In systems that host many containers, the size of the base image is less important than how many different base images are used. Remember, each image is cached on the server and reused across all containers that use it. If all your containers are, for example, extending from the *debian* image, the same cached copy will be reused in all cases meaning that it will be downloaded only once.

What we use as a base image is a container like any other. That means that you can use your containers as a base for others. For example, you might have many cases with applications that require NodeJS in combination with Gulp and few scripts specific to your organization. This scenario would be a good candidate for a container that would be extended (through the *FROM* instruction) by others.

Let us move to the next instruction.

```
1   MAINTAINER Viktor Farcic "viktor@farcic.com"
```

The maintainer is purely informational providing information about the author; a person who maintains the container. Not much to do here. Moving on.

```
1   RUN apt-get update && \
2       apt-get install -y --force-yes --no-install-recommends openjdk-7-jdk && \
3       apt-get clean && \
4       rm -rf /var/lib/apt/lists/*
```

The *RUN* instruction executes any set of commands that run in the same way as if those commands are run in the command prompt. You might have noticed that each but the last line in our example ends with && \. We are joining several separate commands instead of running each of them as a separate RUN instruction. The same result (from the operational perspective) could be accomplished with the following.

---

[46]https://hub.docker.com/_/debian/

[47]https://hub.docker.com/_/centos/

[48]https://hub.docker.com/_/alpine/

[49]https://hub.docker.com/_/mongo/

```
1  RUN apt-get update
2  RUN apt-get install -y --force-yes --no-install-recommends openjdk-7-jdk
3  RUN apt-get clean
4  RUN rm -rf /var/lib/apt/lists/*
```

That certainly looks cleaner and easier to maintain. However, it has its set of problems. One of them is that each instruction in the Dockerfile generates a separate image. A container is a collection of images stacked one on top of the other. Knowing that, last two RUN instructions (`clean` and `rm`) do not provide any value. Let's illustrate it by putting (invented numbers) of the size of each image. First two instructions (`apt-get update` and `apt-get install`) are adding packages (let's say 100 MB). The second two (`apt-get clean` and `rm`) are removing files (let's say 10 MB). While removal of files on a "normal" system does reduce the size of what we have stored on the HD, in the case of Docker containers it only removes things from the current image. Since each image is *immutable*, previous two images continue to have the size of 100 MB thus not removing the overall size of the container even though files removed later on are not accessible within the container. The size of those four images continues being 100 MB. If we go back to the first example where all commands are executed within the same *RUN* instruction thus creating a single image, the size is smaller (100 MB - 10 MB = 90 MB).

The important thing to note is that the size is not the only important consideration and we should try to balance it with maintainability. *Dockerfile* needs to be readable, easy to maintain and with a clear intention behind it. That means that in some cases the benefits of having one huge *RUN* instruction might not be the best option if that means that it will be hard to maintain it later on.

All that being said, the purpose of the RUN command in our example is to update the system with latest packages (`apt-get update`), install JDK 7 (`apt-get install`) and remove unnecessary files created during the process (`apt-get clean` and `rm`).

The next set of instructions provides the container with environment variables that can be changed at runtime.

```
1  ENV DB_DBNAME books
2  ENV DB_COLLECTION books
```

In this particular case, we are declaring variables *DB_DBNAME* and *DB_COLLECTION* with default values. The code of the service uses those variables to create the connection to the *Mongo DB*. If, for some reason, we'd like to change those values, we could set them when executing the `docker run` command (as we'll see later on throughout the book).

In the "container world", we are discouraged from passing environment specific files to containers running on different servers. Ideally, we should run a container without any other external files. While that is in some cases impractical (as, for example, with *nginx* that we'll use later on for reverse proxy), environment variables are a preferred way of passing environment specific information to the container at runtime.

Next, in our example, are a couple of *COPY* instructions.

```
1   COPY run.sh /run.sh
2   RUN chmod +x /run.sh
3
4   COPY target/scala-2.10/books-ms-assembly-1.0.jar /bs.jar
5   COPY client/components /client/components
```

COPY instruction is true to its name. It copies files from the host file system to the container we are building. It should be written in the COPY ‹source›... ‹destination› format. The *source* is relative to the location of the *Dockerfile* and must be inside the context of the build. What the latter statement means is that you cannot copy files that are not inside the directory where *Dockerfile* resides or one of its child directories. For example, COPY ../something /something is not allowed. The source can be a file or a whole directory and can accept wildcards matching the Go's filepath.Match[50] rules. The *destination* can also be a file or a directory. Destination matches the type of the source. If the source is a file, destination will be a file as well. Same is true when the source is a directory. To force destination to be a directory, end it with a slash (/).

While we haven't used *ADD* in our example, it is worth noting that it is very similar to *COPY*. In most cases I encourage you to use *COPY* unless you need additional features that *ADD* provides (most notably TAR extraction and URL support).

In our example, we are copying *run.sh* and making it executable through the chmod *RUN* instruction. Next, we are copying the rest of the files (back-end *JAR* and front-end *components*).

Let us go through the last two instructions from our Dockerfile.

```
1   CMD ["/run.sh"]
2   EXPOSE 8080
```

CMD specifies the command that will be executed when the container starts. The format is ["executable", "parameter1", "parameter2"...]. In our case /run.sh will run without any parameters. At the moment, the script contains a single command java -jar bs.jar that will start the Scala/Spray server. Keep in mind that *CMD* provides only the default executor that can be easily overwritten when a container is run.

The *EXPOSE* instruction specifies which port inside the container will be available at runtime.

The example *Dockerfile* we explained does not contain all the instructions we could use. Throughout this book, we'll work with a couple of others and get more familiar with the format. In the meantime, please visit the Dockerfile reference[51] for more information.

Equipped with this knowledge, let us build the container. The command is as follows.

---

[50]http://golang.org/pkg/path/filepath/#Match

[51]https://docs.docker.com/reference/builder/

```
1  docker build -t 10.100.198.200:5000/books-ms .
```

Let us use the time it takes for this command run (the first build always takes longer than the others) and go through the arguments we used. The first argument is `build` used for building containers. Argument `-t` allows us to tag the container with a particular name. If you'd like to push this container to the public Hub, the tag would be using the *<username>/<container_name>* format. If you have the account on Docker Hub[52], the username is used to identify you and can be used later on to push the container making it available for pulling on any server connected to the internet. Since I'm not willing to share my password, we took a different approach and used the *registry* IP and port instead of the Docker Hub username. That allows us to push it to the private registry instead. This alternative is usually better because it provides us with a complete control over our containers, tends to be faster over the local network and won't give CEO of your company a heart attack for sending your applications to the cloud. Finally, the last argument is a dot (.) specifying that the Dockerfile is located in the current directory.

One important thing left to discuss is the order of instructions in the *Dockerfile*. On one hand, it needs to be in logical. We can not, for example, run an executable before installing it or, as in our example, change permissions of the *run.sh* file before we copy it. On the other hand, we need to take in account Docker caching. When a `docker build` command is run, Docker will go instruction by instruction and check whether some other build process already created the image. Once an instruction that will build a new image is found, Docker will build not only that instruction but of all those that follow. That means that, in most cases, *COPY* and *ADD* instructions should be placed near the bottom of the *Dockerfile*. Even within a group of *COPY* and *ADD* instructions, we should make sure to place higher those files that are less likely to change. In our example, we're adding *run.sh* before the *JAR* file and front-end components since latter are likely to change with every build. If you execute the `docker build` command the second time you'll notice that Docker outputs `---> Using cache` in all steps. Later on, when we change the source code, Docker will continue outputting `---> Using cache` only until it gets to one of the last two *COPY* instructions (which one it will be, depends on whether we changed the *JAR* file or the front-end components).

We'll be using Docker commands a lot, and you'll have plenty opportunity to get more familiar with them. In the meantime, please visit the Using the command line[53] page for more information.

Hopefully, by this time, the container is already built. If not, take a short break. We are about to run our newly built container.

Running Containers

Running containers is easy as long as you know which arguments to use. The container we just built can be run with the following commands.

---

[52]https://hub.docker.com/

[53]https://docs.docker.com/reference/commandline/cli/

```
1  docker run -d --name books-db mongo
2
3  docker run -d --name books-ms \
4      -p 8080:8080 \
5      --link books-db:db \
6      10.100.198.200:5000/books-ms
```

The first command started the database container required by our service. The argument -d allows us to run a container in detached mode, meaning that it will run in the background. The second one, --name books-db, gives the container a name. If not specified, Docker would assign a random one. Finally, the last argument is the name of the image we want to use. In our case, we're using *mongo*, the official Docker MongoDB image.

This command shows one of very useful Docker features. Just as GitHub revolutionized the way we share code between different developers and projects, Docker Hub changed the way we deploy not only applications we are building but also those built by others. Please feel free to visit Docker Hub[54] and search for your favorite application, service, or a database. Chances are you'll find not only one (often official docker container) but many others done by the community. Efficient usage of Docker is often a combination of running images built by yourself and those built by others. Even if no image serves your purpose, it is often a good idea to use existing one as a base image. For example, you might want MongoDB with *replication set* enabled. The best way to obtain such an image would be to use *mongo* as the *FROM* instruction in your *Dockerfile* and add replication commands below it.

The second docker run is a little bit more complicated. Besides running in detached mode and giving it a name, it also exposes port 8080 and links with the *books-ms-db* container. Exposing port is easy. We can provide a single port, for example -p 8080. In such a case, Docker will expose its internal port 8080 as a random port. We'll use this approach later on when we start working with *service discovery tools*. In this example, we used two ports separated by a colon (-p 8080:8080). With such argument, Docker exposed its internal port 8080 to 8080. The next argument we used is --link books-db:db and allows us to link two containers. In this example, the name of the container we want to link to is *books-ms-db*. Inside the container, this link will be converted into environment variables. Let see how those variables look like.

We can enter the running container using the *exec* command.

```
1  docker exec -it books-ms bash
2
3  env | grep DB
4
5  exit
```

Arguments -it tells Docker that we want this execution to be interactive and with a terminal. It is followed by the name of the running container. Finally, we are overwriting the default command

---

[54]https://hub.docker.com/

specified as the *CMD* instruction in the *Dockerfile* with *bash*. In other words, we entered into the running container by running *bash*. Once inside the container, we listed all environment variables and filtered them so that only those containing *DB* are output. When we run the container, we specified that it should link with *books-ms-db* as *db*. Since all environment variables are always in uppercase, Docker created quite a few of them with names starting with *DB*. The output of env was as follows.

```
1  DB_NAME=/books-ms/db
2  DB_PORT_27017_TCP=tcp://172.17.0.5:27017
3  DB_PORT=tcp://172.17.0.5:27017
4  DB_ENV_MONGO_VERSION=3.0.5
5  DB_PORT_27017_TCP_PORT=27017
6  DB_ENV_MONGO_MAJOR=3.0
7  DB_PORT_27017_TCP_PROTO=tcp
8  DB_PORT_27017_TCP_ADDR=172.17.0.5
9  DB_COLLECTION=books
10 DB_DBNAME=books
```

All but the last two are a result of linking with the other container. We got the name of the link, TCP, port, and so on. The last two (*DB_COLLECTION* and *DB_DBNAME*) are not the result of linking but variables we defined inside the *Dockerfile*.

Finally, we exited the container.

There are few more things we can do to ensure that everything is running correctly.

```
1  docker ps -a
2
3  docker logs books-ms
```

The ps -a command listed all (-a) containers. This command should output both *books-ms* and *books-ms-db*. The logs command, as the name says, outputs logs of the container *books-ms*.

Even though it was very easy to run the Mongo DB and our container, *books-ms*, we are still required to remember all the arguments. Much easier way to accomplish the same result is with Docker Compose[55]. Before we see it in action, let us remove the container we are running.

```
1  docker rm -f books-ms books-db
2
3  docker ps -a
```

---

[55]https://docs.docker.com/compose/

The first command (rm) removes all listed containers. The argument -f forces that removal. Without it, only stopped containers could be removed. The rm command combined with the -f argument is equivalent to stopping containers with the stop command and then removing them with rm.

Let us run the same two containers (*mongo* and *books-ms*) with *Docker Compose.*

```
1  docker-compose -f docker-compose-dev.yml up -d app
```

The output of the command is as follows.

```
1  Creating booksms_db_1
2  Creating booksms_app_1
```

This time, we run both containers with a single docker-compose command. The -f argument specifies the specification file we want to use. I tend to define all development configurations in *docker-compose-dev.yml* and production in the default *docker-compose.yml*. When default file name is used, there is no need for the -f argument. Next is the up command that brought up the app container in detached mode (-d).

Let's take a look at the contents of the docker-compose-dev.yml[56] file.

```
1  app:
2    image: 10.100.198.200:5000/books-ms
3    ports:
4      - 8080:8080
5    links:
6      - db:db
7
8  db:
9    image: mongo
10   ...
```

The above output only displays the targets we are interested right now. There are others primarily dedicated to testing and compiling. We used them before when we set up the development environment. We'll use them again later on. For now, let us discuss the *app* and *db* targets. Their definition is very similar to Docker commands and arguments we already used and should be easy to understand. The interesting one is links. Unlike linking with manual commands where we need first to start the source container (in our case *mongo*) and then the one that links to it (*books-ms*), *docker-compose* will start all dependant containers automatically. We run the *app* target and Docker compose realized that it depends on the *db* target, so it started it first.

As before, we can verify that both containers are up and running. This time, we'll do it with the Docker Compose.

---

[56]https://github.com/vfarcic/books-ms/blob/master/docker-compose-dev.yml

```
1  docker-compose ps
```

The output should be similar to the following.

```
1      Name                Command            State           Ports
2  ------------------------------------------------------------------------
3  booksms_app_1   /run.sh                   Up      0.0.0.0:8080->8080/tcp
4  booksms_db_1    /entrypoint.sh mongod     Up      27017/tcp
```

Docker Compose, by default, names running containers using the combination of the project name (which default to the name of the directory), the name of the target (*app*) and the instance number (*1*). Later on, we'll run multiple instances of the same container distributed across multiple servers, and you'll have the chance to see this number increase.

With both containers up and running, we can check the logs of the containers we run with Docker Compose.

```
1  docker-compose logs
```

Please note that Docker Compose logs are in the *follow* mode, and you need to press *CTRL+c* to stop it.

I prefer as much testing as possible to be automatic, but that subject is left for later chapters so a brief manual verification will have to do for now.

```
1  curl -H 'Content-Type: application/json' -X PUT -d \
2    '{"_id": 1,
3    "title": "My First Book",
4    "author": "John Doe",
5    "description": "Not a very good book"}' \
6    http://localhost:8080/api/v1/books | jq '.'
7
8  curl -H 'Content-Type: application/json' -X PUT -d \
9    '{"_id": 2,
10   "title": "My Second Book",
11   "author": "John Doe",
12   "description": "Not a bad as the first book"}' \
13   http://localhost:8080/api/v1/books | jq '.'
14
15 curl -H 'Content-Type: application/json' -X PUT -d \
16   '{"_id": 3,
17   "title": "My Third Book",
```

```
18    "author": "John Doe",
19    "description": "Failed writers club"}' \
20    http://localhost:8080/api/v1/books | jq '.'
21
22 curl http://localhost:8080/api/v1/books | jq '.'
23
24 curl http://localhost:8080/api/v1/books/_id/1 | jq '.'
```

For those unfamiliar with *cURL*, it is a command line tool and library for transferring data with URL syntax. In our case, we're using it to send three *PUT* requests to the service that, in turn, stored data to the MongoDB. Last two commands invoked the service APIs to retrieve a list of all books, as well as data related to a particular book with the ID 1. With those manual verifications, we confirmed that the service works and can communicate with the database. Please note that we used *jq* to format JSON output.

Remember, this service also contains front-end Web components, but we won't try them out at this time. That is reserved for later, when we deploy this service to production together with the Web site that will import them.

Containers that we are running are misplaced. The VM that we're using is supposed to be dedicated to continuous deployment, and the containers that we built should run on a separate production server (or in our case a separate VM that should simulate such a server). Before we start deploying to production, we should go through *configuration management* that will allow us not only to streamline the deployment but also to setup the servers. We already used *Ansible* to create the *cd* VM, but we haven't had time to explain how it works. Even worst, we are yet to make a choice which tool to use.

For now, let us stop and remove the *books-ms* container and its dependencies thus freeing the *cd* server to do what it was intended to do in the first place; enable continuous deployment pipeline.

```
1 docker-compose stop
2
3 docker-compose rm -f
```

Pushing Containers to the Registry

Docker Registry can be used to store and retrieve containers. We already run it with the *cd* VM we created at the beginning of this chapter. With the *books-ms* built, we can push it to the registry. That will allow us to pull the container from any place that can access the *cd* server. Please run the following command.

```
1 docker push 10.100.198.200:5000/books-ms
```

Earlier in this chapter, we built the container using the *10.100.198.200:5000/books-ms* tag. That was a special format used for pushing to private registries; *<registry_ip>:<registry_port>/<container_-name>*. After the container has been tagged, we pushed it to the registry running on IP *10.100.198.200* and port *5000*. 10.100.198.200 is the IP of our *cd* VM.

With the container safely stored to the registry, we can run it on any server. Soon, once we go through *configuration management*, we'll have additional servers where we'll run containers stored in this registry.

Let's finish this chapter by destroying all the VMs. The next chapter will create those we need. That way you can take a break before continuing our adventure or jump into any chapter without the fear that something will fail due to tasks we did before. Each chapter is fully autonomous. While you will benefit from the knowledge obtained from previous chapters, technically, each of them works on its own. Before we destroy everything we did, we'll push the tests container so that we do not have to re-built it again from scratch. Registry container has a volume that maps our host directory to the internal path where images are stored. That way, all pushed images are stored on the host (directory *registry*) and do not depend on the VM where it's running.

```
1  docker push 10.100.198.200:5000/books-ms-tests
2
3  exit
4
5  vagrant destroy -f
```

The Checklist

We are still a few steps short of the basic implementation of the deployment pipeline. As a reminder, the steps are following.

1. Checkout the code - Done
2. Run pre-deployment tests - Done
3. Compile and/or package the code - Done
4. Build the container - Done
5. Push the container to the registry - Done
6. Deploy the container to the production server - Pending
7. Integrate the container - Pending
8. Run post-deployment tests - Pending
9. Push the tests container to the registry - Pending

It is important to notice that all the steps we run by now were performed on the *cd* VM. We want to reduce the impact on the production environment as much as possible so we'll continue running steps (or part of them) outside the destination server as much as possible.

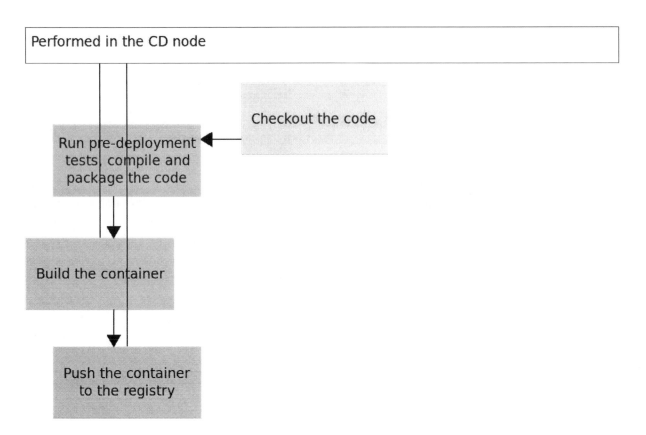

Figure 5-2: The initial stages of the deployment pipeline with Docker

We did the first five steps, or, at least, their manual version. The rest will have to wait until we set up our production server. In the next chapter, we'll discuss the options we have to accomplish this task.

Configuration Management in the Docker World

Anyone managing more than a few servers can confirm that doing such a task manually is a waste of time and risky. *Configuration management (CM)* exists for a long time, and there is no single reason I can think of why one would not use one of the tools. The question is not whether to adopt one of them but which one to choose. Those that already embraced one or the other and invested a lot of time and money will probably argue that the best tool is the one they chose. As things usually go, the choices change over time and the reasons for one over the other might not be the same today as they were yesterday. In most cases, decisions are not based on available options but by the architecture of the legacy system, we are sworn to maintain. If such systems are to be ignored, or someone with enough courage and deep pockets would be willing to modernize them, today's reality would be dominated by containers and microservices. In such a situation, the choices we made yesterday are different from choices we could make today.

CFEngine

CFEngine[57] can be considered the father of configuration management. It was created in 1993 and revolutionized the way we approach server setups and configurations. It started as an open source project and become commercialized in 2008 when the first enterprise version was released.

CFEngine is written in C, has only a few dependencies and is lightning fast. Actually, as to my knowledge, no other tool managed to overcome CFEngine's speed. That was, and still is its main strength. However, it had its weaknesses, with the requirement for coding skills being probably the main one. In many cases, an average operator was not able to utilize CFEngine. It requires a C developer to manage it. That did not prevent it from becoming widely adopted in some of the biggest enterprises. However, as youth usually wins over age, new tools were created, and today rarely anyone chooses CFEngine without being "forced" to do so due to the investment the company made into it.

Puppet

Later on, Puppet[58] came into being. It also started as an open source project followed by the enterprise version. It was considered more "operations friendly" thanks to its model-driven approach and small

---

[57]http://cfengine.com/
[58]https://puppetlabs.com/

learning curve when compared to CFEngine. Finally, there was a configuration management tool that operations department could leverage. Unlike C utilized by CFEngine, Ruby proved to be easier to reason with and more accepted by ops. CFEngine's learning curve was probably the main reason Puppet got its footing into the configuration management market and slowly sent CFEngine into history. That does not mean that CFEngine is not used any more. It is, and it doesn't seem it will disappear anytime soon in the same way as Cobol is still present in many banks and other finance related businesses. However, it lost its reputation for being the weapon of choice.

Chef

Then came Chef[59] promising to solve some of the nuances of Puppet. And it did, for a while. Later, as the popularity of both Puppet and Chef continued increasing, they entered the "zero sum game". As soon as one of them came up with something new or some improvement, the other one adopted it. Both feature an ever increasing number of tools that tend to increase their learning curves and complexity. Chef is a bit more "developer friendly" while Puppet could be considered more oriented towards operations and sysadmin type of tasks. Neither has a clear enough advantage over the other, and the choice is often based on personal experience than anything else. Both Puppet and Chef are mature, widely adopted (especially in enterprise environments) and have an enormous number of open source contributions. The only problem is that they are too complicated for what we are trying to accomplish. Neither of them was designed with containers in mind. Neither of them could know that the "game" would change with Docker since it didn't exist at the time they were designed.

All of the configuration management tools we mentioned thus far are trying to solve problems that we should not have the moment we adopt containers and immutable deployments. The server mess that we had before is no more. Instead of hundreds or even thousands of packages, configuration files, users, logs, and so on, we are now trying to deal with a lot of containers and very limited amount of anything else. That does not mean that we do not need configuration management. We do! However, the scope of what the tool of choice should do is much smaller. In most cases, we need a user or two, Docker service up and running and a few more things. All the rest are containers. Deployment is becoming a subject of a different set of tools and redefining the scope of what CM should do. *Docker Compose, Mesos, Kubernetes,* and *Docker Swarm,* are only a few of a rapidly increasing number of deployment tools we might use today. In such a setting, our configuration management choice should value simplicity and immutability over other things. Syntax should be simple and easy to read even to those who never used the tool. Immutability can be accomplished by enforcing a push model that does not require anything to be installed on the destination server.

Ansible

Ansible[60] tries to solve the same problems as other configuration management tools but in a very different way. One significant difference is that it performs all its operations over SSH. CFEngine

---

[59]https://www.chef.io/

[60]http://www.ansible.com/

and Puppet require clients to be installed on all servers they are supposed to manage. While Chef claims that it doesn't, its support for agent-less running has limited features. That in itself is a huge difference when compared to Ansible that does not require servers to have anything special since SSH is (almost) always present. It leverages well defined and widely used protocol to run whatever commands need to be run to make sure that the destination servers comply with our specifications. The only requirement is Python that is already pre-installed on most Linux distributions. In other words, unlike competitors that are trying to force you to setup servers in a certain way, Ansible leverages existing realities and does not require anything. Due to its architecture, all you need is a single instance running on a Linux or OS X computer. We can, for example, manage all our servers from a laptop. While that is not advisable and Ansible should probably run on a "real" server (preferably the same one where other continuous integration and deployment tools are installed), laptop example illustrates its simplicity. In my experience, push-based systems like Ansible are much easier to reason with than pull based tools we discussed earlier.

Learning Ansible takes a fraction of the time when compared to all the intricacies required to master the other tools. Its syntax is based on YAML (Yet Another Markup Language) and with a single glimpse over a playbook, even a person who never used the tool would understand what's going on. Unlike Chef, Puppet and, especially CFEngine that are written by developers for developers, Ansible is written by developers for people who have better things to do than learn yet another language and/or DSL.

Some would point out that the major downside is Ansible's limited support for Windows. The client does not even run on Windows, and the number of modules that can be used in playbooks and run on it is very limited. This downside, assuming that we are using containers is, in my opinion, an advantage. Ansible developers did not waste time trying to create an all around tool and concentrated on what works best (commands over SSH on Linux). In any case, Docker is not yet ready to run containers in Windows. It might be in the future but at this moment (or, at least, the moment I was writing this text), this is on the roadmap. Even if we ignore containers and their questionable future on Windows, other tools are also performing much worse on Windows than Linux. Simply put, Windows architecture is not as friendly to the CM objectives than Linux is.

I probably went too far and should not be too harsh on Windows and question your choices. If you do prefer Windows servers over some Linux distribution, all my praise of Ansible is in vain. You should choose Chef or Puppet and, unless you already use it, ignore CFEngine.

Final Thoughts

If someone asked me few years ago which tool should we use I would have a hard time answering. Today, if one has the option to switch to containers (be it Docker or some other type) and immutable deployments, the choice is clear (at least among tools I mentioned). Ansible (when combined with Docker and Docker deployment tools) wins any time of the day. We might even argue whether CM tools are needed at all. There are examples when people fully rely upon, let's say, CoreOS, containers, and deployment tools like Docker Swarm or Kubernetes. I do not have such a radical opinion (yet) and think that CM continues being a valuable tool in the arsenal. Due to the scope of the tasks CM tools needs to perform, Ansible is just the tool we need. Anything more complicated or harder to learn would be overkill. I am yet to find a person who had trouble maintaining Ansible playbooks. As a result, configuration management can quickly become the responsibility of the whole team. I'm not trying to say that infrastructure should be taken lightly (it definitely shouldn't). However, having contributions from the entire team working on a project is a significant advantage for any type of tasks and CM should not be an exception. CFEngine, Chef, and Puppet are an overkill with their complex architecture and their steep learning curve, at least, when compared with Ansible.

The four tools we briefly went through are by no means the only ones we can choose from. You might easily argue that neither of those is the best and vote for something else. Fair enough. It all depends on preferences and objectives we are trying to archive. However, unlike the others, Ansible can hardly be a waste of time. It is so easy to learn that, even if you choose not to adopt it, you won't be able to say that a lot of valuable time was wasted. Besides, everything we learn brings something new and makes us better professionals.

You probably guessed by now that Ansible will be the tool we'll use for configuration management.

Configuring the Production Environment

Let us see Ansible[61] in action and then discuss how it is configured. We'll need two VMs up and running; the *cd* will be used as a server from which we'll set up the *prod* node.

```
1   vagrant up cd prod --provision
2
3   vagrant ssh cd
4
5   ansible-playbook /vagrant/ansible/prod.yml -i /vagrant/ansible/hosts/prod
```

The output should be similar to the following.

```
1    PPLAY [prod] *********************************************************
2
3    GATHERING FACTS *****************************************************
4    The authenticity of host '10.100.198.201 (10.100.198.201)' can't be established.
5    ECDSA key fingerprint is 2c:05:06:9f:a1:53:2a:82:2a:ff:93:24:d0:94:f8:82.
6    Are you sure you want to continue connecting (yes/no)? yes
7    ok: [10.100.198.201]
8
9    TASK: [common | JQ is present] ************************************
10   changed: [10.100.198.201]
11
```

---

[61]http://www.ansible.com/home

```
12   TASK: [docker | Debian add Docker repository and update apt cache] ***********
13   changed: [10.100.198.201]
14
15   TASK: [docker | Debian Docker is present] ***********************************
16   changed: [10.100.198.201]
17
18   TASK: [docker | Debian python-pip is present] *******************************
19   changed: [10.100.198.201]
20
21   TASK: [docker | Debian docker-py is present] ********************************
22   changed: [10.100.198.201]
23
24   TASK: [docker | Debian files are present] ***********************************
25   changed: [10.100.198.201]
26
27   TASK: [docker | Debian Daemon is reloaded] **********************************
28   skipping: [10.100.198.201]
29
30   TASK: [docker | vagrant user is added to the docker group] ******************
31   changed: [10.100.198.201]
32
33   TASK: [docker | Debian Docker service is restarted] *************************
34   changed: [10.100.198.201]
35
36   TASK: [docker-compose | Executable is present] ******************************
37   changed: [10.100.198.201]
38
39   PLAY RECAP ******************************************************************
40   10.100.198.201             : ok=11    changed=9    unreachable=0    failed=0
```

The important thing about Ansible (and configuration management in general) is that we are in most cases specifying the desired state of something instead commands we want to run. Ansible, in turn, will do its best to make sure that the servers are in that state. From the output above we can see that statuses of all tasks are *changed* or *skipping*. For example, we specified that we want Docker service. Ansible noticed that we do not have it on the destination server (*prod*) and installed it.

What happens if we run the playbook again?

```
1   ansible-playbook /vagrant/ansible/prod.yml -i /vagrant/ansible/hosts/prod
```

You'll notice that the status of all the tasks is *ok*.

```
 1   PLAY [prod] ************************************************************
 2
 3   GATHERING FACTS *******************************************************
 4   ok: [10.100.198.201]
 5
 6   TASK: [common | JQ is present] ***************************************
 7   ok: [10.100.198.201]
 8
 9   TASK: [docker | Debian add Docker repository and update apt cache] ***********
10   ok: [10.100.198.201]
11
12   TASK: [docker | Debian Docker is present] ****************************
13   ok: [10.100.198.201]
14
15   TASK: [docker | Debian python-pip is present] ***********************
16   ok: [10.100.198.201]
17
18   TASK: [docker | Debian docker-py is present] ***********************
19   ok: [10.100.198.201]
20
21   TASK: [docker | Debian files are present] ***************************
22   ok: [10.100.198.201]
23
24   TASK: [docker | Debian Daemon is reloaded] *************************
25   skipping: [10.100.198.201]
26
27   TASK: [docker | vagrant user is added to the docker group] ****************
28   ok: [10.100.198.201]
29
30   TASK: [docker | Debian Docker service is restarted] *********************
31   skipping: [10.100.198.201]
32
33   TASK: [docker-compose | Executable is present] *********************
34   ok: [10.100.198.201]
35
36   PLAY RECAP ***********************************************************
37   10.100.198.201             : ok=10    changed=0    unreachable=0    failed=0
```

Ansible went to the server and checked the status of all tasks, one at the time. Since this is the second run and we haven't modified anything in the server, Ansible concluded that there is nothing to do. The current state is as expected.

The command we just run (ansible-playbook prod.yml -i hosts/prod) is simple. The first argument is the path to the playbook and the second argument's value represents the path to the inventory file that contains the list of servers where this playbook should run.

That was a very simple example. We had to setup the production environment and, at this moment, all we needed is Docker, Docker Compose, and a few configuration files. Later on, we'll see more complicated examples.

Now that we've seen Ansible in action let us go through the configuration of the *playbook* we just run (twice).

Setting Up the Ansible Playbook

The content of the prod.yml[62] Ansible playbook is as follows.

```
1  - hosts: prod
2    remote_user: vagrant
3    serial: 1
4    sudo: yes
5    roles:
6      - common
7      - docker
```

Just by reading the playbook one should be able to understand what's it about. It is running on hosts called *prod* as the user *vagrant* and executes commands as *sudo*. At the bottom is the list of roles that, in our case, consists of only two; *common* and *docker*. Role is a set of tasks that we usually organize around one functionality, product, type of operations, and so on. The Ansible playbook organization is based on tasks that are grouped into roles that can be combined into playbooks.

Before we take a look at it, let us discuss what are the objectives of the *docker* role. We want to make sure that the Docker Debian repository is present and that the latest *docker-engine* package is installed. Later on, we'll need the docker-py[63] (Python API client for Docker) that can be installed with pip[64] so we're making sure that both are present in our system. Next, we need the standard Docker configuration to be replaced with our file located in the *files* directory. Docker configurations require Docker service to be restarted, so we have to do just that every time there is a change to the *files/docker* file. Finally, we're making sure that the user *vagrant* is added to the group *docker* and, therefore, able to run Docker commands.

Let us take a look at the *roles/docker* directory that defines the role we're using. It consists of two sub-directories, *files*, and *tasks*. Tasks are the heart of any role and, by default, requires them to be defined in the *main.yml* file.

The content of the roles/docker/tasks/main.yml[65] file is as follows.

[62]https://github.com/vfarcic/ms-lifecycle/blob/master/ansible/prod.yml
[63]https://github.com/docker/docker-py
[64]https://pypi.python.org/pypi/pip
[65]https://github.com/vfarcic/ms-lifecycle/blob/master/ansible/roles/docker/tasks/main.yml

```
1  - include: debian.yml
2    when: ansible_distribution == 'Debian' or ansible_distribution == 'Ubuntu'
3
4  - include: centos.yml
5    when: ansible_distribution == 'CentOS' or ansible_distribution == 'Red Hat Ent\
6  erprise Linux'
```

Since we'll be running Docker on both *Debian* (*Ubuntu*) and *CentOS* or *Red Hat*, roles are split into *debian.yml* and *centos.yml* files. Right now, we'll be using Ubuntu so let's take a look at the roles/docker/tasks/debian.yml[66] role.

```
1  - name: Debian add Docker repository and update apt cache
2    apt_repository:
3      repo: deb https://apt.dockerproject.org/repo ubuntu-{{ debian_version }} main
4      update_cache: yes
5      state: present
6    tags: [docker]
7
8  - name: Debian Docker is present
9    apt:
10     name: docker-engine
11     state: latest
12     force: yes
13   tags: [docker]
14
15 - name: Debian python-pip is present
16   apt: name=python-pip state=present
17   tags: [docker]
18
19 - name: Debian docker-py is present
20   pip: name=docker-py version=0.4.0 state=present
21   tags: [docker]
22
23 - name: Debian files are present
24   template:
25     src: "{{ docker_cfg }}"
26     dest: "{{ docker_cfg_dest }}"
27   register: copy_result
28   tags: [docker]
29
30 - name: Debian Daemon is reloaded
```

---

[66]https://github.com/vfarcic/ms-lifecycle/blob/master/ansible/roles/docker/tasks/debian.yml

```
31      command: systemctl daemon-reload
32      when: copy_result|changed and is_systemd is defined
33      tags: [docker]
34
35    - name: vagrant user is added to the docker group
36      user:
37        name: vagrant
38        group: docker
39      register: user_result
40      tags: [docker]
41
42    - name: Debian Docker service is restarted
43      service:
44        name: docker
45        state: restarted
46      when: copy_result|changed or user_result|changed
47      tags: [docker]
```

If this would be a different framework or a tool, I would pass through each of the tasks and explain them one by one, and you would be very grateful for acquiring more pieces of wisdom. However, I do not think there is a reason to do that. Ansible is very straightforward. Assuming that you have a basic Linux knowledge, I bet you can understand each of the tasks without any further explanation. In case I was wrong, and you do need an explanation, please look for the module in question in the All Modules[67] section of the Ansible documentation. For example, if you'd like to know what the second task does, you'd open the apt module[68]. The only important thing to know for now is how the indentation works. YAML is based on *key: value, parent/child* structure. For example, the last task has *name* and *state* keys that are children of the *service* that, in turn, is one of the Ansible modules.

There is one more thing we used with our *prod.yml* playbook. The command we executed had the -i hosts/prod argument that we used to specify the inventory file with the list of hosts the playbook should run on. The hosts/prod[69] inventory is quite big since it is used throughout the whole book. At the moment, we are interested only in the *prod* section since that is the value of the *hosts* argument we specified in the playbook.

```
1    ...
2    [prod]
3    10.100.198.201
4    ...
```

If we'd like to apply the same configuration to more than one server all we'd have to do is add another IP.

---

[67]http://docs.ansible.com/ansible/list_of_all_modules.html

[68]http://docs.ansible.com/ansible/apt_module.html

[69]https://github.com/vfarcic/ms-lifecycle/blob/master/ansible/hosts/prod

We'll see more complex examples later on. I intentionally said more complex since nothing is truly complicated in Ansible but, depending on some tasks and their interdependency, some roles can be more or less complex. I hope that the playbook we just run gave you an approximation of the type of the tool Ansible is and I hope you liked it. We'll rely on it for all the configuration management tasks and more.

You might have noticed that we never entered the *prod* environment but run everything remotely from the *cd* server. The same practice will continue throughout the book. With Ansible and few other tools we'll get introduced to, later on, there is no need to ssh into servers and do manual tasks. In my opinion, our knowledge and creativity should be used for coding and everything else should be automatic; testing, building, deployment, scaling, logging, monitoring, and so on. That is one of the takeaways of this book. The key to success is massive automation that frees us to do exciting and more productive tasks.

As before, we'll end this chapter by destroying all the VMs. The next chapter will create those we need.

```
1  exit
2
3  vagrant destroy -f
```

With the first production server up and running (at the moment only with Ubuntu OS, Docker, and Docker Compose) we can continue working on the basic implementation of the deployment pipeline.

Implementation of the Deployment Pipeline: Intermediate Stages

We could not complete the basic implementation of the deployment pipeline without the production server being set up. We didn't need much. At the moment, Docker is our only prerequisite for the deployment and that gave us a good excuse to make a side trip into the world of *configuration management*. Now, with the Ansible playbook that will set up our *prod* server, we can continue where we left and deploy the container to the production server.

1. Checkout the code - Done
2. Run pre-deployment tests - Done
3. Compile and/or package the code - Done
4. Build the container - Done
5. Push the container to the registry - Done
6. Deploy the container to the production server - Pending
7. Integrate the container - Pending
8. Run post-deployment tests - Pending
9. Push the tests container to the registry - Pending

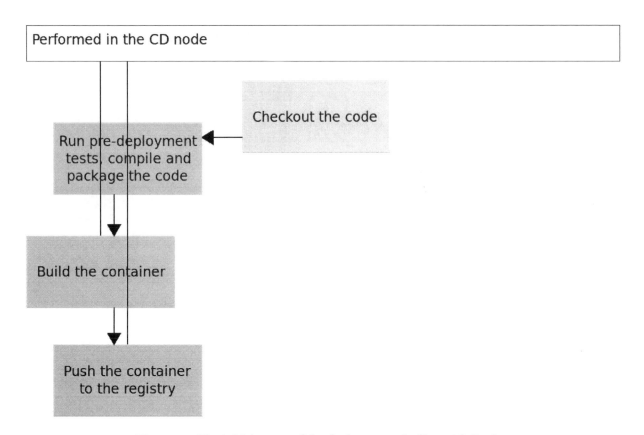

Figure 7-1: **The initial stages of the deployment pipeline with Docker**

We are missing only four steps from the manual deployment pipeline.

Deploying Containers to the Production Server

Let's create and configure VMs we'll use throughout this chapter.

```
1  vagrant up cd prod
2
3  vagrant ssh cd
4
5  ansible-playbook /vagrant/ansible/prod.yml \
6      -i /vagrant/ansible/hosts/prod
```

The first command brought up the *cd* and *prod* VMs while the second got us inside the *cd* VM. Finally, the last command configured the *prod* VM.

Now that the production server is properly configured, we can deploy the *books-ms* container. Even though we don't have it pulled to the destination server, we already pushed it to the Docker registry in the *cd* node (that maps into the host directory) and can retrieve it from there. What we do not have, however, is the Docker Compose configuration that specifies how the container should be run. I prefer keeping everything related to a service in the same repository and *docker-compose.yml* is no exception. We can retrieve it GitHub.

```
1  wget https://raw.githubusercontent.com/vfarcic\
2  /books-ms/master/docker-compose.yml
```

With the docker-compose.yml[70] downloaded, let us take a quick look at it (targets that won't be used in this chapter have been excluded).

```
1  base:
2    image: 10.100.198.200:5000/books-ms
3    ports:
4      - 8080
5    environment:
6      - SERVICE_NAME=books-ms
7
8  app:
9    extends:
10     service: base
11   links:
12     - db:db
13
14 db:
15   image: mongo
```

The *base* target contains the base definition of our container. The next target (*app*) is extending the *base* service allowing us to avoid duplicating the definitions. By extending services, we can override arguments or add new ones. The *app* target will run the container we stored in the registry on the *cd* server and is linked to the third target that represent the database required by the service. You might notice that we changed the way ports are specified. In the docker-compose-dev.yml[71] we had two numbers separated by a colon (*8080:8080*). The first one was the port Docker would expose to the host while the second one is the internal port used by the server inside the container. The *docker-compose.yml* is a bit different and has only the internal port set. The reason behind that is the elimination of potential conflicts. While in the development environment we tend to run only a small number of services (those we need at the moment), in production we might run tens, hundreds, or even thousands of them at the same time. Having predefined ports can easily result in conflicts. If two of them are using the same port, the result will be a failure. For that reason, we'll let Docker expose a random port to the host.

Let us run the Docker Compose *app* target.

```
1  export DOCKER_HOST=tcp://prod:2375
2
3  docker-compose up -d app
```

We exported the *DOCKER_HOST* variable that tells local Docker client to send commands to the remote one located on the *prod* node and port *2375*. The second command run the Docker Compose target *app*. Since *DOCKER_HOST* is pointing to the remote host, the *app* target and linked container *db* were deployed to the *prod* server. We did not even have to enter the destination server. The deployment was done remotely.

For security reasons, the ability to invoke remote Docker API is disabled by default. However, one of the Ansible playbook tasks was to change that behaviour by modifying the */etc/default/docker* configuration file. Its content is as follows.

```
1  DOCKER_OPTS="$DOCKER_OPTS --insecure-registry 10.100.198.200:5000 -H tcp://0.0.0\
2  .0:2375 -H unix:///var/run/docker.sock"
```

The *–insecure-registry* allows Docker to pull images from our private registry located in the *cd* node (*10.100.198.200*). The *-H* argument tells Docker to listen to remote requests from any address (*0.0.0.0*) on the port *2375*. Please note that in the "real" production environment, we would need to be much more restrictive and allow only trusted addresses to access the remote Docker API.

We can confirm that both containers are indeed running on the *prod* VM by executing another remote call.

```
1  docker-compose ps
```

The output is as follows.

```
1     Name              Command              State           Ports
2  ----------------------------------------------------------------------
3  vagrant_app_1    /run.sh                  Up       0.0.0.0:32770->8080/tcp
4  vagrant_db_1     /entrypoint.sh mongod    Up       27017/tcp
```

Since Docker assigned a random port to the service's internal port 8080, we need to find it out. That can be done with the *inspect* command.

```
1  docker inspect vagrant_app_1
```

The part of the output that interests us should be similar to the following.

```
1   ...
2   "NetworkSettings": {
3       "Bridge": "",
4       "EndpointID": "45a8ea03cc2514b128448...",
5       "Gateway": "172.17.42.1",
6       "GlobalIPv6Address": "",
7       "GlobalIPv6PrefixLen": 0,
8       "HairpinMode": false,
9       "IPAddress": "172.17.0.4",
10      "IPPrefixLen": 16,
11      "IPv6Gateway": "",
12      "LinkLocalIPv6Address": "",
13      "LinkLocalIPv6PrefixLen": 0,
14      "MacAddress": "02:42:ac:11:00:04",
15      "NetworkID": "dce90f852007b489f4a2fe...",
16      "PortMapping": null,
17      "Ports": {
18          "8080/tcp": [
19              {
20                  "HostIp": "0.0.0.0",
21                  "HostPort": "32770"
22              }
23          ]
24      },
25      "SandboxKey": "/var/run/docker/netns/f78bc787f617",
26      "SecondaryIPAddresses": null,
27      "SecondaryIPv6Addresses": null
28  },
29  ...
```

The original output is much bigger than this and it contains all the info we might (or might not) need. What we are interested in right now is the *NetworkSettings.Ports* section that, in my case, gives us *HostPort 32770* mapped to the internal port *8080*. We can do better than that and use the *–format* argument.

```
1   PORT=$(docker inspect \
2       --format='{{(index (index .NetworkSettings.Ports "8080/tcp") 0).HostPort}}' \
3       vagrant_app_1)
4
5   echo $PORT
```

Do not get scared by the *–format* value syntax. It uses Go's text/template[72] format and indeed can

---

[72]http://golang.org/pkg/text/template/

be a bit daunting. The good news is that we'll use much better ways to do this once we get to *service discovery* chapter. This is only the temporary workaround.

We got our port and stored it to the *PORT* variable. Now we can repeat *cURL* commands we already got familiar with and confirm that the service is running and is connected to the DB.

```
1   curl -H 'Content-Type: application/json' -X PUT -d \
2       "{\"_id\": 1,
3       \"title\": \"My First Book\",
4       \"author\": \"John Doe\",
5       \"description\": \"Not a very good book\"}" \
6       http://prod:$PORT/api/v1/books \
7       | jq '.'
8
9   curl -H 'Content-Type: application/json' -X PUT -d \
10      "{\"_id\": 2,
11      \"title\": \"My Second Book\",
12      \"author\": \"John Doe\",
13      \"description\": \"Not a bad as the first book\"}" \
14      http://prod:$PORT/api/v1/books \
15      | jq '.'
16
17  curl -H 'Content-Type: application/json' -X PUT -d \
18      "{\"_id\": 3,
19      \"title\": \"My Third Book\",
20      \"author\": \"John Doe\",
21      \"description\": \"Failed writers club\"}" \
22      http://prod:$PORT/api/v1/books \
23      | jq '.'
24
25  curl http://prod:$PORT/api/v1/books \
26      | jq '.'
27
28  curl http://prod:$PORT/api/v1/books/_id/1 \
29      | jq '.'
```

The output of the last command is as follows.

```
1  {
2      "_id": 1,
3      "author": "John Doe",
4      "description": "Not a very good book",
5      "title": "My First Book"
6  }
```

As before, when we run the same command in the development environment, we inserted three books to the database and confirmed that they can be retrieved from the database. However, this is not an efficient way of verifying whether the service was deployed correctly. We can do better than that and run the integration tests.

The important thing to note is that we have not even entered into the *prod* node. All the deployment commands were done through the remote Docker API.

Docker UI

This might be a good opportunity to introduce a nice open source project DockerUI[73]. It is defined as part of the *docker* Ansible role so it is running on all servers where we configure Docker. We can, for example, see the instance running on the *prod* node by opening http://10.100.198.201:9000[74] from any browser.

 Please note that all IPs created through Vagrant are set to be private, meaning that they can be accessed only from the host machine. If that happens to be your laptop, you should not have a problem to open the DockerUI address in your browser. On the other hand, if you are running the examples on one of your corporate servers, please make sure that you can access it's desktop and that a browser is installed. If you need to access that server remotely, please try one of remote desktop solutions like VNC[75].

---

[73]https://github.com/crosbymichael/dockerui

[74]http://10.100.198.201:9000

[75]https://www.realvnc.com/

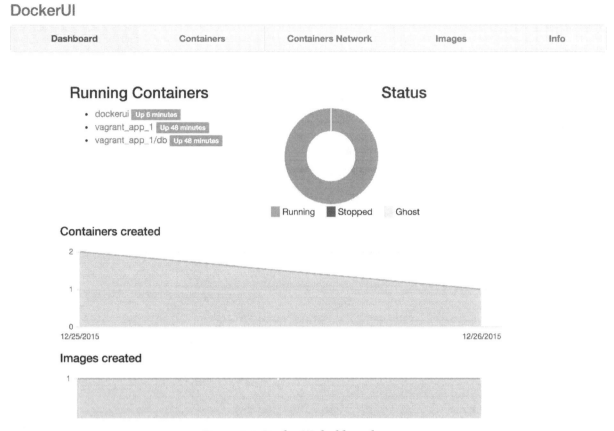

Figure 7-2: DockerUI dashboard screen

While it is much more efficient to operate containers through CLI, the DockerUI provides a very useful way to gain a general overview of the system and details related to each container, network, and images. Its true usefulness can be seen when a big number of containers is running in a cluster. It is very lightweight so it won't use much of your resources.

Unless specified otherwise, you'll find it running on each VM we set up.

The Checklist

Before we move on, let's see where we are with our basic implementation of the deployment pipeline.

1. Checkout the code - Done
2. Run pre-deployment tests - Done
3. Compile and/or package the code - Done
4. Build the container - Done
5. Push the container to the registry - Done
6. Deploy the container to the production server - Done
7. Integrate the container - Pending

8. Run post-deployment tests - Pending

9. Push the tests container to the registry - Pending

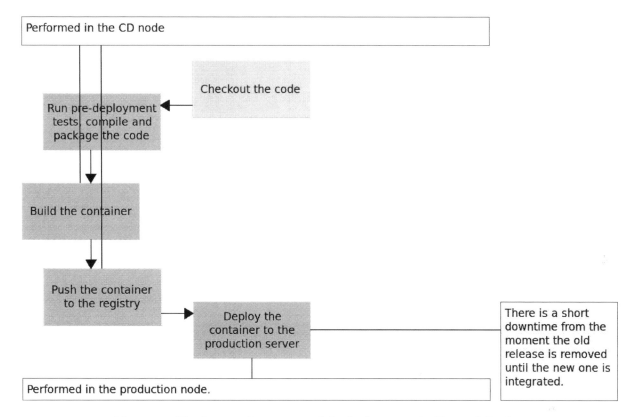

Figure 7-3: The intermediate stages of the deployment pipeline with Docker

Please note that, unlike the steps we did in the previous chapter, the deployment was performed in the production environment through remote Docker API. If we deployed the second release, we would have a period which neither the old nor the new release were operational. One would need to be stopped while the other would require some time to be brought up. No matter whether this period was short or not, we would have *down-time* that, in itself, would prevent us from moving towards *continues deployment*. All we'll do for now is take a note of this problem. Later on, we'll explore the *blue-green deployment* procedure that will help us overcome this issue and proceed towards the quest for zero-downtime deployments.

We're making progress and only three tasks are left on the checklist. However, the application is not yet integrated and, therefore, we cannot run integration tests. In order to proceed, there are two more concepts we need to explore; *service discovery* and *reverse proxy*.

We'll use a new set of virtual machines while experimenting with service discovery tools, so let us save some resources and destroy the VMs we're running. We'll create those that we need in the next chapter.

```
1  exit
2
3  vagrant destroy -f
```

Service Discovery: The Key to Distributed Services

It does not take much strength to do things, but it requires a great deal of strength to decide what to do

– Elbert Hubbard

The more services we have, the bigger the chance for a conflict to occur if we are using predefined ports. After all, there can be no two services listening on the same port. Managing an accurate list of all the ports used by, let's say, a hundred services is a challenge in itself. Add to that list the databases those services need and the number grows even more. For that reason, we should deploy services without specifying ports and letting Docker assign random ones for us. The only problem is that we need to discover the port number and let others know about it.

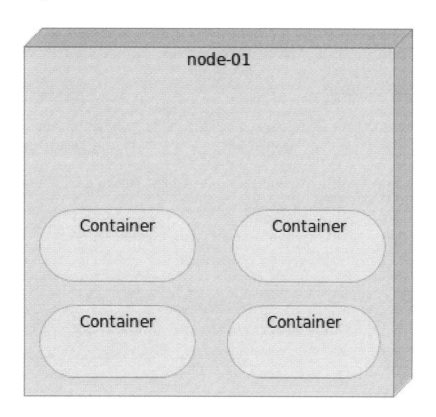

Figure 8-1: Single node with services deployed as Docker containers

Things will get even more complicated later on when we start working on a distributed system with services deployed into one of the multiple servers. We can choose to define in advance which service goes to which server, but that would cause a lot of problems. We should try to utilize server resources as best we can, and that is hardly possible if we define in advance where to deploy each service. Another problem is that automatic scaling of services would be difficult at best, and not to mention automatic recuperation from, let's say, server failure. On the other hand, if we deploy services to the server that has, for example, least number of containers running, we need to add the IP to the list of data needed to be discovered and stored somewhere.

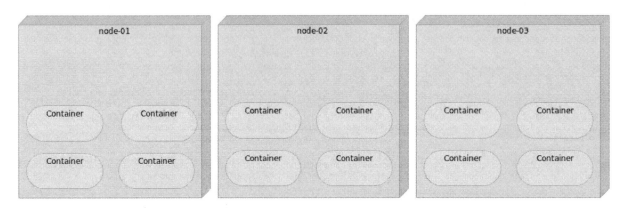

Figure 8-2: Multiple nodes with services deployed as Docker containers

There are many other examples of cases when we need to store and retrieve (discover) some information related to the services we are working with.

To be able to locate our services, we need at least the following two processes to be available for us.

- **Service registration** process that will store, as a minimum, the host and the port service is running on.
- **Service discovery** process that will allow others to be able to discover the information we stored during the registration process.

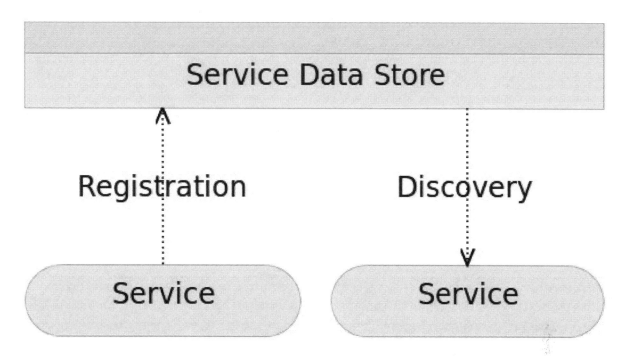

Figure 8-3: Service registration and discovery

Besides those processes, we need to consider several other aspects. Should we unregister the service if it stops working and deploy/register a new instance? What happens when there are multiple copies of the same service? How do we balance the load among them? What happens if a server goes down? Those and many other questions are tightly related to the registration and discovery processes and will be the subject of the next chapters. For now, we'll limit the scope only to the *service discovery* (the common name that envelops both processes mentioned above) and the tools we might use for such a task. Most of them feature highly available distributed key/value storage.

Service Registry

The goal of the service registry is simple. Provide capabilities to store service information, be fast, persistent, fault-tolerant, and so on. In its essence, service registry is a database with a very limited scope. While other databases might need to deal with a vast amount of data, service registry expects a relatively small data load. Due to the nature of the task, it should expose some API so that those in need of it's data can access it easily.

There's not much more to be said (until we start evaluating different tools) so we'll move on to service registration.

Service Registration

Microservices tend to be very dynamic. They are created and destroyed, deployed to one server and then moved to another. They are always changing and evolving. Whenever there is any change in service properties, information about those changes needs to be stored in some database (we'll call it *service registry* or simply *registry*). The logic behind service registration is simple even though the implementation of that logic might become complicated. Whenever a service is deployed, its data (IP and port as a minimum) should be stored in the service registry. Things are a bit more complicated when a service is destroyed or stopped. If that is a result of a purposeful action, service data should be removed from the registry. However, there are cases when service is stopped due to a failure and in such a situation we might choose to do additional actions meant to restore the correct functioning of that service. We'll speak about such a situation in more details when we reach the self-healing chapter.

There are quite a few ways service registration can be performed.

Self-Registration

Self-registration is a common way to register service information. When a service is deployed it notifies the registry about its existence and sends its data. Since each service needs to be capable of sending its data to the registry, this can be considered an anti-pattern. By using this approach, we are breaking *single concern* and *bounded context* principles that we are trying to enforce inside our microservices. We'd need to add the registration code to each service and, therefore, increase the development complexity. More importantly, that would couple services to a specific registry service. Once their number increases, modifying all of them to, for example, change the registry would be a very cumbersome work. Besides, that was one of the reasons we moved away from monolithic applications; freedom to modify any service without affecting the whole system. The alternative would be to create a library that would do that for us and include it in each service. However, this approach would severally limit our ability to create entirely self-sufficient microservices. We'd increase their dependency on external resources (in this case the registration library).

De-registration is, even more, problematic and can quickly become quite complicated with the self-registration concept. When a service is stopped purposely, it should be relatively easy to remove its data from the registry. However, services are not always stopped on purpose. They might fail in unexpected ways and the process they're running in might stop. In such a case it might be difficult (if not impossible) to always be able to de-register the service from itself.

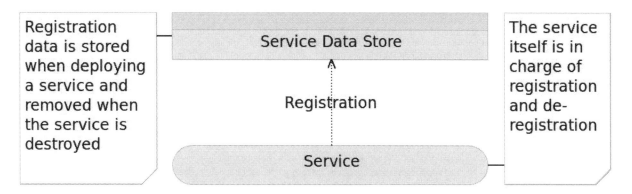

Figure 8-4: Self-registration

While self-registration might be common, it is not an optimum nor productive way to perform this type of operations. We should look at alternative approaches.

Registration Service

Registration service or third party registration is a process that manages registration and de-registration of all services. The service is in charge of checking which microservices are running and should update the registry accordingly. A similar process is applied when services are stopped. The registration service should detect the absence of a microservice and remove its data from the registry. As an additional function, it can notify some other process of the absence of the microservice that would, in turn, perform some corrective actions like re-deployment of the absent microservice, email notifications, and so on. We'll call this registration and de-registration process *service registrator* or simply *registrator* (actually, as you'll soon see, there is a product with the same name).

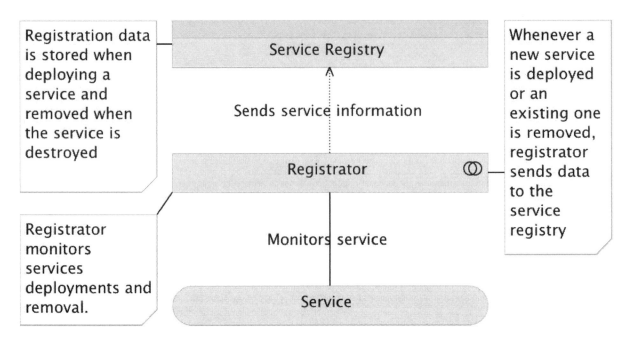

Figure 8-5: Registration service

A separate registration service is a much better option than self-registration. It tends to be more reliable and, at the same time, does not introduce unnecessary coupling inside our microservices code.

Since we established what will be the underlying logic behind the services registration process, it is time to discuss the discovery.

Service Discovery

Service discovery is the opposite of service registration. When a client wants to access a service (the client might also be another service), it must know, as a minimum, where that service is. One approach we can take is self-discovery.

Self-Discovery

Self-discovery uses the same principles as self-registration. Every client or a service that wants to access other services would need to consult the registry. Unlike self-registration that posed problems mostly related to our internal ways to connect services, self-discovery might be used by clients and services outside our control. One example would be a front-end running in user browsers. That front-end might need to send requests to many separate back-end services running on different ports or even different IPs. The fact that we do have the information stored in the registry does not mean that others can, should, or know how to use it. Self-discovery can be effectively used only for the communication between internal services. Even such a limited scope poses a lot of additional problems many of which are the same as those created by self-registration. Due to what we know by now, this option should be discarded.

Proxy Service

Proxy services have been around for a while and proved their worth many times over. The next chapter will explore them in more depth so we'll go through them only briefly. The idea is that each service should be accessible through one or more fixed addresses. For example, the list of books from our *books-ms* service should be available only through the *[DOMAIN]/api/v1/books* address. Notice that there is no IP, port nor any other deployment-specific detail. Since there will be no service with that exact address, something will have to detect such a request and redirect it to the IP and port of the actual service. Proxy services tend to be the best type of tools that can fulfill this task.

Now that we have a general, and hopefully clear, idea of what we're trying to accomplish, let's take a look at some of the tools that can help us out.

Service Discovery Tools

The primary objective of *service discovery tools* is to help services find and talk to one another. To perform their duty, they need to know where each service is. The concept is not new, and many tools existed long before Docker was born. However, containers brought the need for such tools to a whole new level.

The basic idea behind *service discovery* is for each new instance of a service (or application) to be able to identify its current environment and store that information. Storage itself is performed in a registry usually in key/value format. Since the discovery is often used in distributed system, registry needs to be scalable, fault-tolerant and distributed among all nodes in the cluster. The primary usage of such a storage is to provide, as a minimum, IP and port of a service to all interested parties that might need to communicate with it. This data is often extended with other types of information.

Discovery tools tend to provide some API that can be used by a service to register itself as well as by others to find the information about that service.

Let's say that we have two services. One is a provider, and the other one is its consumer. Once we deploy the provider, we need to store its information in the *service registry* of choice. Later on, when the consumer tries to access the provider, it would first query the registry and call the provider using the IP and port obtained from the registry. To decouple the consumer from a particular implementation of the registry, we often employ some *proxy service*. That way the consumer would always request information from the fixed address that would reside inside the proxy that, in turn, would use the discovery service to find out the provider information and redirect the request. Actually, in many cases, there is no need for the proxy to query the service registry if there is a process that updates its configuration every time data in the registry changes. We'll go through *reverse proxy* later on in the book. For now, it is important to understand that the flow that is based on three actors; consumer, proxy, and provider.

What we are looking for in the service discovery tools is data. As a minimum, we should be able to find out where the service is, whether it is healthy and available, and what is its configuration. Since we are building a distributed system with multiple servers, the tool needs to be robust, and failure of one node should not jeopardize data. Also, each of the nodes should have the same data replica. Further on, we want to be able to start services in any order, be able to destroy them, or to replace them with newer versions. We should also be able to reconfigure our services and see the data change accordingly.

Let's take a look at a few of the tools we can use to accomplish the goals we set.

Manual Configuration

Most of the services are still managed manually. We decide in advance where to deploy the service, what is its configuration and hope beyond reason that it will continue working properly until the end of days. Such approach is not easily scalable. Deploying a second instance of the service means that we need to start the manual process all over. We have to bring up a new server or find out which one has low utilization of resources, create a new set of configurations and deploy it. The situation is even more complicated in the case of, let's say, a hardware failure since the reaction time is usually slow when things are managed manually. Visibility is another sore point. We know what the static configuration is. After all, we prepared it in advance. However, most of the services have a lot of information generated dynamically. That information is not easily visible. There is no single location we can consult when we are in need of that data.

Reaction time is inevitably slow, failure resilience questionable at best and monitoring difficult to manage due to a lot of manually handled moving parts.

While there was an excuse to do this job manually in the past or when the number of services and/or servers is small, with the emergence of service discovery tools, this excuse quickly evaporated.

Zookeeper

ZooKeeper[76] is one of the oldest projects of this type. It originated out of the Hadoop world, where it was built to help the maintenance of various components in a Hadoop cluster. It is mature, reliable and used by many big companies (YouTube, eBay, Yahoo, and so on). The format of the data it stores is similar to the organization of the file system. If run on a server cluster, Zookeeper will share the state of the configuration across all of the nodes. Each cluster elects a leader and clients can connect to any of the servers to retrieve data.

The main advantages Zookeeper brings to the table is its maturity, robustness, and feature richness. However, it comes with its set of disadvantages, with Java and complexity being main culprits. While Java is great for many use cases, it is massive for this type of work. Zookeeper's usage of Java, together with a considerable number of dependencies, makes Zookeeper much more resource

---

[76]http://zookeeper.apache.org/

hungry that its competition. On top of those problems, Zookeeper is complex. Maintaining it requires considerably more knowledge than we should expect from an application of this type. That is the part where feature richness converts itself from an advantage to a liability. The more features an application has, the bigger the chances that we won't need all of them. Thus, we end up paying the price in the form of complexity for something we do not fully need.

Zookeeper paved the way that others followed with considerable improvements. "Big players" are using it because there were no better alternatives at the time. Today, Zookeeper shows its age, and we are better off with alternatives.

We'll skip Zookeeper examples and skip straight into better options.

etcd

etcd[77] is a key/value store accessible through HTTP. It is distributed and features hierarchical configuration system that can be used to build service discovery. It is very easy to deploy, setup and use, provides reliable data persistence, it's secure and with excellent documentation.

etcd is a better option than Zookeeper due to its simplicity. However, it needs to be combined with a few third-party tools before it can serve service discovery objectives.

Setting Up etcd

Let us set up the *etcd*. First, we should create the first node in the cluster (*serv-disc-01*) together with the, already familiar, *cd* VM.

```
1  vagrant up cd serv-disc-01 --provision
2
3  vagrant ssh serv-disc-01
```

With the cluster node *serv-disc-01* up and running, we can install *etcd* and *etcdctl* (etcd command line client).

---

[77]https://github.com/coreos/etcd

```
1   curl -L https://github.com/coreos/etcd/releases/\
2   download/v2.1.2/etcd-v2.1.2-linux-amd64.tar.gz \
3       -o etcd-v2.1.2-linux-amd64.tar.gz
4
5   tar xzf etcd-v2.1.2-linux-amd64.tar.gz
6
7   sudo mv etcd-v2.1.2-linux-amd64/etcd* /usr/local/bin
8
9   rm -rf etcd-v2.1.2-linux-amd64*
10
11  etcd >/tmp/etcd.log 2>&1 &
```

We downloaded, uncompressed and moved the executables to */usr/local/bin* so that they are easily accessible. Then, we removed unneeded files and, finally, run the *etcd* with output redirected to */tmp/etcd.log*.

Let's see what we can do with etcd.

Basic operations are *set* and *get*. Please note that we can set a key/value inside a directory.

```
1   etcdctl set myService/port "1234"
2
3   etcdctl set myService/ip "1.2.3.4"
4
5   etcdctl get myService/port # Outputs: 1234
6
7   etcdctl get myService/ip # Outputs: 1.2.3.4
```

The first command put the key *port* with the value *1234* into the directory *myService*. The second did the same with the key *ip*, and the last two commands were used to output values of those two keys.

We can also list all the keys in the specified directory or delete a key with its value.

```
1   etcdctl ls myService
2
3   etcdctl rm myService/port
4
5   etcdctl ls myService
```

The last command output only the */myService/ip* value since previous command removed the port.

Besides *etcdctl*, we can also run all commands through HTTP API. Before we try it out, let's install *jq* so that we can see the formatted output.

```
1  sudo apt-get install -y jq
```

We can, for example, put a value into *etcd* through its HTTP API and retrieve it through a GET request.

```
1  curl http://localhost:2379/v2/keys/myService/newPort \
2    -X PUT \
3    -d value="4321" | jq '.'
4
5  curl http://localhost:2379/v2/keys/myService/newPort \
6    | jq '.'
```

The jq '.' is not required, but I tend to use it often to format JSON. The output should be similar to the following.

```
1  {
2      "action": "set",
3      "node": {
4          "createdIndex": 16,
5          "key": "/myService/newPort",
6          "modifiedIndex": 16,
7          "value": "4321"
8      }
9  }
10
11  {
12      "action": "get",
13      "node": {
14          "createdIndex": 16,
15          "key": "/myService/newPort",
16          "modifiedIndex": 16,
17          "value": "4321"
18      }
19  }
```

HTTP API is especially useful when we need to query etcd remotely. In most, I prefer the *etcdctl*, when running ad-hoc commands while HTTP is a preferred way to interact with *etcd* through some code.

Now that we've seen (briefly) how etcd works on a single server, let us try it inside a cluster. The cluster setup requires a few additional arguments to be passed to *etcd*. Let's say that we'll have a cluster of three nodes with IPs *10.100.197.201* (*serv-disc-01*), *10.100.197.202* (*serv-disc-02*) and *10.100.197.203* (*serv-disc-03*). The etcd command that should be run on the first server would be the following (please don't run it yet).

```
1  NODE_NAME=serv-disc-0$NODE_NUMBER
2  NODE_IP=10.100.197.20$NODE_NUMBER
3  NODE_01_ADDRESS=http://10.100.197.201:2380
4  NODE_01_NAME=serv-disc-01
5  NODE_01="$NODE_01_NAME=$NODE_01_ADDRESS"
6  NODE_02_ADDRESS=http://10.100.197.202:2380
7  NODE_02_NAME=serv-disc-02
8  NODE_02="$NODE_02_NAME=$NODE_02_ADDRESS"
9  NODE_03_ADDRESS=http://10.100.197.203:2380
10 NODE_03_NAME=serv-disc-03
11 NODE_03="$NODE_03_NAME=$NODE_03_ADDRESS"
12 CLUSTER_TOKEN=serv-disc-cluster
13
14 etcd -name $NODE_NAME \
15     -initial-advertise-peer-urls http://$NODE_IP:2380 \
16     -listen-peer-urls http://$NODE_IP:2380 \
17     -listen-client-urls \
18     http://$NODE_IP:2379,http://127.0.0.1:2379 \
19     -advertise-client-urls http://$NODE_IP:2379 \
20     -initial-cluster-token $CLUSTER_TOKEN \
21     -initial-cluster \
22     $NODE_01,$NODE_02,$NODE_03 \
23     -initial-cluster-state new
```

I extracted parts that would change from one server (or a cluster) to another into variables so that you can see them clearly. We won't go into details of what each argument means. You can find more information in the etcd clustering guide[78]. Suffice to say that we specified the IP and the name of the server where this command should run as well as the list of all the servers in the cluster.

Before we start working on the etcd deployment to the cluster, let us kill the currently running instance and create the rest of servers (there should be three in total).

```
1  pkill etcd
2
3  exit
4
5  vagrant up serv-disc-02 serv-disc-03
```

Doing the same set of tasks manually across multiple servers is tedious and error prone. Since we already worked with Ansible, we can use it to set up etcd across the cluster. This should be a fairly easy task since we already have all the commands, and all we have to do is translate those we already

---

[78]https://github.com/coreos/etcd/blob/master/Documentation/clustering.md

run into the Ansible format. We can create the *etcd role* and add it to the playbook with the same name. The role is fairly simple. It copies the executables to the */usr/local/bin* directory and runs etcd with the cluster arguments (the very long command we examined above). Let us take a look at it before running the playbook.

The first task in the roles/etcd/tasks/main.yml[79] is as follows.

```
1  - name: Files are copied
2    copy:
3      src: "{{ item.src }}"
4      dest: "{{ item.dest }}"
5      mode: 0755
6    with_items: files
7    tags: [etcd]
```

The name is purely descriptive and followed with the copy module[80]. Then, we are specifying few of the module options. The copy option *src* indicates the name of the local file we want to copy and is relative to the *files* directory inside the role. The second copy option (*dest*) is the destination path on the remote server. Finally, we are setting the mode to be *755*. The user that runs with roles will have *read/write/execute* permissions, and those belonging to the same group and everyone else will be assigned *read/execute* permissions. Next is the *with_items* declaration that allows us to use a list of values. In this case, the values are specified in the roles/etcd/defaults/main.yml[81] file and are as follows.

```
1  files: [
2    {src: 'etcd', dest: '/usr/local/bin/etcd'},
3    {src: 'etcdctl', dest: '/usr/local/bin/etcdctl'}
4  ]
```

Externalizing variables is a good way to keep things that might change in the future separated from the tasks. If, for example, we are to copy another file through this role, we'd add it here and avoid even opening the tasks file. The task that uses the *files* variable will iterate for each value in the list and, in this case, run twice; once for *etcd* and the second time for *etcdctl*. Values from variables are represented with the variable key surrounded with *{{* and *}}* and use the Jinja2 format[82]. Finally, we set *etcd* to be the tag associated with this task. Tags can be used to filter tasks when running playbooks and are very handy when we want to run only a subset of them or when we want to exclude something.

The second task is as follows.

[79]https://github.com/vfarcic/ms-lifecycle/blob/master/ansible/roles/etcd/tasks/main.yml
[80]http://docs.ansible.com/ansible/copy_module.html
[81]https://github.com/vfarcic/ms-lifecycle/blob/master/ansible/roles/etcd/defaults/main.yml
[82]http://docs.ansible.com/ansible/playbooks_variables.html#using-variables-about-jinja2

```
 1  - name: Is running
 2    shell: "nohup etcd -name {{ ansible_hostname }} \
 3      -initial-advertise-peer-urls \
 4      http://{{ ip }}:2380 \
 5      -listen-peer-urls \
 6      http://{{ ip }}:2380 \
 7      -listen-client-urls \
 8      http://{{ ip }}:2379,http://127.0.0.1:2379 \
 9      -advertise-client-urls \
10      http://{{ ip }}:2379 \
11      -initial-cluster-token {{ cl_token }} \
12      -initial-cluster \
13      {{ cl_node_01 }},{{ cl_node_02 }},{{ cl_node_03 }} \
14      -initial-cluster-state new \
15      >/var/log/etcd.log 2>&1 &"
16    tags: [etcd]
```

Shell module[83] is often the last resort since it does not work with states. In most cases, commands run as through shell will not check whether something is in the correct state or not and run every time we execute Ansible playbook. However, etcd always runs only a single instance and there is no risk that multiple executions of this command will produce multiple instances. we have a lot of arguments and all those that might change are put as variables. Some of them, like *ansible_hostname*, are discovered by Ansible. Others were defined by us and placed in the roles/etcd/defaults/main.yml[84]. With all the tasks defined, we can take a look at the playbook etcd.yml[85].

```
 1  - hosts: etcd
 2    remote_user: vagrant
 3    serial: 1
 4    sudo: yes
 5    roles:
 6      - common
 7      - etcd
```

When this playbook is run, Ansible will configure all the servers defined in an inventory, use *vagrant* as the remote user, run commands as *sudo* and execute the *common* and *etcd* roles.

Let us take a look at the hosts/serv-disc[86] file. It is our inventory that contains the list of all hosts we're using.

---

[83]http://docs.ansible.com/ansible/shell_module.html

[84]https://github.com/vfarcic/ms-lifecycle/blob/master/ansible/roles/etcd/defaults/main.yml

[85]https://github.com/vfarcic/ms-lifecycle/blob/master/ansible/etcd.yml

[86]https://github.com/vfarcic/ms-lifecycle/blob/master/ansible/hosts/serv-disc

```
1  [etcd]
2  10.100.194.20[1:3]
```

In this example, you can a different way to define hosts. The second line is Ansible's way of saying that all addresses between *10.100.194.201* and *10.100.194.203* should be used. In total, we have three IPs specified for this purpose.

Let's run the *etcd* playbook and see it in action.

```
1  vagrant ssh cd
2
3  ansible-playbook \
4      /vagrant/ansible/etcd.yml \
5      -i /vagrant/ansible/hosts/serv-disc
```

We can check whether etcd cluster was correctly set by putting a value through one server and getting it from the another.

```
1  curl http://serv-disc-01:2379/v2/keys/test \
2    -X PUT \
3    -d value="works" | jq '.'
4
5  curl http://serv-disc-03:2379/v2/keys/test \
6    | jq '.'
```

The output of those commands should be similar to the following.

```
1  {
2      "action": "set",
3      "node": {
4          "createdIndex": 8,
5          "key": "/test",
6          "modifiedIndex": 8,
7          "value": "works"
8      }
9  }
10
11 {
12     "action": "get",
13     "node": {
14         "createdIndex": 8,
15         "key": "/test",
```

```
16        "modifiedIndex": 8,
17        "value": "works"
18      }
19  }
```

We sent the HTTP PUT request to the *serv-disc-01* server (10.100.197.201) and retrieved the stored value through the HTTP GET request from the *serv-disc-03* (10.100.197.203) node. In other words, data set through any of the servers in the cluster is available in all of them. Isn't that neat?

Our cluster (after we deploy few containers), would look as presented in the figure 8-6.

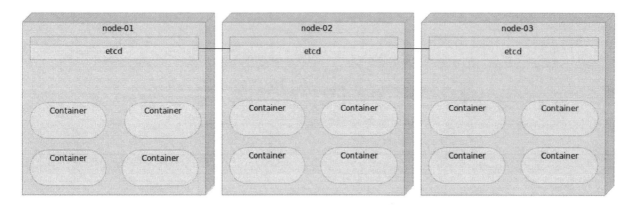

Figure 8-6: Multiple nodes with Docker containers and etcd

Now that we have a place to store the information related to our services, we need a tool that will send that information to etcd automatically. After all, why would we put data to etcd manually if that can be done automatically? Even if we would want to put the information manually to etcd, we often don't know what that information is. Remember, services might be deployed to a server with least containers running and it might have a random port assigned. Ideally, that tool should monitor Docker on all nodes and update etcd whenever a new container is run, or an existing one is stopped. One of the tools that can help us with this goal is *Registrator*.

Setting Up Registrator

Registrator[87] automatically registers and deregisters services by inspecting containers as they are brought online or stopped. It currently supports *etcd*, *Consul* and *SkyDNS 2*.

Setting up Registrator with etcd registry is easy. We can simply run the Docker container as follows (please do not run it yourself).

---

[87]https://github.com/gliderlabs/registrator

```
1  docker run -d --name registrator \
2      -v /var/run/docker.sock:/tmp/docker.sock \
3      -h serv-disc-01 \
4      gliderlabs/registrator \
5      -ip 10.100.194.201 etcd://10.100.194.201:2379
```

With this command we are sharing */var/run/docker.sock* as Docker volume. Registrator will monitor and intercept Docker events and, depending on the event type, put or remove service information to/from etcd. With the *-h* argument we are specifying the hostname. Finally, we are passing two arguments to Registrator. The first one is the *-ip* and represents the IP of the host and the second one is the protocol (*etcd*), the IP (*serv-disc-01*) and the port (*2379*) of the registration service.

Before we proceed, let's create a new Ansible role called *registrator* and deploy it to all nodes inside the cluster. The roles/registrator/tasks/main.yml[88] file is as follows.

```
1  - name: Container is running
2    docker:
3      name: "{{ registrator_name }}"
4      image: gliderlabs/registrator
5      volumes:
6        - /var/run/docker.sock:/tmp/docker.sock
7      hostname: "{{ ansible_hostname }}"
8      command: -ip {{ facter_ipaddress_eth1 }} {{ registrator_protocol }}://{{ fac\
9  ter_ipaddress_eth1 }}:2379
10     tags: [etcd]
```

This Ansible role is equivalent to the manual command we saw earlier. Please note that we changed the hard-coded *etcd* protocol with a variable. That way we can reuse this role with other registries as well. Keep in mind that having quotes is not mandatory in Ansible except when value starts with *{{* as in the case of the *hostname* value.

Let's take a look at the registrator-etcd.yml[89] playbook.

---

[88]https://github.com/vfarcic/ms-lifecycle/blob/master/ansible/roles/registrator/tasks/main.yml

[89]https://github.com/vfarcic/ms-lifecycle/blob/master/ansible/registrator-etcd.yml

```
 1  - hosts: all
 2    remote_user: vagrant
 3    serial: 1
 4    sudo: yes
 5    vars:
 6      - registrator_protocol: etcd
 7      - registrator_port: 2379
 8    roles:
 9      - common
10      - docker
11      - etcd
12      - registrator
```

Most of the playbook is similar to those we used before except the *vars* key. In this case, we're using it to define the Registrator protocol as *etcd* and port of the registry as *2379*.

With everything in place, we can run the playbook.

```
 1  ansible-playbook \
 2      /vagrant/ansible/registrator-etcd.yml \
 3      -i /vagrant/ansible/hosts/serv-disc
```

Once the playbook is finished executing, Registrator will be running on all three nodes of our cluster.

Let's give Registrator a spin and run one container inside one of the three cluster nodes.

```
 1  export DOCKER_HOST=tcp://serv-disc-02:2375
 2
 3  docker run -d --name nginx \
 4      --env SERVICE_NAME=nginx \
 5      --env SERVICE_ID=nginx \
 6      -p 1234:80 \
 7      nginx
```

We exported the *DOCKER_HOST* variable so that Docker commands are sent to the cluster node 2 (*serv-disc-02*) and run the *nginx* container exposing port *1234*. We'll use *nginx* later on, and there will be plenty of opportunities to get familiar with it. For now, we are not interested in what nginx does, but that Registrator detected it and stored the information in etcd. In this case, we put a few environment variables (*SERVICE_NAME* and *SERVICE_ID*) that Registrator can use to identify better the service.

Let us take a look at Registrator's log.

```
1  docker logs registrator
```

The output should be similar to the following.

```
1  2015/08/30 19:18:12 added: 5cf7dd974939 nginx
2  2015/08/30 19:18:12 ignored: 5cf7dd974939 port 443 not published on host
```

We can see that Registrator detected nginx container with the ID *5cf7dd974939*. We can also see that it ignored the port 443. The *nginx* container internally exposes ports 80 and 443. However, we exposed only 80 to the outside world, so Registrator decided to ignore the port *443*. After all, why would we store the information about the port not accessible to anyone?

Now, let us take a look at data stored in etcd.

```
1  curl http://serv-disc-01:2379/v2/keys/ | jq '.'
2
3  curl http://serv-disc-01:2379/v2/keys/nginx-80/ | jq '.'
4
5  curl http://serv-disc-01:2379/v2/keys/nginx-80/nginx | jq '.'
```

The output of the last command is as follows.

```
1  {
2    "node": {
3      "createdIndex": 13,
4      "modifiedIndex": 13,
5      "value": "10.100.194.202:1234",
6      "key": "/nginx-80/nginx"
7    },
8    "action": "get"
9  }
```

The first command listed all keys at the root, the second listed all those inside *nginx-80* and the last one retrieved the final value. Registrator stored values in the format *<NAME>/<ID>* that matches environment variables we used when running the container. Please note that in case that more that one port is defined for a service, Registrator adds it as a suffix (e.g. nginx-80). The value that Registrator put corresponds with the IP of the host where the container is running and the port that we exposed.

Please note that even though the container is run on the node 2, we queried etcd running on the node 1. It was yet another demonstration that data is replicated across all nodes etcd is running on.

What happens when we remove the container?

```
1  docker rm -f nginx
2
3  docker logs registrator
```

The output of Registrator logs should be similar to the following.

```
1  ...
2  2015/08/30 19:32:31 removed: 5cf7dd974939 nginx
```

Registrator detected that we removed the container and sent a request to etcd to remove corresponding values. We can confirm that with the following command.

```
1  curl http://serv-disc-01:2379/v2/keys/nginx-80/nginx | jq '.'
```

The output is as follows.

```
1  {
2    "index": 14,
3    "cause": "/nginx-80/nginx",
4    "message": "Key not found",
5    "errorCode": 100
6  }
```

The service with the ID *nginx/nginx* disappeared.

Registrator combined with *etcd* is a powerful, yet simple, combination that will allow us to practice many advanced techniques. Whenever we bring up a container, data will be stored in etcd and propagated to all nodes in the cluster. What we'll do with that information will be the subject of the next chapter.

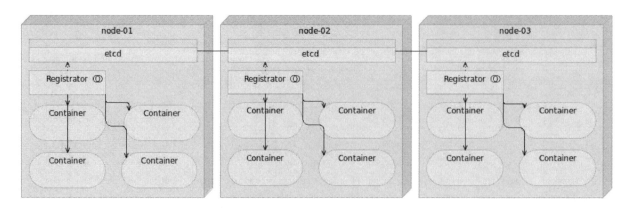

Figure 8-7: **Multiple nodes with Docker containers, etcd and Registrator**

There is one more piece of the puzzle missing. We need a way to create configuration files with data stored in *etcd* as well as run some commands when those files are created.

Setting Up confd

confd[90] is a lightweight tool that can be used to maintain configuration files. The most common usage of the tool is keeping configuration files up-to-date using data stored in *etcd*, *consul*, and few other data registries. It can also be used to reload applications when configuration files change. In other words, we can use it as a way to reconfigure services with the information stored in etcd (or few other registries).

Installing *confd* is straightforward. The commands are as follows (please don't run them yet).

```
1  wget https://github.com/kelseyhightower/confd/releases\
2  /download/v0.10.0/confd-0.10.0-linux-amd64
3
4  sudo mv confd-0.10.0-linux-amd64 /usr/local/bin/confd
5
6  sudo chmod 755 /usr/local/bin/confd
7
8  sudo mkdir -p /etc/confd/{conf.d,templates}
```

In order for confd to work, we need a configuration file located in the */etc/confd/conf.d/* directory and a template in the */etc/confd/templates*.

Example configuration file is as follows.

```
1  [template]
2  src = "nginx.conf.tmpl"
3  dest = "/tmp/nginx.conf"
4  keys = [
5      "/nginx/nginx"
6  ]
```

As a minimum, we need to specify template source, destination file, and keys that will be fetched from the registry.

Templates use GoLang text templates[91] format. An example template is as follows.

```
1  The address is {{getv "/nginx/nginx"}};
```

When this template is processed, it will substitute {{getv "/nginx/nginx"}} with the value from the registry.

Finally, *confd* can be run in two modes. In the *Daemon mode*, it polls a registry and updates destination configuration whenever relevant values change. The *onetime* mode is run once. An example of the *onetime* mode is as follows (please do not run it yet).

---

[90]https://github.com/kelseyhightower/confd
[91]http://golang.org/pkg/text/template/#pkg-overview

```
1  confd -onetime -backend etcd -node 10.100.197.202:2379
```

This command would run in the *onetime* mode, would use *etcd* as the backend running on the specified node. When executed, destination configuration would be updated with values from the *etcd* registry.

Now that we know basics of how confd works, let's take a look at the Ansible role *confd* that will make sure that it is installed on all servers in the cluster.

The roles/confd/tasks/main.yml[92] file is as follows.

```
1  - name: Directories are created
2    file:
3      path: "{{ item }}"
4      state: directory
5    with_items: directories
6    tags: [confd]
7
8  - name: Files are copied
9    copy:
10     src: "{{ item.src }}"
11     dest: "{{ item.dest }}"
12     mode: "{{ item.mode }}"
13   with_items: files
14   tags: [confd]
```

This Ansible role is even simpler than the one we created for *etcd* since we are not even running the binary. It makes sure that directories are created and that files are copied to the destination servers. Since there are multiple directories and files involved, we defined them as variables in the roles/confd/defaults/main.yml[93] file.

```
1  directories:
2    - /etc/confd/conf.d
3    - /etc/confd/templates
4
5  files: [
6    { src: 'example.toml', dest: '/etc/confd/conf.d/example.toml', mode: '0644' },
7    { src: 'example.conf.tmpl', dest: '/etc/confd/templates/example.conf.tmpl', mo\
8  de: '0644' },
9    { src: 'confd', dest: '/usr/local/bin/confd', mode: '0755' }
10 ]
```

---

[92]https://github.com/vfarcic/ms-lifecycle/blob/master/ansible/roles/confd/tasks/main.yml

[93]https://github.com/vfarcic/ms-lifecycle/blob/master/ansible/roles/confd/defaults/main.yml

We defined directories where we'll put configurations and templates. We also defined files that need to be copied; one binary, one configuration, and one template file that we'll use to try out confd.

Finally, we need confd.yml[94] file that will act as the Ansible playbook.

```
1  - hosts: confd
2    remote_user: vagrant
3    serial: 1
4    sudo: yes
5    roles:
6      - common
7      - confd
```

There's nothing new to discuss since this file is almost the same the other playbooks we worked with.

With everything set up, we can deploy confd to all the cluster servers.

```
1  ansible-playbook \
2      /vagrant/ansible/confd.yml \
3      -i /vagrant/ansible/hosts/serv-disc
```

With confd installed on all nodes in the cluster, we can try it out.

Let's run the nginx container again so that Registrator can put some data to etcd.

```
1  export DOCKER_HOST=tcp://serv-disc-01:2375
2
3  docker run -d --name nginx \
4      --env SERVICE_NAME=nginx \
5      --env SERVICE_ID=nginx \
6      -p 4321:80 \
7      nginx
8
9  confd -onetime -backend etcd -node 10.100.194.203:2379
```

We run the nginx container on the *serv-disc-01* node and exposed the port 4321. Since *Registrator* is already running on that server, it put data to *etcd*. Finally, we run the local instance of *confd* that checked all its configuration files and compared keys with those stored in etcd. Since *nginx/nginx* key has been changed in etcd, it processed the template and updated the destination config. That can be seen from the output that should be similar to the following (timestamp has been removed for brevity).

---

[94]https://github.com/vfarcic/ms-lifecycle/blob/master/ansible/confd.yml

```
1  cd confd[15241]: INFO Backend set to etcd
2  cd confd[15241]: INFO Starting confd
3  cd confd[15241]: INFO Backend nodes set to 10.100.194.203:2379
4  cd confd[15241]: INFO Target config /tmp/example.conf out of sync
5  cd confd[15241]: INFO Target config /tmp/example.conf has been updated
```

It found that the */tmp/example.conf* is out of sync and updated it. Let us confirm that.

```
1  cat /tmp/example.conf
```

The output is as follows.

```
1  The address is 10.100.194.201:4321
```

If any of the changes in templates or *etcd* data is updated, running *confd* will make sure that all destination configurations are updated accordingly.

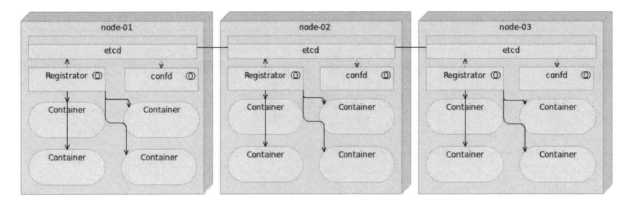

Figure 8-8: Multiple nodes with Docker containers, etcd, Registrator and confd

Combining etcd, Registrator, and confd

When etcd, Registrator, and confd are combined, we get a simple yet powerful way to automate all our service discovery and configuration needs. That will come in handy when we start working on more advanced deployment strategies. The combination also demonstrates the effectiveness of having the right mix of "small" tools. Those three do what we need them to do. Less than this and we would not be able to accomplish the goals set in front of us. If, on the other hand, they were designed with bigger scope in mind, we would introduce unnecessary complexity and overhead on server resources and maintenance.

Before we make the final verdict, let's take a look at another combination of tools with similar goals. After all, we should never settle for some solution without investigating alternatives.

Consul

Consul[95] is strongly consistent datastore that uses gossip to form dynamic clusters. It features hierarchical key/value store that can be used not only to store data but also to register watches that can be used for a variety of tasks, from sending notifications about data changes, to running health checks and custom commands depending on their output.

Unlike Zookeeper and etcd, Consul implements service discovery system embedded, so there is no need to build your own or use a third-party one. This discovery includes, among other things, health checks of nodes and services running on top of them.

ZooKeeper and etcd provide only a primitive K/V store and require that application developers build their own system to provide service discovery. Consul, on the other hand, provides a built-in framework for service discovery. Clients only need to register services and perform discovery using the DNS or HTTP interface. The other two tools require either a hand-made solution or the usage of third-party tools.

Consul offers out of the box native support for multiple data centers and the gossip system that works not only with nodes in the same cluster but across data centers as well.

Consul has another nice feature that distinguishes it from the others. Not only that it can be used to discover information about deployed services and nodes they reside on, but it also provides easy to extend health checks through HTTP and TCP requests, TTLs (time-to-live), custom scripts and even Docker commands.

Setting Up Consul

As before, we'll start by exploring manual installation commands and, later on, automate them with Ansible. We'll configure it on the *cd* node as an exercise.

```
1  sudo apt-get install -y unzip
2
3  wget https://releases.hashicorp.com/consul/0.6.4/consul_0.6.4_linux_amd64.zip
4
5  unzip consul_0.6.4_linux_amd64.zip
6
7  sudo mv consul /usr/local/bin/consul
8
9  rm -f consul_0.6.4_linux_amd64.zip
10
11 sudo mkdir -p /data/consul/{data,config,ui}
```

---

[95]https://www.consul.io/

We started by installing *unzip* since it is not included in default Ubuntu distribution. Then we downloaded the Consul ZIP, unpacked it, moved it to the */usr/local/bin* directory, removed the ZIP file since we won't need it anymore and, finally, created few directories. Consul will place its information to the *data* directory and configuration files into *config*.

Next we can run Consul.

```
1   sudo consul agent \
2       -server \
3       -bootstrap-expect 1 \
4       -data-dir /data/consul/data \
5       -config-dir /data/consul/config \
6       -node=cd \
7       -bind=10.100.198.200 \
8       -client=0.0.0.0 \
9       -ui \
10      >/tmp/consul.log &
```

Running Consul was very straight forward. We specified that it should run the *agent* as a *server* and that there will be only one server instance (*-bootstrap-expect 1*). That is followed by locations of key directories; *ui*, *data* and *config*. Then we specified the name of the *node*, address it will *bind* to and which *client* can connect to it (*0.0.0.0* refers to all). Finally, we redirected the output and made sure that it's running in the background (*&*).

Let's verify that Consul started correctly.

```
1   cat /tmp/consul.log
```

The output of the log file should be similar to the following (timestamps are removed for brevity).

```
1   ==> Starting Consul agent...
2   ==> Starting Consul agent RPC...
3   ==> Consul agent running!
4              Node name: 'cd'
5             Datacenter: 'dc1'
6                 Server: true (bootstrap: true)
7            Client Addr: 0.0.0.0 (HTTP: 8500, HTTPS: -1, DNS: 8600, RPC: 8400)
8           Cluster Addr: 10.100.198.200 (LAN: 8301, WAN: 8302)
9         Gossip encrypt: false, RPC-TLS: false, TLS-Incoming: false
10                 Atlas: <disabled>
11
12  ==> Log data will now stream in as it occurs:
13
```

```
14  [INFO] serf: EventMemberJoin: cd 10.100.198.200
15  [INFO] serf: EventMemberJoin: cd.dc1 10.100.198.200
16  [INFO] raft: Node at 10.100.198.200:8300 [Follower] entering Follower state
17  [WARN] serf: Failed to re-join any previously known node
18  [INFO] consul: adding LAN server cd (Addr: 10.100.198.200:8300) (DC: dc1)
19  [WARN] serf: Failed to re-join any previously known node
20  [INFO] consul: adding WAN server cd.dc1 (Addr: 10.100.198.200:8300) (DC: dc1)
21  [ERR] agent: failed to sync remote state: No cluster leader
22  [WARN] raft: Heartbeat timeout reached, starting election
23  [INFO] raft: Node at 10.100.198.200:8300 [Candidate] entering Candidate state
24  [INFO] raft: Election won. Tally: 1
25  [INFO] raft: Node at 10.100.198.200:8300 [Leader] entering Leader state
26  [INFO] consul: cluster leadership acquired
27  [INFO] consul: New leader elected: cd
28  [INFO] raft: Disabling EnableSingleNode (bootstrap)
```

We can see that the Consul agent we run in server mode elected itself as the leader (which is to be expected since it's the only one).

With Consul up and running, let's see how we can put some data into it.

```
1  curl -X PUT -d 'this is a test' \
2      http://localhost:8500/v1/kv/msg1
3
4  curl -X PUT -d 'this is another test' \
5      http://localhost:8500/v1/kv/messages/msg2
6
7  curl -X PUT -d 'this is a test with flags' \
8      http://localhost:8500/v1/kv/messages/msg3?flags=1234
```

The first command created the *msg1* key with the value *this is a test*. The second had nested the key *msg2* into a parent key *messages*. Finally, the last command added the *flag* with the value *1234*. Flags can be used to store version number or any other information that can be expressed as an integer.

Let's take a look how to retrieve the information we just stored.

```
1  curl http://localhost:8500/v1/kv/?recurse \
2      | jq '.'
```

The output of the command is as follows (order is not guaranteed).

```
1  [
2      {
3          "CreateIndex": 141,
4          "Flags": 0,
5          "Key": "messages/msg2",
6          "LockIndex": 0,
7          "ModifyIndex": 141,
8          "Value": "dGhpcyBpcyBhbm90aGVyIHRlc3Q="
9      },
10     {
11         "CreateIndex": 142,
12         "Flags": 1234,
13         "Key": "messages/msg3",
14         "LockIndex": 0,
15         "ModifyIndex": 147,
16         "Value": "dGhpcyBpcyBhIHRlc3Qgd210aCBmbGFncw=="
17     },
18     {
19         "CreateIndex": 140,
20         "Flags": 0,
21         "Key": "msg1",
22         "LockIndex": 0,
23         "ModifyIndex": 140,
24         "Value": "dGhpcyBpcyBhIHRlc3Q="
25     }
26 ]
```

Since we used the *recurse* query, keys were returned from the root recursively.

Here we can see all the keys we inserted. However, the value is base64 encoded. Consul can store more than "text" and, in fact, it stores everything as binary under the hood. Since not everything can be represented as text, you can store anything in Consul's K/V, but there are size limitations.

We can also retrieve a single key.

```
1  curl http://localhost:8500/v1/kv/msg1 \
2      | jq '.'
```

The output is the same as before but limited to the key *msg1*.

```
1  [
2      {
3          "CreateIndex": 140,
4          "Flags": 0,
5          "Key": "msg1",
6          "LockIndex": 0,
7          "ModifyIndex": 140,
8          "Value": "dGhpcyBpcyBhIHRlc3Q="
9      }
10 ]
```

Finally, we can request only the value.

```
1  curl http://localhost:8500/v1/kv/msg1?raw
```

This time, we put the *raw* query parameter and the result is only the value of the requested key.

```
1  this is a test
```

As you might have guessed, Consul keys can easily be deleted. The command to, for example, delete the *messages/msg2* key is as follows.

```
1  curl -X DELETE http://localhost:8500/v1/kv/messages/msg2
```

We can also delete recursively.

```
1  curl -X DELETE http://localhost:8500/v1/kv/?recurse
```

The Consul agent we deployed was set up to be the server. However, most agents do not need to run in the server mode. Depending on the number of nodes, we might opt for three Consul agents running in the server mode and many non-server agents joining it. If, on the other hand, the number of nodes is indeed big, we might increase the number of agents running in the server mode to five. If only one server is running, there will be data loss in case of its failure. In our case, since the cluster consists of only three nodes and this is a demo environment, one Consul agent running in the server mode is more than enough.

The command to run an agent on the *serv-disc-02* node and make it join the cluster is as follows (please don't run it yet).

```
1  sudo consul agent \
2      -data-dir /data/consul/data \
3      -config-dir /data/consul/config \
4      -node=serv-disc-02 \
5      -bind=10.100.197.202 \
6      -client=0.0.0.0 \
7      >/tmp/consul.log &
```

The only difference we did when compared with the previous execution is the removal of arguments *-server* and *-bootstrap-expect 1*. However, running Consul in one of the cluster servers is not enough. We need to join it with the Consul agent running on the other server. The command to accomplish that is as follows (please don't run it yet).

```
1  consul join 10.100.198.200
```

The effect of running this command is that agents of both servers would be clustered and data synchronized between them. If we continued adding Consul agents to other servers and joining them, the effect would be an increased number of cluster nodes registered in Consul. There is no need to join more than one agent since Consul uses a gossip protocol to manage membership and broadcast messages to the cluster. That is one of the useful improvements when compared to *etcd* that requires us to specify the list of all servers in the cluster. Managing such a list tends to be more complicated when the number of servers increases. With the gossip protocol, Consul is capable of discovering nodes in the cluster without us telling it where they are.

With Consul basics covered, let's see how we can automate its configuration across all servers in the cluster. Since we are already committed to Ansible, we'll create a new role for Consul. While the configuration we're about to explore is very similar to those we did by now, there are few new details we have not yet seen.

The first two tasks from the Ansible role roles/consul/tasks/main.yml[96] are as follows.

```
1  - name: Directories are created
2    file:
3      path: "{{ item }}"
4      state: directory
5    with_items: directories
6    tags: [consul]
7
8  - name: Files are copied
9    copy:
10      src: "{{ item.src }}"
```

---

[96]https://github.com/vfarcic/ms-lifecycle/blob/master/ansible/roles/consul/tasks/main.yml

```
11      dest: "{{ item.dest }}"
12      mode: "{{ item.mode }}"
13    with_items: files
14    tags: [consul]
```

We started by creating directories and copying files. Both tasks use variables array specified in the *with_items* tag.

Let's take a look at those variables. They are defined in the roles/consul/defaults/main.yml[97].

```
1  logs_dir: /data/consul/logs
2
3  directories:
4    - /data/consul/data
5    - /data/consul/config
6    - "{{ logs_dir }}"
7
8  files: [
9    { src: 'consul', dest: '/usr/local/bin/consul', mode: '0755' },
10   { src: 'ui', dest: '/data/consul', mode: '0644' }
11 ]
```

Even though we could specify all those variables inside the roles/consul/tasks/main.yml[98] file, having them separated allows us to change their values more easily. In this case, have a simple list of directories and the list of files in JSON format with source, destination and mode.

Let's continue with the tasks in the roles/consul/tasks/main.yml[99]. The third one is as follows.

```
1  - name: Is running
2    shell: "nohup consul agent {{ consul_extra }} \
3      -data-dir /data/consul/data \
4      -config-dir /data/consul/config \
5      -node={{ ansible_hostname }} \
6      -bind={{ ip }} \
7      -client=0.0.0.0 \
8      >{{ logs_dir }}/consul.log 2>&1 &"
9    tags: [consul]
```

Since Consul makes sure that there is only one process running at the time, there is no danger running this task multiple times. It is equivalent to the command we run manually with an addition of a few variables.

---

[97]https://github.com/vfarcic/ms-lifecycle/blob/master/ansible/roles/consul/defaults/main.yml

[98]https://github.com/vfarcic/ms-lifecycle/blob/master/ansible/roles/consul/tasks/main.yml

[99]https://github.com/vfarcic/ms-lifecycle/blob/master/ansible/roles/consul/tasks/main.yml

If you remember the manual execution of Consul, one node should run Consul in the server node and the rest should join at least one node so that Consul can gossip that information to the whole cluster. We defined those differences as the (*consul_extra*) variable. Unlike those we used before that are defined in roles/consul/defaults/main.yml[100] file inside the role, *consul_extra* is defined in the hosts/serv-disc[101] inventory file. Let's take a look at it.

```
1  [consul]
2  10.100.194.201 consul_extra="-server -bootstrap"
3  10.100.194.20[2:3] consul_server_ip="10.100.194.201"
```

We defined variables to the right of the server IPs. In this case, the *.201* is acting as a server. The rest is defining the *consul_server_ip* variables that we'll discuss very soon.

Let's jump into the fourth (and last) task defined in the roles/consul/tasks/main.yml[102] file.

```
1  - name: Has joined
2    shell: consul join {{ consul_server_ip }}
3    when: consul_server_ip is defined
4    tags: [consul]
```

This task makes sure that every Consul agent, except the one running in the server mode, joins the cluster. The task runs the same command like the one we executed manually, with the addition of the *consul_server_ip* variable that has a double usage. The first usage is to provide value for the *shell* command. The second usage is to decide whether this task is run at all. We accomplished that using the when: consul_server_ip is defined definition.

Finally, we have the consul.yml[103] playbook, that is as follows.

```
1  - hosts: consul
2    remote_user: vagrant
3    serial: 1
4    sudo: yes
5    roles:
6      - common
7      - consul
```

There's not much to say about it since it follows the same structure as the playbooks we used before.

Now that we have the playbook, let us execute it and take a look at Consul nodes.

---

[100]https://github.com/vfarcic/ms-lifecycle/blob/master/ansible/roles/consul/defaults/main.yml

[101]https://github.com/vfarcic/ms-lifecycle/blob/master/ansible/hosts/serv-disc

[102]https://github.com/vfarcic/ms-lifecycle/blob/master/ansible/roles/consul/tasks/main.yml

[103]https://github.com/vfarcic/ms-lifecycle/blob/master/ansible/consul.yml

```
1  ansible-playbook \
2      /vagrant/ansible/consul.yml \
3      -i /vagrant/ansible/hosts/serv-disc
```

We can confirm whether Consul is indeed running on all nodes by sending the *nodes* request to one of its agents.

```
1  curl serv-disc-01:8500/v1/catalog/nodes \
2      | jq '.'
```

The output of the command is as follows.

```
1  [
2      {
3          "Address": "10.100.194.201",
4          "Node": "serv-disc-01"
5      },
6      {
7          "Address": "10.100.194.202",
8          "Node": "serv-disc-02"
9      },
10     {
11         "Address": "10.100.194.203",
12         "Node": "serv-disc-03"
13     }
14 ]
```

All three nodes in the cluster are now running Consul. With that out of the way, we can move back to Registrator and see how it behaves when combined with Consul.

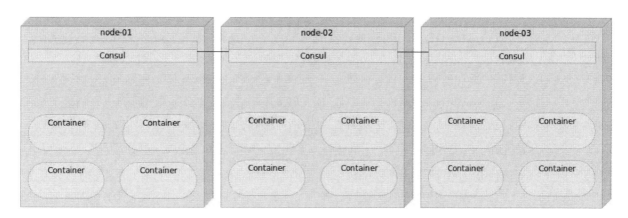

Figure 8-9: Multiple nodes with Docker containers and Consul

Setting Up Registrator

Registrator[104] has two Consul protocols. We'll take a look at *consulkv* first since its results should be very similar to those obtained with the etcd protocol.

```
1  export DOCKER_HOST=tcp://serv-disc-01:2375
2
3  docker run -d --name registrator-consul-kv \
4      -v /var/run/docker.sock:/tmp/docker.sock \
5      -h serv-disc-01 \
6      gliderlabs/registrator \
7      -ip 10.100.194.201 consulkv://10.100.194.201:8500/services
```

Let's take a look at the Registrator log and check whether everything seems to be working correctly.

```
1  docker logs registrator-consul-kv
```

The output should be similar to the following (timestamps were removed for brevity).

```
1  Starting registrator v6 ...
2  Forcing host IP to 10.100.194.201
3  consulkv: current leader  10.100.194.201:8300
4  Using consulkv adapter: consulkv://10.100.194.201:8500/services
5  Listening for Docker events ...
6  Syncing services on 1 containers
7  ignored: 19c952849ac2 no published ports
8  ignored: 46267b399098 port 443 not published on host
9  added: 46267b399098 nginx
```

The result is the same as when we run Registrator with the etcd protocol. It found the nginx container running (the one that we started previously while practicing etcd) and published the exposed port 4321 to Consul. We can confirm that by querying Consul.

```
1  curl http://serv-disc-01:8500/v1/kv/services/nginx-80/nginx?raw
```

As expected, the output is the IP and the port exposed through the nginx container.

---

[104]https://github.com/gliderlabs/registrator

```
1  10.100.194.201:4321
```

However, Registrator has another protocol called *consul* (the one we just used is *consulkv*) that utilizes Consul's format for storing service information.

```
1  docker run -d --name registrator-consul \
2      -v /var/run/docker.sock:/tmp/docker.sock \
3      -h serv-disc-01 \
4      gliderlabs/registrator \
5      -ip 10.100.194.201 consul://10.100.194.201:8500
```

Let's see what information Registrator sent to Consul this time.

```
1  curl http://serv-disc-01:8500/v1/catalog/service/nginx-80 | jq '.'
```

This time, the data is a bit more complete yet still in a very simple format.

```
1  [
2    {
3      "ModifyIndex": 185,
4      "CreateIndex": 185,
5      "Node": "serv-disc-01",
6      "Address": "10.100.194.201",
7      "ServiceID": "nginx",
8      "ServiceName": "nginx-80",
9      "ServiceTags": [],
10     "ServiceAddress": "10.100.194.201",
11     "ServicePort": 4321,
12     "ServiceEnableTagOverride": false
13   }
14 ]
```

Besides the IP and the port that is normally stored with *etcd* or *consulkv* protocols, this time, we got more information. We know the node the service is running on, service ID and the name. We can do even better than that with few additional environment variables. Let's bring up another nginx container and see the data stored in Consul.

```
1  docker run -d --name nginx2 \
2      --env "SERVICE_ID=nginx2" \
3      --env "SERVICE_NAME=nginx" \
4      --env "SERVICE_TAGS=balancer,proxy,www" \
5      -p 1111:80 \
6      nginx
7
8  curl http://serv-disc-01:8500/v1/catalog/service/nginx-80 | jq '.'
```

The output of the last command is as follows.

```
1  [
2    {
3      "ModifyIndex": 185,
4      "CreateIndex": 185,
5      "Node": "serv-disc-01",
6      "Address": "10.100.194.201",
7      "ServiceID": "nginx",
8      "ServiceName": "nginx",
9      "ServiceTags": [],
10     "ServiceAddress": "10.100.194.201",
11     "ServicePort": 4321,
12     "ServiceEnableTagOverride": false
13   },
14   {
15     "ModifyIndex": 202,
16     "CreateIndex": 202,
17     "Node": "serv-disc-01",
18     "Address": "10.100.194.201",
19     "ServiceID": "nginx2",
20     "ServiceName": "nginx",
21     "ServiceTags": [
22       "balancer",
23       "proxy",
24       "www"
25     ],
26     "ServiceAddress": "10.100.194.201",
27     "ServicePort": 1111,
28     "ServiceEnableTagOverride": false
29   }
30 ]
```

The second container (*nginx2*) was registered and, this time, Consul got tags that we might find useful later on. Since both containers are listed under the same name Consul considers them to be two instances of the same service.

Now that we know how Registrator works in conjunction with Consul, let's configure it in all nodes of the cluster. The good news is that the role is already created, and we set the protocol to be defined with the variable *protocol*. We also put the name of the container as the *registrator_name* variable so that we can bring the Registrator container with the consul protocol without getting in conflict with the etcd one we configured earlier.

The playbook registrator.yml[105] is as follows.

```
1  - hosts: registrator
2    remote_user: vagrant
3    serial: 1
4    sudo: yes
5    vars:
6      - registrator_name: registrator-consul
7    roles:
8      - docker
9      - consul
10     - registrator
```

The registrator-etcd.yml[106] has the *registrator_protocol* variable set to *etcd* and *registrator_port* to *2379*. We didn't need it in this case since we already had default values set to *consul* and *8500* in the roles/registrator/defaults/main.yml[107] file. On the other hand, we did overwrite the default value of the *registrator_name*.

With everything ready, we can run the playbook.

```
1  ansible-playbook \
2      /vagrant/ansible/registrator.yml \
3      -i /vagrant/ansible/hosts/serv-disc
```

Once the execution of this playbook is finished, Registrator with the consul protocol will be configured on all nodes in the cluster.

---

[105]https://github.com/vfarcic/ms-lifecycle/blob/master/ansible/registrator.yml

[106]https://github.com/vfarcic/ms-lifecycle/blob/master/ansible/registrator-etcd.yml

[107]https://github.com/vfarcic/ms-lifecycle/blob/master/ansible/roles/registrator/defaults/main.yml

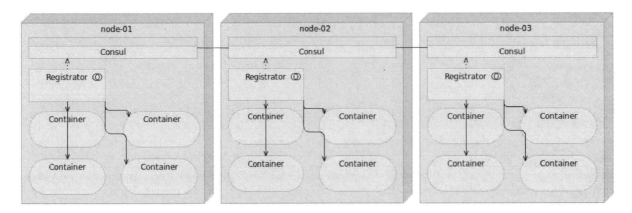

Figure 8-10: Multiple nodes with Docker containers, Consul and Registrator

How about templating? Should we use confd or something else?

Setting Up Consul Template

We can use confd with Consul in the same way as we used it with etcd. However, Consul has its own templating service with features more in line with what Consul offers.

Consul Template[108] is a very convenient way to create files with values obtained from Consul. As a bonus, it can also run arbitrary commands after the files have been updated. Just as confd, Consul Template also uses Go Template[109] format.

By now, you're probably accustomed to the routine. First we'll try Consul Template manually. As with all other tools, we set up in this chapter, installation consists of downloading the release, unpacking it and making sure that the executable is in the system path.

```
1  wget https://releases.hashicorp.com/consul-template/0.12.0/\
2  consul-template_0.12.0_linux_amd64.zip
3
4  sudo apt-get install -y unzip
5
6  unzip consul-template_0.12.0_linux_amd64.zip
7
8  sudo mv consul-template /usr/local/bin
9
10 rm -rf consul-template_0.12.0_linux_amd64*
```

With Consul Template available on the node, we should create one template.

---

[108]https://github.com/hashicorp/consul-template

[109]http://golang.org/pkg/text/template/

```
1  echo '
2  {{range service "nginx-80"}}
3  The address is {{.Address}}:{{.Port}}
4  {{end}}
5  ' >/tmp/nginx.ctmpl
```

When this template is processed, it will iterate (*range*) over all services with the name *nginx-80*. Each iteration will produce the text with service *Address* and *Port*. Template has been created as */tmp/nginx.ctmpl*.

Before we run the Consul Template, let's take another look at what we have stored in Consul for the nginx services.

```
1  curl http://serv-disc-01:8500/v1/catalog/service/nginx-80 | jq '.'
```

The output is as follows.

```
1  [
2    {
3      "ModifyIndex": 185,
4      "CreateIndex": 185,
5      "Node": "serv-disc-01",
6      "Address": "10.100.194.201",
7      "ServiceID": "nginx",
8      "ServiceName": "nginx-80",
9      "ServiceTags": [],
10     "ServiceAddress": "10.100.194.201",
11     "ServicePort": 4321,
12     "ServiceEnableTagOverride": false
13   },
14   {
15     "ModifyIndex": 202,
16     "CreateIndex": 202,
17     "Node": "serv-disc-01",
18     "Address": "10.100.194.201",
19     "ServiceID": "nginx2",
20     "ServiceName": "nginx-80",
21     "ServiceTags": [
22       "balancer",
23       "proxy",
24       "www"
25     ],
```

```
26      "ServiceAddress": "10.100.194.201",
27      "ServicePort": 1111,
28      "ServiceEnableTagOverride": false
29    }
30  ]
```

We have two nginx services up and running and registered in Consul. Let's see the result of applying the template we created.

```
1  consul-template \
2      -consul serv-disc-01:8500 \
3      -template "/tmp/nginx.ctmpl:/tmp/nginx.conf" \
4      -once
5
6  cat /tmp/nginx.conf
```

The result of the second command is as follows.

```
1  The address is 10.100.194.201:4321
2
3  The address is 10.100.194.201:1111
```

The Consul Template command we executed found both services and generated the output in the format we specified. We specified that it should run only once. The alternative is to run it in daemon mode. In such a case, it would monitor the registry for changes and apply them to specified configuration files.

We will go into details of how Consul Template works later on when we start using it in our deployment pipeline. Until then, please consult Consul documentation[110] yourself. For now, it is important to understand that it can obtain any information stored in Consul and apply it to the template we specify. Besides creating the file, it can also run custom commands. That will come in handy with *reverse proxy*, that is the subject of our next chapter.

We didn't try Consul Template applied to Consul's key/value format. In that combination, there is no significant difference when compared to confd.

The major downside Consul Template has is its tight coupling with Consul. Unlike confd that can be used with many different registries, Consul Template is created as a templating engine tightly integrated with Consul. That is, at the same time, an advantage, since it understands Consul's service format. If you choose to use Consul, Consul Template is a great fit.

Before we move on to the next subject, let's create Consul Template role and configure it on all nodes. The roles/consul-template/tasks/main.yml[111] file is as follows.

---

[110]https://github.com/hashicorp/consul-template

[111]https://github.com/vfarcic/ms-lifecycle/blob/master/ansible/roles/consul-template/tasks/main.yml

```
1  - name: Directory is created
2    file:
3      path: /data/consul-template
4      state: directory
5    tags: [consul-template]
6
7  - name: File is copied
8    copy:
9      src: consul-template
10     dest: /usr/local/bin/consul-template
11     mode: 0755
12   tags: [consul-template]
```

There's nothing exciting with this role. It's probably the simplest one we did by now. The same holds true for the consul-template.yml[112] playbook.

```
1  - hosts: consul-template
2    remote_user: vagrant
3    serial: 1
4    sudo: yes
5    roles:
6      - common
7      - consul-template
```

And, finally, we can configure it on all nodes.

```
1  ansible-playbook \
2      /vagrant/ansible/consul-template.yml \
3      -i /vagrant/ansible/hosts/serv-disc
```

The end result is very similar to the etcd/Registrator combination with the difference in data format sent to Consul.

---

[112]https://github.com/vfarcic/ms-lifecycle/blob/master/ansible/consul-template.yml

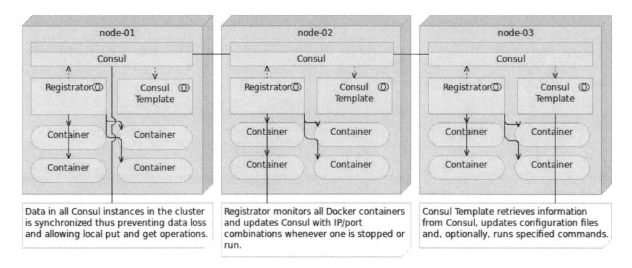

Figure 8-11: Multiple nodes with Docker containers, Consul, Registrator and Consul Template

Up to this point, we covered Consul's features that are, somewhat, similar to the etcd/registrator/-confd combination. It's time to take a look at the characteristics that make Consul indeed stand up from the crowd.

Consul Health Checks, Web UI, and Data Centers

Monitoring health of cluster nodes and services is as important as testing and deployment itself. While we should aim towards having stable environments that never fail, we should also acknowledge that unexpected failures happen and be prepared to act accordingly. We can, for example, monitor memory usage and, if it reaches a certain threshold, move some services to a different node in the cluster. That would be an example of preventive actions performed before the "disaster" would happen. On the other hand, not all potential failures can be detected in time for us to act on time. A single service can fail. A whole node can stop working due to a hardware failure. In such cases, we should be prepared to act as fast as possible by, for example, replacing a node with a new one and moving failed services. We won't go into details how Consul can help us in this task since there is a whole chapter dedicated to *self-healing systems* and Consul will play a major role in it. For now, suffice to say that Consul has a simple, elegant and, yet, powerful way to perform health checks that can help us define what actions should be performed when health thresholds are reached.

If you googled "etcd ui" or "etcd dashboard" you probably saw that there are a few solutions available, and you might be asking why we haven't presented them. The reason is simple; etcd is a key/value store and not much more. Having a UI to present data is not of much use since we can easily obtain it through the etcdctl. That does not mean that etcd UI is of no use but that it does not make much difference due to its limited scope.

Consul is much more than a simple key/value store. As we've already seen, besides storing key/value pairs, it has a notion of a service together with data that belong to it. It can also perform health checks, thus becoming a good candidate for a dashboard that can be used to see the status of our nodes and services running on top of them. Finally, it understands the concept of multiple data centers. All those features combined, let us see the need for a dashboard in a different light.

With the Consul Web UI, we can view all services and nodes, monitor health checks and their statuses, read and set key/value data as well as switch from one data center to another. To see it in action, please open http://10.100.194.201:8500/ui[113] in your favorite browser. You'll see items in the top menu that correspond to the steps we performed earlier through the API.

The *Services* menu item lists all the services we registered. There's not much at the moment since only Consul server, Docker UI and two instances of the nginx service are up and running. We can filter them by name or status and see details by clicking on one of the registered services.

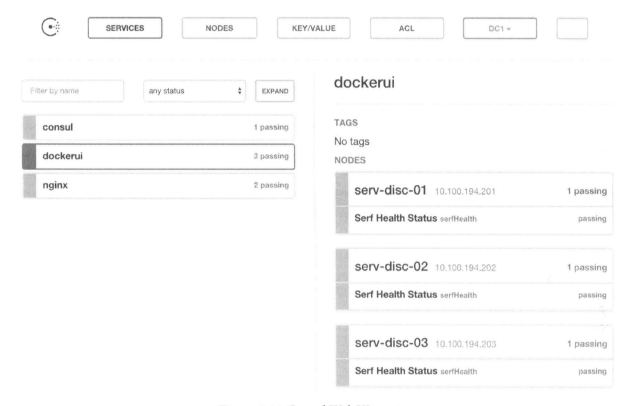

Figure 8-12: Consul Web UI services

Nodes show us the list of all nodes belonging to the selected data center. In our case, we have three nodes. The first one has three registered services.

---

[113]http://10.100.194.201:8500/ui

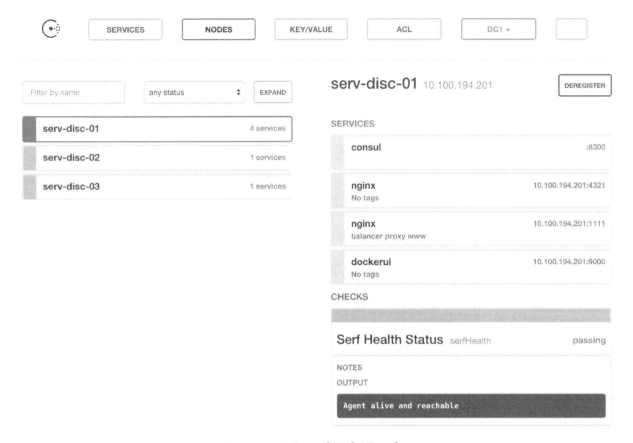

Figure 8-13: Consul Web UI nodes

The *Key/Value* screen can be used to both display and modify data. In it, you can see data put to Consul by the Registrator instance set to use *consulkv* as the protocol. Please feel free to add data yourself and see how they are visualized in the UI. Besides working with Consul key/value data with the API we used before, you can also manage them through the UI.

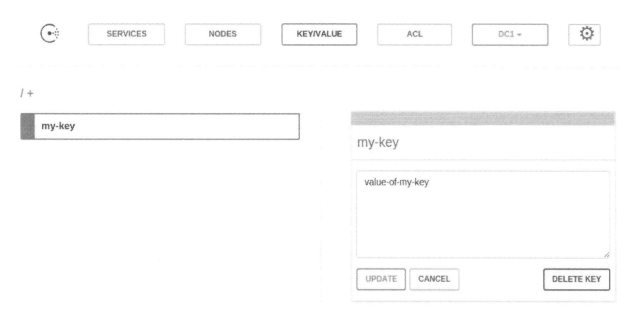

Figure 8-14: Consul Web UI key/value

Please note that Consul allows us to group nodes into data centers. We haven't used this feature since we are running only three nodes. When nodes in the cluster start increasing, splitting them into data centers is often a good idea and Consul helps us to visualize them through its UI.

Combining Consul, Registrator, Template, Health Checks and WEB UI

Consul, together with the tools we explored, is in many cases a better solution than what etcd offers. It was designed with services architecture and discovery in mind. It is simple, yet powerful. It provides a complete solution without sacrificing simplicity and, in many cases, it is the best tool for service discovery and health checking needs (at least among those we evaluated).

Service Discovery Tools Compared

All of the tools are based on similar principles and architecture. They run on nodes, require a quorum to operate and are strongly consistent. They all provide some form of key/value storage.

Zookeeper is the oldest of the three, and the age shows in its complexity, utilization of resources and goals it's trying to accomplish. It was designed in a different age than the rest of the tools we evaluated (even though it's not much older).

etcd with *Registrator* and *confd* is a very simple, yet very powerful combination that can solve most, if not all, of our service discovery needs. It showcases the power we can obtain when we combine simple and very specific tools. Each of them performs a very specific task, communicates through well-established API and is capable of working with relative autonomy. They are *microservices* both in their architectural as well as their functional approach.

What distinguishes *Consul* is the support for multiple data centers and health checking without the usage of third-party tools. That does not mean that the usage of third-party tools is wrong. Actually, throughout this book we are trying to combine different tools by choosing those that are performing better than others without introducing unnecessary features overhead. The best results are obtained when we use right tools for the job. If the tool does more than the job we require, its efficiency drops. On the other hand, a tool that doesn't do what we need it to do is useless. Consul strikes the right balance. It does very few things, and it does them well.

The way Consul uses the gossip protocol to propagate knowledge about the cluster makes it easier to set up than etcd, especially in the case of a big data center. The ability to store data as a service makes it more complete and useful than key/value storage used in etcd (even though Consul has that option as well). While we could accomplish the same by inserting multiple keys in etcd, Consul's service achieves a more compact result that often requires a single query to retrieve all the data related to the service. On top of that, Registrator has quite a good implementation of the Consul protocol making the two an excellent combination, especially when Consul Template is added to this mixture. Consul's Web UI is like a cherry on top of a cake and provides a good way to visualize your services and their health.

I can't say that Consul is a clear winner. Instead, it has a slight edge when compared with etcd. Service discovery as a concept, as well as the tools we can use, is so new that we can expect a lot of changes in this field. By the time you read this book, it's likely that new tools will come, or those we evaluated will change enough that some of the exercises we did will become obsolete. Have an open mind and try to take bits of advice from this chapter with a grain of salt. The logic we employed is solid and is not likely to change anytime soon. The same can not be said for tools. They are bound to evolve rapidly soon.

We are left with one more subject before we can get back to our deployment procedure. The integration step will require that we go through *reverse proxy*.

Before we move on, let's destroy the virtual machines we created for the purpose of service discovery practice and free some resources for the next chapter.

```
1   exit
2
3   vagrant destroy -f
```

Proxy Services

We reached the point where we need something that will tie together the containers we're deploying. We need to simplify the access to the services and unify all the servers and ports our containers are (or will be) deployed on. Multiple solutions are trying to solve this problem, with *Enterprise Service Bus (ESB)* products being most commonly used. That is not to say that their only goal is redirection towards destination services. It indeed isn't, and that is one of the reasons we rejected ESB as (part of) the solution for our architecture. The significant difference in the approach is that ESBs tend to do a lot (much more than we need) while we are trying to compose our system by using very specific small components or services that do (almost) exactly what we need. Not more, not less. ESBs are an antithesis of microservices and, in a way, are betraying the initial ideas behind service-oriented architecture. With us being committed to microservices and looking for more concrete solutions, the alternative is a proxy service. It stands to reason that we should dedicate a bit more time discussing what proxy services are and which products might be able to help us in our architecture and processes.

A *proxy service* is a service that acts as an intermediary between clients performing requests and services that serve those requests. A client sends a request to the proxy service that, in turn, redirects that request to the destination service thus simplifying and controlling complexity laying behind the architecture where the services reside.

There are at least three different types of proxy services.

- A *gateway or tunneling service* is the kind of a proxy service that redirect requests to the destination services and responses back to the clients that made those requests.
- A *forward proxy* is used for retrieving data from different (mostly internet) sources.
- A *reverse proxy* is usually used to control and protect access to a server or services on a private network. Besides its primary function, a reverse proxy often also performs tasks such as load-balancing, decryption, caching and authentication.

A reverse proxy is probably the best solution for the problem at hand, so we'll spend a bit more time trying to understand it better.

Reverse Proxy Service

The main purpose of the proxy service is to hide the rest of the services as well as to redirect requests to their final destination. The same holds true for responses. Once a service responds to a request, that response goes back to the proxy service and from there is redirected to the client that initially requested it. For all purposes, from the point of view of the destination service, the request came from the proxy. In other words, neither the client that generates the request knows what is behind the proxy nor the service responding to the request knows that it originated from beyond the proxy. In other words, both clients and services know only about the existence of the proxy service.

We'll concentrate on usages of a proxy service in the context of an architecture based on (micro)services. However, most of the concepts are the same if a proxy service would be used on whole servers (except that it would be called proxy server).

Some of the main purposes of a proxy services (beyond orchestration of requests and responses) are as follows.

- While almost any applications server can provide **encryption** (most commonly Secure Sockets Layer (SSL)), it is often easier to let the "middle man" be in charge of it.
- **Load balancing** is the process when, in this case, proxy service balances loads between multiple instances of the same service. In most cases, those instances would be scaled over multiple servers. With that combination (load balancing and scaling), especially when architecture is based on microservices, we can quickly accomplish performance improvements and avoid timeouts and downtimes.
- **Compression** is another candidate for a feature that is easily accomplished when centralized in a single service. Main products that act as proxy services are very efficient in compression and allow relatively easy setup. The primary reason for a compression of the traffic is a speedup of the load time. The smaller the size, the faster the load.
- **Caching** is another one of the features that are easy to implement within a proxy service that (in some cases) benefits from being centralized. By caching responses, we can offload part of the work our services need to do. The gist of caching is that we set up the rules (for example, cache requests related to the products listing) and cache timeouts. From there on, the proxy service will send a request to the destination service only the first time and store the responses internally. From there on, as long as the request is the same, it will be served directly by the proxy without even sending the request to the service. That is, until the timeout is reached and the process is repeated. The are much more complicated combinations we can employ, but the most common usage is the one we described.
- Most proxy services serve as a **single point of entry** to the public APIs exposed through services. That in itself increases **security**. In most cases only ports 80 (HTTP) and 443 (HTTPS) would be available to the public usage. All other ports required by services should be open only to the internal use.
- Different types of **authentication** (for example OAuth) can be implemented through the proxy service. When the request does not have the user identification, the proxy service can be set to return with an appropriate response code to the caller. On the other hand, when identification is present, a proxy can choose to continue going to the destination and leave the verification of that identification to the target service or perform it itself. Of course, many variations can be used to implement the authentication. The crucial thing to note is that if a proxy is used, it will most likely be involved in this process one way or another.

This list is by no means extensive nor final but contains some of the most commonly used cases. Many other combinations are possible involving both legal and illegal purposes. As an example, a proxy is an indispensable tool for any hacker that wants to stay anonymous.

Throughout this books, we'll focus mostly on its primary function; we'll use proxy services to act as proxies. They will be in charge of the orchestration of all traffic between microservices we'll be deploying. We'll start with simple usages used in deployments and slowly progress towards more complicated orchestration, namely *blue-green deployment*.

To some, it might sound that a proxy service deviates from microservices approach since it can do (as is often the case) multiple things. However, when looking from the functional point of view, it has a single purpose. It provides a bridge between the outside world and all the services we host internally. At the same time, it tends to have a very low resource usage and can be handled with only a few configuration files.

Equipped with the basic understanding about proxy services, the time has come to take a look at some of the products we can use.

From now on, we'll refer to *reverse proxy* as, simply, *proxy*.

How Can Proxy Service Help Our Project?

By now we managed to have a controlled way to deploy our services. Due to the nature of deployments we are trying to accomplish, those services should be deployed on ports and, potentially, servers that are unknown to us in advance. Flexibility is the key to scalable architecture, fault tolerance, and many other concepts we'll explore further on. However, that flexibility comes at a cost. We might not know in advance where will the services be deployed nor which ports they are exposing. Even if this information would be available before the deployment, we should not force users of our services to specify different ports and IPs when sending requests. The solution is to centralize all communications both from third parties as well as from internal services at a single point. The singular place that will be in charge of redirecting requests is a proxy service. We'll explore some of the tools that are at our disposal and compare their strengths and weaknesses.

As before, we'll start by creating virtual machines that we'll use to experiment with different proxy services. We'll recreate the *cd* node and use it to provision the *proxy* server with different proxy services.

```
1  vagrant up cd proxy
```

The first tool we'll explore is *nginx*.

nginx

nginx[114] (engine x) is an HTTP and reverse proxy server, a mail proxy server, and a generic TCP proxy server. Igor Sysoev originally wrote it. In the beginning, it powered many Russian sites. Since then, it become a server of choice for some of the busiest sites in the world (NetFlix, Wordpress, and FastMail are only a few of the examples). According to Netcraft, nginx served or proxied around 23% of busiest sites[115] in September 2015. That makes it second to Apache. While numbers provided by Netcraft might be questionable, it is clear that nginx is highly popular and probably is closer to the third place after Apache and IIS. Since everything we did by now is based on Linux, Microsoft IIS should be discarded. That leaves us with Apache as a valid candidate to be our proxy service of choice. Stands to reason that the two should be compared.

Apache[116] has been available for many years and built a massive user base. Its huge popularity is partly thanks to Tomcat[117] that runs on top of Apache and is one of the most popular application servers today. Tomcat is only one out of many examples of Apache's flexibility. Through its modules, it can be extended to process almost any programming language.

Being most popular does not necessarily makes something the best choice. Apache can slow down to a crawl under a heavy load due to its design deficiencies. It spawns new processes that, in turn, consume quite a lot of memory. On top of that, it creates new threads for all requests making them compete with each others for access to CPU and memory. Finally, if it reaches the configurable limit of processes, it just refuses new connections. Apache was not designed to serve as a proxy service. That function is very much an after-thought.

nginx was created to address some of the problems Apache has, in particular, the C10K problem. At the time, C10K was a challenge for web servers to begin handling ten thousand concurrent connections. nginx was released in 2004 and met the goal of the challenge. Unlike Apache, its architecture is based on asynchronous, non-blocking, event-driven architecture. Not only that it beats Apache in the number of concurrent requests it can handle, but its resource usage was much lower. It was born after Apache and designed from ground up as a solution for concurrency problems. We got a server capable of handling more requests and a lower cost.

nginx' downside is that it is designed to serve static content. If you need a server to serve content generated by Java, PHP, and other dynamic languages, Apache is a better option. In our case, this downside is of almost no importance since we are looking for a proxy service with the capability to do load balancing and few more features. We will not be serving any content (static or dynamic) directly by the proxy, but redirect requests to specialized services.

All in all, while Apache might be a good choice in a different setting, nginx is a clear winner for the task we're trying to accomplish. It will perform much better than Apache if its only task is to act as a proxy and load balancing. It's memory consumption will be minuscule and it will be capable

---

[114]http://nginx.org/

[115]http://news.netcraft.com/archives/2015/09/16/september-2015-web-server-survey.html

[116]http://httpd.apache.org/

[117]http://tomcat.apache.org/

of handling a vast amount of concurrent requests. At least, that is the conclusion before we get to other contestants for the proxy supremacy.

Setting Up nginx

Before we set up the nginx proxy service, let's take a quick look at the Ansible files that we're about to run. The nginx.yml[118] playbook is similar to those we used before. We'll be running the roles we already run before with the addition of nginx.

```
 1  - hosts: proxy
 2    remote_user: vagrant
 3    serial: 1
 4    sudo: yes
 5    roles:
 6      - common
 7      - docker
 8      - docker-compose
 9      - consul
10      - registrator
11      - consul-template
12      - nginx
```

The roles/nginx/tasks/main.yml[119] role also doesn't contain anything extraordinary.

```
 1  - name: Directories are present
 2    file:
 3      dest: "{{ item }}"
 4      state: directory
 5    with_items: directories
 6    tags: [nginx]
 7
 8  - name: Container is running
 9    docker:
10      image: nginx
11      name: nginx
12      state: running
13      ports: "{{ ports }}"
14      volumes: "{{ volumes }}"
15    tags: [nginx]
```

---

[118]https://github.com/vfarcic/ms-lifecycle/blob/master/ansible/nginx.yml
[119]https://github.com/vfarcic/ms-lifecycle/blob/master/ansible/roles/nginx/tasks/main.yml

```
16
17  - name: Files are present
18    copy:
19      src: "{{ item.src }}"
20      dest: "{{ item.dest }}"
21    with_items: files
22    register: result
23    tags: [nginx]
24
25  - name: Container is reloaded
26    shell: docker kill -s HUP nginx
27    when: result|changed
28    tags: [nginx]
29
30  - name: Info is sent to Consul
31    uri:
32      url: http://localhost:8500/v1/kv/proxy/ip
33      method: PUT
34      body: "{{ ip }}"
35    ignore_errors: yes
36    tags: [nginx]
```

We are creating few directories, making sure that the nginx container is running, passing few files and, if any of them changed, reloading nginx. Finally, we are putting the nginx IP to Consul in case we need it for later. The only important thing to notice is the nginx configuration file roles/nginx/files/services.conf[120].

```
1  log_format upstreamlog
2       '$remote_addr - $remote_user [$time_local] '
3       '"$request" $status $bytes_sent '
4       '"$http_referer" "$http_user_agent" "$gzip_ratio" '
5       '$upstream_addr';
6
7  server {
8    listen 80;
9    server_name _;
10
11   access_log /var/log/nginx/access.log upstreamlog;
12
13   include includes/*.conf;
14 }
```

---

[120]https://github.com/vfarcic/ms-lifecycle/blob/master/ansible/roles/nginx/files/services.conf

```
15
16    include upstreams/*.conf;
```

For the moment, you can ignore log formatting and jump to the *server* specification. We specified that nginx should *listen* to the standard HTTP port *80* and accept requests sent to any server (server_name _). Next are the *include* statements. Instead of specifying all the configuration in one place, with includes we'll be able to add configuration for each service separately. That, in turn, will allow us to focus on one service at a time and make sure that the one we deploy is configured correctly. Later on, we'll explore in more depth which types of configurations go into each of those includes.

Let's run the nginx playbook and start "playing" with it. We'll enter the *cd* node and execute the playbook that will provision the *proxy* node.

```
1    vagrant ssh cd
2
3    ansible-playbook /vagrant/ansible/nginx.yml \
4        -i /vagrant/ansible/hosts/proxy
```

Living Without a Proxy

Before we see nginx in action, it might be worthwhile to refresh our memory of the difficulties we are facing without a proxy service. We'll start by running the *books-ms* application.

```
1    wget https://raw.githubusercontent.com/vfarcic\
2    /books-ms/master/docker-compose.yml
3
4    export DOCKER_HOST=tcp://proxy:2375
5
6    docker-compose up -d app
7
8    docker-compose ps
9
10   curl http://proxy/api/v1/books
```

The output of the last command is as follows.

```
1  <html>
2  <head><title>404 Not Found</title></head>
3  <body bgcolor="white">
4  <center><h1>404 Not Found</h1></center>
5  <hr><center>nginx/1.9.9</center>
6  </body>
7  </html>
```

Even though we run the application with *docker-compose* and confirmed that it is running on the *proxy* node by executing docker-compose ps, we observed through *curl* that the service is not accessible on the standard HTTP port 80 (there was a "404 Not Found" message served through nginx). This result was to be expected since our service is running on a random port. Even if we did specify the port (we already discussed why that is a bad idea), we could not expect users to memorize a different port for each separately deployed service. Besides, we already have service discovery with Consul in place.

```
1  curl http://10.100.193.200:8500/v1/catalog/service/books-ms | jq '.'
```

The output of the last command is as follows.

```
1  [
2    {
3      "ModifyIndex": 42,
4      "CreateIndex": 42,
5      "Node": "proxy",
6      "Address": "10.100.193.200",
7      "ServiceID": "proxy:vagrant_app_1:8080",
8      "ServiceName": "books-ms",
9      "ServiceTags": [],
10     "ServiceAddress": "10.100.193.200",
11     "ServicePort": 32768,
12     "ServiceEnableTagOverride": false
13   }
14 ]
```

We can also obtain the port by inspecting the container.

```
1  PORT=$(docker inspect \
2      --format='{{(index (index .NetworkSettings.Ports "8080/tcp") 0).HostPort}}' \
3      vagrant_app_1)
4
5  echo $PORT
6
7  curl http://proxy:$PORT/api/v1/books | jq '.'
```

We inspected the container, applied formatting to retrieve only the port of the service and stored that information in the *PORT* variable. Later on, we used that variable to make a proper request to the service. As expected, this time, the result was correct. Since there is no data, the service returned an empty JSON array (this time without the 404 error).

Be it as it may, while this operation was successful, it is even less acceptable one for our users. They cannot be given access to our servers only so that they can query Consul or inspect containers to obtain the information they need. Without a proxy, services are unreachable. They are running, but no one can use them.

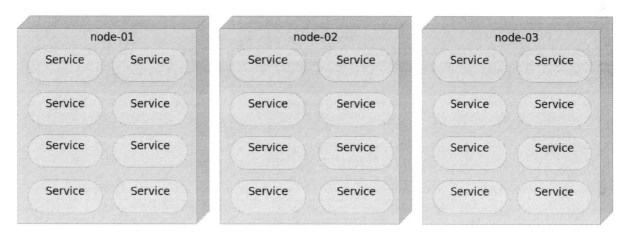

Figure 9-1: Services without proxy

Now that we felt the pain our users would feel without a proxy, let us configure nginx correctly. We'll start with manual configuration, and from there on, progress towards automated one.

Manually Configuring nginx

Do you remember the first *includes* statement in the nginx configuration? Let's use it. We already have the *PORT* variable, and all that we have to do is make sure that all requests coming to nginx on port 80 and starting with the address */api/v1/books* are redirected to the correct port. We can accomplish that by running the following commands.

```
1  echo "
2  location /api/v1/books {
3    proxy_pass http://10.100.193.200:$PORT/api/v1/books;
4  }
5  " | tee books-ms.conf
6
7  scp books-ms.conf \
8      proxy:/data/nginx/includes/books-ms.conf # pass: vagrant
9
10 docker kill -s HUP nginx
```

We created the *books-ms.conf* file that will proxy all requests for */api/v1/books* to the correct IP and port. The *location* statement will match all requests starting with */api/v1/books* and proxy them to the same address running on the specified IP and port. While IP was not necessary, it is a good practice to use it since, in most cases, the proxy service will run on a separate server. Further on, we used *scp* (secure copy) to transfer the file to the */data/nginx/includes/* directory in the *proxy* node. Once the configuration was copied, all we had to do was reload nginx using `kill -s HUP` command.

Let's see whether the change we just did works correctly.

```
1  curl -H 'Content-Type: application/json' -X PUT -d \
2      "{\"_id\": 1,
3      \"title\": \"My First Book\",
4      \"author\": \"John Doe\",
5      \"description\": \"Not a very good book\"}" \
6      http://proxy/api/v1/books | jq '.'
7
8  curl http://proxy/api/v1/books | jq '.'
```

We successfully made a PUT request that inserted a book to the database and queried the service that returned that same book. Finally, we can make requests without worrying about the ports.

Are our problems solved? Only partly. We still need to figure out the way to make these updates to the nginx configuration automatic. After all, if we'll be deploying our microservices often, we cannot rely on human operators to continuously monitor deployments and perform configuration updates.

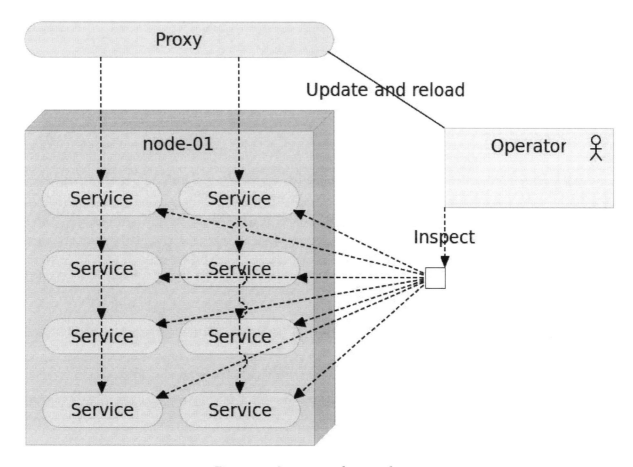

Figure 9-2: Services with manual proxy

Automatically Configuring nginx

We already discussed service discovery tools and the nginx playbook we run earlier made sure that Consul, Registrator, and Consul Template are properly configured on the *proxy* node. That means that Registrator detected the service container we ran and stored that information to the Consul registry. All that is left is to make a template, feed it to Consul Template that will output the configuration file and reload nginx.

Let's make the situation a bit more complicated and scale our service by running two instances. Scaling with Docker Compose is relatively easy.

```
1  docker-compose scale app=2
2
3  docker-compose ps
```

The output of the latter command is as follows.

```
1        Name                 Command              State          Ports
2        -------------------------------------------------------------------------
3        vagrant_app_1        /run.sh              Up        0.0.0.0:32768->8080/tcp
4        vagrant_app_2        /run.sh              Up        0.0.0.0:32769->8080/tcp
5        vagrant_db_1         /entrypoint.sh mongod  Up      27017/tcp
```

We can observe that there are two instances of our service, both using different random ports. Concerning nginx, this means several things, most important being that we cannot proxy in the same way as before. It would be pointless to run two instances of the service and redirect all requests only to one of them. We need to combine proxy with *load balancing*.

We won't go into all possible load balancing techniques. Instead, we'll use the simplest one called *round robin* that is used by nginx by default. Round robin means that the proxy will distribute requests equally among all services. As before, things closely related to a project should be stored in the repository together with the code and nginx configuration files and templates should not be an exception.

Let us first take a look at the nginx-includes.conf[121] configuration file.

```
1    location /api/v1/books {
2      proxy_pass http://books-ms/api/v1/books;
3      proxy_next_upstream error timeout invalid_header http_500;
4    }
```

This time, instead of specifying IP and port, we're using *books_ms*. Obviously, that domain does not exist. It is a way for us to tell nginx to proxy all requests from the location to an upstream. Additionally, we also added *proxy_next_upstream* instruction. If an error, timeout, invalid header or an error 500 is received as a service response, nginx will pass to the next upstream connection.

That is the moment when we can start using the second include statement from the main configuration file. However, since we do not know the IPs and ports the service will use, the upstream is the Consul Template file nginx-upstreams.ctmpl[122].

```
1    upstream books-ms {
2        {{range service "books-ms" "any"}}
3        server {{.Address}}:{{.Port}};
4        {{end}}
5    }
```

What this means is that the upstream request *books-ms* we set as the proxy upstream will be load balanced between all instances of the service and that data will be obtained from Consul. We'll see the result once we run Consul Template.

First things first. Let's download the two files we just discussed.

---

[121]https://github.com/vfarcic/books-ms/blob/master/nginx-includes.conf
[122]https://github.com/vfarcic/books-ms/blob/master/nginx-upstreams.ctmpl

```
1  wget http://raw.githubusercontent.com/vfarcic\
2  /books-ms/master/nginx-includes.conf
3
4  wget http://raw.githubusercontent.com/vfarcic\
5  /books-ms/master/nginx-upstreams.ctmpl
```

Now that the proxy configuration and the upstream template are on the *cd* server, we should run Consul Template.

```
1  consul-template \
2      -consul proxy:8500 \
3      -template "nginx-upstreams.ctmpl:nginx-upstreams.conf" \
4      -once
5
6  cat nginx-upstreams.conf
```

Consul Template took the downloaded template as the input and created the *books-ms.conf* upstream configuration. The second command output the result that should look similar to the following.

```
1  upstream books-ms {
2
3      server 10.100.193.200:32768;
4
5      server 10.100.193.200:32769;
6
7  }
```

Since we are running two instances of the same service, Consul template retrieved their IPs and ports and put them in the format we specified in the *books-ms.ctmpl* template.

Please note that we could have passed the third argument to Consul Template, and it would run any command we specify. We'll use it later on throughout the book.

Now that all the configuration files are created, we should copy them to the *proxy* node and reload nginx.

```
1  scp nginx-includes.conf \
2      proxy:/data/nginx/includes/books-ms.conf # Pass: vagrant
3
4  scp nginx-upstreams.conf \
5      proxy:/data/nginx/upstreams/books-ms.conf # Pass: vagrant
6
7  docker kill -s HUP nginx
```

All that's left is to double check that proxy works and is balancing requests among those two instances.

```
1  curl http://proxy/api/v1/books | jq '.'
2
3  curl http://proxy/api/v1/books | jq '.'
4
5  curl http://proxy/api/v1/books | jq '.'
6
7  curl http://proxy/api/v1/books | jq '.'
8
9  docker logs nginx
```

After making four requests we output nginx logs that should look like following (timestamps are removed for brevity).

```
1  "GET /api/v1/books HTTP/1.1" 200 268 "-" "curl/7.35.0" "-" 10.100.193.200:32768
2  "GET /api/v1/books HTTP/1.1" 200 268 "-" "curl/7.35.0" "-" 10.100.193.200:32769
3  "GET /api/v1/books HTTP/1.1" 200 268 "-" "curl/7.35.0" "-" 10.100.193.200:32768
4  "GET /api/v1/books HTTP/1.1" 200 268 "-" "curl/7.35.0" "-" 10.100.193.200:32769
```

While ports might be different in your case, it is obvious that the first request was sent to the port *32768*, the next one to the *32769*, then to the *32768* again, and, finally, to the *32769*. It is a success, with nginx not only acting as a proxy but also load balancing requests among all instances of the service we deployed.

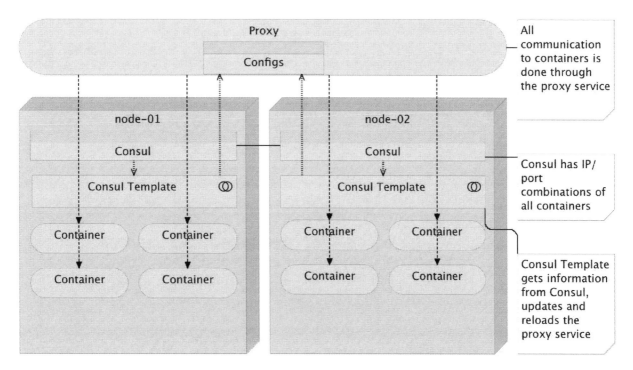

Figure 9-3: Services with automatic proxy with Consul Template

We still haven't tested the error handling we set up with the *proxy_next_upstream* instruction. Let's remove one of the service instances and confirm that nginx handles failures correctly.

```
1  docker stop vagrant_app_2
2
3  curl http://proxy/api/v1/books | jq '.'
4
5  curl http://proxy/api/v1/books | jq '.'
6
7  curl http://proxy/api/v1/books | jq '.'
8
9  curl http://proxy/api/v1/books | jq '.'
```

We stopped one service instance and made several requests. Without the *proxy_next_upstream* instruction, nginx would fail on every second request since one of the two services set as upstreams are not working anymore. However, all four requests worked correctly. We can observe what nginx did by taking a look at its logs.

```
1  docker logs nginx
```

The output should be similar to the following (timestamps are removed for brevity).

```
 1  "GET /api/v1/books HTTP/1.1" 200 268 "-" "curl/7.35.0" "-" 10.100.193.200:32768
 2  [error] 12#12: *98 connect() failed (111: Connection refused) while connecting t\
 3  o upstream, client: 172.17.42.1, server: _, request: "GET /api/v1/books HTTP/1.1\
 4  ", upstream: "http://10.100.193.200:32769/api/v1/books", host: "localhost"
 5  [warn] 12#12: *98 upstream server temporarily disabled while connecting to upstr\
 6  eam, client: 172.17.42.1, server: _, request: "GET /api/v1/books HTTP/1.1", upst\
 7  ream: "http://10.100.193.200:32768/api/v1/books", host: "localhost"
 8  "GET /api/v1/books HTTP/1.1" 200 268 "-" "curl/7.35.0" "-" 10.100.193.200:32768,\
 9   10.100.193.200:32768
10  "GET /api/v1/books HTTP/1.1" 200 268 "-" "curl/7.35.0" "-" 10.100.193.200:32768
11  "GET /api/v1/books HTTP/1.1" 200 268 "-" "curl/7.35.0" "-" 10.100.193.200:32768
```

The first request went to the port *32768* served by the instance that is still running. As expected, nginx sent the second request to the port *32768*. Since the response was *111* (Connection refused), it decided to temporarily disable this upstream and try with the next one in line. From there on, all the rest of requests were proxied to the port *32768*.

With only a few lines in configuration files, we managed to set up the proxy and combine it with load balancing and failover strategy. Later on, when we get to the chapter that will explore *self-healing systems*, we'll go even further and make sure not only that proxy works only with running services, but also how to restore the whole system to a healthy state.

When nginx is combined with service discovery tools, we have an excellent solution. However, we should not use the first tool that comes along, so we'll evaluate a few more options. Let us stop the nginx container and see how *HAProxy* behaves.

```
 1  docker stop nginx
```

HAProxy

Just like nginx, HAProxy[123] is a free, very fast and reliable solution offering high availability, load balancing, and proxying. It is particularly suited for very high traffic websites and powers quite many of the world's most visited ones.

We'll speak about the differences later on when we compare all proxy solutions we're exploring. For now, suffice to say that HAProxy is an excellent solution and probably the best alternative to nginx.

We'll start with practical exercises and try to accomplish with HAProxy the same behavior as the one with have with nginx. Before we provision the *proxy* node with HAProxy, let us take a quick look at the tasks in the Ansible role haproxy[124].

---

[123]http://www.haproxy.org/
[124]https://github.com/vfarcic/ms-lifecycle/blob/master/ansible/roles/haproxy/tasks/main.yml

```
1   - name: Directories are present
2     file:
3       dest: "{{ item }}"
4       state: directory
5     with_items: directories
6     tags: [haproxy]
7
8   - name: Files are present
9     copy:
10      src: "{{ item.src }}"
11      dest: "{{ item.dest }}"
12    with_items: files
13    register: result
14    tags: [haproxy]
15
16  - name: Container is running
17    docker:
18      image: million12/haproxy
19      name: haproxy
20      state: running
21      ports: "{{ ports }}"
22      volumes: /data/haproxy/config/:/etc/haproxy/
23    tags: [haproxy]
```

The *haproxy* role is very similar to the one we used for nginx. We created some directories and copied some files (we'll see them later on). The major thing to note is that, unlike most other containers not built by us, we're not using the official *haproxy* container. The main reason is that the official image has no way to reload HAProxy configuration. We'd need to restart the container every time we update HAProxy configuration, and that would produce some downtime. Since one of the goals is to accomplish zero-downtime, restarting the container is not an option. Therefore, we had to look at alternatives, and the user *million12* has just what we need. The million12/haproxy[125] container comes with *inotify* (*inode notify*). It is a Linux kernel subsystem that acts by extending filesystems to notice changes, and report them to applications. In our case, inotify will reload HAProxy whenever we change its configuration.

Let us proceed and provision HAProxy on the *proxy* node.

```
1   ansible-playbook /vagrant/ansible/haproxy.yml \
2       -i /vagrant/ansible/hosts/proxy
```

Manually Configuring HAProxy

We'll start by checking whether HAProxy is running.

---

[125]https://hub.docker.com/r/million12/haproxy/

```
1  export DOCKER_HOST=tcp://proxy:2375
2
3  docker ps -a
4
5  docker logs haproxy
```

The docker ps command showed that the *haproxy* container has the status *Exited*, and the logs produced the output similar to the following.

```
1   [2015-10-16 08:55:40] /usr/local/sbin/haproxy -f /etc/haproxy/haproxy.cfg -D -p \
2   /var/run/haproxy.pid
3   [2015-10-16 08:55:40] Current HAProxy config /etc/haproxy/haproxy.cfg:
4   ==================================================================\
5   ===================
6   cat: /etc/haproxy/haproxy.cfg: No such file or directory
7   ==================================================================\
8   ===================
9   [ALERT] 288/085540 (9) : Could not open configuration file /etc/haproxy/haproxy.\
10  cfg : No such file or directory
11  [ALERT] 288/085540 (10) : Could not open configuration file /etc/haproxy/haproxy\
12  .cfg : No such file or directory
```

HAProxy complained that there is no *haproxy.cfg* configuration file and stopped the process. Actually, the "fault" is in the playbook we run. The only file we created is *haproxy.cfg.orig* (more about it later) and that there is no *haproxy.cfg*. Unlike nginx, HAPRoxy cannot be run without having, at least, one proxy set. We'll set up the first proxy soon but, at the moment, we have none. Since creating the configuration without any proxy is a waste of time (HAProxy fails anyway) and we cannot provide one when provisioning the node for the first time since at that point there would be no services running, we just skipped the creation of the *haproxy.cfg*.

Before we proceed with the configuration of the first proxy, let us comment another difference that might complicate the process. Unlike nginx, HAProxy does not allow includes. The complete configuration needs to be in a single file. That will pose certain problems since the idea is to add or modify only configurations of the service we are deploying and ignore the rest of the system. We can, however, simulate includes by creating parts of the configuration as separate files and concatenate them every time we deploy a new container. For this reason, we copied the haproxy.cfg.orig[126] file as part of the provisioning process. Feel free to take a look at it. We won't go into details since it contains mostly the default settings and HAProxy has a decent documentation that you can consult. The important thing to note is that the *haproxy.cfg.orig* file contains settings without a single proxy being set.

We'll create the HAProxy configuration related to the service we have running in the similar way as we did before.

---

[126]https://github.com/vfarcic/ms-lifecycle/blob/master/ansible/roles/haproxy/files/haproxy.cfg.orig

```
1  PORT=$(docker inspect \
2      --format='{{(index (index .NetworkSettings.Ports "8080/tcp") 0).HostPort}}' \
3      vagrant_app_1)
4
5  echo $PORT
6
7  echo "
8  frontend books-ms-fe
9      bind *:80
10     option http-server-close
11     acl url_books-ms path_beg /api/v1/books
12     use_backend books-ms-be if url_books-ms
13
14 backend books-ms-be
15     server books-ms-1 10.100.193.200:$PORT check
16 " | tee books-ms.service.cfg
```

We started by inspecting the *vagrant_app_1* container in order to assign the current port to the *PORT* variable and use it to create the *books-ms.service.cfg* file.

HAProxy uses similar logic as nginx even though things are named differently. The *frontend* defines how requests should be forwarded to *backends*. In a way, the *frontend* is analogous to the nginx' *location* instruction and the *backend* to the *upstream*. What we did can be translated to the following. Define a frontend called *books-ms-fe*, bind it to the port *80* and, whenever the request part starts with */api/v1/books*, use the backend called *books-ms-be*. The backend *books-ms-be* has (at the moment) only one server defined with the IP *10.100.193.200* and the port assigned by Docker. The *check* argument has (more or less) the same meaning as in nginx and is used to skip proxying to services that are not healthy.

Now that we have the general settings in the file *haproxy.cfg.orig* and those specific to services we're deploying (named with the *.service.cfg* extension), we can concatenate them into a single *haproxy.cfg* configuration file and copy it to the *proxy* node.

```
1  cat /vagrant/ansible/roles/haproxy/files/haproxy.cfg.orig \
2      *.service.cfg | tee haproxy.cfg
3
4  scp haproxy.cfg proxy:/data/haproxy/config/haproxy.cfg
```

Since the container is not running, we'll need to start it (again), and then we can check whether the proxy is working correctly by querying the service.

```
1  curl http://proxy/api/v1/books | jq '.'
2
3  docker start haproxy
4
5  docker logs haproxy
6
7  curl http://proxy/api/v1/books | jq '.'
```

The first request returned the "Connection refused" error. We used it to confirm that no proxy is running. Then we started the *haproxy* container and saw through the container logs that the configuration file we created is valid and indeed used by the proxy service. Finally, we sent the request again, and, this time, it returned a valid response.

So far, so good. We can proceed and automate the process using Consult Template.

Automatically Configuring HAProxy

We'll try to do the same or very similar steps as what we did before with nginx. That way you can compare the two tools more easily.

We'll start by scaling the service.

```
1  docker-compose scale app=2
2
3  docker-compose ps
```

Next we should download the haproxy.ctmpl[127] template from the code repository. Before we do that, let us take a quick look at its contents.

```
1  frontend books-ms-fe
2      bind *:80
3      option http-server-close
4      acl url_books-ms path_beg /api/v1/books
5      use_backend books-ms-be if url_books-ms
6
7  backend books-ms-be
8      {{range service "books-ms" "any"}}
9      server {{.Node}}_{{.Port}} {{.Address}}:{{.Port}} check
10     {{end}}
```

The way we created the template follows the same pattern as the one we used with nginx. The only difference is that HAProxy needs each server to be uniquely identified so we added the service *Node* and *Port* that will serve as the server ID.

Let's download the template and run it through Consul Template.

---

[127]https://github.com/vfarcic/books-ms/blob/master/haproxy.ctmpl

```
1  wget http://raw.githubusercontent.com/vfarcic\
2  /books-ms/master/haproxy.ctmpl \
3      -O haproxy.ctmpl
4
5  sudo consul-template \
6      -consul proxy:8500 \
7      -template "haproxy.ctmpl:books-ms.service.cfg" \
8      -once
9
10 cat books-ms.service.cfg
```

We downloaded the template using *wget* and run the *consul-template* command.

Let us concatenate all the files into haproxy.cfg, copy it to the *proxy* node and take a look at *haproxy* logs.

```
1  cat /vagrant/ansible/roles/haproxy/files/haproxy.cfg.orig \
2      *.service.cfg | tee haproxy.cfg
3
4  scp haproxy.cfg proxy:/data/haproxy/config/haproxy.cfg
5
6  docker logs haproxy
7
8  curl http://proxy/api/v1/books | jq '.'
```

All that's left is to double check whether the proxy balancing works with two instances.

```
1  curl http://proxy/api/v1/books | jq '.'
2
3  curl http://proxy/api/v1/books | jq '.'
4
5  curl http://proxy/api/v1/books | jq '.'
6
7  curl http://proxy/api/v1/books | jq '.'
```

Unfortunately, HAProxy cannot output logs to stdout (preferred way to log Docker containers) so we cannot confirm that balancing works. We could output logs to syslog, but that is outside of the scope of this chapter.

We still haven't tested the error handling we set up with the *backend* instruction. Let's remove one of the service instances and confirm that HAProxy handles failures correctly.

```
1  docker stop vagrant_app_1
2
3  curl http://proxy/api/v1/books | jq '.'
4
5  curl http://proxy/api/v1/books | jq '.'
6
7  curl http://proxy/api/v1/books | jq '.'
8
9  curl http://proxy/api/v1/books | jq '.'
```

We stopped one service instance and made several requests, and all of them worked properly.

Without the possibility to include files into HAProxy configuration, our job was slightly more complicated. Not being able to log to stdout can be solved with syslog but will go astray from one of the containers best practices. There is a reason for this HAProxy behavior. Logging to stdout slows it down (noticeable only with an enormous number of requests). However, it would be better if that is left as our choice and maybe the default behavior, instead of not being supported at all. Finally, not being able to use the official HAProxy container might be considered a minor inconvenience. None of those problems are of great importance. We solved the lack of includes, could log into syslog and ended up using the container from *million12/haproxy* (we could also create our own that would extend from the official one).

Proxy Tools Compared

Apache, nginx and HAProxy are by no means the only solutions we could use. There are many projects available and making a choice is harder than ever.

One of the open source projects worth trying out is lighttpd[128] (pron. lighty). Just like nginx and HAProxy, it was designed for security, speed, compliance, flexibility and high performance. It features a small memory footprint and efficient management of the CPU-load.

If JavaScript is your language of preference, [node-http-proxy] could be a worthy candidate. Unlike other products we explored, node-http-proxy uses JavaScript code to define proxies and load balancing.

VulcanD[129] is a project to keep an eye on. It is programmable proxy and load balancer backed by etcd. A similar process that we did with Consul Template and nginx/HAProxy is incorporated inside VulcanD. It can be combined with Sidekick[130] to provide functionality similar to *check* arguments in nginx and HAProxy.

---

[128]http://www.lighttpd.net/

[129]https://github.com/mailgun/vulcand

[130]https://github.com/lokalebasen/sidekick

There are many similar projects available, and it is certain that new and existing ones are into making. We can expect more "unconventional" projects to appear that will combine proxy, load balancing, and service discovery in many different ways.

However, my choice, for now, stays with nginx or HAProxy. None of the other products we spoke about has anything to add and, in turn, each of them, at least, one deficiency.

Apache is process based, making its performance when faced with a massive traffic less than desirable. At the same time, its resource usage skyrockets easily. If you need a server that will serve dynamic content, Apache is a great option, but should not be used as a proxy.

Lighttpd was promising when it appeared but faced many obstacles (memory leaks, CPU usage, and so on) that made part of its users switch to alternatives. The community maintaining it is much smaller than the one working on nginx and HAProxy. While it had its moment and many had high expectations from it, today it is not the recommended solution.

What can be said about *node-http-proxy*? Even though it does not outperform nginx and HAProxy, it is very close. The major obstacle would be its programmable configuration that is not well suited for continuously changing proxies. If your language of choice is JavaScript and proxies should be relatively static, node-http-proxy is a valid option. However, it still doesn't provide any benefit over nginx and HAProxy.

VulcanD, in conjunction with Sidekick, is a project to keep an eye on, but it is not yet production ready (at least, not at the time this text was written). It is very unlikely that it will manage to outperform main players. The potential problem with VulcanD is that it is bundled with etcd. If that's what you're already using, great. On the other hand, if your choice fell to some other type of Registry (for example Consul or Zookeeper), there is nothing VulcanD can offer. I prefer keeping proxy and service discovery separated and put the glue between them myself. Real value VulcanD provides is in a new way of thinking that combines proxy service with service discovery, and it will probably be considered as one of the pioneers that opened the door for new types of proxy services.

That leaves us with nginx and HAProxy. If you spend some more time investigating opinions, you'll see that both camps have an enormous number of users defending one over the other. There are areas where nginx outperforms HAProxy and others where it underperforms. There are some features that HAProxy doesn't have and other missing in nginx. But, the truth is that both are battle-tested, both are an excellent solution, both have a huge number of users, and both are successfully used in companies that have colossal traffic. If what you're looking for is a proxy service with load balancing, you cannot go wrong with either of them.

I am slightly more inclined towards nginx due to its better (official) Docker container (for example, it allows configuration reloads with a HUP signal), option to log to stdout and the ability to include configuration files. Excluding Docker container, HAProxy made the conscious decision not to support those features due to possible performance issues they can create. However, I prefer having the ability to choose when it's appropriate to use them and when it isn't. All those are truly preferences of no great importance and, in many cases, the choice is made depending on a particular use case one is trying to accomplish. However, there is one critical nginx feature that HAProxy does not support. HAProxy can drop traffic during reloads. If microservices architecture, continuous deployment, and blue-green processes are adopted, configuration reloads are very common. We can have several or even hundreds of reloads each day. No matter the reload frequency, with HAProxy there is a possibility of downtime.

We have to make a choice, and it falls to nginx. It will be out proxy of choice throughout the rest of the book.

With that being said, let us destroy the VMs we used in this chapter and finish the implementation of the deployment pipeline. With service discovery and the proxy, we have everything we need.

```
1  exit
2
3  vagrant destroy -f
```

Implementation of the Deployment Pipeline: The Late Stages

We had to make a break from the implementation of our deployment pipeline and explore service discovery and proxy services. Without a proxy service, our containers would not be accessible in an easy and reliable manner. To provide all the data proxy service needs, we spent some time exploring different options and came up with a few combinations that could serve as service discovery solutions.

With service discovery and proxy services in our tool-belt, we can continue where we left and finalize manual execution of the deployment pipeline.

1. Checkout the code - Done
2. Run pre-deployment tests - Done
3. Compile and/or package the code - Done
4. Build the container - Done
5. Push the container to the registry - Done
6. Deploy the container to the production server - Done
7. Integrate the container - Pending
8. Run post-deployment tests - Pending
9. Push the tests container to the registry - Pending

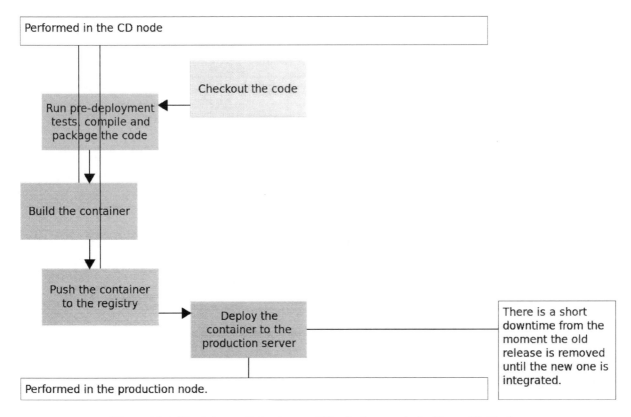

Figure 10-1: The intermediate stages of the deployment pipeline with Docker

We are missing three steps in our deployment pipeline. We should integrate our container and, once that is done, run post-deployment tests. Finally, we should push our tests container to the registry so that everyone can use it.

We'll start by bringing up the two nodes we're using for our deployment pipeline.

```
1  vagrant up cd prod
```

We'll use the prod2.yml[131] Ansible playbook to provision the *prod* node. It contains service discovery and proxy roles that we already discussed in the previous chapter.

---

[131]https://github.com/vfarcic/ms-lifecycle/blob/master/ansible/prod2.yml

```
1  - hosts: prod
2    remote_user: vagrant
3    serial: 1
4    sudo: yes
5    roles:
6      - common
7      - docker
8      - docker-compose
9      - consul
10     - registrator
11     - consul-template
12     - nginx
```

Once run, our *prod* node will have Consul, Registrator, Consul Template and nginx up and running. They will allow us to proxy all requests to their destination services (at the moment only *books-ms*). Let us run the playbook from the *cd* node.

```
1  vagrant ssh cd
2
3  ansible-playbook /vagrant/ansible/prod2.yml \
4      -i /vagrant/ansible/hosts/prod
```

Starting the Containers

Before we proceed with the integration, we should run the containers.

```
1  wget https://raw.githubusercontent.com/vfarcic\
2  /books-ms/master/docker-compose.yml
3
4  export DOCKER_HOST=tcp://prod:2375
5
6  docker-compose up -d app
```

Since we provisioned this node with Consul and Registrator, IPs and ports from those two containers should be available in the registry. We can confirm this by visiting the Consul UI from a browser by opening http://10.100.198.201:8500/ui[132].

If we click on the *Nodes* button, we can see that the *prod* node is registered. Further on, clicking the *prod* node button should reveal that it contains two services; *consul* and *books-ms*. The *mongo* container that we started is not registered because it does not expose any ports.

---

[132]http://10.100.198.201:8500/ui

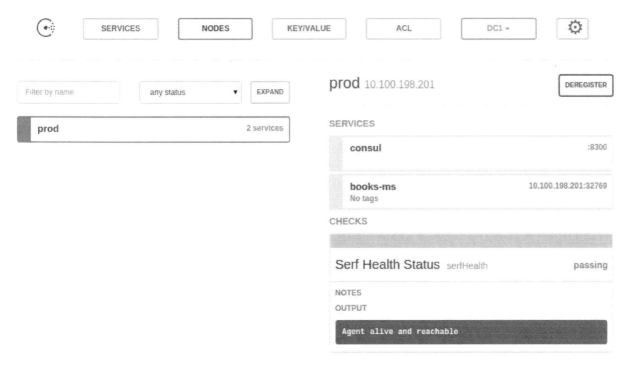

Figure 10-2: Consul screenshot with the prod node and services running on it

We can see the same information by sending a request to Consul.

```
1  curl prod:8500/v1/catalog/services | jq '.'
2
3  curl prod:8500/v1/catalog/service/books-ms | jq '.'
```

The first command listed all services registered in Consul. The output is as follows.

```
1  {
2    "dockerui": [],
3    "consul": [],
4    "books-ms": []
5  }
```

The second command output all the information related to the *books-ms* services.

```
 1  [
 2    {
 3      "ModifyIndex": 27,
 4      "CreateIndex": 27,
 5      "Node": "prod",
 6      "Address": "10.100.198.201",
 7      "ServiceID": "prod:vagrant_app_1:8080",
 8      "ServiceName": "books-ms",
 9      "ServiceTags": [],
10      "ServiceAddress": "10.100.198.201",
11      "ServicePort": 32768,
12      "ServiceEnableTagOverride": false
13    }
14  ]
```

With the containers up and running and their information stored in the service registry, we can reconfigure nginx so that the *books-ms* service is accessible through the standard HTTP port 80.

Integrating the Service

We'll start by confirming that nginx does not know about the existence of our service.

```
 1  curl http://prod/api/v1/books
```

After sending the request, nginx responded with the "404 Not Found" message. Let's change this.

```
 1  exit
 2
 3  vagrant ssh prod
 4
 5  wget https://raw.githubusercontent.com/vfarcic\
 6  /books-ms/master/nginx-includes.conf \
 7      -O /data/nginx/includes/books-ms.conf
 8
 9  wget https://raw.githubusercontent.com/vfarcic\
10  /books-ms/master/nginx-upstreams.ctmpl \
11      -O /data/nginx/upstreams/books-ms.ctmpl
12
13  consul-template \
14      -consul localhost:8500 \
15      -template "/data/nginx/upstreams/books-ms.ctmpl:\
```

```
16   /data/nginx/upstreams/books-ms.conf:\
17   docker kill -s HUP nginx" \
18       -once
```

We already did most of those steps in the previous chapter so we'll go through them very briefly. We entered the *prod* node and downloaded the includes file and upstreams template from the code repository. Then we run *consul-template* that fetched data from Consul and applied them to the template. The result is the nginx upstreams configuration file. Please note that, this time, we added the third argument docker kill -s HUP nginx. Not only that *consul-template* created the configuration file from the template, but it also reloaded nginx. The reason that we did those command from the *prod* server instead of doing everything remotely like in the previous chapters lies in automation. The steps we just run are much closer to the way we'll automate this part of the process in the next chapter.

Now we can test whether our service is indeed accessible through the port 80.

```
1    exit
2
3    vagrant ssh cd
4
5    curl -H 'Content-Type: application/json' -X PUT -d \
6        "{\"_id\": 1,
7        \"title\": \"My First Book\",
8        \"author\": \"John Doe\",
9        \"description\": \"Not a very good book\"}" \
10       http://prod/api/v1/books | jq '.'
11
12   curl http://prod/api/v1/books | jq '.'
```

Running Post-Deployment Tests

While we did confirm that the service is accessible from nginx by sending the request and observing the proper response, this way of verification is not reliable if we are trying to accomplish full automation of the process. Instead, we should repeat the execution of our integration tests but, this time, using port 80 (or no port at all since 80 is standard HTTP port).

```
1  git clone https://github.com/vfarcic/books-ms.git
2
3  cd books-ms
4
5  docker-compose \
6      -f docker-compose-dev.yml \
7      run --rm \
8      -e DOMAIN=http://10.100.198.201 \
9      integ
```

The output is as follows.

```
1   [info] Loading project definition from /source/project
2   [info] Set current project to books-ms (in build file:/source/)
3   [info] Compiling 2 Scala sources to /source/target/scala-2.10/classes...
4   [info] Compiling 2 Scala sources to /source/target/scala-2.10/test-classes...
5   [info] ServiceInteg
6   [info]
7   [info] GET http://10.100.198.201/api/v1/books should
8   [info] + return OK
9   [info]
10  [info] Total for specification ServiceInteg
11  [info] Finished in 23 ms
12  [info] 1 example, 0 failure, 0 error
13  [info] Passed: Total 1, Failed 0, Errors 0, Passed 1
14  [success] Total time: 27 s, completed Sep 17, 2015 7:49:28 PM
```

As expected, the output shows that integration tests passed successfully. The truth is that we have only one test that makes the same request as the *curl* command we run earlier. However, in a "real world" situation, the number of tests would increase, and using proper testing frameworks is much more reliable than running *curl* requests.

Pushing the Tests Container to the Registry

Truth be told, we already pushed this container to the registry to avoid building it every time we need it and, therefore, save you from waiting. However, this time, we should push it as part of the deployment pipeline process. We are trying to run tasks in order of their importance so that we get feedback as fast as possible. Pushing containers with tests is very low on our list of priorities, so we left it for the end. Now that everything else was run successfully, we can push the container and let others pull it from the registry and use it as they see fit.

```
1   docker push 10.100.198.200:5000/books-ms-tests
```

The Checklist

We managed to go through the whole deployment pipeline. It took us quite a lot of time since we had to take a few breaks and explore different ways to proceed. We could not deploy to production without exploring configuration management concepts and tools. Later on, we got stuck again and had to learn about service discovery and proxy before being able to integrate the service container.

1. Checkout the code - Done
2. Run pre-deployment tests - Done
3. Compile and/or package the code - Done
4. Build the container - Done
5. Push the container to the registry - Done
6. Deploy the container to the production server - Done
7. Run post-deployment tests - Done
8. Push the tests container to the registry - Done

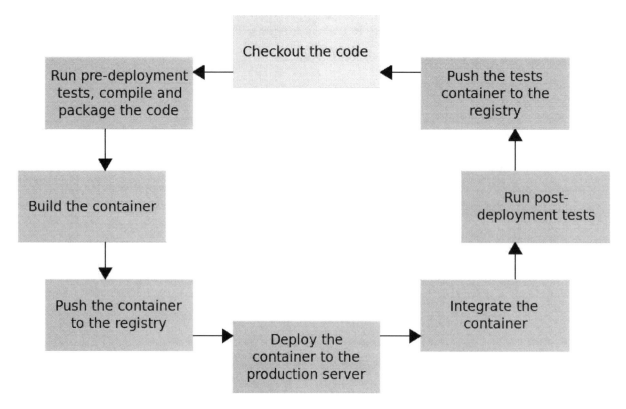

Figure 10-3: The late stages of the deployment pipeline with Docker

Now we are all set. We are capable of running the deployment procedure manually. The next step is to automate all those commands and start running the pipeline automatically from the beginning to the end. We'll destroy the nodes we used so that we can start over fresh and confirm that the automated procedure indeed works.

```
1  exit
2
3  vagrant destroy -f
```

Automating Implementation of the Deployment Pipeline

Now that we are in control of the process of manually executing the deployment pipeline, we can start working on the creation of a fully automated version. After all, our goal is not to employ an army of operators that will sit in front of their computers and continuously execute deployment commands. Before we proceed, let us quickly go through the process one more time.

Deployment Pipeline Steps

The steps of the pipeline are as follows.

1. Check out the code
2. Run pre-deployment tests, compile and package the code
3. Build the container
4. Push the container to the registry
5. Deploy the container to the production server
6. Integrate the container
7. Run post-deployment tests
8. Push the tests container to the registry

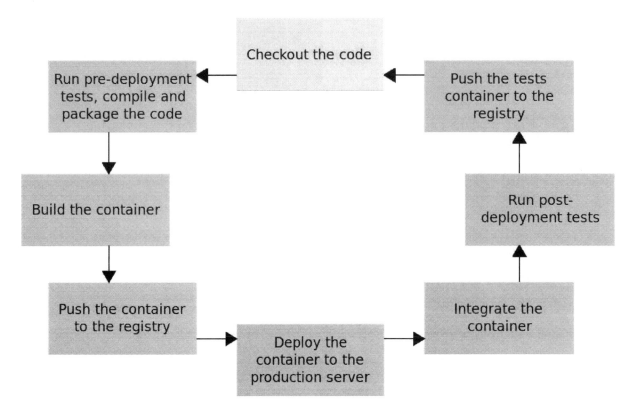

Figure 11-1: Deployment pipeline

To minimize the impact the pipeline has on our business, we tried our best to run as many tasks as possible outside the production server. The only two steps that we had to perform on the *prod* node is deployment itself and the integrations (at the moment only with the proxy service). All the rest of the steps were done inside the *cd* server.

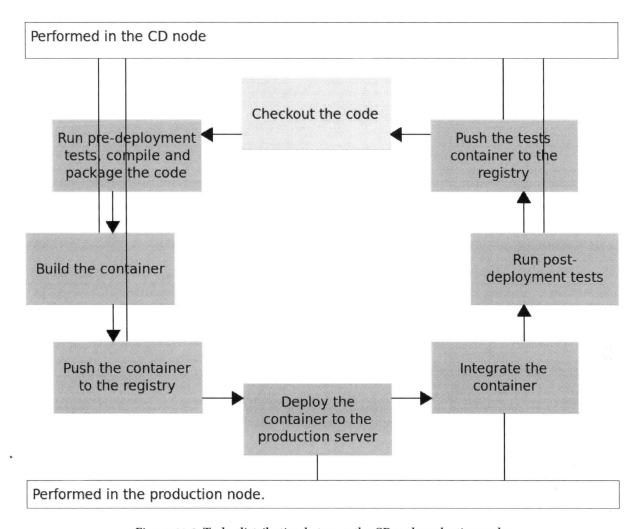

Figure 11-2: Tasks distribution between the CD and production nodes

We already chose Ansible as the tool we're using for servers provisioning. We used it in several occasions to install packages, setup configurations and so on. Up until now, all those usages were aimed at providing all the requirements necessary for the deployment of our containers. We'll extend the usage of Ansible playbooks and add the deployment pipeline to it.

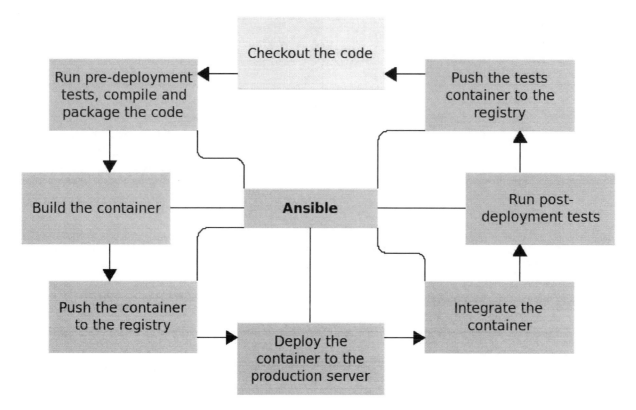

Figure 11-3: Automated deployment pipeline with Ansible

Of all the steps involved, we'll leave only one of them outside of the automation scope. We won't check out the code with Ansible. The reason behind this is not that Ansible is not capable of cloning a Git repository. It certainly is. The problem is that Ansible is not a tool designed to run continuously and monitor code repositories for changes. There are a few more problems that we did not yet tackle. For example, we do not have a set of actions that should be run in case of a failure of the process. Another hole in the current pipeline is that there is a short downtime related to each deployment. The process stops the running release and brings up the new one. Between those two actions, there is a (short) period the service we're deploying is not operational. We'll leave those and other possible improvements for later on.

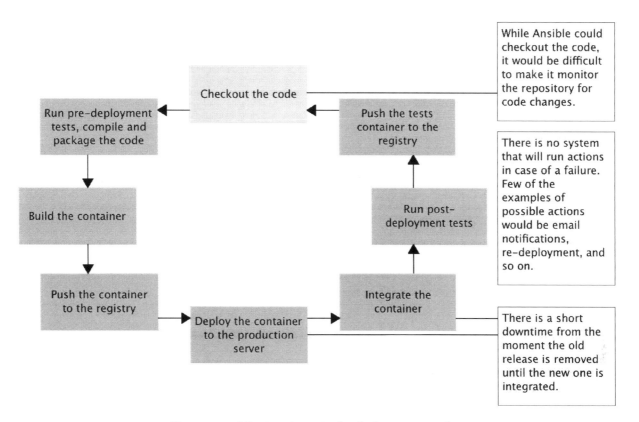

Figure 11-4: Missing pieces in the deployment pipeline

To get a better grasp on the process, we'll go through each manual step we performed earlier and see how it can be done with Ansible.

We'll start by creating up the nodes and cloning the code.

```
1  vagrant up cd prod
2
3  vagrant ssh cd
4
5  git clone https://github.com/vfarcic/books-ms.git
```

The Playbook and the Role

If you already tried automated deployment, the chances are that the scripts you created were mostly related to the deployment itself. With Ansible (and CM tools in general), we have the option to do the process from scratch every time. Not only that we'll automate the deployment, but we'll set up the whole server. We cannot be confident in which state the server is. For example, maybe it has nginx or maybe it doesn't. Maybe it did have the nginx container up and running but, for some reason, its process stopped. Even if the process is running, maybe some crucial configuration changed. The same logic can be applied to anything, directly or indirectly, related to the service we want to deploy.

The approach we'll take is to have a playbook that will make sure that everything is set correctly. Ansible is intelligent enough to check the status of all those dependencies and applies changes only if something is wrong.

Let us take a look at the service.yml[133] playbook.

```
 1  - hosts: prod
 2    remote_user: vagrant
 3    serial: 1
 4    sudo: yes
 5    roles:
 6      - common
 7      - docker
 8      - docker-compose
 9      - consul
10      - registrator
11      - consul-template
12      - nginx
13      - service
```

The *service* role will contain tasks directly related to the deployment and all the others before them are dependencies our service needs to work correctly. Since we already went through all but the last role from this playbook, stands to reason that we should jump directly to the definition of the list of tasks in the *service* role defined in the roles/service/tasks/main.yml[134] file.

```
 1  - include: pre-deployment.yml
 2
 3  - include: deployment.yml
 4
 5  - include: post-deployment.yml
```

Since this role will be a bit bigger than those we used before, we made the decision to split them into logical groups (*pre-deployment*, *deployment* and *post-deployment*) and include them into the *main.yml* file. That way we won't be dealing with too many tasks at a time, and we'll increase the readability of the role.

Pre-Deployment Tasks

The first thing we should do is build the tests container. We already used the following command (please don't run it).

---

[133]https://github.com/vfarcic/ms-lifecycle/blob/master/ansible/service.yml
[134]https://github.com/vfarcic/ms-lifecycle/blob/master/ansible/roles/service/tasks/main.yml

```
1  docker pull \
2      -t 10.100.198.200:5000/books-ms-tests
3
4  docker build \
5      -t 10.100.198.200:5000/books-ms-tests \
6      -f Dockerfile.test \
7      .
```

Replicating the same command in Ansible is very easy with the Shell module[135].

```
1  - name: Tests container is pulled
2    shell: docker pull \
3      {{ registry_url }}{{ service_name }}-tests
4    delegate_to: 127.0.0.1
5    ignore_errors: yes
6    tags: [service, tests]
7
8  - name: Tests container is built
9    shell: docker build \
10     -t {{ registry_url }}{{ service_name }}-tests \
11     -f Dockerfile.test \
12     .
13   args:
14     chdir: "{{ repo_dir }}"
15   delegate_to: 127.0.0.1
16   tags: [service, tests]
```

We changed the command itself so that parts that might be prone to change are used as variables. The first one is the *registry_url* that should contain the IP and the port of the Docker registry. The default value is specified in the group_vars/all[136] file. The second one is more interesting. We are not creating this role to work with the service *books-ms* but as something that can be used with (almost) any service since all of them can follow the same pattern. We can do this sorts of things without sacrificing the freedom since the key instructions are stored in a few files located in the repository of each service. The most important ones are the *Dockerfile.test* and the *Dockerfile* that define testing and service containers, Docker Compose configurations that define how should containers be run and, finally, the proxy configuration and template. All those files are separated from the process we're creating, and people in charge of the project have the full freedom to tailor them to their needs. That showcases a very important aspect I'm trying to promote. It is crucial not only to have the right process in place but also to have the scripts, configurations and the code properly located. Everything that is common to multiple projects should be centralized (as is the case with Ansible

---

[135]http://docs.ansible.com/ansible/shell_module.html

[136]https://github.com/vfarcic/ms-lifecycle/blob/master/ansible/group_vars/all

playbooks located in the vfarcic/ms-lifecycle[137] repository). On the other hand, things that might be specific to a project should be stored in the repository that project resides in. Storing everything in one centralized place would introduce quite a lot of waiting time since a project team would need to request a change from the delivery team. The other extreme is just as wrong. If everything is stored in the project repositories, there would be quite a lot of duplication. Each project would need to come up with scripts to set up servers, deploy a service, and so on.

Next we specified a single argument *chdir*. It will make sure that the command is run from the directory that, in this case, contains the *Dockerfile.test* file. The *chdir* value is the variable *repo_dir* that, unlike *registry_url* does not have the default value. We'll specify it at runtime when we run the playbook. Then comes the *delegate_to* instruction. Since we are committed to disrupting the destination server as little as possible, tasks like this one will be run on the localhost (127.0.0.1). Finally, we set few tags that can be used to filter which tasks will or will not be run.

The reason behind pulling the tests container before building it is to save the time. The execution of the playbook might change from one server to another and, if such a thing happens, without first pulling the container from the Registry, Docker would build all the layers even though most of them are likely to be the same as before. Take a note that we introduced the *ignore_errors* instruction. Without it, the playbook would fail if this is the first build of the container and there is nothing to be pulled.

Please keep in mind that the *shell* module should be avoided in most cases. The idea behind Ansible is to specify the desired behavior and not the action that should be performed. Once that "desire" is run, Ansible will try to "do the right thing". If, for example, we specify that some package should be installed, Ansible will check whether such a package already exists and do the installation only if it doesn't. The shell module that we used, in this case, will always run, no matter the state of the system. In this particular situation, that is OK, because Docker itself will make sure that only changed layers are built. It won't build the whole container every time. Please keep this in mind when designing your roles.

The rest of the commands we used in the pre-deployment phase are as follows (please don't run them).

```
1  docker-compose -f docker-compose-dev.yml \
2      run --rm tests
3
4  docker pull 10.100.198.200:5000/books-ms
5
6  docker build -t 10.100.198.200:5000/books-ms .
7
8  docker push 10.100.198.200:5000/books-ms
```

When translated to the Ansible format, the result is as follows.

---

[137]https://github.com/vfarcic/ms-lifecycle

```
 1  - name: Pre-deployment tests are run
 2    shell: docker-compose \
 3      -f docker-compose-dev.yml \
 4      run --rm tests
 5    args:
 6      chdir: "{{ repo_dir }}"
 7    delegate_to: 127.0.0.1
 8    tags: [service, tests]
 9
10  - name: Container is built
11    shell: docker build \
12      -t {{ registry_url }}{{ service_name }} \
13      .
14    args:
15      chdir: "{{ repo_dir }}"
16    delegate_to: 127.0.0.1
17    tags: [service]
18
19  - name: Container is pushed
20    shell: docker push \
21      {{ registry_url }}{{ service_name }}
22    delegate_to: 127.0.0.1
23    tags: [service]
```

There's not much to be said about those tasks. They all use the shell module and are all running on localhost. We run the tests container that, besides the obvious function of checking the quality of the code, compiles the service. The result of that compilation is used to build the service container that is later on pushed to the Docker registry.

The final result can be seen in the roles/service/tasks/pre-deployment.yml[138] file and we can proceed with the deployment tasks.

Deployment Tasks

The next set of commands we did when manually running the deployment pipeline had the goal of creating directories and files required for the process. They were as follows (please don't run them).

---

[138]https://github.com/vfarcic/ms-lifecycle/blob/master/ansible/roles/service/tasks/pre-deployment.yml

```
1  mkdir -p /data/books-ms
2
3  cd /data/books-ms
4
5  wget https://raw.githubusercontent.com/vfarcic\
6  /books-ms/master/docker-compose.yml
7
8  wget https://raw.githubusercontent.com/vfarcic\
9  /books-ms/master/nginx-includes.conf \
10      -O /data/nginx/includes/books-ms.conf
11
12 wget https://raw.githubusercontent.com/vfarcic\
13 /books-ms/master/nginx-upstreams.ctmpl \
14      -O /data/nginx/upstreams/books-ms.ctmpl
```

We created the service directory and downloaded the *docker-compose.yml, nginx-includes.conf* and *nginx-upstreams.ctmpl* files from the code repository. The latter two we'll download later when the time comes to change the proxy, but we can group them all together as a single Ansible task. With Ansible, we'll do it a bit differently. Since we already checked out the code, there is no reason to download those files. We can just copy them to the destination server. Ansible tasks that replicate this same set of commands are as follows.

```
1  - name: Directory is created
2    file:
3      path: /data/{{ service_name }}
4      recurse: yes
5      state: directory
6    tags: [service]
7
8  - name: Files are copied
9    copy:
10     src: "{{ item.src }}"
11     dest: "{{ item.dest }}"
12   with_items: files
13   tags: [service]
```

We created two tasks. The first one uses the Ansible module *file* to create the service directory. Since this role is supposed to be generic and apply to (almost) any service, the name of the service is a variable that we'll set at runtime when we run the playbook. The second task uses the *copy* module to copy all the files that we'll need on the destination server. We're using the *with_items* instruction that will repeat this task for each entry into the *files_ variable. The variable is defined in the roles/service/defaults/main.yml[139] file and is as follows.

---

[139]https://github.com/vfarcic/ms-lifecycle/blob/master/ansible/roles/service/defaults/main.yml

```
 1  files: [
 2    {
 3      src: "{{ repo_dir }}/docker-compose.yml",
 4      dest: "/data/{{ service_name }}/docker-compose.yml"
 5    }, {
 6      src: "{{ repo_dir }}/nginx-includes.conf",
 7      dest: "/data/nginx/includes/{{ service_name }}.conf"
 8    }, {
 9      src: "{{ repo_dir }}/nginx-upstreams.ctmpl",
10      dest: "/data/nginx/upstreams/{{ service_name }}.ctmpl"
11    }
12  ]
```

The source of all of those files utilizes the *repo_dir* variable that we already used in the pre-deployment tasks. Similarly, file destinations are using the *service_name* variable.

Once we're sure that all the files we'll need are on the destination server, we can proceed with the actual deployment that consists of two steps (please don't run them).

```
 1  docker-compose pull app
 2
 3  docker-compose up -d app
 4
 5  consul-template \
 6      -consul localhost:8500 \
 7      -template "/data/nginx/upstreams/books-ms.ctmpl:\
 8  /data/nginx/upstreams/books-ms.conf:\
 9  docker kill -s HUP nginx" \
10      -once
```

First we pulled the latest image from the Docker registry and then we brought it up. When `docker-compose up` is run, it checks whether the container image or its configuration changed when compared with the running container. If it is indeed different, Docker Compose will stop the running containers and run the new ones while preserving mounted volumes. We already discussed that, during some time (between the stopping the current version and running the new one), our service will be unavailable. We'll deal with this problem later on. For now, a (very short) downtime will be something we'll have to live with. Finally, we run *consul-template* that updates configurations and reloads nginx.

As you probably guessed, we'll run those two commands through the Ansible *shell* module.

```
1  - name: Containers are pulled
2    shell: docker-compose pull app
3    args:
4      chdir: /data/{{ service_name }}
5    tags: [service]
6
7  - name: Containers are running
8    shell: docker-compose up -d app
9    args:
10     chdir: /data/{{ service_name }}
11   tags: [service]
12
13 - name: Proxy is configured
14   shell: consul-template \
15     -consul localhost:8500 \
16     -template "{{ ct_src }}:{{ ct_dest }}:{{ ct_cmd }}" \
17     -once
18   tags: [service]
```

We're not doing anything new. It's the same pattern as the shell tasks we defined as pre-deployment tasks. The only thing worth noting is that we used variables as the -template value. The only reason behind this is that the length of the book has a maximum limit of characters per line, and all the parameters would not fit. Those variables are defined in the roles/service/defaults/main.yml[140] file and are as follows.

```
1  ct_src: /data/nginx/upstreams/{{ service_name }}.ctmpl
2  ct_dest: /data/nginx/upstreams/{{ service_name }}.conf
3  ct_cmd: docker kill -s HUP nginx
```

The final result can be seen in the roles/service/tasks/deployment.yml[141] file. Please note that, unlike the pre-deployment tasks, all those in this group are indeed going to run on the destination server. That can be seen by the lack of the `delegate_to: 127.0.0.1` instruction.

We're done with deployment and can turn our attention to the last group of tasks.

Post-Deployment Tasks

All that is left is to run integration tests and push the tests container to the registry. As a reminder, the commands are as follows (please don't run them).

---

[140]https://github.com/vfarcic/ms-lifecycle/blob/master/ansible/roles/service/defaults/main.yml

[141]https://github.com/vfarcic/ms-lifecycle/blob/master/ansible/roles/service/tasks/deployment.yml

```
1  docker-compose \
2      -f docker-compose-dev.yml \
3      run --rm \
4      -e DOMAIN=http://10.100.198.201 \
5      integ
6
7  docker push 10.100.198.200:5000/books-ms-tests
```

Ansible equivalent of those commands is as follows.

```
1  - name: Post-deployment tests are run
2    shell: docker-compose \
3      -f docker-compose-dev.yml \
4      run --rm \
5      -e DOMAIN={{ proxy_url }} \
6      integ
7    args:
8      chdir: "{{ repo_dir }}"
9    delegate_to: 127.0.0.1
10   tags: [service, tests]
11
12 - name: Tests container is pushed
13   shell: docker push \
14     {{ registry_url }}{{ service_name }}-tests
15   delegate_to: 127.0.0.1
16   tags: [service, tests]
```

There's nothing new here so we won't go into details. The complete version of post-deployment tasks can be found in the roles/service/tasks/post-deployment.yml[142] file.

Running the Automated Deployment Pipeline

Let us see the *service* playbook in action.

---

[142]https://github.com/vfarcic/ms-lifecycle/blob/master/ansible/roles/service/tasks/post-deployment.yml

```
1   cd ~/books-ms
2
3   ansible-playbook /vagrant/ansible/service.yml \
4       -i /vagrant/ansible/hosts/prod \
5       --extra-vars "repo_dir=$PWD service_name=books-ms"
```

We run the playbook service.yml[143] with the inventory pointing to the hosts/prod[144] file and few extra variables. The first one is the *repo_dir* with the value of the current directory ($PWD). The second represents the name of the service we want to deploy (*books-ms*). At the moment, we have only this service. If there would be more, they could all be deployed with this same playbook by changing the value of this variable.

We managed to have not only the fully automated deployment but also provisioning of the destination server. The first of the playbook was done against a "virgin" Ubuntu server, so Ansible made sure that everything needed for the deployment is properly configured. The result is not perfect, but it is a good start.

Feel free to repeat the execution of the playbook and observe the differences when compared to the first run. You'll notice that most of the Ansible tasks will be in the status *ok* since there was nothing to be done and that the playbook runs much faster.

What could be the things that we might be missing? There are quite a few. However, before we proceed and try to fix them, we should set up a proper *Continuous Deployment* platform and see whether it can help with the current process. Until then, let us destroy the VMs and let your computer take a break.

```
1   exit
2
3   vagrant destroy -f
```

---

[143]https://github.com/vfarcic/ms-lifecycle/blob/master/ansible/service.yml
[144]https://github.com/vfarcic/ms-lifecycle/blob/master/ansible/hosts/prod

Continuous Integration (CI), Delivery and Deployment (CD) Tools

We have most of the process already automated with Ansible. Until now, we used playbooks to automate two types of tasks; server provisioning and configuration and the deployment process. While Ansible shines as a tool intended to provision and configure our servers, deployment (at least in our context) is not its strongest side. We used it mostly as a substitute for bash scripts. Most of the deployment tasks we have right now are using the Ansible *shell* module. We could have used shell scripts instead, and the result would be, more or less, the same. Ansible is designed to use *promises* as a way to ensure that the system is in the correct state. It does not work very well with deployments when conditionals, try/catch statements and other types of logic are needed. The main reason for using Ansible to deploy containers was avoidance to split the process into multiple commands (provision with ansible, run a script, provision more, run more scripts, and so on). The second, and more important, reason was that we did not cover CI/CD tools, so we used what we had. That will change very soon.

What are we missing in our deployment pipeline? We are using Ansible to configure and provision servers, and that works great. We are still looking for a better way to deploy software (calling Ansible *shell* module is a bit cumbersome). We are also missing a way to monitor the repository so that new deployments can be executed whenever there is a change in the code. When part of the process fails, we do not have a mechanism to send notifications. We are also missing visual representation of all our builds and deployments. The list can go on and on. What all those missing features have in common is that they can be easily solved with CI/CD tools. Therefore, we should start looking at the CI/CD platform we could use and adopt one of them.

CI/CD Tools Compared

One way to divide CI/CD tools is to put them into cloud services and self-hosted solutions groups. There are a plethora of cloud services both for free and paid. Most of them are great for the more simplified process than the one we're trying to accomplish. If you have a small application consisting out of few services and residing on no more than a few servers, cloud solutions are excellent. I used many of them for my "pet" projects. Travis[145], Shippable[146], CircleCI[147] and Drone.io[148] are only a few of them. They will run your scripts, build your applications and services and pack them into containers. Most of them are neither designed nor capable of handling a cluster of servers especially

---

[145]https://travis-ci.org/

[146]https://app.shippable.com/

[147]https://circleci.com/

[148]https://drone.io/

when it is private or self-hosted. That is not to say that there are no cloud solutions that would fit this scenario. There are, but they tend to be too expensive on a large scale. With that in mind, we should look for self-hosted solutions.

There's a hell of a lot of self-hosted CI/CD tools, ranging from free offerings all the way to very expensive ones. Some of the commonly used self-hosted CI/CD tools like Jenkins[149], Bamboo[150], GoCD[151], Team City[152] and Electric Cloud[153] are only a few among many others. All of them have their strengths and weaknesses. However, Jenkins sticks out from the crowd thanks to its community. No other tool has such a big number of people contributing on a daily basis. It has an excellent support and, through its plugins, it can be extended to do almost anything we might need. You will hardly find yourself in a need of something that is not already covered with one or more plugins. Even if you find a use case that is not covered, writing your own plugin (and hopefully making it public for others to use) is a very easy thing to do. Community and plugins are its greatest strength that makes it more widely adopted than any other tool.

The chances are that you already used Jenkins, or, at least, heard of it. One of the main reasons companies are choosing some other tool (especially Bamboo and Team City) are their enterprise offerings. When an organization becomes big, it needs support and reliability that comes with it. It needs those extra features and know-how that enterprise offerings provide. Cloud Bees[154] is one such company formed recently. They offer Jenkins Enterprise version and have an excellent support capable of handling almost any scenario related to continuous integration, delivery or deployment. They have the community version of Jenkins that can be obtained for free but also offer paid enterprise features and support. That is another reason one should choose Jenkins. No other tool (at least among those previously mentioned) has fully free tool and, at the same time, offers paid support and additional features. Team City can be downloaded for free but has a limited number of agents. GoCD is free but it doesn't provide any support. Bamboo is similar to Team City regarding limitations imposed on the free version. By choosing Jenkins, we are choosing battle tested and most widely used tool supported by a vast community that has, if such a need arises, paid support and features through CloudBees.

 While writing this book, I chose to join the CloudBees team (the company behind Enterprise Jenkins). The decision to promote Jenkins throughout this book was not based on my employment in CloudBees. It's the other way around. I chose to join them because I believe that Jenkins is the best CI/CD tool in the market.

---

[149]https://jenkins-ci.org/

[150]https://www.atlassian.com/software/bamboo/

[151]http://www.go.cd/

[152]https://www.jetbrains.com/teamcity/

[153]http://electric-cloud.com/

[154]https://www.cloudbees.com/

The Short History of CI/CD Tools

Jenkins[155] (forked from Hudson[156] after a dispute with Oracle) has been around for a long time and established itself as the leading platform for the creation of *continuous integration (CI) and continuous delivery/deployment (CD)* pipelines. The idea behind it is that we should create jobs that perform operations like building, testing, deploying, and so on. Those jobs should be chained together to create a CI/CD pipeline. The success was so big that other products followed its lead and we got Bamboo[157], Team City[158], and others. They all used a similar logic of having jobs and chaining them together. Operations, maintenance, monitoring, and the creation of jobs is mostly done through their UIs. However, none of the other products managed to suppress Jenkins due to its strong community support. There are over one thousand plugins, and one would have a hard time imagining a task that is not supported by, at least, one of them. The support, flexibility, and extensibility featured by Jenkins allowed it to maintain its reign as the most popular and widely used CI/CD tool throughout all this time. The approach based on heavy usage of UIs can be considered the first generation of CI/CD tools (even though there were others before).

With time, new products come into being and, with them, new approaches were born. Travis[159], CircleCI[160], and the like, moved the process to the cloud and based themselves on auto-discovery and, mostly YML, configurations that reside in the same repository as the code that should be moved through the pipeline. The idea was good and provided quite a refreshment. Instead of defining your jobs in a centralized location, those tools would inspect your code and act depending on the type of the project. If, for example, they find *build.gradle* file, they would assume that your project should be tested and built using Gradle[161]. As the result, they would run `gradle check` to test your code and, if tests passed, follow it by `gradle assemble` to produce the artifacts. We can consider those products to be the second generation of CI/CD tools.

The first and the second generation of tools suffer from different problems. Jenkins and the like feature power and flexibility that allow us to create custom tailored pipelines that can handle almost any level of complexity. This power comes with a price. When you have tens of jobs, their maintenance is quite easy. However, when that number increases to hundreds, managing them can become quite tedious and time demanding.

Let's say that an average pipeline has five jobs (building, pre-deployment testing, deployment to a staging environment, post-deployment testing, and deployment to production). In reality, there are often more than five jobs but let's keep it an optimistic estimate. If we multiply those jobs with, let's say, twenty pipelines belonging to twenty different projects, the total number reaches one hundred. Now, imagine that we need to change all those jobs from, let's say, Maven to Gradle. We can choose to start modifying them through the Jenkins UI or be brave and apply changes directly in Jenkins

---

[155]https://jenkins-ci.org/

[156]http://hudson-ci.org/

[157]https://www.atlassian.com/software/bamboo/

[158]https://www.jetbrains.com/teamcity/

[159]https://travis-ci.org/

[160]https://circleci.com/

[161]http://gradle.org/

XML files that represent those jobs. Either way, this, seemingly simple, change would require quite some dedication. Moreover, due to its nature, everything is centralized in one location making it hard for teams to manage jobs belonging to their projects. Besides, project specific configurations and code belong to the same repository where the rest of application code resides and not in some central location. And Jenkins is not alone with this problem. Most of the other self-hosted tools have it as well. It comes from the era when heavy centralization and horizontal division of tasks was thought to be a good idea. At approximately the same time, we felt that UIs should solve most of the problems. Today, we know that many of the types of tasks are easier to define and maintain as code, than through some UI.

I remember the days when Dreamweaver was big. That was around the end of the nineties and the beginning of year two thousand (bear in mind that at that time Dreamweaver was quite different than today). It looked like a dream come true (hence the name?). I could create a whole web page with my mouse. Drag and drop a widget, select few options, write a label, repeat. We could create things very fast. What was not so obvious at that time was that the result was a loan that would need to be paid with interests. The code Dreamweaver created for us was anything but maintainable. As a matter a fact, sometimes it was easier to start over than modify pages created with it. That was especially true when we had to do something not included in one of its widgets. It was a nightmare. Today, almost no one writes HTML and JavaScript by using drag & drop tools. We write the code ourselves instead of relying on other tools to write it for us. There are plenty of other examples. For example, Oracle ESB, at least in its infancy, was similarly wrong. Drag & drop was not a thing to rely on (but good for sales). That does not mean that GUIs are not used any more. They are, but for very specific purposes. A web designer might rely on drag & drop before passing the result to a coder.

What I'm trying to say is that different approaches belong to different contexts and types of tasks. Jenkins and similar tools benefit greatly from their UIs for monitoring and visual representations of statuses. The part it fails with is the creation and maintenance of jobs. That type of tasks would be much better done through code. With Jenkins, we had the power but needed to pay the price for it in the form of maintenance effort.

The "second generation" of CI/CD tools (Travis, CircleCI, and the like) reduced that maintenance problem to an almost negligible effort. In many cases, there is nothing to be done since they will discover the type of the project and "do the right thing". In some other cases, we have to write a *travis.yml*, a *circle.yml*, or a similar file, to give the tool additional instructions. Even in such a case, that file tends to have only a few lines of specifications and resides together with the code thus making it easy for the project team to manage it. However, these tools do not replace "the first generation" since they tend to work well only on small projects with a very simple pipeline. The "real" continuous delivery/deployment pipeline is much more complex than what those tools are capable of. In other words, we gained low maintenance but lost the power and, in many cases, flexibility.

Today, old-timers like Jenkins, Bamboo, and Team City, continue dominating the market and are recommended tools to use for anything but small projects. At the same time, cloud tools like Travis and CircleCI dominate smaller settings. The team maintaining Jenkins codebase recognized the need to introduce a few significant improvements that will bring it to the next level by combining the best of both generations, and some more. I'll call that change the "third generation" of CI/CD tools. They introduced Jenkins Workflow[162] and *Jenkinsfile*. Together, they bring some very useful and powerful features. With Jenkins Workflow, we can write a whole pipeline using Groovy-based DSL. The process can be written as a single script that utilizes most of the existing Jenkins features. The result is an enormous reduction in code (Workflow scripts are much smaller than traditional Jenkins job definitions in XML) and reduction in jobs (one Workflow job can substitute many traditional Jenkins jobs). That results in much easier management and maintenance. On the other hand, newly introduced *Jenkinsfile* allows us to define the Workflow script inside the repository together with the code. That means that developers in charge of the project can be in control of the CI/CD pipeline as well. That way, responsibilities are much better divided. Overall Jenkins management is centralized while individual CI/CD pipelines are placed where they belong (together with the code that should be moved through it). Moreover, if we combine all that with the *Multibranch Workflow* job type, we can even fine tune the pipeline depending on the branch. For example, we might have the full process defined in the Jenkinsfile residing in the *master* branch and shorter flows in each feature branch. What is put into each Jenkinsfile is up to those maintaining each repository/branch. With the *Multibranch Workflow* job, Jenkins will create jobs whenever a new branch is created and run whatever is defined in the file. Similarly, it will remove jobs when branches are removed. Finally, *Docker Workflow* has been introduced as well, making Docker the first class citizen in Jenkins.

 Jenkins has a long history that led it to the *Pipeline* plugin. There was the *Build Pipeline* plugin that provided visualizations for connected jobs, then came the *Build Flow* plugin that introduced the concept of Groovy DSL as a way to define Jenkins jobs. The latter hit many obstacles that led its authors to start over and create the *Workflow* plugin, only to rename it, later on, into the *Pipeline* plugin.

All those improvements brought Jenkins to a whole new level confirming its supremacy among CI/CD platforms.

If even more is needed, there is the CloudBees Jenkins Platform - Enterprise Edition[163] that provides fantastic features, especially when we need to run Jenkins at scale.

 Workflow authors decided to rename the plugin into *Pipeline*. However, at this moment, not all the source code has been renamed and there are references to both *pipeline* and *workflow*. For consistency, and to avoid possible failures, I chose to stick with the old name and use the word *Workflow* throughout the book. The change is only semantic and does not introduce any functional changes.

---

[162]https://wiki.jenkins-ci.org/display/JENKINS/Workflow+Plugin

[163]https://www.cloudbees.com/products/cloudbees-jenkins-platform/enterprise-edition

Jenkins

Jenkins shines with its plugins. There are so many of them that it would be hard to find something we'd like to accomplish that is not already covered with at least one plugin. Want to connect to a code repository? There is a plugin. Want to send notifications to Slack? There is a plugin. Want to parse logs using your formulas? There is a plugin.

Being able to choose from so many plugins is a double edged sword. People tend to abuse it and install plugins for many more things than its needed. One example would be the Ansible plugin.

We can select it as a build step and fill in the fields like *Playbook path*, *Inventory*, *Tags to skip*, *Additional parameters* and so on. The screen could look like the one presented in the figure 12-01.

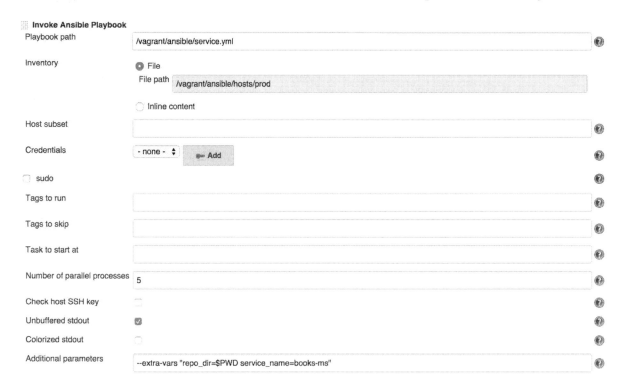

Figure 12-01: Ansible plugin used inside a Jenkins job

Alternative to the Ansible plugin would be just to use the *Execute Shell* build step (part of the Jenkins core) and put the command we'd like to run. We wrote the automation ourselves and are familiar with commands that should be run. By using those same commands there are fewer fields to be filled or ignored, we know what will be run and can use those same commands as a reference if the same process should be repeated outside of Jenkins.

Figure 12-02: Running Ansible playbook as a shell command

In many cases, automation should be something done outside Jenkins (or any other CI/CD tool). From there on, all we have to do is tell Jenkins which script to run. That script can be in the repository together with the code of the service we are deploying (for example *deploy.sh*) or, as in our case, be generalized through few naming conventions and used for all services. No matter the way automation scripts are organized, in most cases the best and the easiest way to use them inside Jenkins is to just run the command associated with those scripts. That held true until recently. Now, with the addition of Jenkinsfile, we can follow the same logic of creating project specific scripts and keeping them in the project repository. The additional benefit it brings is that we can utilize Jenkins specific features inside the Workflow script residing in the Jenkinsfile. If you need to run something on a particular node, there is a module for it. If you need to use authentication stored in Jenkins, there is a module for it. The list goes on and on, but the gist is that with Jenkinsfile and the Workflow we can continue relying on scripts residing inside the code repository and, at the same time, utilize advanced Jenkins features.

The time has come to get our hands dirty and set up Jenkins.

Setting Up Jenkins

As always, we'll start by creating virtual machines that we'll use for our exploration of Jenkins. We'll create the *cd* node that will host our Jenkins server as well as Ansible playbooks that we'll run through it.

```
1  vagrant up cd prod
```

Once both servers are up and running, we can proceed and provision the *prod* node in the same way as we did before.

```
1  vagrant ssh cd
2
3  ansible-playbook /vagrant/ansible/prod2.yml \
4      -i /vagrant/ansible/hosts/prod
```

Now we are ready to bring up Jenkins. Setting up the basic installation is very easy with Docker. All we have to do is run a container with a few arguments.

```
1  sudo mkdir -p /data/jenkins
2
3  sudo chmod 0777 /data/jenkins
4
5  docker run -d --name jenkins \
6      -p 8080:8080 \
7      -v /data/jenkins:/var/jenkins_home \
8      -v /vagrant/.vagrant/machines:/machines \
9      jenkins
```

Docker detected that there is no local copy of the Jenkins container and started pulling it from the Docker Hub. Once pulling is done, we'll have a running instance that exposes the port 8080 and shares a few volumes. The */var/jenkins_home* directory contains all Jenkins configuration. It is handy to have it shared for the sake of configuration management that we'll explore soon. We gave full permissions (0777) to that directory in the host since the container processes run as the *jenkins* user that does not exist in our system. It's not a good solution security-wise, but it should do for now. The second shared directory is */machines* that is mapped to the host's directory */vagrant/.vagrant/machines*. That's the location where Vagrant keeps all SSH keys that we'll need to set up Jenkins nodes on which the actual jobs will be run. Please note that, if you'd run this on production servers, you should generate keys with ssh-copy-id and share them instead of those generated by Vagrant.

Once the Jenkins container is going, we can open http://10.100.198.200:8080[164] and explore the GUI.

---

[164]http://10.100.198.200:8080

Figure 12-03: Jenkins home screen after the standard installation

If this is the first time you are in front of Jenkins[165], please take a break from this book and spend some time getting familiar with it. Its GUI is very intuitive, and there are a lot of online sources that will help you get a basic understanding of how it works. We are about to dive into automation of Jenkins administration. Even though we won't use the GUI for that, understanding how it works visually will help you understand better the tasks we are about to perform. Take your time with it and, once you feel comfortable, return here for more.

Most people I know use Jenkins exclusively through its GUI. Some might use its API to run jobs or automate some basic operations. And that's fine, for a while. You start by installing a few plugins, create a few jobs and feel great for accomplishing a lot very quickly. With time, the number of jobs increases and with them the maintenance effort. It is not uncommon to have tens, hundreds or even thousands of jobs defined and running periodically or being triggered by some events (for example code commit). Administrating all those jobs through the GUI is hard and time demanding. Imagine, for instance, that you want to add Slack[166] notifications to all jobs. Modifying jobs one by one is not a good option when there's a significant number of them.

There are different ways we can tackle the problem of Jenkins automation that is, primarily, focused on creation and maintenance of its jobs. One approach would be to use some of the Jenkins plugins that could help us out. A few of those are Job DSL[167] and Job Generator[168] plugins. We'll take a different approach. All Jenkins settings are stored as XML files located in the */var/jenkins_home*

---

[165]https://jenkins-ci.org/

[166]https://slack.com/

[167]https://wiki.jenkins-ci.org/display/JENKINS/Job+DSL+Plugin

[168]https://wiki.jenkins-ci.org/display/JENKINS/Job+Generator+Plugin

directory (we exposed it as a Docker volume). We can simply add new files or modify existing ones when we need to change some Jenkins behavior. Since we are already familiar with Ansible, we can continue using it as a tool to not only install but also maintain Jenkins. In that spirit, we'll remove the current Jenkins installation and start over with Ansible.

```
1  docker rm -f jenkins
2
3  sudo rm -rf /data/jenkins
```

We removed the Jenkins container and deleted the directory we exposed as a volume. Now we can install it and configure it through Ansible.

Setting Up Jenkins with Ansible

Setting up Jenkins with Ansible is easy even though the role we'll use has few complications we haven't encountered previously. Since it will take a few minutes for the playbook to finish executing, let's run it first and discuss its definition while waiting for it to finish.

```
1  ansible-playbook /vagrant/ansible/jenkins-node.yml \
2      -i /vagrant/ansible/hosts/prod
3
4  ansible-playbook /vagrant/ansible/jenkins.yml \
5      -c local
```

First we set up Jenkins nodes that we'll use later on. It should not take long to execute the first playbook since all it has to do is make sure that JDK is installed (required by Jenkins, to be able to connect to a node) and that the single directory */data/jenkins_slaves*. Jenkins will use that directory to store files when executing processes on those nodes. The *jenkins* role is in the *jenkins.yml* playbook is a bit longer and will be worthwhile spending some time with. Let's explore it in more details. The jenkins.yml[169] playbook is as follows.

```
1  - hosts: localhost
2    remote_user: vagrant
3    serial: 1
4    sudo: yes
5    roles:
6      - consul-template
7      - jenkins
```

---

[169]https://github.com/vfarcic/ms-lifecycle/blob/master/ansible/jenkins.yml

It installs Consul Template that we're already familiar with so we'll move straight to the roles/-jenkins[170] role. The tasks are defined in the roles/jenkins/tasks/main.yml[171] file and we'll go through them one by one.

The first task creates directories that we'll need. As before, variables are defined in the roles/jenkins/defaults/main.yml[172]

```
1  - name: Directories are created
2    file:
3      path: "{{ item.dir }}"
4      mode: 0777
5      recurse: yes
6      state: directory
7    with_items: configs
8    tags: [jenkins]
```

With directories created, we can run the *jenkins* container. Even though it takes no time for the container to start running, Jenkins itself requires a bit of patience until it is fully operational. Later on, we'll be issuing some commands to Jenkins API, so we'll have to pause the playbook, for, let's say, half a minute, to be sure that Jenkins is operational. At the same time, this gives us the opportunity to see *pause* module in action (even though it should be rarely used). Please notice that we are registering the variable *container_result* and, later on, pausing so that Jenkins application inside the container is fully operational before proceeding with the rest of tasks. This pause is performed if the state of the Jenkins container changed.

```
1  - name: Container is running
2    docker:
3      name: jenkins
4      image: jenkins
5      ports: 8080:8080
6      volumes:
7        - /data/jenkins:/var/jenkins_home
8        - /vagrant/.vagrant/machines:/machines
9    register: container_result
10   tags: [jenkins]
11
12 - pause: seconds=30
13   when: container_result|changed
14   tags: [jenkins]
```

Next we should copy a few configuration files. We'll start with roles/jenkins/files/credentials.xml[173],

---

[170]https://github.com/vfarcic/ms-lifecycle/tree/master/ansible/roles/jenkins

[171]https://github.com/vfarcic/ms-lifecycle/blob/master/ansible/roles/jenkins/tasks/main.yml

[172]https://github.com/vfarcic/ms-lifecycle/blob/master/ansible/roles/jenkins/defaults/main.yml

[173]https://github.com/vfarcic/ms-lifecycle/blob/master/ansible/roles/jenkins/files/credentials.xml

followed by few nodes (roles/jenkins/files/cd_config.xml[174], roles/jenkins/files/prod_config.xml[175], and so on) and a several other less important configurations. Feel free to see contents of those files. At the moment, it is only important to understand that we need those configurations.

```
1  - name: Configurations are present
2    copy:
3      src: "{{ item.src }}"
4      dest: "{{ item.dir }}/{{ item.file }}"
5      mode: 0777
6    with_items: configs
7    register: configs_result
8    tags: [jenkins]
```

Next, we should make sure that several plugins are installed. Since our code is in GitHub, we'll need the *Git Plugin*. Another useful plugin that we'll use is the *Log Parser*. Since Ansible logs are quite big, we'll use this plugin to break them into more manageable pieces. Few other plugins will be installed as well, and we'll discuss each of them when the time comes to use them.

Most people tend just to download plugins they need. Even the official Jenkins container that we are using has a way to specify which plugins to download. However, that approach is very dangerous since we'd need to define not only plugins we need but also their dependencies, dependencies of those dependencies and so on. It would be easy to forget one of them or specify a wrong dependency. If such a thing happens, at best, the plugin we wanted to use would not work. In some cases, even the whole Jenkins server could stop functioning. We'll take a different approach. Plugins can be installed by sending an HTTP request to */pluginManager/installNecessaryPlugins* with XML in the body. Jenkins, upon receiving the request will download both the plugin we specify and its dependencies. Since we don't want to send the request if the plugin is already installed, we'll use the *creates* instruction specifying the path to the plugin. If the plugin exists, the task will not be run.

Most plugins require a restart of the application, so we'll restart the container if any of the plugins was added. Since the request to install a plugin is asynchronous, first we'll have to wait until plugin directory is created (Jenkins unpacks plugins into directories with the same name). Once it is confirmed that all plugins are installed, we'll restart Jenkins and wait (again) for some time before it is fully operational. In other words, we send requests to Jenkins to install plugins and, if they are not already installed, wait until Jenkins is finished with installations, restart the container so that new plugins are used and wait for a while until the restart is finished.

---

[174]https://github.com/vfarcic/ms-lifecycle/blob/master/ansible/roles/jenkins/files/cd_config.xml

[175]https://github.com/vfarcic/ms-lifecycle/blob/master/ansible/roles/jenkins/files/prod_config.xml

```
1   - name: Plugins are installed
2     shell: "curl -X POST \
3       -d '<jenkins><install plugin=\"{{ item }}@latest\" /></jenkins>' \
4       --header 'Content-Type: text/xml' \
5       http://{{ ip }}:8080/pluginManager/installNecessaryPlugins"
6     args:
7       creates: /data/jenkins/plugins/{{ item }}
8     with_items: plugins
9     register: plugins_result
10    tags: [jenkins]
11
12  - wait_for:
13      path: /data/jenkins/plugins/{{ item }}
14    with_items: plugins
15    tags: [jenkins]
16
17  - name: Container is restarted
18    docker:
19      name: jenkins
20      image: jenkins
21      state: restarted
22    when: configs_result|changed or plugins_result|changed
23    tags: [jenkins]
24
25  - pause: seconds=30
26    when: configs_result|changed or plugins_result|changed
27    tags: [jenkins]
```

Now we are ready to create jobs. Since all of them will work in (more or less) the same way, we can use a single template that will serve for all our jobs related with service deployments. We need to create a separate directory for each job, apply the template, copy the result to the destination server and, finally, if any of the jobs changed, reload Jenkins. Unlike plugins that require a full restart, Jenkins will start using new jobs after the reload which is a very fast (almost instantaneous) action.

```
1  - name: Job directories are present
2    file:
3      path: "{{ home }}/jobs/{{ item.name }}"
4      state: directory
5      mode: 0777
6    with_items: jobs
7    tags: [jenkins]
8
9  - name: Jobs are present
10   template:
11     src: "{{ item.src }}"
12     dest: "{{ home }}/jobs/{{ item.name }}/config.xml"
13     mode: 0777
14   with_items: jobs
15   register: jobs_result
16   tags: [jenkins]
17
18 - name: Jenkins is reloaded
19   uri:
20     url: http://{{ ip }}:8080/reload
21     method: POST
22     status_code: 200,302
23   when: jobs_result|changed
24   ignore_errors: yes
25   tags: [jenkins]
```

In the future, if we'd like to add more jobs, all we'd need to do is add more entries to the *jobs* variable. With a system like that, we can easily create as many Jenkins jobs as there are services with almost no effort. Not only that but, if jobs need to be updated, all we'd need to do is change the template and re-run the playbook, and the changes would be propagated to all the jobs in charge of building, testing and deploying our services.

The *jobs* variable defined in the roles/jenkins/defaults/main.yml[176] file is as follows.

[176]https://github.com/vfarcic/ms-lifecycle/blob/master/ansible/roles/jenkins/defaults/main.yml

```
1  jobs: [
2    {
3      name: "books-ms-ansible",
4      service_name: "books-ms",
5      src: "service-ansible-config.xml"
6    },
7    ...
8  ]
```

The *name* and *service_name* values should be easy to understand. They represent the name of the job and the name of the service. The third value is the source template we'll use to create the job configuration.

Finally, let's take a look at the roles/jenkins/templates/service-ansible-config.xml[177] template.

```
1   <?xml version='1.0' encoding='UTF-8'?>
2   <project>
3     <actions/>
4     <description></description>
5     <logRotator class="hudson.tasks.LogRotator">
6       <daysToKeep>-1</daysToKeep>
7       <numToKeep>25</numToKeep>
8       <artifactDaysToKeep>-1</artifactDaysToKeep>
9       <artifactNumToKeep>-1</artifactNumToKeep>
10    </logRotator>
11    <keepDependencies>false</keepDependencies>
12    <properties>
13    </properties>
14    <scm class="hudson.plugins.git.GitSCM" plugin="git@2.4.1">
15      <configVersion>2</configVersion>
16      <userRemoteConfigs>
17        <hudson.plugins.git.UserRemoteConfig>
18          <url>https://github.com/vfarcic/{{ item.service_name }}.git</url>
19        </hudson.plugins.git.UserRemoteConfig>
20      </userRemoteConfigs>
21      <branches>
22        <hudson.plugins.git.BranchSpec>
23          <name>*/master</name>
24        </hudson.plugins.git.BranchSpec>
25      </branches>
26      <doGenerateSubmoduleConfigurations>false</doGenerateSubmoduleConfigurations>
```

---

[177]https://github.com/vfarcic/ms-lifecycle/blob/master/ansible/roles/jenkins/templates/service-ansible-config.xml

```
27     <submoduleCfg class="list"/>
28     <extensions/>
29   </scm>
30   <canRoam>true</canRoam>
31   <disabled>false</disabled>
32   <blockBuildWhenDownstreamBuilding>false</blockBuildWhenDownstreamBuilding>
33   <blockBuildWhenUpstreamBuilding>false</blockBuildWhenUpstreamBuilding>
34   <triggers/>
35   <concurrentBuild>false</concurrentBuild>
36   <builders>
37     <hudson.tasks.Shell>
38       <command>export PYTHONUNBUFFERED=1
39
40 ansible-playbook /vagrant/ansible/service.yml \
41     -i /vagrant/ansible/hosts/prod \
42     --extra-vars &quot;repo_dir=${PWD} service_name={{ item.service_name }}&quot\
43 ;</command>
44     </hudson.tasks.Shell>
45   </builders>
46   <publishers/>
47   <buildWrappers/>
48 </project>
```

It is a relatively big XML definition of a Jenkins job. I created it manually through the GUI, copied the file and replaced values with variables. One of the key entries is the one that tells Jenkins the location of the code repository.

```
1   <url>https://github.com/vfarcic/{{ item.service_name }}.git</url>
```

As you can see, we are, again, using naming conventions. The name of the repository is the same as the name of the service and will be replaced with the value of the variable we saw earlier.

The second entry is the one that executes the command that runs Ansible playbook and builds, packages, tests and deploys the service.

```
1       <command>export PYTHONUNBUFFERED=1
2
3 ansible-playbook /vagrant/ansible/service.yml \
4     -i /vagrant/ansible/hosts/prod \
5     --extra-vars &quot;repo_dir=${PWD} service_name={{ item.service_name }}&quot\
6 ;</command>
```

As you can see, we're running the same Ansible playbook that we created in the previous chapter.

Finally, the last task in the *jenkins* role is as follows.

```
1  - name: Scripts are present
2    copy:
3      src: scripts
4      dest: /data
5      mode: 0766
6    tags: [jenkins]
```

It copies scripts to the */data* directory. We'll explore those scripts later on.

The Ansible role *jenkins* is a good example of a more complicated use case. Until this chapter, most of the provisioning and configurations we did with Ansible were much simpler. In most instances we would update APT repository, install a package and, maybe, copy some configuration file. In some other cases, we would only run a Docker container. There were many other cases but, in the essence, they were all very simple since none of the other tools required much configuration. Jenkins was quite different. Besides running a container, we had to create quite a quite a few configuration files, install several plugins, create some jobs, and so on. As an alternative, we could (and probably should) have created our container that would have everything but jobs inside it. That would simplify the setup and, at the same time, provide a more reliable solution. However, I wanted to show you a bit more complicated Ansible process.

I'll leave the creation of a custom Jenkins image as an exercise. The image should contain everything but jobs inside it. Create a Dockerfile, build and push the image to Docker Hub and modify Ansible role *jenkins* so that the new container is used. It should share volumes with SSH keys and jobs so that they can be updated from outside a container.

Running Jenkins Jobs

By now, the Ansible playbook we run earlier should have finished the execution. Not only that Jenkins is up and running, but the *books-ms* job is created and waiting for us to use it.

Let's take a look at the Jenkins GUI. Please open http://10.100.198.200:8080[178]. You'll see the home page with a few jobs. The one we'll be exploring first is the *book-ms-ansible* job. In a different situation, our code repository would trigger a request to Jenkins to execute the build. However, since we're using public GitHub repo and this Jenkins instance is (probably) running on your laptop and is not accessible from a public network, we'll have to execute the job manually. Let's click the *Schedule a build for books-ms-ansible* button (icon with a clock and play arrow). You'll see that the first build of the *books-ms-ansible* job is running on the *cd* node located in the left-hand side of the screen.

---

[178]http://10.100.198.200:8080

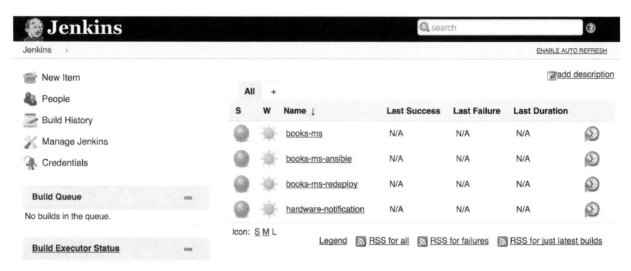

Figure 12-04: Jenkins home screen with a few jobs

Let's click the *books-ms-ansible* job, then click *#1* link inside the *Build History* and, finally, the *Console Output*. The same can be accomplished by opening the http://10.100.198.200:8080/job/books-ms-ansible/lastBuild/console[179] URL. You will be presented with the output of the last build of that job. As you probably noticed, the log is a bit big and it would be hard to find information about a particular task. Luckily, we installed the Log Parser[180] plugin that can help us drill through logs easier. But, first things first, we need to wait until the build is finished. We'll use that time wisely and explore the job configuration.

Please go back to the *books-ms-ansible* job main screen and click the *Configure* link located in the left-hand menu (or open the link http://10.100.198.200:8080/job/books-ms-ansible/configure[181]).

The *books-ms-ansible* is a very simple job and yet, in most cases, we won't need anything more complicated if our automation scripts are done correctly (with or without Ansible). You'll see that the job is restricted to the *cd* node meaning that it can run only on servers named or labeled *cd*. That way we can control which jobs are run on which servers. Part of the Jenkins setup was to create one node called *cd*.

Source Code Management section has the reference to the GitHub repository. Please note that we are missing a trigger that will run this job whenever there is a new commit. That can be accomplished in a variety of ways. We could set *Build Trigger* to *Poll SCM* and schedule it to run periodically (let's say every 10 seconds). Please note that the scheduling format uses the *cron* syntax. In such a case, Jenkins would regularly check the repository and, if anything changed (if there was a commit), it would run the job. A better way would be to create a *webhook* directly in the repository. That hook would invoke a Jenkins build on every commit. In such a case, the build would start running almost instantaneously after the commit. At the same time, there would be no overhead created by jobs periodically checking the repository. However, this approach would require Jenkins being accessible from the repository (in this case GitHub) and we are currently running Jenkins inside a private

---

[179]http://10.100.198.200:8080/job/books-ms-ansible/lastBuild/console

[180]https://wiki.jenkins-ci.org/display/JENKINS/Log+Parser+Plugin

[181]http://10.100.198.200:8080/job/books-ms-ansible/configure

network. We choose neither since it is very unlikely that there will be a commit to the *books-ms* repository while you are reading this book. It is up to you to investigate different ways to trigger this job. We'll simulate the same process by running builds manually. No matter the way the job is run, the first thing it will do is clone the repository using information provided in the *Source Code Management* section.

Now we reached the main part of the job; the *Build* section. I already mentioned that we could have used the *Ansible* plugin to help us run the playbook. However, the command we should run is so simple that using a plugin would only introduce additional complications. Inside the *Build* section, we have the *Execute shell* step that runs the *service.yml* playbook is the same way as we run it manually. We are using Jenkins only as a tool to detect changes to the code repository and run the same commands we would run without it.

Figure 12-05: Jenkins books-ms-ansible job configuration screen

Finally, we have the *Console output (build log) parsing* set as the *Post-build actions* step. It parses (in this case) Ansible logs so that they are displayed in a more user-friendly fashion. By this time, the execution of the build probably finished, and we can take a look at the parsed log.

Go back to the build *#1* of the *books-ms* job and click the *Parsed Console Output* link in the left-hand menu or open the URL http://10.100.198.200:8080/job/books-ms-ansible/lastBuild/parsed_console/[182]. Under the section *Info*, you'll see each Ansible task separated and can click any of them to jump to the part of the output related to that task. If there were some problems during the execution, they would appear under the link *Error*. We won't go into details how the *Log Parser* plugin works. I included it into this job mostly as a demonstration of the power Jenkins provides through its plugins. There's over a thousand of them available and new ones coming. Plugins are probably the main advantage Jenkins has over other CI/CD tools. There is such a big community behind them that you can rest assured that almost any need you have is (probably) covered. Even better, just by

---

[182]http://10.100.198.200:8080/job/books-ms-ansible/lastBuild/parsed_console/

exploring available plugins, you will get new ideas.

Even though this job fulfills all the essential purposes required to deploy the service (checkout the code and run the Ansible playbook), there are a few additional tasks we could add to the job. Probably the most interesting thing we could do is add notifications in case of a job failure. That can be an email message, Slack notification or (almost) any other type of notification we're used to. I'll leave that part to you as an exercise. Spend some time checking out plugins that would help to send notifications, select one and install it. The *Manage Plugins* screen can be accessed by clicking the *Manage Jenkins* located in the left-hand menu on the home screen. As an alternative, the same screen can be accessed by opening the URL http://10.100.198.200:8080/pluginManager/[183]. Once inside, follow plugin instructions and add it to the *books-ms-ansible* job. Once you're comfortable with it, try to do the same through Ansible. Add the new plugin to the *plugins* variable and put the required entries to the *service-ansible-config.xml* template. The easiest way to do that is to apply the changes through the UI, and then check the changes Jenkins did to the */data/jenkins/jobs/books-ms-ansible/config.xml* file in the *cd* node.

Setting Up Jenkins Workflow Jobs

Is there a better way to structure a job that will deploy the *books-ms* service? What we have right now is a job consisting of multiple steps. One step checks out the code while the another runs the Ansible script. We specified that it should run on the *cd* node and did few more minor steps. Notifications are missing at the moment (unless you implemented them yourself) and they would be another step in the job. Each step is a separate plugin. Some of them are distributed with Jenkins core while others were added by us. With time, the number of steps might increase considerably. At the same time, while Ansible is great for provisioning and configuring servers when used as a tool to build, test and deploy services, it proved to be a bit cumbersome and lacking some of the features that could be done easier with a simple bash script. On the other hand, bash scripts lack some of the characteristics Ansible has. For example, Ansible is much better at running commands in remote locations. The third option would be to move the deployment process to "traditional" Jenkins jobs. That would also not be a great solution. We'd end up with quite a few jobs that would probably run bash scripts as well. One job would do pre-deployment tasks on the *cd* node, another would be in charge of deployment in the *prod* node, and we'd need a third one that would execute post-deployment steps in the *cd* node. As a minimum, we would have three chained jobs. More likely, there would be more. Maintaining many jobs is time-demanding and complicated at best.

We can utilize Jenkins' Workflow Plugin[184] to write a script that does all the steps for us. We can use it as an alternative to deployment we're currently doing with Ansible. We already discussed that Ansible shines at servers provisioning and configuration, but the deployment part could be improved. The Workflow plugin allows us to script the whole job. This feature in itself is a great way to continue relying heavily on automation. That is especially true since Jenkins XML is

---

[183]http://10.100.198.200:8080/pluginManager/

[184]https://wiki.jenkins-ci.org/display/JENKINS/Workflow+Plugin

very cumbersome and hard to write and read. It is enough to take a look at the service-ansible-config.xml[185] that we used to define a simple job that deploys our services. Jenkins XML is cryptic and with a lot of boilerplate definitions, Ansible is not designed to be used with conditionals nor it has a decent substitute for try/catch statements and bash scripts are just an extra layer of complexity. It is true that, at this point, our process is complicated, and we should strive to keep things as simple as possible without sacrificing the goals we set in front of us.

Let's give Workflow plugin a go and see whether it can help. We'll combine it with the CloudBees Docker Workflow Plugin[186].

We'll begin by taking a look at the configuration of the *books-ms* job. We can navigate through the Jenkins UI all the way to the job settings screen or simply open the http://10.100.198.200:8080/job/books-ms/configure[187] URL.

Figure 12-06: Configuration screen of the *books-ms* Jenkins workflow job

Once inside the *books-ms* configuration, you'll notice that the whole job consists only of a few parameters and the workflow script. Unlike "regular" jobs, workflow allows us to script (almost) everything. That, in turn, makes managing Jenkins jobs much easier. The roles/jenkins/templates/service-flow.groovy[188] script we're using is as follows.

---

[185]https://github.com/vfarcic/ms-lifecycle/blob/master/ansible/roles/jenkins/templates/service-ansible-config.xml

[186]https://wiki.jenkins-ci.org/display/JENKINS/CloudBees+Docker+Workflow+Plugin

[187]http://10.100.198.200:8080/job/books-ms/configure

[188]https://github.com/vfarcic/ms-lifecycle/blob/master/ansible/roles/jenkins/templates/service-flow.groovy

```
1  node("cd") {
2      git url: "https://github.com/vfarcic/${serviceName}.git"
3      def flow = load "/data/scripts/workflow-util.groovy"
4      flow.provision("prod2.yml")
5      flow.buildTests(serviceName, registryIpPort)
6      flow.runTests(serviceName, "tests", "")
7      flow.buildService(serviceName, registryIpPort)
8      flow.deploy(serviceName, prodIp)
9      flow.updateProxy(serviceName, "prod")
10     flow.runTests(serviceName, "integ", "-e DOMAIN=http://${proxyIp}")
11 }
```

The script starts with the node definition telling Jenkins that all the instructions should be run on the *cd* node.

The first instruction inside the node is to check out the code from the Git repository. The *git* module is one of the examples of the DSL created for the Jenkins Workflow. This instruction uses the *serviceName* parameter defined in the Jenkins job.

Next, we're using the *load* instruction that will include all the utility functions defined in the *workflow-util.groovy* script. That way we won't repeat ourselves when we create jobs with different goals and processes. We'll explore the *workflow-util.groovy* script very soon. The result of the load is assigned to the *flow* variable.

From this point on, the rest of the script should be self-explanatory. We're calling the *provision* function passing it *prod2.yml* as variable. Then we're calling the *buildTest* function and passing it *serviceName* and *registryIpPort* job parameters as variables. And so on, and so forth. The functions we are invoking are performing the same actions like those we implemented through Ansible, and represent the deployment pipeline. With this separation between utility functions loaded as a separate file and the workflow script itself, we can properly divide responsibilities. The utility script provides functions multiple workflow scripts can use and benefits greatly from being centralized so that improvements are done once. On the other hand, one workflow might not be the same as the other so, in this case, it mostly contains invocations of utility functions.

Let's take a closer look at the functions inside the workflow-util.groovy[189] script.

```
1  def provision(playbook) {
2      stage "Provision"
3      env.PYTHONUNBUFFERED = 1
4      sh "ansible-playbook /vagrant/ansible/${playbook} \
5          -i /vagrant/ansible/hosts/prod"
6  }
```

---

[189]https://github.com/vfarcic/ms-lifecycle/blob/master/ansible/roles/jenkins/files/scripts/workflow-util.groovy

The *provision* function is in charge of provisioning our servers before deployment. It defines *stage* that helps us better identify the set of tasks this function is in charge of. That is followed by the declaration of the *PYTHONUNBUFFERED* environment variable that tells Ansible to skip buffering logs and display the output as soon as possible. Finally, we are invoking the Ansible playbook using the workflow module *sh* that runs any shell script. Since we might run different playbooks depending on the type of the Jenkins job, we are passing the playbook name as the function variable.

The next function we'll explore is in charge of building tests.

```
1  def buildTests(serviceName, registryIpPort) {
2      stage "Build tests"
3      def tests = docker.image("${registryIpPort}/${serviceName}-tests")
4      try {
5          tests.pull()
6      } catch(e) {}
7      sh "docker build -t \"${registryIpPort}/${serviceName}-tests\" \
8          -f Dockerfile.test ."
9      tests.push()
10 }
```

This time, we are using the *docker* module to declare the Docker image and assigning the result to the *tests* variable. From there on, we are pulling the image, running a Shell script that builds a new one in case something changed and, finally, pushing the result to the registry. Please note that image pulling is inside a *try/catch* statement. The workflow is run for the first time, there will be no image to pull, and, without a *try/catch* statement, the script would fail.

Next in line are functions for running tests and building the service image.

```
1  def runTests(serviceName, target, extraArgs) {
2      stage "Run ${target} tests"
3      sh "docker-compose -f docker-compose-dev.yml \
4          -p ${serviceName} run --rm ${extraArgs} ${target}"
5  }
6
7  def buildService(serviceName, registryIpPort) {
8      stage "Build service"
9      def service = docker.image("${registryIpPort}/${serviceName}")
10     try {
11         service.pull()
12     } catch(e) {}
13     docker.build "${registryIpPort}/${serviceName}"
14     service.push()
15 }
```

Those two functions use the same instructions as those we already discussed so we'll jump over them.

The function for deploying the service might need further explanation.

```
1  def deploy(serviceName, prodIp) {
2      stage "Deploy"
3      withEnv(["DOCKER_HOST=tcp://${prodIp}:2375"]) {
4          try {
5              sh "docker-compose pull app"
6          } catch(e) {}
7          sh "docker-compose -p ${serviceName} up -d app"
8      }
9  }
```

The new instruction is the *withEnv*. We're using it to create the environment variable that has a limited scope. It will exist only for instructions declared inside curly braces. In this case, environment variable *DOCKER_HOST* is used only to pull and run the *app* container on a remote host.

The last function updates the proxy service.

```
1  def updateProxy(serviceName, proxyNode) {
2      stage "Update proxy"
3      stash includes: 'nginx-*', name: 'nginx'
4      node(proxyNode) {
5          unstash 'nginx'
6          sh "sudo cp nginx-includes.conf /data/nginx/includes/${serviceName}.conf"
7          sh "sudo consul-template \
8              -consul localhost:8500 \
9              -template \"nginx-upstreams.ctmpl:/data/nginx/upstreams/${serviceNam\
10 e}.conf:docker kill -s HUP nginx\" \
11             -once"
12     }
13 }
```

The new instructions are *stash* and *unstash*. Since we are updating the proxy on a different node (defined as the *proxyNode* variable), we had to stash few files from the *cd* server and unstash them in the proxy node. In other words, stash/unstash combination is equivalent to copying the files from one server or directory to another.

All in all, the approach with Jenkins Workflow and Groovy DSL removes the need for deployment defined in Ansible. We'll keep using Ansible playbooks for provisioning and configuration since those are the areas it truly shines. On the other hand, Jenkins Workflow and Groovy DSL provide much more power, flexibility, and freedom when defining the deployment process. The main difference is that Groovy is a scripting language and, therefore, provides a better syntax for this type of tasks. At the same time, its integration with Jenkins allows us to utilize some powerful features. For example, we could define five nodes with a label *tests*. Later on, if we specify that some Workflow instructions should be run on a *tests* node, Jenkins would make sure that the least utilized of those five nodes is used (or there might be a different logic depending on the way we set it up).

At the same time, by using Jenkins Workflow, we're avoiding complicated and not easy to understand XML definitions required by traditional Jenkins jobs and reducing the overall number of jobs. There are many other advantages Workflow provides and we'll discuss them later. The result is a single script, much shorter than Ansible deployment tasks we had before, and, at the same time, something easier to understand and update. We embraced Jenkins for tasks it is good at while keeping Ansible for servers provisioning and configuration. The result is the combination that uses the best of both worlds.

Let's take another look at the configuration of the *books-ms* job. Please open the books-ms configuration[190] screen in your favorite browser. You'll see that the job contains only two set of specifications. It starts with parameters and ends with the Workflow script we discussed earlier. The script itself can be very generic since differences are declared through parameters. We could multiply this job for all our services, and the only differences would be Jenkins parameters. That way, management of those jobs can be handled through a single Ansible template defined in the roles/jenkins/templates/service-workflow-config.xml[191] file.

Let's build the job and see how it fares. Please open the books-ms build[192] screen. You'll see that the parameters are already pre-defined with reasonable values. The name of the service is the *books-ms* parameter, the IP of the production server is the *prodIp* parameter, the IP of the proxy server is the *proxyIp* parameter and, finally, the IP and the port of the Docker registry is defined as the *registryIpPort* parameter. Once you click the *Build* button, the deployment will be initiated.

---

[190]http://10.100.198.200:8080/job/books-ms/configure

[191]https://github.com/vfarcic/ms-lifecycle/blob/master/ansible/roles/jenkins/templates/service-workflow-config.xml

[192]http://10.100.198.200:8080/job/books-ms/build?delay=0sec

Workflow books-ms

This build requires parameters:

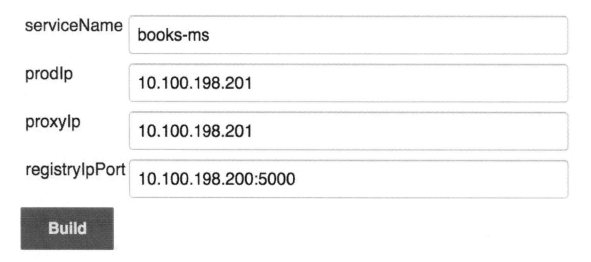

Figure 12-07: Build screen of the *books-ms* Jenkins workflow job

We can monitor the execution of the job by opening the books-ms Console screen of the last build[193].

---

[193]http://10.100.198.200:8080/job/books-ms/lastBuild/console

Console Output

```
Started by user anonymous
[Workflow] Allocate node : Start
Running on cd in /data/jenkins_slaves/cd/workspace/books-ms
[Workflow] node {
[Workflow] git
 > git rev-parse --is-inside-work-tree # timeout=10
Fetching changes from the remote Git repository
 > git config remote.origin.url https://github.com/vfarcic/books-ms.git #
timeout=10
Fetching upstream changes from https://github.com/vfarcic/books-ms.git
 > git --version # timeout=10
 > git -c core.askpass=true fetch --tags --progress
https://github.com/vfarcic/books-ms.git +refs/heads/*:refs/remotes/origin/*
 > git rev-parse refs/remotes/origin/master^{commit} # timeout=10
 > git rev-parse refs/remotes/origin/origin/master^{commit} # timeout=10
Checking out Revision 0e10f5d070252e1a7e46ca13aaefac494c3177a2
(refs/remotes/origin/master)
 > git config core.sparsecheckout # timeout=10
 > git checkout -f 0e10f5d070252e1a7e46ca13aaefac494c3177a2
 > git rev-list 0e10f5d070252e1a7e46ca13aaefac494c3177a2 # timeout=10
[Workflow] load: Loaded script: /data/scripts/workflow-util.groovy
[Workflow] load {
[Workflow] } //load
[Workflow] stage: Provision
Entering stage Provision
Proceeding
```

Figure 12-08: Console screen of the *books-ms* Jenkins workflow job

As you already know, many things are done as part of our deployment process and the logs can be too big for us to find something fast. Luckily, Jenkins workflow jobs have the *Workflow Steps* feature that can help. When the execution is finished, please click the Workflow Steps[194] link after navigating to the last books-ms build[195]. You'll see that each stage and step is presented with a link (icon representing a terminal screen) that allow us to investigate only logs belonging to the step in question.

[194]http://10.100.198.200:8080/job/books-ms/lastBuild/flowGraphTable/

[195]http://10.100.198.200:8080/job/books-ms/lastBuild/

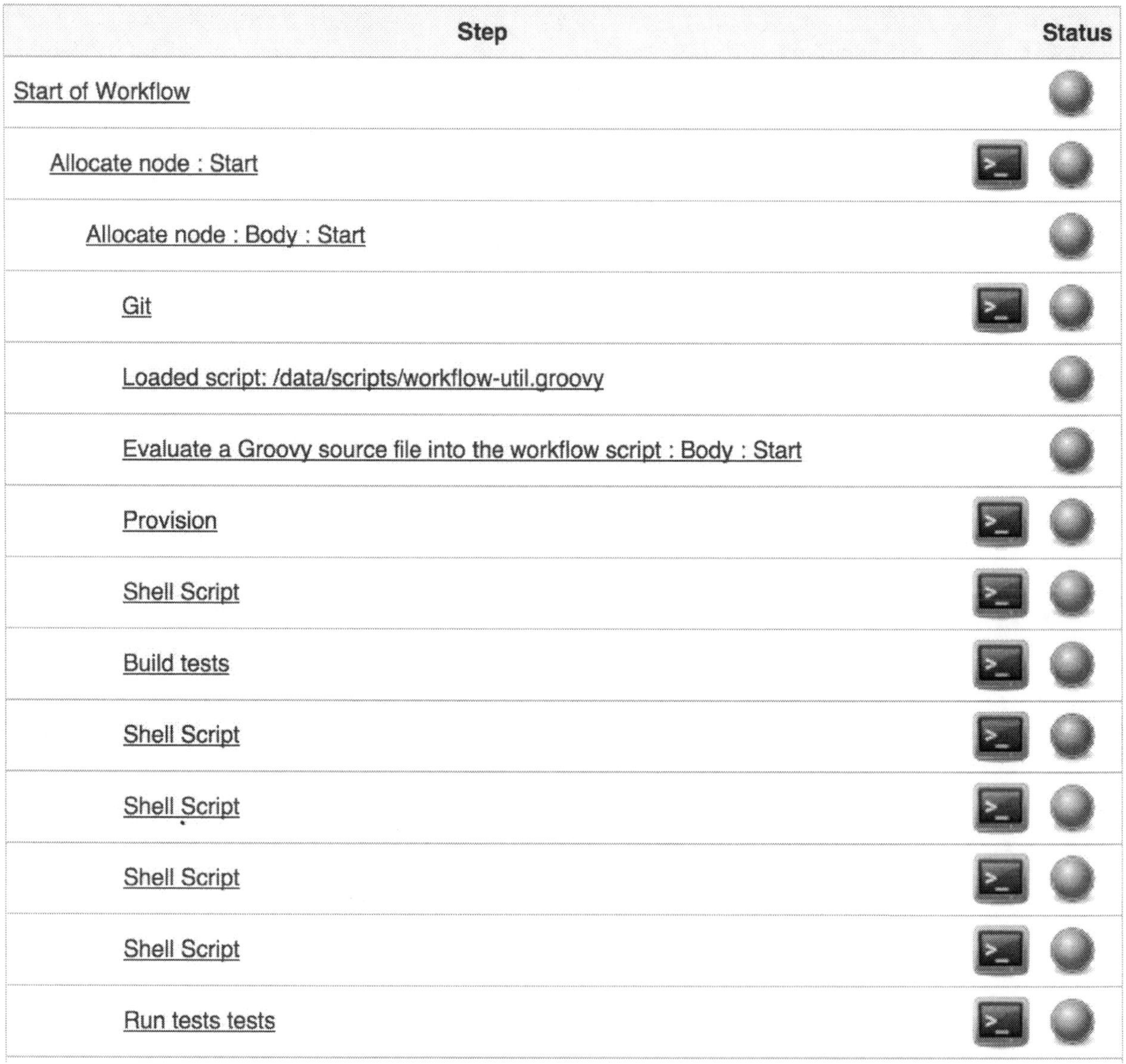

Step	Status
Start of Workflow	
Allocate node : Start	
Allocate node : Body : Start	
Git	
Loaded script: /data/scripts/workflow-util.groovy	
Evaluate a Groovy source file into the workflow script : Body : Start	
Provision	
Shell Script	
Build tests	
Shell Script	
Shell Script	
Shell Script	
Shell Script	
Run tests tests	

Figure 12-09: Workflow Steps screen of the *books-ms* Jenkins workflow job

There's much more to Jenkins workflow than what we presented here. Please spend some time with the online tutorial[196] to get more familiar with it. As an exercise, add, for example, email notifications to the script. While exploring Jenkins Workflow, make sure to select the *Snippet Generator* checkbox located below the script in the books-ms configuration[197] screen. It is a very useful way to discover what each snippet does and how it can be used.

Even though Workflow provided a lot of benefits over deployment defined through the playbook, managing the script through Ansible is still the sub-optimum solution. A better way would be to set the deployment pipeline as a script inside the code repository together with the rest of the service

---

[196]https://github.com/jenkinsci/workflow-plugin/blob/master/TUTORIAL.md
[197]http://10.100.198.200:8080/job/books-ms/configure

code. That way, the team maintaining the service would be in full control of deployment. Besides the need to have the workflow script inside the code repository, it would be highly beneficial if a Jenkins job would be capable not only of handling the main branch but all of them or those we select to be worth the trouble. Luckily, both of those improvements can be accomplished with the *Multibranch Workflow* plugin and *Jenkinsfile*.

Setting Up Jenkins Multibranch Workflow and Jenkinsfile

The *Jenkins Multibranch Workflow* plugin adds a new job type that allows us to keep the Workflow script inside a code repository. Such a job would create a subproject for each branch it finds in the repository and expects to find *Jenkinsfile* in each of them. That allows us to keep the Workflow script inside the repository instead having it centralized inside Jenkins. That, in turn, enables developers in charge of a project full freedom to define the deployment pipeline. Since each branch creates a separate Jenkins project with a different Jenkinsfile, we can fine-tune the process depending on the type of branch. For example, we might decide to define a full pipeline in the Jenkinsfile residing in the master branch and choose to have only building and testing tasks defined for feature branches. There's more. Not only that Jenkins will detect all branches and keep that list updated, but it will also remove a subproject if a corresponding branch is removed.

Let's give Multibranch Workflow and Jenkinsfile a spin. We'll start by opening the books-ms-multibranch job[198]. You'll see the message stating that "this project scans branches in your SCM and generate a job for each of them, but you have no branches configured". Please click the *Branch Indexing* and, then, *Run Now* links from the left-hand menu. Jenkins will index all branches that match the filter we specified in the configuration. Once branches are indexed, it will create subprojects for each and initiate building. Let's explore the configuration of the job while building is in progress.

Please open the books-ms-multibranch configuration[199] screen. The only important part of the job configuration is *Branch Sources*. We used it to define the code repository. Please note the *Advanced* button. When clicked, you'll see that only branches that contain *workflow* in their names are included. This setting is configured for two reasons. The first one is to demonstrate the option to filter which branches will be included and, the other, to save you from building too many branches inside the VM with such a limited capacity (the *cd* node has only 1 CPU and 1 GB of RAM).

By this time, branch indexing is probably finished. If you go back to the books-ms-multibranch job[200] screen, you'll see that two subject projects matched the filter, *jenkins-workflow* and *jenkins-workflow-simple*, and that Jenkins initiated builds of both. Since the *cd* node is configured to have only one executor, the second build will wait until the first is finished.

Let's take a look at the *Jenkinsfile* in those branches.

---

[198]http://10.100.198.200:8080/job/books-ms-multibranch/

[199]http://10.100.198.200:8080/job/books-ms-multibranch/configure

[200]http://10.100.198.200:8080/job/books-ms-multibranch/

The Jenkinsfile[201] in the jenkins-workflow[202] branch is as follows.

```
 1   node("cd") {
 2       def serviceName = "books-ms"
 3       def prodIp = "10.100.198.201"
 4       def proxyIp = "10.100.198.201"
 5       def registryIpPort = "10.100.198.200:5000"
 6
 7       git url: "https://github.com/vfarcic/${serviceName}.git"
 8       def flow = load "/data/scripts/workflow-util.groovy"
 9       flow.provision("prod2.yml")
10       flow.buildTests(serviceName, registryIpPort)
11       flow.runTests(serviceName, "tests", "")
12       flow.buildService(serviceName, registryIpPort)
13       flow.deploy(serviceName, prodIp)
14       flow.updateProxy(serviceName, "prod")
15       flow.runTests(serviceName, "integ", "-e DOMAIN=http://${proxyIp}")
16   }
```

The script is almost the same as the one we defined earlier when we worked with Jenkins Workflow embedded in the Jenkins job books-ms[203]. The only difference is that, this time, variables are defined inside the script instead of using Jenkins properties. Since the project team is now in full charge of the process, there is no need to externalize those variables. We accomplished the same result as before but this time we moved the script to the code repository.

The Jenkinsfile[204] in the jenkins-workflow-simple[205] branch is a bit simpler.

```
 1   node("cd") {
 2       def serviceName = "books-ms"
 3       def registryIpPort = "10.100.198.200:5000"
 4
 5       git url: "https://github.com/vfarcic/${serviceName}.git"
 6       def flow = load "/data/scripts/workflow-util.groovy"
 7       flow.buildTests(serviceName, registryIpPort)
 8       flow.runTests(serviceName, "tests", "")
 9   }
```

By inspecting the script, we can conclude that the developer who made that branch wants to benefit from tests being run through Jenkins every time he pushes a commit. He removed deployment and

---

[201]https://github.com/vfarcic/books-ms/blob/jenkins-workflow/Jenkinsfile

[202]https://github.com/vfarcic/books-ms/tree/jenkins-workflow

[203]http://10.100.198.200:8080/job/books-ms/

[204]https://github.com/vfarcic/books-ms/blob/jenkins-workflow-simple/Jenkinsfile

[205]https://github.com/vfarcic/books-ms/tree/jenkins-workflow-simple

post-deployment tests from it since the code is probably not ready to be deployed to production or the policy is that only the code in the master or other selected branches is deployed. Once he merges his code, a different script will be run and his changes will be deployed to production assuming that he didn't introduce any bugs, and the process was successful.

The introduction of *Multibranch Workflow* and *Jenkinsfile* improved our deployment pipeline quite a lot. We have a utility script located in the *cd* node so that others can reuse common functions. From there on, we allowed every team to host their script inside the *Jenkinsfile* located in their repository. Moreover, we gave them freedom not only to decide what is the proper way to build, test, and deploy their services but also the flexibility to fine-tune the process based on each branch.

Final Thoughts

That was a very brief introduction to CI/CD tools and Jenkins in particular. Apart from the need to have a CI/CD tool, Jenkins will be one of the cornerstones of the next chapter. We'll use it as part of the *blue-green deployment* toolset. If you are new to Jenkins, I suggest you take a break from this book. Spend some time with it, read few tutorials and play around with different plugins. Time invested in Jenkins is indeed a valuable investment that will be paid off quickly.

The introduction of Jenkins Workflow together with Docker and Multibranch plugins proved to be invaluable additions to our toolbelt. We are using all the power Jenkins UI can offer while still maintaining the flexibility that scripting provides for the deployment pipeline. Workflow DLS and Groovy combine the best of both worlds. Through Workflow domain specific language (DSL), we have syntax and functionality specifically tailored to serve deployment purposes. On the other hand, Groovy itself provides everything we might need when DSL cuts short. At the same time, we can access almost any functionality Jenkins offers. Docker addition to the Workflow provided few helpful shortcuts and Multibranch together with Jenkinsfile allowed us to have the pipeline (or part of it) applied to all branches (or those we select). All in all, we combined high level with low-level tools into one powerful and easy to use combination.

The way we created Jenkins jobs through Ansible was far from great. We could have used one of the Jenkins plugins like Template Project Plugin[206] to create templates. However, none of them are truly great and they all suffer from some deficiencies. Jenkins Enterprise Edition[207] from CloudBees[208] does have tools that solve templating and many other problems. However, all the examples we used by now were based on open source software, and we'll continue in the same fashion throughout the rest of the book. That does not mean that paid solutions are not worth the investment. They often are and should be evaluated. If you choose to use Jenkins and the size of your project or organization warrants the investment, I recommend you evaluate Jenkins Enterprise Edition[209]. It brings a lot of improvements over the open source version.

---

[206]https://wiki.jenkins-ci.org/display/JENKINS/Template+Project+Plugin

[207]https://www.cloudbees.com/products/cloudbees-jenkins-platform/enterprise-edition

[208]https://www.cloudbees.com/

[209]https://www.cloudbees.com/products/cloudbees-jenkins-platform/enterprise-edition

Given the tools we have at our disposal and the relatively uniform way to run our deployment steps, the current solution is probably the best we could do, and it is time for us to move to the next subject and explore the benefits we can obtain from *blue-green deployment.*

Before we move on, let's destroy the VMs we used in this chapter.

```
1  exit
2
3  vagrant destroy -f
```

Blue-Green Deployment

Traditionally, we deploy a new release by replacing the current one. The old release is stopped, and the new one is brought up in its place. The problem with this approach is the downtime occurring from the moment the old release is stopped until the new one is fully operational. No matter how quickly you try to do this process, there will be some downtime. That might be only a millisecond, or it can last for minutes or, in extreme situations, even hours. Having monolithic applications introduces additional problems like, for example, the need to wait a considerable amount of time until the application is initialized. People tried to solve this issue in various ways, and most of them used some variation of the *blue-green deployment process*. The idea behind it is simple. At any time, one of the releases should be running meaning that, during the deployment process, we must deploy a new release in parallel with the old one. The new and the old releases are called blue and green.

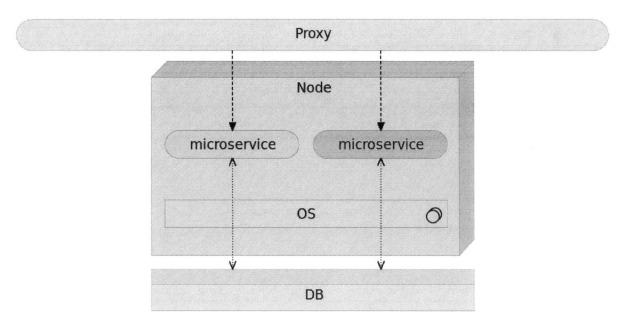

Figure 13-1: At any given moment, at least, one service release is up and running

We run one color as a current release, bring up the other color as a new release and, once it is fully operational, switch all the traffic from the current to the new release. This switch is often made with a router or a proxy service.

With the blue-green process, not only that we are removing the deployment downtime, but we are also reducing the risk the deployment might introduce. No matter how well we tested our software before it reached the production node(s), there is always a chance that something will go wrong. When that happens, we still have the current version to rely on. There is no real reason to switch the traffic to the new release until it is tested enough that any reasonable possibility of a failure due to some specifics of the production node is verified. That usually means that integration testing is performed after the deployment and before the "switch" is made. Even if those verifications returned false negatives and there is a failure after the traffic is redirected, we can quickly switch back to the old release and restore the system to the previous state. We can roll back much faster than if we'd need to restore the application from some backup or do another deployment.

If we combine the blue-green process with immutable deployments (through VMs in the past and though containers today), the result is a very powerful, secure and reliable deployment procedure that can be performed much more often. If architecture is based on microservices in conjunction with containers, we don't need two nodes to perform the procedure and can run both releases side by side.

The significant challenges with this approach are databases. In many cases, we need to upgrade a database schema in a way that it supports both releases and then proceed with the deployment. The problems that might arise from this database upgrade are often related to the time that passes between releases. When releases are done often, changes to the database schema tend to be small, making it easier to maintain compatibility across two releases. If weeks, or months, passed between releases, database changes could be so big that backward compatibility might be impossible or not worthwhile doing. If we are aiming towards continuous delivery or deployment, the period between two releases should be short or, if it isn't, involve a relatively small amount of changes to the code base.

The Blue-Green Deployment Process

The blue-green deployment procedure, when applied to microservices packed as containers, is as follows.

The current release (for example blue), is running on the server. All traffic to that release is routed through a proxy service. Microservices are immutable and deployed as containers.

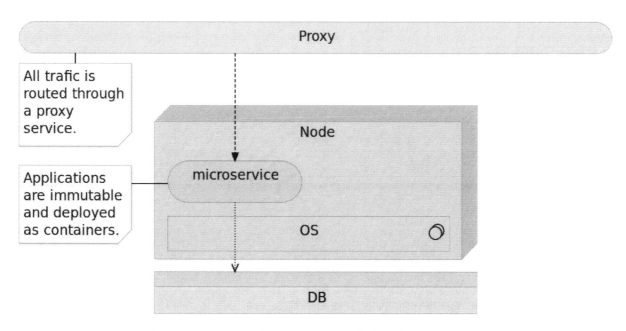

Figure 13-2: Immutable microservice deployed as a container

When a new release (for example green) is ready to be deployed, we run it in parallel with the current release. This way we can test the new release without affecting the users since all the traffic continues being sent to the current release.

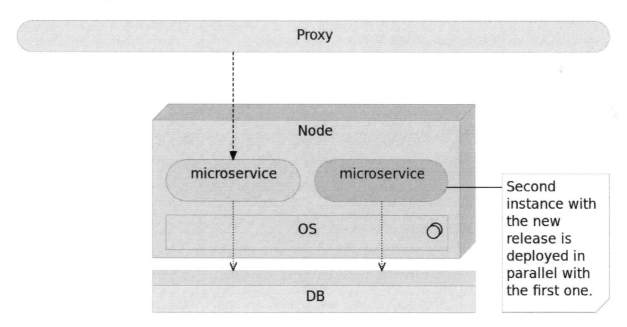

Figure 13-3: New release of the immutable microservice deployed alongside the old release

Once we think that the new release is working as expected, we change the proxy service configuration so that the traffic is redirected to that release. Most proxy services will let the existing requests finish their execution using the old proxy configuration so that there is no interruption.

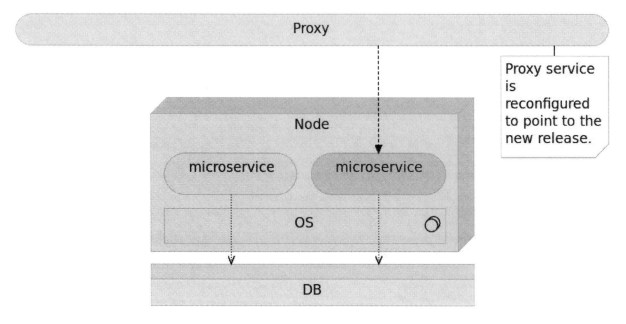

Figure 13-4: Poxy is re-configured to point to the new release

When all the requests sent to the old release received responses, the previous version of a service can be removed or, even better, stopped from running. If the latter option is used, rollback in case of a failure of the new release will be almost instantaneous since all we have to do is bring the old release back up.

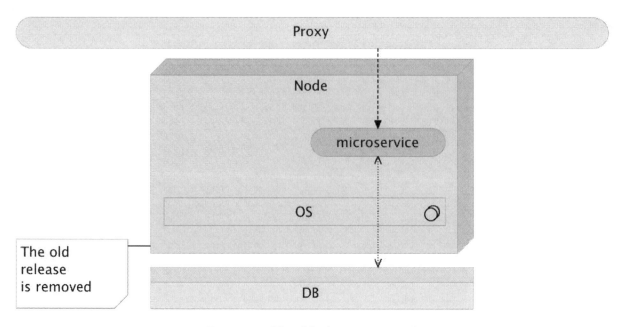

Figure 13-5: The old release is removed

Equipped with the basic logic behind the blue-green process, we can try setting it up. We'll start with manual commands and, once we're familiar with the practical part of the process, we'll attempt to automate the procedure.

We'll need the usual two nodes (*cd* and *prod*) to be up and running so let us create and provision the VMs.

```
1  vagrant up cd prod
2
3  vagrant ssh cd
4
5  ansible-playbook /vagrant/ansible/prod2.yml \
6      -i /vagrant/ansible/hosts/prod
```

Manually Running the Blue-Green Deployment

Please note that we'll go through the whole blue-green process within the context of what we tried to accomplish earlier. We will not only run two releases in parallel but make sure that, among other things, everything is thoroughly tested during multiple phases. That will complicate the process more than if we follow the blue-green procedure assuming that everything works. Most implementations do not take into account the need for testing before making the change to the proxy service. We can, and will, do better than that. Another thing to note is that we'll explore manual steps for you to understand the process. Later on, we'll automate everything using the tools we're already familiar with. I choose this approach in order to be sure that you grasp the complexity behind the combination of the continuous deployment and the blue-green processes. By truly understanding how to do it manually, you will be able to make an informed decision whether benefits of tools we're will explore throughout the rest of the book are greater than things they are missing.

We'll start by downloading the Docker Compose and nginx configurations that we used in the previous chapter.

```
1  mkdir books-ms
2
3  cd books-ms
4
5  wget https://raw.githubusercontent.com/vfarcic\
6  /books-ms/master/docker-compose.yml
7
8  wget https://raw.githubusercontent.com/vfarcic\
9  /books-ms/master/nginx-includes.conf
10
11 wget https://raw.githubusercontent.com/vfarcic\
12 /books-ms/master/nginx-upstreams-blue.ctmpl
13
14 wget https://raw.githubusercontent.com/vfarcic\
15 /books-ms/master/nginx-upstreams-green.ctmpl
```

With all the configuration files available, let us deploy the first release. The tools we explored earlier will come in handy. We'll use Consul as the service registry, Registrator to register and de-register containers, nginx as a proxy service and Consul Template to generate configurations and reload nginx.

Deploying the Blue Release

Since, at this moment, we do not have the *books-ms* service up and running, we'll call the first release *blue*. The only thing we need to do for now is to make sure that the name of the container we are about to run contains the word *blue* so that it does not collide with the next release. We'll be using Docker Compose to run containers so let us take a quick look at the targets defined in the docker-compose.yml[210] file that we just downloaded (only relevant targets are presented).

```
1   ...
2   base:
3     image: 10.100.198.200:5000/books-ms
4     ports:
5       - 8080
6     environment:
7       - SERVICE_NAME=books-ms
8
9   app-blue:
10    extends:
11      service: base
12    environment:
13      - SERVICE_NAME=books-ms-blue
14    links:
15      - db:db
16
17  app-green:
18    extends:
19      service: base
20    environment:
21      - SERVICE_NAME=books-ms-green
22    links:
23      - db:db
24  ...
```

We cannot use the *app* target directly since we'll be deploying two different targets (one for each color) and in that way avoid them overriding each other. Also, we'll want to differentiate them in

---

[210]https://github.com/vfarcic/books-ms/blob/master/docker-compose.yml

Consul as well, so the *SERVICE_NAME* environment variable should be unique. To accomplish that, we have two new targets called *app-blue* and *app-green*. Those targets extend the *base* service in the same way the *app* target extended it in previous chapters. The only difference between the targets *app-blue* and *app-green* on one hand and the *base* on the other is (besides the name of the target) the environment variable *SERVICE_NAME*.

With those two targets defined, we can deploy the blue release.

```
1  export DOCKER_HOST=tcp://prod:2375
2
3  docker-compose pull app-blue
4
5  docker-compose up -d app-blue
```

We pulled the latest version from the registry and brought it up as the blue release of the service. Just to be on the safe side, let us quickly check whether the service is running and is registered in Consul.

```
1  docker-compose ps
2
3  curl prod:8500/v1/catalog/service/books-ms-blue \
4      | jq '.'
```

The output of both commands combined is as follows.

```
1         Name              Command           State          Ports
2  --------------------------------------------------------------------------
3  booksms_app-blue_1   /run.sh              Up     0.0.0.0:32768->8080/tcp
4  booksms_db_1         /entrypoint.sh mongod Up     27017/tcp
5  ...
6  [
7    {
8      "ModifyIndex": 38,
9      "CreateIndex": 38,
10     "Node": "prod",
11     "Address": "10.100.198.201",
12     "ServiceID": "prod:booksms_app-blue_1:8080",
13     "ServiceName": "books-ms-blue",
14     "ServiceTags": [],
15     "ServiceAddress": "10.100.198.201",
16     "ServicePort": 32768,
17     "ServiceEnableTagOverride": false
18   }
19 ]
```

The first command showed that both the *app-blue* and the *db* containers are running. The second command displayed the details of the *books-ms-blue* service registered in Consul. Now we have the first release of our service up and running but still not integrated with nginx and, therefore, not accessible through the port 80. We can confirm that by sending a request to the service.

```
1  curl -I prod/api/v1/books
```

The output is as follows.

```
1  HTTP/1.1 404 Not Found
2  Server: nginx/1.9.9
3  Date: Sun, 03 Jan 2016 20:47:59 GMT
4  Content-Type: text/html
5  Content-Length: 168
6  Connection: keep-alive
```

The request response is the *404 Not Found* error message proving that we are yet to configure the proxy.

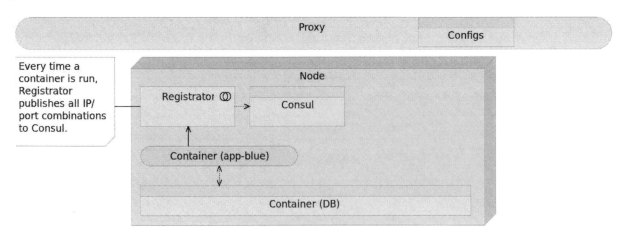

Figure 13-6: The blue container is deployed

Integrating the Blue Release

We can integrate the service in a similar way as we did before. The only difference is in the target of the service we registered in Consul.

Let us start by taking a look at the nginx Consul template nginx-upstreams-blue.ctmpl[211] that we downloaded earlier.

---

[211]https://github.com/vfarcic/books-ms/blob/master/nginx-upstreams-blue.ctmpl

```
1  upstream books-ms {
2      {{range service "books-ms-blue" "any"}}
3      server {{.Address}}:{{.Port}};
4      {{end}}
5  }
```

The service name is *books-ms-blue* and we can proceed by running Consul Template that will generate the final nginx upstreams configuration.

```
1  consul-template \
2      -consul prod:8500 \
3      -template "nginx-upstreams-blue.ctmpl:nginx-upstreams.conf" \
4      -once
```

The command run Consul Template that produced the nginx upstreams configuration file and reloaded the service.

Let's check whether the configuration file was indeed created correctly.

```
1  cat nginx-upstreams.conf
```

The output is as follows.

```
1  upstream books-ms {
2      server 10.100.198.201:32769;
3  }
```

Finally, all that's left is to copy the configuration files to the *prod* server and reload *nginx*. When asked, please use *vagrant* as the password.

```
1  scp nginx-includes.conf \
2      prod:/data/nginx/includes/books-ms.conf
3
4  scp nginx-upstreams.conf \
5      prod:/data/nginx/upstreams/books-ms.conf
6
7  docker kill -s HUP nginx
```

We copied the two configuration files to the server and reloaded *nginx* by sending the *HUP* signal.

Let's check whether our service is indeed integrated with the proxy.

```
1  curl -I prod/api/v1/books
```

The output is as follows.

```
1  HTTP/1.1 200 OK
2  Server: nginx/1.9.9
3  Date: Sun, 03 Jan 2016 20:51:12 GMT
4  Content-Type: application/json; charset=UTF-8
5  Content-Length: 2
6  Connection: keep-alive
7  Access-Control-Allow-Origin: *
```

This time, the response code is *200 OK* indicating that the service indeed responded to the request.

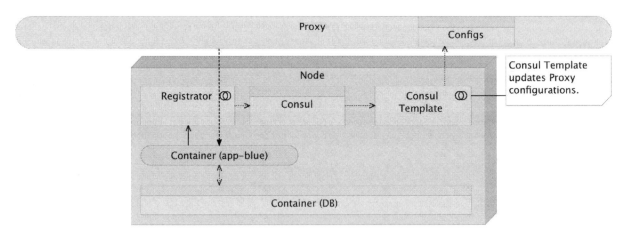

Figure 13-7: **The blue container integrated with the proxy service**

We finished the simplest scenario by deploying the first (blue) release. As you will soon see, the process of deploying the second (green) release will not be much different.

Deploying the Green Release

Deployment of the second (green) release can be done using the same steps as those we executed for the first (blue) release. The only difference is that this time we'll deploy the *books-ms-green* instead of the *books-ms-blue* target.

Unlike the previous deployment, this time, the new release (green) will run in parallel with the current release (blue).

```
1  docker-compose pull app-green
2
3  docker-compose up -d app-green
```

The new release has been pulled and run. We can confirm that by running the `docker-compose ps` command.

```
1  docker-compose ps
```

The result is as follows.

```
1       Name                Command              State           Ports
2  --------------------------------------------------------------------------------
3  booksms_app-blue_1      /run.sh                Up      0.0.0.0:32769->8080/tcp
4  booksms_app-green_1     /run.sh                Up      0.0.0.0:32770->8080/tcp
5  booksms_db_1            /entrypoint.sh mongod  Up      27017/tcp
```

The output shows that the two services (blue and green) are running in parallel. Similarly, we can confirm that both releases are registered in Consul.

```
1  curl prod:8500/v1/catalog/services \
2      | jq '.'
```

The output is as follows.

```
1  {
2    "dockerui": [],
3    "consul": [],
4    "books-ms-green": [],
5    "books-ms-blue": []
6  }
```

As before, we can also check the details of the newly deployed service.

```
1  curl prod:8500/v1/catalog/service/books-ms-green \
2      | jq '.'
```

Finally, we can confirm that the old release is still accessible through the proxy.

```
1  curl -I prod/api/v1/books
2
3  docker logs nginx
```

The output of the last command should be similar to the following (timestamps are removed for brevity).

```
1  "GET /api/v1/books HTTP/1.1" 200 201 "-" "curl/7.35.0" "-" 10.100.198.201:32769
2  "GET /api/v1/books HTTP/1.1" 200 201 "-" "curl/7.35.0" "-" 10.100.198.201:32769
```

Please keep in mind that the port of the service deployed on your computer might be different than the one from the example above.

The output of nginx logs should display that the request we made is redirected to the port of the blue release. That can be observed by checking that the last request went to the same port as the one we made before deploying the *green* release.

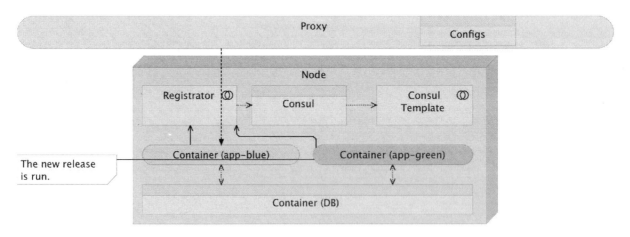

Figure 13-8: The green container is deployed in parallel with the blue

Right now, we have two releases (blue and green) running in parallel and the proxy service is still redirecting all requests to the old release (blue). The next step should be to test the new release before we change the proxy configuration. We'll skip testing until we reach the automation part and dive straight into the integration of the green release with nginx.

Integrating the Green Release

The process to integrate the second (green) release with the proxy service is similar to the one we already did.

```
1  consul-template \
2      -consul prod:8500 \
3      -template "nginx-upstreams-green.ctmpl:nginx-upstreams.conf" \
4      -once
5
6  scp nginx-upstreams.conf \
7      prod:/data/nginx/upstreams/books-ms.conf
8
9  docker kill -s HUP nginx
```

We can send a request to the proxy and check its logs to see whether it truly points to the new (green) release.

```
1  curl -I prod/api/v1/books
2
3  docker logs nginx
```

The nginx logs should be similar to the following (timestamps are removed for brevity).

```
1  "GET /api/v1/books HTTP/1.1" 200 201 "-" "curl/7.35.0" "-" 10.100.198.201:32769
2  "GET /api/v1/books HTTP/1.1" 200 201 "-" "curl/7.35.0" "-" 10.100.198.201:32769
3  "GET /api/v1/books HTTP/1.1" 200 201 "-" "curl/7.35.0" "-" 10.100.198.201:32770
```

It is obvious that the last request went to a different port (32770) than those we made before (32769). We switched the proxy from the blue to the green release. There was no downtime during this process since we waited until the new release is fully up and running before changing the proxy. Also, nginx is intelligent enough not to apply the configuration change to all requests but only to those made after the reload. In other words, all requests started before the reload continued using the old release while all those initiated afterward were sent to the new release. We managed to accomplish zero-downtime with minimum effort and without resorting to any new tool. We used nginx as a proxy and Consul (together with Registrator and Consul Template) to store and retrieve service information.

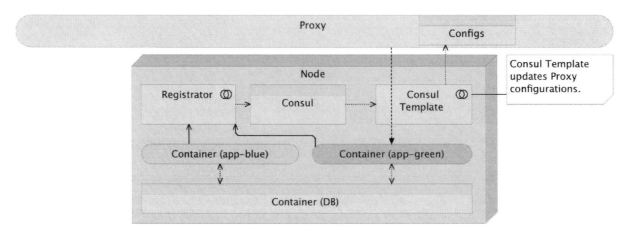

Figure 13-9: The green container integrated with the proxy service

As a result of what we did by now, the new release was deployed in parallel with the old one and proxy was changed to point to that new release. Now we can safely remove the old release.

Removing the Blue Release

Removing a release is easy, and we did it many times before. All we have to do is make sure that the correct target is used when running the stop command.

```
1  docker-compose stop app-blue
2
3  docker-compose ps
```

The first command stopped the blue release, and the second listed all processes specified as Docker Compose targets. The output of the command that list processes is as follows.

```
1       Name              Command              State              Ports
2  ------------------------------------------------------------------------------
3  booksms_app-blue_1    /run.sh              Exit 137
4  booksms_app-green_1   /run.sh              Up        0.0.0.0:32770->8080/tcp
5  booksms_db_1          /entrypoint.sh mongod Up        27017/tcp
```

Please note that the state of the *booksms_app-blue_1* is *Exit 137*. Only the green release and the database containers are running.

We can also confirm the same by sending a request to Consul.

```
1  curl prod:8500/v1/catalog/services | jq '.'
```

The Consul response is as follows.

```
1  {
2    "dockerui": [],
3    "consul": [],
4    "books-ms-green": []
5  }
```

Registrator detected the removal of the blue release and removed it from Consul.

We should also check that the green release is still integrated with the proxy service.

```
1  curl -I prod/api/v1/books
```

As expected, nginx is still sending all requests to the green release and our work is done (for now). To summarize, we deployed a new release in parallel with the old one, changed the proxy service to point to the new release and, once all requests invoked with the old release received their responses, removed the old release.

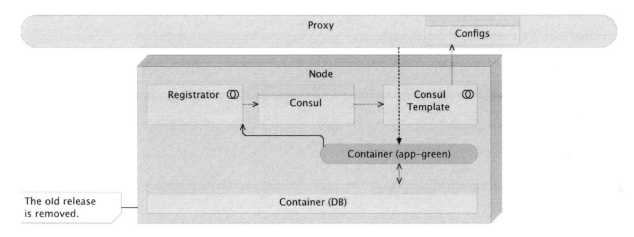

Figure 13-10: The blue container is removed

The only thing left, before we proceed with the automation, is to find a better way to discover which release to deploy (blue or green). While running manually, we can easily find that information by simply listing docker processes or services registered in Consul and observing which color is not running. The automated deployment will require a bit different approach. We should discover which release to run.

Let us remove the containers and start over.

```
1  docker-compose stop
2
3  docker-compose rm -f
```

Discovering Which Release to Deploy and Rolling Back

One way to know which color to deploy next would be to store the deployed color to Consul and use that information for the next deployment. In other words, we should have two processes; color discovery and color registration.

Let's think about use cases of the color discovery. There are three possible combinations

1. We are deploying the first release, and no color is stored in the registry.
2. The blue release is running and stored in the registry.
3. The green release is running and stored in the registry.

We can reduce those combinations to two. If blue color is registered, the next one is green. Otherwise, the next color is blue covering both the case when the current color is green or when no color is registered (when service has never been deployed). With this strategy, we can create the following bash script (please do not run it yet).

```bash
1   #!/usr/bin/env bash
2
3   SERVICE_NAME=$1
4   PROD_SERVER=$2
5
6   CURR_COLOR=`curl \
7       http://$PROD_SERVER:8500/v1/kv/$SERVICE_NAME/color?raw`
8
9   if [ "$CURR_COLOR" == "blue" ]; then
10      echo "green"
11  else
12      echo "blue"
13  fi
```

Since we could use the same script for many services, it accepts two arguments; the name of the service we are about to deploy and the destination (production) server. Then, we query Consul on the production server and put the result into the *CURR_COLOR* variable. That is followed by a simple *if/else* statement that sends the *green* or the *blue* string to *STDOUT*. With such a script, we can easily retrieve the color we should use to deploy a service.

Let's create the script.

```
1   echo '#!/usr/bin/env bash
2
3   SERVICE_NAME=$1
4   PROD_SERVER=$2
5
6   CURR_COLOR=`curl \
7       http://$PROD_SERVER:8500/v1/kv/$SERVICE_NAME/color?raw`
8
9   if [ "$CURR_COLOR" == "blue" ]; then
10      echo "green"
11  else
12      echo "blue"
13  fi
14  ' | tee get-color.sh
15
16  chmod +x get-color.sh
```

We created the *get-color.sh* script and gave it executable permissions. Now we can use it to retrieve the next color and repeat the procedure we practiced before.

```
1   NEXT_COLOR=`./get-color.sh books-ms prod`
2
3   export DOCKER_HOST=tcp://prod:2375
4
5   docker-compose pull app-$NEXT_COLOR
6
7   docker-compose up -d app-$NEXT_COLOR
```

The only difference when compared with the commands we run earlier, is that we're using the *NEXT_COLOR* variable instead of hard-coded values *blue* and *green*. As a result, we have the first release (blue) up and running.

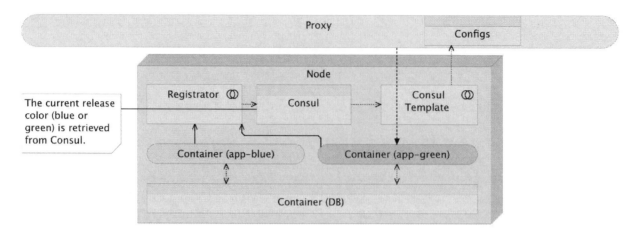

Figure 13-11: The color of the current release is retrieved from Consul

Let's use this opportunity to have a short discussion about testing. On one hand, we want to test as much as possible before we change the proxy to point to the new release. On the other hand, we still need to make one round of tests, after the proxy is changed, to be sure that everything (including the change of the proxy) is running as expected. We'll call those two types *pre-integration tests* and *post-integration tests*. Keep in mind that their scope should be limited to those cases that could not be covered with *pre-deployment* tests. In the case of the (relatively small) *books-ms* service, it should be enough if pre-integration tests verify that the service can communicate with the database. In such a case, the only thing left to check after the integration with the proxy service, is that nginx has been reconfigured correctly.

Let's start with *pre-integration* tests. We'll simulate testing using curl. Since the proxy is still not changed to point to the newly deployed service, we need to find out what the port the newly released service is. We can find the port from Consul and create a script similar to the *get-color.sh*. The script can be created with the following command.

```
1   echo '#!/usr/bin/env bash
2
3   SERVICE_NAME=$1
4   PROD_SERVER=$2
5   COLOR=$3
6
7   echo `curl \
8     $PROD_SERVER:8500/v1/catalog/service/$SERVICE_NAME-$COLOR \
9     | jq ".[0].ServicePort"`
10  ' | tee get-port.sh
11
12  chmod +x get-port.sh
```

This time, we created the script named *get-port.sh* with three arguments; the name of the service, the address of the production server, and the color. With those three arguments, we are querying the information from Consul and sending the result to STDOUT.

Let's try it out.

```
1  NEXT_PORT=`./get-port.sh books-ms prod $NEXT_COLOR`
2
3  echo $NEXT_PORT
```

The output will vary from case to case depending on the random port Docker assigned to our service. With the port stored inside the variable, we can test the service before integrating it with the proxy.

```
1  curl -I prod:$NEXT_PORT/api/v1/books
```

Service returned the status code *200 OK* so we can proceed with the integration in a similar way we did before. When asked, please use *vagrant* as the password.

```
1  consul-template \
2      -consul prod:8500 \
3      -template "nginx-upstreams-$NEXT_COLOR.ctmpl:nginx-upstreams.conf" \
4      -once
5
6  scp nginx-upstreams.conf \
7      prod:/data/nginx/upstreams/books-ms.conf
8
9  docker kill -s HUP nginx
```

With the service integrated, we can test it again but this time without the port.

```
1  curl -I prod/api/v1/books
```

Finally, we should stop one of the containers. Which one should be stopped depends on the testing results. If pre-integration tests failed, we should stop the new release. There is no need to do anything with the proxy since, at this time, it is still sending all requests to the old release. On the other hand, if post-integration tests failed, not only that the new release should be stopped, but we should also revert changes to the proxy service so that all traffic goes back to the old release. At this moment we won't go through all the paths we might need to take in case of tests failures. That will be reserved for the automation that we will explore soon. For now, we'll put the color to Consul registry and stop the old release.

```
1  curl -X PUT -d $NEXT_COLOR \
2      prod:8500/v1/kv/books-ms/color
3
4  CURR_COLOR=`./get-color.sh books-ms prod`
5
6  docker-compose stop app-$CURR_COLOR
```

This set of commands put the new color to the registry, obtained the next color that should be equivalent to the color of the old release, and, finally, stopped the old release. Since we started over and this is the first release, there was no old release to be stopped. Never the less, the next time we run the process, the old release will indeed be stopped.

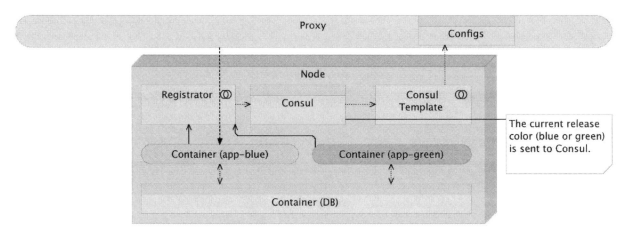

Figure 13-12: The color of the current release is sent to Consul

With this, we concluded the manual process of blue-green deployment. It is done in a way that it can easily be automated. Before we move forward, let's run all those commands few more times and observe that the color changes from blue to green, from green to blue and so on. All the commands grouped together are as follows.

```
1  NEXT_COLOR=`./get-color.sh books-ms prod`
2
3  docker-compose pull app-$NEXT_COLOR
4
5  docker-compose up -d app-$NEXT_COLOR
6
7  NEXT_PORT=`./get-port.sh books-ms prod $NEXT_COLOR`
8
9  consul-template \
10     -consul prod:8500 \
11     -template "nginx-upstreams-$NEXT_COLOR.ctmpl:nginx-upstreams.conf" \
12     -once
```

```
13
14  scp nginx-upstreams.conf \
15      prod:/data/nginx/upstreams/books-ms.conf
16
17  docker kill -s HUP nginx
18
19  curl -I prod/api/v1/books
20
21  curl -X PUT -d $NEXT_COLOR \
22      prod:8500/v1/kv/books-ms/color
23
24  CURR_COLOR=`./get-color.sh books-ms prod`
25
26  docker-compose stop app-$CURR_COLOR
27
28  curl -I prod/api/v1/books
29
30  docker-compose ps
```

The last command showed Docker processes. You will see that, after the first run, the green release will be running, and the blue will be in Exited state, and then, after the next run, the blue release will be running, and the green will be in the Exited state, and so on. We managed to deploy new releases without any downtime. The only exception is if post-integration tests fail, which is very unlikely to happen since the only cause for that would be a failure of the proxy service itself due to the wrong configuration. Since the process will soon be fully automated, such a thing is indeed very unlikely to happen. Another reason for post-integration tests to fail would be if proxy service itself fails. The only way to remove this possibility is to have multiple instances of the proxy service (out of the scope of this book).

That being said, let's see the nginx logs.

```
1  docker logs nginx
```

You'll notice that each request we made was sent to a different port meaning that a new container was indeed deployed and running on a new port.

Now, after all those commands and experiments, we are ready to start working on the automation of the blue-green deployment procedure.

We'll destroy the virtual machines and start over to be sure that everything works correctly.

```
1  exit
2
3  vagrant destroy -f
```

Automating the Blue-Green Deployment with Jenkins Workflow

We'll start by creating the VMs, provisioning the *prod* node, and bringing up Jenkins, our deployment tool of choice.

```
1  vagrant up cd prod
2
3  vagrant ssh cd
4
5  ansible-playbook /vagrant/ansible/prod2.yml \
6      -i /vagrant/ansible/hosts/prod
7
8  ansible-playbook /vagrant/ansible/jenkins-node.yml \
9      -i /vagrant/ansible/hosts/prod
10
11 ansible-playbook /vagrant/ansible/jenkins.yml \
12     -c local
```

Since it will take a couple of minutes until everything is set, let us discuss what should be automated and how. We are already familiar with the Jenkins Workflow. It served us well, so there is no real reason to change the tool at this time. We'll use it to automate the blue-green deployment procedure. The flow will have quite a lot of steps so we'll break them into functions to digest the process more easily and, at the same time, to extend our workflow utilities script. More detailed discussion and implementation of those functions follow.

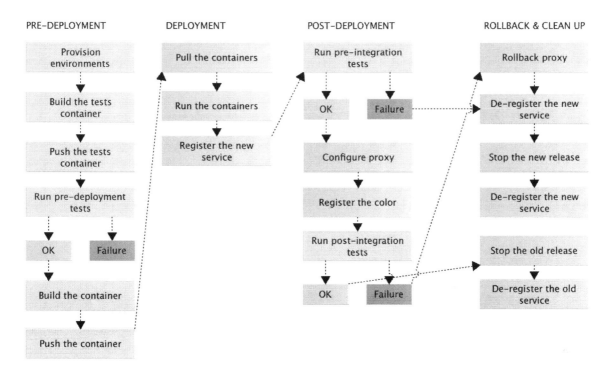

Figure 13-13: Blue-green deployment automation flow

Blue-Green Deployment Role

We'll use the *Multibranch Workflow* jenkins job books-ms-blue-green[212]. It filters branches of the vfarcic/books-ms[213] repository so that only those containing *blue-green* in their names are included.

Since the first run might take a considerable amount of time, let's index branches so that Jenkins can run the subprojects while we explore the script.

Please open the Jenkins Multibranch Workflow job books-ms-blue-green[214], click the *Branch Indexing* and, then, *Run Now* links from the left-hand menu. Once branches are indexed, Jenkins will find that the *blue-green* branch matches the filter set inside the job, create the subproject with the same name and start running it. The indexing status can be seen in the *master* node executor located in the bottom-left part of the screen.

---

[212]http://10.100.198.200:8080/job/books-ms-blue-green/

[213]https://github.com/vfarcic/books-ms/

[214]http://10.100.198.200:8080/job/books-ms-blue-green/

books-ms-blue-green

S	W	Name ↓	Last Success	Last Failure	Last Duration	
		blue-green	10 hr - #14	10 hr - #13	5 min 56 sec	

Icon: S M L

Legend   RSS for all   RSS for failures   RSS for just latest builds

Figure 13-14: The Jenkins Multibranch Workflow job *books-ms-blue-green* with the *blue-green* subproject

We'll leave Jenkins running the build and explore the Jenkinsfile[215] inside the blue-green branch[216].

```
1  node("cd") {
2      def serviceName = "books-ms"
3      def prodIp = "10.100.198.201"
4      def proxyIp = "10.100.198.201"
5      def proxyNode = "prod"
6      def registryIpPort = "10.100.198.200:5000"
7
8      def flow = load "/data/scripts/workflow-util.groovy"
9
10     git url: "https://github.com/vfarcic/${serviceName}.git"
11     flow.provision("prod2.yml")
12     flow.buildTests(serviceName, registryIpPort)
13     flow.runTests(serviceName, "tests", "")
14     flow.buildService(serviceName, registryIpPort)
15
16     def currentColor = flow.getCurrentColor(serviceName, prodIp)
17     def nextColor = flow.getNextColor(currentColor)
18
19     flow.deployBG(serviceName, prodIp, nextColor)
20     flow.runBGPreIntegrationTests(serviceName, prodIp, nextColor)
21     flow.updateBGProxy(serviceName, proxyNode, nextColor)
22     flow.runBGPostIntegrationTests(serviceName, prodIp, proxyIp, proxyNode, curr\
23 entColor, nextColor)
24 }
```

---

[215]https://github.com/vfarcic/books-ms/blob/blue-green/Jenkinsfile
[216]https://github.com/vfarcic/books-ms/tree/blue-green

The file starts with the declaration of a few variables followed by the load of the workflow-util.groovy[217] script. That is followed with invocations of the functions that provision the environments, build and run tests, and build the service. Up until now, the script is the same as the one we explored in the previous chapter.

The first new additions are invocations of the utilities functions[218] *getCurrentColor* and *getNextColor* and assignment of values they return to the *currentColor* and the *nextColor* variables. The functions are as follows.

```groovy
1  def getCurrentColor(serviceName, prodIp) {
2      try {
3          return sendHttpRequest("http://${prodIp}:8500/v1/kv/${serviceName}/color\
4  ?raw")
5      } catch(e) {
6          return ""
7      }
8  }
9
10 def getNextColor(currentColor) {
11     if (currentColor == "blue") {
12         return "green"
13     } else {
14         return "blue"
15     }
16 }
```

As you can see, those functions follow the same logic as the one we practiced with manual commands but, this time, translated to Groovy. The current color is retrieved from Consul and used to deduce the next color we should deploy.

Now that we know what the currently running color is as well as what the next color should be, we can deploy the new release using the *deployBG*. The function is as follows.

```groovy
1  def deployBG(serviceName, prodIp, color) {
2      stage "Deploy"
3      withEnv(["DOCKER_HOST=tcp://${prodIp}:2375"]) {
4          sh "docker-compose pull app-${color}"
5          sh "docker-compose -p ${serviceName} up -d app-${color}"
6      }
7  }
```

[217]https://github.com/vfarcic/ms-lifecycle/blob/master/ansible/roles/jenkins/files/scripts/workflow-util.groovy
[218]https://github.com/vfarcic/ms-lifecycle/blob/master/ansible/roles/jenkins/files/scripts/workflow-util.groovy

We created the *DOCKER_HOST* environment variable pointing to Docker CLI running on the production node. The variable scope is limited to the commands within its curly braces. Inside them, we are pulling the latest release and running it through Docker Compose. The only important difference when, compared with the *Jenkinsfile* script we explored in the previous chapter, is the dynamic generation of the target through the *color* variable. The target that will be used depends on the actual value of the *nextColor* used to invoke this function.

At this point in the script, a new release is deployed but still not integrated with the proxy service. The users of our service would still be using the old release thus giving us the opportunity to test the newly deployed version before making it publicly available. We'll call them *pre-integration tests*. They are run by invoking the utility function *runBGPreIntegrationTests* located in the workflow-util.groovy[219] script.

```
 1  def runBGPreIntegrationTests(serviceName, prodIp, color) {
 2      stage "Run pre-integration tests"
 3      def address = getAddress(serviceName, prodIp, color)
 4      try {
 5          runTests(serviceName, "integ", "-e DOMAIN=http://${address}")
 6      } catch(e) {
 7          stopBG(serviceName, prodIp, color);
 8          error("Pre-integration tests failed")
 9      }
10  }
```

The function starts by retrieving the address of the newly deployed service from Consul. This retrieval is accomplished through invocation of the *getAddress* function. Please consult the details of the function by examining the workflow-util.groovy[220] script. Next, we run the tests inside a *try/catch* block. Since the new release is still not integrated with *nginx* and, therefore, not accessible through the port *80*, we are passing the *address* of the release as an environment variable *DOMAIN*. If the execution of tests fails, the script will jump to the *catch* block and call the *stopBG* function that will stop the new release. Since our servers are running [Registrator], once the new release is stopped, its data will be removed from Consul. There's nothing else to be done. Proxy service will continue pointing to the old release, and, through it, our users will continue using the old version of our service that is proven to work correctly. Please consult the workflow-util.groovy[221] script to see details of the *stopBG* function.

If the *pre-integration* tests passed, we are invoking the *updateBGProxy* function that updates the proxy service thus making our new release available to our users. The function is as follows.

---

[219]https://github.com/vfarcic/ms-lifecycle/blob/master/ansible/roles/jenkins/files/scripts/workflow-util.groovy

[220]https://github.com/vfarcic/ms-lifecycle/blob/master/ansible/roles/jenkins/files/scripts/workflow-util.groovy

[221]https://github.com/vfarcic/ms-lifecycle/blob/master/ansible/roles/jenkins/files/scripts/workflow-util.groovy

```
 1  def updateBGProxy(serviceName, proxyNode, color) {
 2      stage "Update proxy"
 3      stash includes: 'nginx-*', name: 'nginx'
 4      node(proxyNode) {
 5          unstash 'nginx'
 6          sh "sudo cp nginx-includes.conf /data/nginx/includes/${serviceName}.conf"
 7          sh "sudo consul-template \
 8              -consul localhost:8500 \
 9              -template \"nginx-upstreams-${color}.ctmpl:/data/nginx/upstreams/${s\
10  erviceName}.conf:docker kill -s HUP nginx\" \
11              -once"
12          sh "curl -X PUT -d ${color} http://localhost:8500/v1/kv/${serviceName}/c\
13  olor"
14      }
15  }
```

The major difference, when compared with the *updateProxy* function we used in the previous chapter, is the usage of *nginx-upstreams-${color}.ctmpl* as the name of the template. Depending on the value we pass to the function, *nginx-upstreams-blue.ctmpl* or *nginx-upstreams-green.ctmpl* will be used. As an additional instruction, we are sending a request to Consul to store the color related to the newly deployed release. The rest of this function is the same as the *updateProxy*.

Finally, now that the new release is deployed, and the proxy service has been reconfigured, we are doing another round of testing to confirm that the integration with the proxy was indeed correct. We're doing that by invoking the *runBGPostIntegrationTests* function located in the workflow-util.groovy[222] script.

```
 1  def runBGPostIntegrationTests(serviceName, prodIp, proxyIp, proxyNode, currentCo\
 2  lor, nextColor) {
 3      stage "Run post-integration tests"
 4      try {
 5          runTests(serviceName, "integ", "-e DOMAIN=http://${proxyIp}")
 6      } catch(e) {
 7          if (currentColor != "") {
 8              updateBGProxy(serviceName, proxyNode, currentColor)
 9          }
10          stopBG(serviceName, prodIp, nextColor);
11          error("Post-integration tests failed")
12      }
13      stopBG(serviceName, prodIp, currentColor);
14  }
```

---

[222]https://github.com/vfarcic/ms-lifecycle/blob/master/ansible/roles/jenkins/files/scripts/workflow-util.groovy

We start by running integration tests that are, this time, using the public domain that points to the proxy. If tests fail, we are reverting the changes to the proxy service by invoking the *updateBGProxy* function. By passing the *currentColor* as the variable, *updateBGProxy* will reconfigure nginx to work with the old release of the service. The second instruction in case of a failure of tests is to stop the new release by invoking the *stopBG* function with *nextColor*. On the other hand, if all tests passed, we are stopping the old release.

If you are new to Groovy, this script might have been overwhelming. However, with a little bit of practice, you'll see that, for our purposes, Groovy is very simple and with the addition of Jenkins Workflow DSL, many things are made even easier.

It is worth noting that the Workflow plugin is restrictive. For security reasons, invocation of some Groovy classes and functions needs to be approved. I already did that for you as part of the provisioning and configuration process defined through the jenkins.yml[223] Ansible playbook. If you'd like to see the end result or would need to make new approvals, please open In-process Script Approval[224] screen located inside *Manage Jenkins*. At first, those security restrictions might seem over-the-top, but the reasoning behind them is essential. Since Workflow scripts can access almost any part of the Jenkins platform, letting anything run inside it might have very severe consequences. For that reason, some instructions are allowed by default while others need to be approved. If a Workflow script fails due to this restriction, you'll see a new entry in the In-process Script Approval[225] screen waiting for your approval (or disapproval). The XML behind those approvals is located in the */data/jenkins/scriptApproval.xml* file.

Running the Blue-Green Deployment

Hopefully, by this time, the subproject finished running. You can monitor the process by opening blue-green subproject Console screen[226]. Once the first run of the subproject is finished, we can manually confirm that everything run correctly. We'll use this opportunity to showcase few *ps* arguments we haven't used. The first one will be *–filter* that can be used to (you guessed it) filter containers returned with the *ps* command. The second one is *–format*. Since the standard output of the *ps* command can be very long, we'll use it to retrieve only names of the containers.

```
1  export DOCKER_HOST=tcp://prod:2375
2
3  docker ps -a --filter name=books --format "table {{.Names}}"
```

The output of the *ps* command is as follows.

---

[223]https://github.com/vfarcic/ms-lifecycle/blob/master/ansible/jenkins.yml
[224]http://10.100.198.200:8080/scriptApproval/
[225]http://10.100.198.200:8080/scriptApproval/
[226]http://10.100.198.200:8080/job/books-ms-blue-green/branch/blue-green/lastBuild/console

```
1  NAMES
2  booksms_app-blue_1
3  booksms_db_1
```

We can see that the *blue* release has been deployed together with the linked database. We can also confirm that the service has been stored in Consul.

```
1  curl prod:8500/v1/catalog/services | jq '.'
2
3  curl prod:8500/v1/catalog/service/books-ms-blue | jq '.'
```

The combined output of the two requests to Consul is as follows.

```
1  {
2    "dockerui": [],
3    "consul": [],
4    "books-ms-blue": []
5  }
6  ...
7  [
8    {
9      "ModifyIndex": 461,
10     "CreateIndex": 461,
11     "Node": "prod",
12     "Address": "10.100.198.201",
13     "ServiceID": "prod:booksms_app-blue_1:8080",
14     "ServiceName": "books-ms-blue",
15     "ServiceTags": [],
16     "ServiceAddress": "10.100.198.201",
17     "ServicePort": 32780,
18     "ServiceEnableTagOverride": false
19   }
20 ]
```

The *books-ms-blue* has been registered as a service besides the *dockerui* and *consul*. The second output shows all the details of the service.

Finally, we should verify that the color has been stored in Consul and that the service itself is indeed integrated with *nginx*.

```
1  curl prod:8500/v1/kv/books-ms/color?raw
2
3  curl -I prod/api/v1/books
```

The first command returned *blue*, and the status of the request to the service through the proxy is *200 OK*. Everything seems to be working correctly.

Please run the job a couple of more times by opening the books-ms-blue-green[227] job and clicking the *Schedule a build for blue-green* icon located on the right-hand side.

You can monitor the process by opening the blue-green subproject Console screen[228].

 **Console Output**

```
Started by user anonymous
Setting origin to https://github.com/vfarcic/books-ms.git
Fetching origin...
 > git rev-parse --is-inside-work-tree # timeout=10
Fetching changes from the remote Git repository
 > git config remote.origin.url https://github.com/vfarcic/books-ms.git # timeout=10
Fetching upstream changes from https://github.com/vfarcic/books-ms.git
 > git --version # timeout=10
 > git -c core.askpass=true fetch --tags --progress https://github.com/vfarcic/books-ms.git
+refs/heads/*:refs/remotes/origin/*
Checking out Revision 9bd4831c78439cdaa7d48abc8fa7ca7df4734cc6 (blue-green)
 > git config core.sparsecheckout # timeout=10
 > git checkout -f 9bd4831c78439cdaa7d48abc8fa7ca7df4734cc6
 > git rev-list 9bd4831c78439cdaa7d48abc8fa7ca7df4734cc6 # timeout=10
[Workflow] Allocate node : Start
Running on cd in /data/jenkins_slaves/cd/workspace/books-ms-blue-green/blue-green
[Workflow] node {
[Workflow] load: Loaded script: /data/scripts/workflow-util.groovy
[Workflow] load {
[Workflow] } //load
[Workflow] echo
CURRENT COLOR: green
[Workflow] echo
NEXT COLOR: blue
[Workflow] git
 > git rev-parse --is-inside-work-tree # timeout=10
Fetching changes from the remote Git repository
 > git config remote.origin.url https://github.com/vfarcic/books-ms.git # timeout=10
Fetching upstream changes from https://github.com/vfarcic/books-ms.git
 > git --version # timeout=10
 > git -c core.askpass=true fetch --tags --progress https://github.com/vfarcic/books-ms.git
+refs/heads/*:refs/remotes/origin/*
 > git rev-parse refs/remotes/origin/master^{commit} # timeout=10
 > git rev-parse refs/remotes/origin/origin/master^{commit} # timeout=10
Checking out Revision 0e10f5d070252e1a7e46ca13aaefac494c3177a2 (refs/remotes/origin/master)
```

Figure 13-15: The Jenkins *blue-green* subproject Console screen

If you repeat the manual verifications, you'll notice that the second time the *green* release will be running, and the *blue* will be stopped. The third run will invert colors and the *blue* release will be

---

[227]http://10.100.198.200:8080/job/books-ms-blue-green/

[228]http://10.100.198.200:8080/job/books-ms-blue-green/branch/blue-green/lastBuild/console

running while the *green* will be stopped. The correct color will be stored in Consul, proxy service will always redirect requests to the latest release, and there will be no downtime during the deployment process.

Even though we are reaching the end of this chapter, we are not finished practicing the blue-green deployment. Even though we will change the way we are running the procedure, it will be the integral part of a couple of more practices we'll explore throughout the rest of this book. We accomplished zero-downtime deployments, but there is still a lot of work left before we reach zero-downtime system. The fact that our current process does not produce downtime during deployments does not mean that the whole system is fault tolerant.

We reached a significant milestone, yet there are still a lot of obstacles left to overcome. One of them is clustering and scaling. The solution we have works well on a single server. We could easily extend it to support a few more, maybe even ten. However, the bigger the number of our servers, the greater the need to look for a better way to manage clustering and scaling. That will be the subject of the next chapter. Until then, let us destroy the environments we've been using so that we can start fresh.

```
1  exit
2
3  vagrant destroy -f
```

Clustering And Scaling Services

Organizations which design systems ... are constrained to produce designs which are copies of the communication structures of these organizations

– M. Conway

Many will tell you that they have a *scalable system*. After all, scaling is easy. Buy a server, install WebLogic (or whichever other monster application server you're using) and deploy your applications. Then wait for a few weeks until you discover that everything is so "fast" that you can click a button, have some coffee, and, by the time you get back to your desk, the result will be waiting for you. What do you do? You scale. You buy few more servers, install your monster applications servers and deploy your monster applications on top of them. Which part of the system was the bottleneck? Nobody knows. Why did you duplicate everything? Because you must. And then some more time passes, and you continue scaling until you run out of money and, simultaneously, people working for you go crazy. Today we do not approach scaling like that. Today we understand that scaling is about many other things. It's about elasticity. It's about being able to quickly and easily scale and de-scale depending on variations in your traffic and growth of your business, and that, during that process, you should not go bankrupt. It's about the need of almost every company to scale their business without thinking that IT department is a liability. It's about getting rid of those monsters.

Scalability

Let us, for a moment take a step back and discuss why we want to scale applications. The main reason is *high availability*. Why do we want high availability? We want it because we want our business to be available under any load. The bigger the load, the better (unless you are under DDoS). It means that our business is booming. With high availability our users are happy. We all want speed, and many of us simply leave the site if it takes too long to load. We want to avoid having outages because every minute our business is not operational can be translated into a money loss. What would you do if an online store is not available? Probably go to another. Maybe not the first time, maybe not the second, but, sooner or later, you would get fed up and switch it for another. We are used to everything being fast and responsive, and there are so many alternatives that we do not think twice before trying something else. And if that something else turns up to be better... One man's loss is another man's gain. Do we solve all our problems with scalability? Not even close. Many other factors decide the availability of our applications. However, scalability is an important part of it, and it happens to be the subject of this chapter.

What is scalability? It is a property of a system that indicates its ability to handle increased load in a graceful manner or its potential to be enlarged as demand increases. It is the ability to accept increased volume or traffic.

The truth is that the way we design our applications dictates the scaling options available. Applications will not scale well if they are not designed to scale. That is not to say that an application not designed for scaling cannot scale. Everything can scale, but not everything can scale well.

Commonly observed scenario is as follows.

We start with a simple architecture, sometimes with load balancer sometimes without, setup a few application servers and one database. Everything is great, complexity is low, and we can develop new features very fast. The cost of operations is low, income is high (considering that we just started), and everyone is happy and motivated.

Business is growing, and the traffic is increasing. Things are beginning to fail, and performance is dropping. Firewalls are added, additional load balancers are set up, the database is scaled, more application servers are added and so on. Things are still relatively simple. We are faced with new challenges, but obstacles can be overcome in time. Even though the complexity is increasing, we can still handle it with relative ease. In other words, what we're doing is still more or less the same but bigger. Business is doing well, but it is still relatively small.

And then it happens. The big thing you've been waiting for. Maybe one of the marketing campaigns hit the spot. Maybe there was a negative change in your competition. Maybe that last feature was indeed a killer one. No matter the reasons, business got a big boost. After a short period of happiness due to this change, your pain increases tenfold. Adding more databases does not seem to be enough. Multiplying application servers does not appear to fulfill the needs. You start adding caching and what so not. You start getting the feeling that every time you multiply something, benefits are not equally big. Costs increase, and you are still not able to meet the demand. Database replications are too slow. New application servers do not make such a big difference anymore. Operational costs are increasing faster than you expected. The situation hurts the business and the team. You are starting to realize that the architecture you were so proud of cannot fulfill this increase in load. You can not split it. You cannot scale things that hurt the most. You cannot start over. All you can do is continue multiplying with ever decreasing benefits of such actions.

The situation described above is quite common. What was good at the beginning, is not necessarily right when the demand increases. We need to balance the need for YAGNI (You Ain't Gonna Need It) principle and the longer term vision. We cannot start with the system optimized for large companies because it is too expensive and does not provide enough benefits when business is small. On the other hand, we cannot lose the focus from one of the main objectives of any business. We cannot not think about scaling from the very first day. Designing scalable architecture does not mean that we need to start with a cluster of a hundred servers. It does not mean that we have to develop something big and complex from the start. It means that we should start small, but in the way that, when it becomes big, it is easy to scale. While microservices are not the only way to accomplish that goal, they are indeed a good way to approach this problem. The cost is not in development but operations. If operations are automated, that cost can be absorbed quickly and does not need to represent a massive investment.

As you already saw (and will continue seeing throughout the rest of the book), there are excellent open source tools at our disposal. The best part of automation is that the investment tends to have lower maintenance cost than when things are done manually.

We already discussed microservices and automation of their deployments on a tiny scale. Now it's time to convert this small scale to something bigger. Before we jump into practical parts, let us explore what are some of the different ways one might approach scaling.

We are often limited by our design and choosing the way applications are constructed limits our choices severely. Although there are many different ways to scale, most common one is called *Axis Scaling*.

Axis Scaling

Axis scaling can be best represented through three dimensions of a cube; *x-axis*, *y-axis* and *z-axis*. Each of those dimensions describes a type of scaling.

- X-Axis: Horizontal duplication
- Y-Axis: Functional decomposition
- Z-Axis: Data partitioning

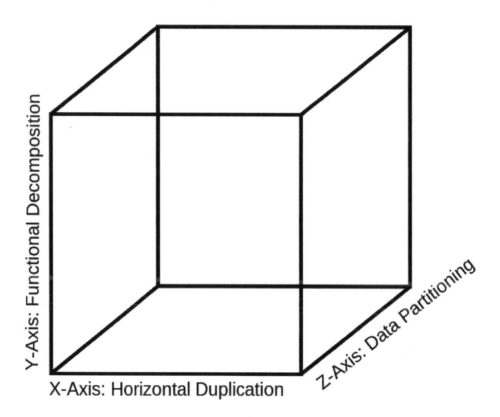

Figure 14-1: Scale cube

Let's go through axes, one at the time.

X-Axis Scaling

In a nutshell, *x-axis scaling* is accomplished by running multiple instances of an application or a service. In most cases, there is a load balancer on top that makes sure that the traffic is shared among all those instances. The biggest advantage of x-axis scaling is simplicity. All we have to do is deploy the same application on multiple servers. For that reason, this is the most commonly used type of scaling. However, it comes with its set of disadvantages when applied to monolithic applications. Having a huge application usually requires big cache that demands heavy usage of memory. When such an application is multiplied, everything is multiplied by it, including the cache. Another, often more important, problem is inappropriate usage of resources. Performance problems are almost never related to the whole application. Not all modules are equally affected, and, yet, we multiply everything. That means that even though we could be better of by scaling only part of the application that require such an action, we scale everything. Never the less, x-scaling is important no matter the architecture. The major difference is the effect that such a scaling has. By using microservices, we are not removing the need for x-axis scaling but making sure that due to their architecture such scaling has more effect than with alternative and more traditional approaches to architecture. With microservices we have the option to fine-tune scaling. We can have many instances of services that suffer a lot under heavy load and only a few instances of those that are used less often or require fewer resources. On top of that, since they are small, we might never reach a limit of a service. A small service in a big server would need to receive a truly massive amount of traffic before the need for scaling arises. Scaling microservices is more often related to fault tolerance than performance problems. We want to have multiple copies running so that, if one of them dies, the others can take over until recovery is performed.

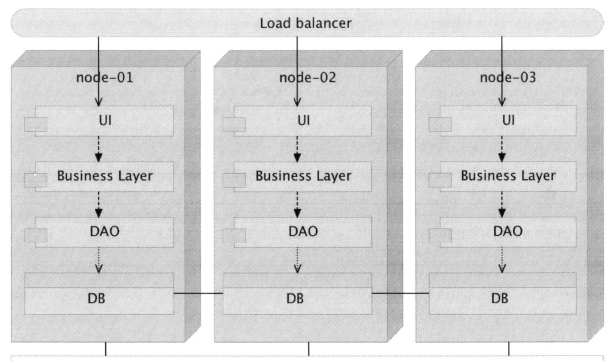

Figure 14-2: Monolithic application scaled inside a cluster

Y-Axis Scaling

Y-axis scaling is all about decomposition of an application into smaller services. Even though there are different ways to accomplish this decomposition, microservices are probably the best approach we can take. When they are combined with immutability and self-sufficiency, there is indeed no better alternative (at least from the prism of y-axis scaling). Unlike x-axis scaling, the y-axis is not accomplished by running multiple instances of the same application but by having multiple different services distributed across the cluster.

Z-Axis Scaling

Z-axis scaling is rarely applied to applications or services. Its primary and most common usage is among databases. The idea behind this type of scaling is to distribute data among multiple servers thus reducing the amount of work that each of them needs to perform. Data is partitioned and distributed so that each server needs to deal only with a subset of the data. This type of the separation is often called sharding, and there are many databases specially designed for this purpose. Benefits of z-axis scaling are most noticeable in I/O and cache and memory utilization.

Clustering

A server cluster consists of a set of connected servers that work together and can be seen as a single system. They are usually connected through fast local area network (LAN). The major difference between a cluster and simply a group of servers is that the cluster acts as a single system trying to provide high availability, load balancing, and parallel processing.

If we deploy applications, or services, to individually managed servers and treat them as separate units, the utilization of resources is sub-optimum. We cannot know in advance which group of services should be deployed to a server and utilize resources to their maximum. More importantly, resource usage tends to fluctuate. While, in the morning, some service might require a lot of memory, during the afternoon that usage might be lower. Having predefined servers does not allow us elasticity that would balance that usage in the best possible way. Even if such a high level of dynamism is not required, predefined servers tend to create problems when something goes wrong, resulting in manual actions to redeploy the affected services to a healthy node.

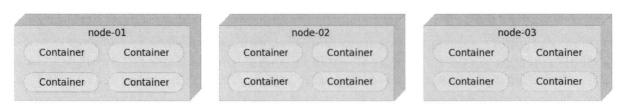

Figure 14-3: Cluster with containers deployed to predefined servers

Real clustering is accomplished when we stop thinking in terms of individual servers and start thinking of a cluster; of all servers as one big entity. That can be better explained if we drop to a bit lower level. When we deploy an application, we tend to specify how much memory or CPU it might need. However, we do not decide which memory slots our application will use nor which CPUs it should utilize. For example, we don't specify that some application should use CPUs 4, 5 and 7. That would be inefficient and potentially dangerous. We only decide that three CPUs are required. The same approach should be taken on a higher level. We should not care where an application or a service will be deployed but what it needs. We should be able to define that the service has certain requirements and tell some tool to deploy it to whichever server in our cluster, as long as it fulfills the needs we have. The best (if not the only) way to accomplish that is to consider the whole cluster as one entity. We can increase or decrease the capacity of that cluster by adding or removing servers but, no matter what we do, it should still be a single entity. We define a strategy and let our services be deployed somewhere inside the cluster. Those using cloud providers like Amazon Web Services (AWS), Microsoft's Azure and Google Cloud Engine (GCP) are already accustomed to this approach, even though they might not be aware of it.

Throughout the rest of this chapter, we'll explore ways to create our cluster and explore tools that can help us with that objective. The fact that we'll be simulating the cluster locally does not mean that the same strategies cannot be applied to public or private clouds and data centers. Quite the opposite.

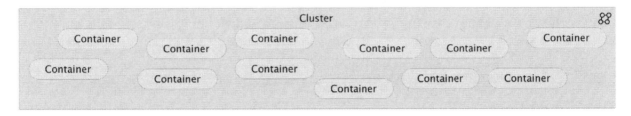

Figure 14-4: Cluster with containers deployed to servers based on a predefined strategy

Docker Clustering Tools Compared: Kubernetes vs Docker Swarm vs Mesos

Kubernetes and Docker Swarm are probably the two most commonly used tools to deploy containers inside a cluster. Both are created as helper platforms that can be used to manage a cluster of containers and treat all servers as a single unit. While their goals are, somewhat, similar, they differ considerably in their approach.

Kubernetes

Kubernetes[229] is based on Google's experience of many years working with Linux containers. It is, in a way, a replica of what Google has been doing for a long time but, this time, adapted to Docker. That approach is great in many ways, most important being that they used their experience from the start. If you started using Kubernetes around Docker version 1.0 (or earlier), the experience with Kubernetes was great. It solved many of the problems that Docker itself had. We can mount persistent volumes that allow us to move containers without losing data, it uses flannel[230] to create networking between containers, it has load balancer integrated, it uses etcd[231] for service discovery, and so on. However, Kubernetes comes at a cost. When compared with Docker, it uses a different CLI, different API, and different YAML definitions. In other words, you cannot use Docker CLI, nor you can use Docker Compose[232] to define containers. Everything needs to be done from scratch exclusively for

---

[229] http://kubernetes.io/
[230] https://github.com/coreos/flannel
[231] https://github.com/coreos/etcd
[232] https://docs.docker.com/compose/

Kubernetes. It's as if the tool was not written for Docker (which is partly true). Kubernetes brought clustering to a new level but at the expense of usability and steep learning curve.

Docker Swarm

Docker Swarm[233] took a different approach. It is a native clustering for Docker. The best part is that it exposes standard Docker API meaning that any tool that you used to communicate with Docker (Docker CLI, Docker Compose, Dokku, Krane, and so on) can work equally well with Docker Swarm. That in itself is both an advantage and a disadvantage at the same time. Being able to use familiar tools of your choosing is great but for the same reasons we are bound by the limitations of Docker API. If the Docker API doesn't support something, there is no way around it through Swarm API, and some clever tricks need to be performed.

Apache Mesos

The next in line of tools that can be used to manage a cluster is Apache Mesos[234]. It is the clustering veteran. Mesos abstracts CPU, memory, storage, and other resources away from machines (physical or virtual), enabling fault-tolerant and elastic distributed systems to be easily built and run efficiently.

Mesos is made using the same principles as the Linux kernel, only at a different level of abstraction. Mesos kernel runs on every machine and provides applications with APIs for resource management and scheduling across entire datacenter and cloud environments. Unlike Kubernetes and Docker Swarm, Mesos is not limited to containers. It can work with almost any type of deployments including Docker containers.

Mesos uses Zookeeper for service discovery. It uses Linux containers to isolate processes. If, for example, we deploy Hadoop without using Docker, Mesos will run it as a native Linux container providing similar features as if we packed it as a Docker container.

Mesos provides few features that Swarm doesn't have at this moment, mainly more powerful scheduler. Apart from the scheduler, what makes Mesos attractive is that we can use it for both Docker and non-Docker deployments. Many organizations might not want to use Docker, or they might decide to use a combination of both Docker and non-Docker deployments. In such a case, Mesos is truly an excellent option if we do not want to deal with two sets of clustering tools; one for containers and the other for the rest of deployments.

However, Mesos is old and too big for what we're trying to accomplish. More importantly, Docker containers are an afterthought. The platform was not designed with them in mind but added Docker support later on. Working with Docker and Mesos feels awkward, and it becomes apparent from the very start that those two were not meant to be used together. Given the existence of Swarm and Kubernetes, there is nothing that Mesos can offer to those decided to embrace Docker. Mesos

---

[233]https://docs.docker.com/swarm/

[234]http://mesos.apache.org/

is falling behind. The main advantage it has over the other two tools is its wide adoption. Many started using it before the emergence of Docker and might choose stick with it. For those that have the option to start fresh, the choice should fall between Kubernetes and Docker Swarm.

We'll explore Docker Swarm in more details and leave Kubernetes and Mesos behind. The exploration will be based on its setup and features it provides for running containers in a cluster.

Setting It Up

Setting up Docker Swarm is easy, straightforward and flexible. All we have to do is install one of the service discovery tools and run the *swarm* container on all nodes. Since the distribution itself is packed in a Docker container, it works in the same way no matter the operating system. We run the *swarm* container, expose a port and inform it about the address of the service discovery. It could hardly be easier than that. We can even start using it without any service discovery tool, see whether we like it and when our usage of it becomes more serious, add etcd[235], Consul[236] or some of the other supported tools.

Kubernetes setup is quite more complicated and obfuscated. Installation instructions differ from OS to OS and provider to provider. Each OS or a hosting provider comes with its set of instructions, each of them having a separate maintenance team with a different set of problems. As an example, if you choose to try it out with Vagrant, you are stuck with Fedora. That does not mean that you cannot run it with Vagrant and, let's say, Ubuntu or CoreOS. You can, but you need to start searching for instructions outside the official Kubernetes Getting Started[237] page. Whatever your needs are, it's likely that the community has the solution, but you still need to spend some time searching for it and hoping that it works from the first attempt. The bigger problem is that the installation relies on a bash script. That would not be a big deal in itself if we would not live in the era where configuration management is a must. We might not want to run a script but make Kubernetes be part of our Puppet[238], Chef[239], or Ansible[240] definitions. Again, this can be overcome as well. You can find Ansible playbooks for running Kubernetes, or you can write your own. None of those issues are a big problem but, when compared with Swarm, they are a bit painful. With Docker, we were supposed not to have installation instructions (aside from a few `docker run` arguments). We were supposed to run containers. Swarm fulfills that promise, and Kubernetes doesn't.

While some might not care about which discovery tool is used, I love the simplicity of Swarm and the logic "batteries included but removable". Everything works out-of-the-box, but we still have the option to substitute one component for the other. Unlike Swarm, Kubernetes is an opinionated tool. You need to live with the choices it made for you. If you want to use Kubernetes, you have to use etcd. I'm not trying to say that etcd is bad (quite contrary), but if you prefer, for example, to use Consul, you're in a very complicated situation and would need to use one for Kubernetes and the

---

[235] https://github.com/coreos/etcd

[236] https://www.consul.io/

[237] http://kubernetes.io/gettingstarted/

[238] https://puppetlabs.com/

[239] https://www.chef.io/

[240] http://www.ansible.com/

other for the rest of your service discovery needs. Another thing I dislike about Kubernetes is its need to know things in advance, before the setup. You need to tell it the addresses of all your nodes, which role each of them has, how many minions there are in the cluster and so on. With Swarm, we just bring up a node and tell it to join the network. Nothing needs to be set in advance since the information about the cluster is propagated through the *gossip* protocol.

Setup might not be the most significant difference between those tools. No matter which tool you choose, sooner or later everything will be up and running, and you'll forget any trouble you might have had during the process. You might say that we should not choose one tool over the other only because one is easier to set up. Fair enough. Let's move on and speak about differences in how you define containers that should be run with those tools.

Running Containers

How do you define all the arguments needed for running Docker containers with Swarm? You don't! Actually, you do, but not in any form or way different from the way you were defining them before Swarm. If you are used to running containers through Docker CLI, you can keep using it with (almost) the same commands. If you prefer to use Docker Compose to run containers, you can continue using it to run them inside the Swarm cluster. Whichever way you've used to run your containers, the chances are that you can continue doing the same with Swarm but on a much larger scale.

Kubernetes requires you to learn its CLI and configurations. You cannot use *docker-compose.yml* definitions you created earlier. You'll have to create Kubernetes equivalents. You cannot use Docker CLI commands you learned before. You'll have to learn Kubernetes CLI and, likely, make sure that the whole organization learns it as well.

No matter which tool you choose for deployments to your cluster, chances are you are already familiar with Docker. You are probably already used to Docker Compose as a way to define arguments for the containers you'll run. If you played with it for more than a few hours, you are using it as a substitute for Docker CLI. You run containers with it, tail their logs, scale them, and so on. On the other hand, you might be a hard-core Docker user who does not like Docker Compose and prefers running everything through Docker CLI or you might have your bash scripts that run containers for you. No matter what you choose, it should work with Docker Swarm.

If you adopt Kubernetes, be prepared to have multiple definitions of the same thing. You will need Docker Compose to run your containers outside Kubernetes. Developers will continue needing to run containers on their laptops, your staging environments might or might not be a big cluster, and so on. In other words, once you adopt Docker, Docker Compose or Docker CLI are unavoidable. You have to use them one way or another. Once you start using Kubernetes you will discover that all your Docker Compose definitions (or whatever else you might be using) need to be translated to Kubernetes way of describing things and, from there on, you will have to maintain both. With Kubernetes, everything will have to be duplicated resulting in higher cost of maintenance. And it's not only about duplicated configurations. Commands you'll run outside the cluster will be different from those inside the cluster. All those Docker commands you learned and love will have to get their Kubernetes equivalents inside the cluster.

Guys behind Kubernetes are not trying to make your life miserable by forcing you to do things "their way". The reason for such a big differences is in different approaches Swarm and Kubernetes are using to tackle the same problem. Swarm team decided to match their API with the one from Docker. As a result, we have (almost) full compatibility. Almost everything we can do with Docker we can do with Swarm as well only on a much larger scale. There's nothing new to do, no configurations to be duplicated and nothing new to learn. No matter whether you use Docker CLI directly or go through Swarm, API is (more or less) the same. The negative side of that story is that if there is something you'd like Swarm to do and that something is not part of the Docker API, you're in for a disappointment. Let us simplify this a bit. If you're looking for a tool for deploying containers in a cluster that will use Docker API, Swarm is the solution. On the other hand, if you want a tool that will overcome Docker limitations, you should go with Kubernetes. It is power (Kubernetes) against simplicity (Swarm). Or, at least, that's how it was until recently. But, I'm jumping ahead of myself.

The only question unanswered is what those limitations are. Two of the major ones were networking, persistent volumes and automatic failover in case one or more containers or a whole node stopped working.

Until Docker Swarm release 1.0 we could not link containers running on different servers. We still cannot link them, but now we have *multi-host networking* to help us connect containers running on different servers. It is a very powerful feature. Kubernetes used flannel[241] to accomplish networking and now, since the Docker release 1.9, that feature is available as part of Docker CLI.

Another problem was persistent volumes. Docker introduced them in release 1.9. Until recently, if you persist a volume, that container was tied to the server that volume resides. It could not be moved around without, again, resorting to some nasty tricks like copying volume directory from one server to another. That in itself is a slow operation that defies the goals of the tools like Swarm. Besides, even if you have time to copy a volume from one to the other server, you do not know where to copy since clustering tools tend to treat your whole datacenter as a single entity. Your containers will be deployed to a location most suitable for them (least number of containers running, most CPUs or memory available, and so on). Now we have persistent volumes supported by Docker natively.

Finally, automatic failover is probably the only feature advantage Kubernetes has over Swarm. However, failover solution provided by Kuberentes is incomplete. If a container goes down, Kubernetes will detect that and start it again on a healthy node. The problem is that containers or whole nodes often do not fail for no reason. Much more needs to be done than a simple re-deployment. Someone needs to be notified, information before a failure needs to be evaluated, and so on. If re-deployment is all you need, Kubernetes is a good solution. If more is needed, Swarm, due to its "batteries included but removable" philosophy, allows you to build your solution. Regarding the failover, it's a question whether to aim for an out-of-the-box solution (Kubernetes) that is hard to extend or go for a solution that is built with the intention to be easily extended (Swarm).

Both networking and persistent volumes problems were one of the features supported by Kubernetes

---

[241]https://github.com/coreos/flannel

for quite some time and the reason many were choosing it over Swarm. That advantage disappeared with Docker release 1.9. Automatic fail-over remains an advantage Kubernetes has over Swarm when looking at out-of-the-box solutions. In the case of Swarm, we need to develop failover strategies ourselves.

The Choice

When trying to make a choice between Docker Swarm and Kubernetes, think in following terms. Do you want to depend on Docker solving problems related to clustering. If you do, choose Swarm. If Docker does not support something, it will be unlikely that it will be supported by Swarm since it relies on Docker API. On the other hand, if you want a tool that works around Docker limitations, Kubernetes might be the right one for you. Kubernetes was not built around Docker but is based on Google's experience with containers. It is opinionated and tries to do things in its own way.

The real question is whether Kubernetes' way of doing things, which is quite different from how we use Docker, is overshadowed by advantages it gives. Or, should we place our bets into Docker itself and hope that it will solve those problems? Before you answer those questions, take a look at the Docker release 1.9. We got persistent volumes and software networking. We also got *unless-stopped* restart policy that will manage our unwanted failures. Now, there are three things less of a difference between Kubernetes and Swarm. Actually, these days there are very few advantages Kubernetes has over Swarm. Automatic failover featured by Kubernetes is a blessing and a curse at the same time. On the other hand, Swarm uses Docker API meaning that you get to keep all your commands and Docker Compose configurations. Personally, I'm placing my bets on Docker engine getting improvements and Docker Swarm running on top of it. The difference between the two is small. Both are production ready but Swarm is easier to set up, easier to use and we get to keep everything we built before moving to the cluster; there is no duplication between cluster and non-cluster configurations.

My recommendation is to go with Docker Swarm. Kubernetes is too opinionated, hard to set up, too different from Docker CLI/API and at the same time, besides automatic failover, it doesn't have real advantages over Swarm since the Docker release 1.9. That doesn't mean that there are no features available in Kubernetes that are not supported by Swarm. There are feature differences in both directions. However, those differences are, in my opinion, not significant ones and the gap is getting smaller with each Docker release. Actually, for many use cases, there is no gap at all while Docker Swarm is easier to set up, learn and use.

Let us give Docker Swarm a spin and see how it fares.

Docker Swarm Walkthrough

To set up Docker Swarm, we need one of the service discovery tools. Consul served us well, and we'll continue using it for this purpose. It is a great tool and works well with Swarm. We'll set up three servers. One will act as master and the other two as cluster nodes.

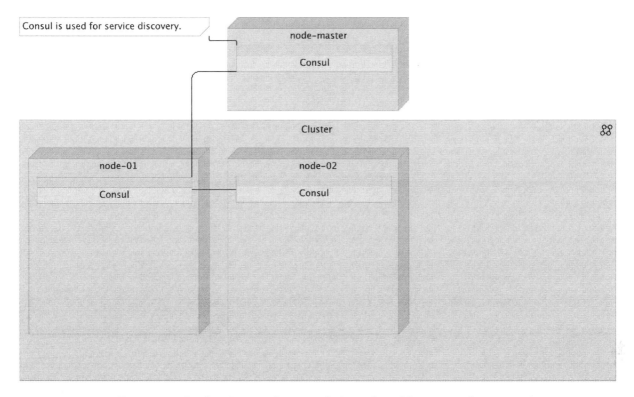

Figure 14-5: Docker Swarm cluster with Consul used for service discovery

Swarm will use Consul instances to register and retrieve information about nodes and services deployed in them. Whenever we bring up a new node or halt an existing one, that information will be propagated to all Consul instances and reach Docker Swarm, which, in turn, will know where to deploy our containers. The master node will have Swarm master running. We'll use its API to instruct Swarm what to deploy and what the requirements are (number of CPUs, the amount of memory, and so on). Node servers will have Swarm nodes deployed. Each time Swarm master receives an instruction to deploy a container, it will evaluate the current situation of the cluster and send instructions to one of the nodes to perform the deployment.

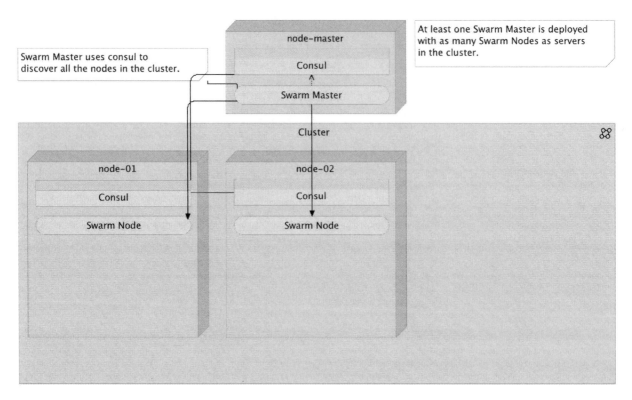

Figure 14-6: Docker Swarm cluster with one master and two nodes

We'll start with the *spread* strategy that will deploy containers to a node that has the least number of containers running. Since, in the beginning, nodes will be empty, when given instruction to deploy the first container, Swarm master will propagate it to one of the nodes since both are empty at the moment.

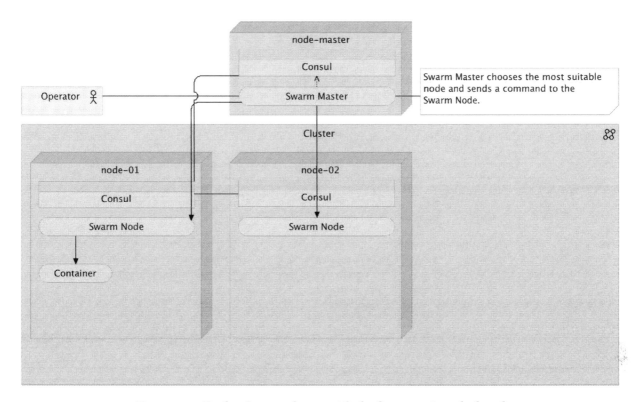

Figure 14-7: Docker Swarm cluster with the first container deployed

When given the second instruction to deploy a container, Swarm master will decide to propagate it to the other Swarm node, since the first already has one container running.

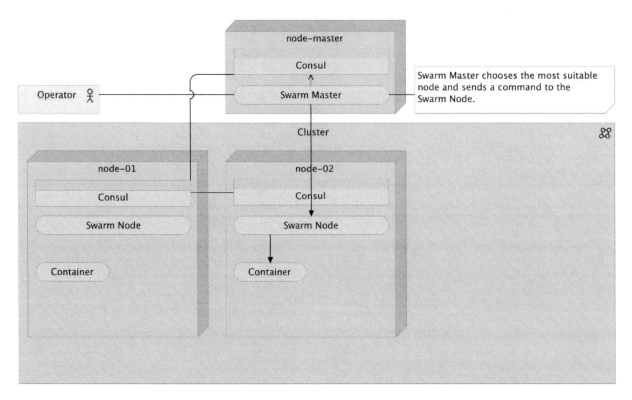

Figure 14-8: Docker Swarm cluster with the second container deployed

If we continue deploying containers, at some point our tiny cluster will become saturated, and something would need to be done before the server collapses.

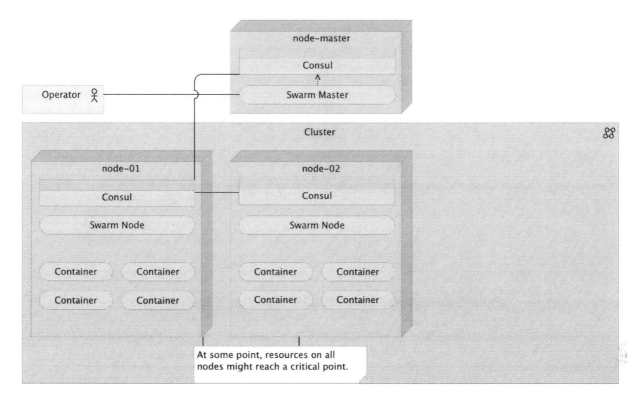

Figure 14-9: Docker Swarm cluster with all nodes full

The only thing we would need to do to increase the cluster capacity is to bring up a new server with Consul and Swarm node. As soon as such a node is brought up, its information would be propagated throughout Consul instances as well as to Swarm master. From that moment on, Swarm would have that node in the account for all new deployments. Since this server would start with no containers and we are using a simple *spread* strategy, all new deployments would be performed on that node until it reaches the same number of running containers as the others.

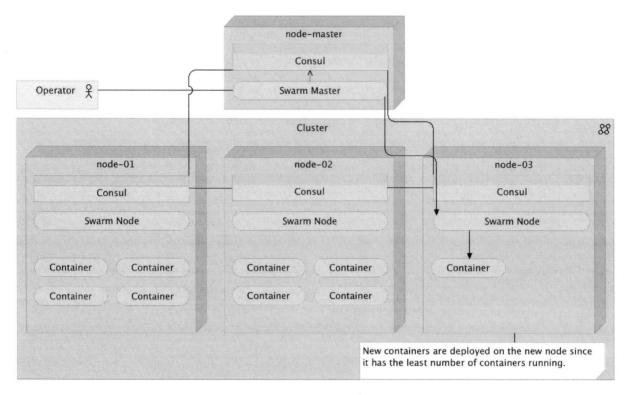

Figure 14-10: Docker Swarm cluster with container deployed to the new node

Opposite scenario can be observed in case one node stops responding due to a failure. Consul cluster would detect that one of it's members is not responding and propagate that information throughout the cluster, thus reaching Swarm master. From that moment on, all new deployments would be sent to one of the healthy nodes.

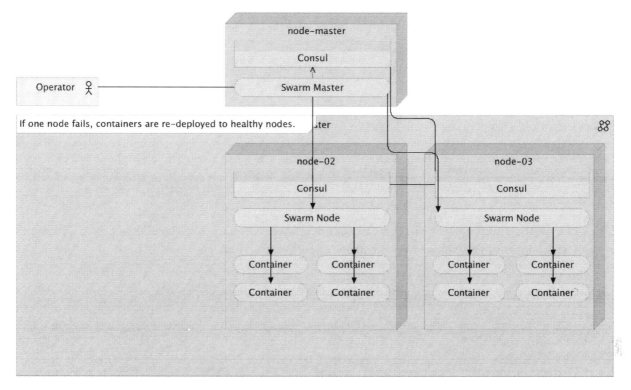

Figure 14-11: Docker Swarm cluster one node failed and containers distributed over healthy nodes

Let us dive into simple examples we just discussed. Later on, we'll explore other strategies as well as the ways Swarm behaves when certain constraints are set; CPU, memory and the like.

Setting Up Docker Swarm

To see Docker Swarm in action, we'll simulate an Ubuntu cluster. We'll bring up the *cd* node that we'll use for orchestration, one node that will act as Swarm master and two nodes that will form the cluster. Up to this point, we always used Ubuntu 14.04 LTS (long term support) since it is considered stable and supported for a long time. The next long term support version will be 15.04 LTS (not released at the time this book was written). Since some of the features we'll explore later on, throughout this chapter, will need a relatively new Kernel, the *swarm* nodes will be running Ubuntu 15.04. If you open the Vagrantfile[242], you'll notice that Swarm master and nodes have the following line:

```
1   d.vm.box = "ubuntu/vivid64"
```

Vivid64 is the code name for Ubuntu 15.04.

Let us bring up the nodes.

---

[242]https://github.com/vfarcic/ms-lifecycle/blob/master/Vagrantfile

```
1  vagrant up cd swarm-master swarm-node-1 swarm-node-2
```

With all the four nodes up and running, we can proceed, and create the Swarm cluster. As before, we'll do the provisioning using Ansible.

```
1  vagrant ssh cd
2
3  ansible-playbook /vagrant/ansible/swarm.yml \
4      -i /vagrant/ansible/hosts/prod
```

Let us use our time wisely and explore the *swarm.yml* playbook, while Ansible is provisioning our servers. The content of the swarm.yml[243] file is as follows.

```
1  - hosts: swarm
2    remote_user: vagrant
3    serial: 1
4    sudo: yes
5    vars:
6      - debian_version: vivid
7      - docker_cfg_dest: /lib/systemd/system/docker.service
8      - is_systemd: true
9    roles:
10     - common
11     - docker
12     - consul
13     - swarm
14     - registrator
```

We started by setting up *docker*. Since this time we're using a different version of Ubuntu, we had to specify those differences as variables, so that the correct repository is used (*debian_version*), as well as to reload service configuration (*is_systemd*). We also set the *docker_cfg_dest* variable so that the configuration file is sent to the correct location.

We have few more variables set in the hosts/prod[244] file.

---

[243]https://github.com/vfarcic/ms-lifecycle/blob/master/ansible/swarm.yml
[244]https://github.com/vfarcic/ms-lifecycle/blob/master/ansible/hosts/prod

```
1  [swarm]
2  10.100.192.200 swarm_master=true consul_extra="-server -bootstrap-expect 1" dock\
3  er_cfg=docker-swarm-master.service
4  10.100.192.20[1:2] swarm_master_ip=10.100.192.200 consul_server_ip=10.100.192.20\
5  0 docker_cfg=docker-swarm-node.service
```

We'll explore *swarm_master* and *swarm_master_ip* later on. For now, please remember that they are defined in the *prod* file so that they can be applied (or omitted) based on the server type (master or node). Depending on whether we are provisioning master or node, Docker configuration file is *docker-swarm-master.service* or *docker-swarm-node.service*.

Let's take a look at the *ExecStart* part of the master node Docker configuration (the rest is the same as the standard one that comes with the Docker package) defined in roles/docker/templates/docker-swarm-master.service[245].

```
1  ExecStart=/usr/bin/docker daemon -H fd:// \
2          --insecure-registry 10.100.198.200:5000 \
3          --registry-mirror=http://10.100.198.200:5001 \
4          --cluster-store=consul://{{ ip }}:8500/swarm \
5          --cluster-advertise={{ ip }}:2375 {{ docker_extra }}
```

We're telling Docker to allow insecure registry on the IP/port where our private registry runs (located in the *cd* node). We're also specifying that Swarm cluster information should be stored in Consul running on the same node, as well as that it should be advertised to the port 2375.

The node configuration defined in roles/docker/templates/docker-swarm-node.service[246] has few more arguments.

```
1  ExecStart=/usr/bin/docker daemon -H fd:// \
2          -H tcp://0.0.0.0:2375 \
3          -H unix:///var/run/docker.sock \
4          --insecure-registry 10.100.198.200:5000 \
5          --registry-mirror=http://10.100.198.200:5001 \
6          --cluster-store=consul://{{ ip }}:8500/swarm \
7          --cluster-advertise={{ ip }}:2375 {{ docker_extra }}
```

Apart from those arguments that are the same as in the master node, we're telling Docker to allow communication on the port 2375 (-H tcp://0.0.0.0:2375) as well as through the socket (-H unix:///var/run/docker.sock).

Both *master* and *node* configurations are following the standard settings recommended by the official Docker Swarm documentation when used in conjunction with Consul.

The rest of the roles used in the swarm.yml[247] playbook are *consul*, *swarm*, and *registrator*. Since we

[245]https://github.com/vfarcic/ms-lifecycle/blob/master/ansible/roles/docker/templates/docker-swarm-master.service
[246]https://github.com/vfarcic/ms-lifecycle/blob/master/ansible/roles/docker/templates/docker-swarm-node.service
[247]https://github.com/vfarcic/ms-lifecycle/blob/master/ansible/swarm.yml

already used and saw Consul and Registrator roles, we'll explore only tasks belonging to the *swarm* role defined in the roles/swarm/tasks/main.yml[248] file.

```
1   - name: Swarm node is running
2     docker:
3       name: swarm-node
4       image: swarm
5       command: join --advertise={{ ip }}:2375 consul://{{ ip }}:8500/swarm
6       env:
7         SERVICE_NAME: swarm-node
8     when: not swarm_master is defined
9     tags: [swarm]
10
11  - name: Swarm master is running
12    docker:
13      name: swarm-master
14      image: swarm
15      ports: 2375:2375
16      command: manage consul://{{ ip }}:8500/swarm
17      env:
18        SERVICE_NAME: swarm-master
19    when: swarm_master is defined
20    tags: [swarm]
```

As you can see, running Swarm is pretty straightforward. All we have to do is run the *swarm* container and, depending on whether it's master or node, specify one command or the other. If server acts as a Swarm node, the command is join --advertise={{ ip }}:2375 consul://{{ ip }}:8500/swarm which, translated into plain words, means that it should join the cluster, advertise its existence on port 2375 and use Consul running on the same server for service discovery. The command that should be used in the Swarm master is even shorter; manage consul://{{ ip }}:8500/swarm. All we had to do is specify that this Swarm container should be used to manage the cluster and, as with Swarm nodes, use Consul for service discovery.

Hopefully, the playbook we run earlier finished its execution. If it didn't, grab a coffee and continue reading once it's done. We're about to check whether our Swarm cluster is working as expected.

Since we are still inside the *cd* node, we should tell Docker CLI to use a different host.

```
1   export DOCKER_HOST=tcp://10.100.192.200:2375
```

With the Docker client running on *cd* and using the *swarm-master* node as a host, we can control the Swarm cluster remotely. For a start, we can check the information of our cluster.

---

[248]https://github.com/vfarcic/ms-lifecycle/blob/master/ansible/roles/swarm/tasks/main.yml

```
1   docker info
```

The output is as follows.

```
1   Containers: 4
2   Images: 4
3   Role: primary
4   Strategy: spread
5   Filters: health, port, dependency, affinity, constraint
6   Nodes: 2
7    swarm-node-1: 10.100.192.201:2375
8     └ Status: Healthy
9     └ Containers: 3
10    └ Reserved CPUs: 0 / 1
11    └ Reserved Memory: 0 B / 1.535 GiB
12    └ Labels: executiondriver=native-0.2, kernelversion=3.19.0-42-generic, operati\
13   ngsystem=Ubuntu 15.04, storagedriver=devicemapper
14    swarm-node-2: 10.100.192.202:2375
15    └ Status: Healthy
16    └ Containers: 3
17    └ Reserved CPUs: 0 / 1
18    └ Reserved Memory: 0 B / 1.535 GiB
19    └ Labels: executiondriver=native-0.2, kernelversion=3.19.0-42-generic, operati\
20   ngsystem=Ubuntu 15.04, storagedriver=devicemapper
21   CPUs: 2
22   Total Memory: 3.07 GiB
23   Name: b358fe59b011
```

Isn't this great? With a single command, we have an overview of the whole cluster. While, at this moment, we have only two servers (*swarm-node-1* and *swarm-node-2*), if there would be hundred, thousand, or even more nodes, docker info would provide information about all of them. In this case, we can see that four containers are running and four images. That is correct since each node is running Swarm and Registrator containers. Further on, we can see the *Role*, *Strategy*, and *Filters*. Next in the line are nodes that constitute our cluster followed by information about each of them. We can see how many containers each is running (currently two), how many CPUs and memory is reserved for our containers, and labels associated with each node. Finally, we can see the total number of CPUs and memory of the whole cluster. Everything presented by docker info acts not only as information but also a functionality of the Swarm cluster. For now, please note that all this information is available for inspection. Later on, we'll explore how to utilize it for our benefit.

The best part of Docker Swarm is that it shares the same API as Docker, so all the commands we already used throughout this book are available. The only difference is that instead of operating Docker on a single server, with Swarm we are operating a whole cluster. For example, we can list all images and processes throughout the entire Swarm cluster.

```
1  docker images
2
3  docker ps -a
```

By running `docker images` and `docker ps -a` we can observe that there are two images pulled into the cluster and four containers running (two containers on each of the two servers). The only visual difference is that names of running containers are prefixed with the name of the server they are running on. For example, the container named *registrator* is presented as *swarm-node-1/registrator* and *swarm-node-2/registrator*. The combined output of those two commands is as follows.

```
1  REPOSITORY                 TAG            IMAGE ID          CREATED        \
2      VIRTUAL SIZE
3  swarm                      latest         a9975e2cc0a3      4 weeks ago    \
4      17.15 MB
5  gliderlabs/registrator     latest         d44d11afc6cc      4 months ago   \
6      20.93 MB
7  ...
8  CONTAINER ID        IMAGE                   COMMAND                  CREATED    \
9          STATUS              PORTS                          NAMES
10 a2c7d156c99d        gliderlabs/registrator  "/bin/registrator -ip"   2 hours ag\
11 o          Up 2 hours                                      swarm-node-2/regis\
12 trator
13 e9b034aa3fc0        swarm                   "/swarm join --advert"   2 hours ag\
14 o          Up 2 hours          2375/tcp                    swarm-node-2/swarm\
15 -node
16 a685cdb09814        gliderlabs/registrator  "/bin/registrator -ip"   2 hours ag\
17 o          Up 2 hours                                      swarm-node-1/regis\
18 trator
19 5991e9bd2a40        swarm                   "/swarm join --advert"   2 hours ag\
20 o          Up 2 hours          2375/tcp                    swarm-node-1/swarm\
21 -node
```

Now that we know that Docker commands work in the same way when run against the remote server (*swarm-master*) and can be used to control the whole cluster (*swarm-node-1* and *swarm-node-2*), let's try to deploy our *books-ms* service.

Deploying with Docker Swarm

We'll start by repeating the same deployment process we did before, but, this time, we'll be sending commands to the Swarm master.

```
1  git clone https://github.com/vfarcic/books-ms.git
2
3  cd ~/books-ms
```

We cloned the *books-ms* repository and, now, we can run the service through Docker Compose.

```
1  docker-compose up -d app
```

Since the *app* target is linked with the *db*, Docker Compose run both. So far, everything looks the same as if we run the same command without Docker Swarm. Let us take a look at the processes that were created.

```
1  docker ps --filter name=books --format "table {{.Names}}"
```

The output is as follows.

```
1  NAMES
2  swarm-node-2/booksms_app_1
3  swarm-node-2/booksms_app_1/booksms_db_1,swarm-node-2/booksms_app_1/db,swarm-node\
4  -2/booksms_app_1/db_1,swarm-node-2/booksms_db_1
```

As we can see, both containers are running on *swarm-node-2*. In your case, it could be *swarm-node-1*. We did not make the decision where to deploy the containers. Swarm did that for us. Since we are using the default strategy that, without specifying additional constraints, runs containers on a server that has the least number of them running. Since both *swarm-node-1* and *swarm-node-2* were equally empty (or full), Swarm had an easy choice and could have placed containers on either one of those servers. In this case, it chose *swarm-node-2*.

The problem with the deployment we just performed is that the two targets (*app* and *db*) are linked. In such a case, Docker has no other option but to place both containers on the same server. That, in a way, defies the objective we're trying to accomplish. We want to deploy containers to the cluster and, as you'll soon discover, be able to scale them easily. If both containers need to be run on the same server, we are limiting Swarm's ability to distribute them properly. In this example, those two containers would be better of running on separate servers. If, before deploying those containers, both servers had the equal number of containers running, it would make more sense to run the *app* on one and the *db* on the other. That way we'd distribute resource usage much better. As it is now, the *swarm-node-2* needs to do all the work, and the *swarm-node-1* is empty. The first thing we should do is to get rid of the link.

Let's stop the containers we're running and start over.

```
1  docker-compose stop
2
3  docker-compose rm -f
```

That was another example of advantages Swarm provides. We sent the *stop* and *rm* commands to the Swarm master and it located containers for us. From now on, all the behavior will be the same, in the sense that, through the Swarm master, we'll treat the whole cluster as one single unit oblivious of the specifics of each server.

Deploying with Docker Swarm Without Links

To deploy containers to Docker Swarm cluster properly, we'll use a different file for Docker Compose definition; docker-compose-no-links.yml[249]. The targets are as follows.

```
1  app:
2    image: 10.100.198.200:5000/books-ms
3    ports:
4      - 8080
5
6  db:
7    image: mongo
```

The only significant difference between *app* and *db* targets defined in *docker-compose.yml* and *docker-compose-swarm-v2.yml* is that the latter does not use links. As you will see soon, this will allow us to distribute freely containers inside the cluster.

Let's take a look at what happens if we bring up *db* and *app* containers without the link.

```
1  docker-compose -f docker-compose-no-links.yml up -d db app
2
3  docker ps --filter name=books --format "table {{.Names}}"
```

The output of the docker ps command is as follows.

```
1  NAMES
2  swarm-node-1/booksms_db_1
3  swarm-node-2/booksms_app_1
```

---

[249]https://github.com/vfarcic/books-ms/blob/master/docker-compose-no-links.yml

As you can see, this time, Swarm decided to place each container on a different server. It brought up the first container and, since from that moment on one server had more containers than the other, it choose to bring up the second on the other node.

By removing linking between containers, we solved one problem but introduced another. Now our containers can be distributed much more efficiently, but they cannot communicate with each other. We can address this issue by using a *proxy* service (nginx, HAProxy, and so on). However, our *db* target does not expose any ports to the outside world. A good practice is to expose only ports of services that are publicly accessible. For that reason, the *app* target exposes port *8080* and the *db* target doesn't expose any. The *db* target is meant to be used internally, and only by the *app*. Since the Docker release 1.9, linking can be considered deprecated, for a new feature called *networking*.

Let's remove the containers and try to bring them up networking enabled.

```
1  docker-compose -f docker-compose-no-links.yml stop
2
3  docker-compose -f docker-compose-no-links.yml rm -f
```

Deploying with Docker Swarm and Docker Networking

At the time I was writing this chapter, Docker introduced the new release 1.9. It is, without a doubt, the most significant release, since version 1.0. It gave us two long awaited features; multi-host networking and persistent volumes. Networking makes linking deprecated and is the feature we need to connect containers across multiple hosts. There is no more need for proxy services to connect containers internally. That is not to say that proxy is not useful, but that we should use a proxy as a public interface towards our services and networking for connecting containers that form a logical group. The new Docker networking and proxy services have different advantages and should be used for different use cases. Proxy services provide load balancing and can control the access to our services. Docker networking is a convenient way to connect separate containers that form a single service and reside on the same network. A typical use case for Docker networking would be a service that requires a connection to a database. We can connect those two through networking. Furthermore, the service itself might need to be scaled and have multiple instances running. A proxy service with load balancer should fulfill that requirement. Finally, other services might need to access this service. Since we want to take advantage of load balancing, that access should also be through a proxy.

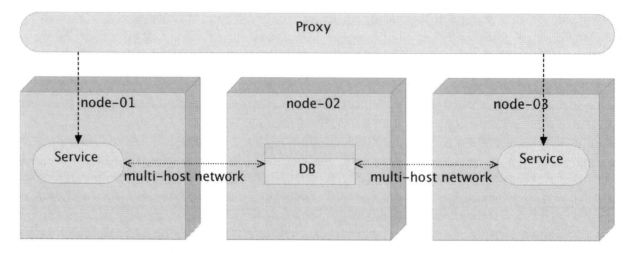

Figure 14-12: Multi-host networking combined with a proxy and load balancing service

The figure 14-12 represents one common use case. We have a scaled service with two instances running on nodes 1 and 3. All communication to those services is performed through a proxy service that takes care of load balancing and security. Any service (be it external or internal) that wants to access our service needs to go through the proxy. Internally, the service uses the database. The communication between the service instances and the database is internal and performed through the multi-host network. This setting allows us to scale easily within the cluster while keeping internal all communication between containers that compose a single service. In other words, all communication between containers that compose a single service is done through networking while the communication between services is performed through the proxy. ·

There are different ways to create a multi-host network. We can set up the network manually.

```
1  docker network create my-network
2
3  docker network ls
```

The output of the network ls command is as follows.

```
1  NETWORK ID              NAME                     DRIVER
2  5fc39aac18bf            swarm-node-2/host        host
3  aa2c17ae2039            swarm-node-2/bridge      bridge
4  267230c8d144            my-network               overlay
5  bfc2a0b1694b            swarm-node-2/none        null
6  b0b1aa45c937            swarm-node-1/none        null
7  613fc0ba5811            swarm-node-1/host        host
8  74786f8b833f            swarm-node-1/bridge      bridge
```

You can see that one of the networks is *my-network* we created earlier. It spans the whole Swarm cluster and we can use it with the *–net* argument.

```
1  docker run -d --name books-ms-db \
2      --net my-network \
3      mongo
4
5  docker run -d --name books-ms \
6      --net my-network \
7      -e DB_HOST=books-ms-db \
8      -p 8080 \
9      10.100.198.200:5000/books-ms
```

We started two containers that compose a single service; *books-ms* is the API that communicates with *books-ms-db* that acts as a database. Since both containers had the *–net my-network* argument, they both belong to the *my-network* network. As a result, Docker updated hosts file providing each container with an alias that can be used for internal communication.

Let's enter the books-ms container and take a look at the hosts file.

```
1  docker exec -it books-ms bash
2
3  cat /etc/hosts
4
5  exit
```

The output of the *exec* command is as follows.

```
1  10.0.0.2          3166318f0f9c
2  127.0.0.1          localhost
3  ::1              localhost ip6-localhost ip6-loopback
4  fe00::0          ip6-localnet
5  ff00::0          ip6-mcastprefix
6  ff02::1          ip6-allnodes
7  ff02::2          ip6-allrouters
8  10.0.0.2          books-ms-db
9  10.0.0.2          books-ms-db.my-network
```

The interesting part of the *hosts* file are the last two entries. Docker detected that the *books-ms-db* container uses the same network as the *books-ms* container, and updated the *hosts* file by adding *books-ms-db* and *books-ms-db.my-network* aliases. If some convention is used, it is trivial to code our services in a way that they use aliases like that one to communicate with resources located in a separate container (in this case with the database).

We also passed an environment variable *DB_HOST* to the *book-ms*. That indicates to our service which host to use to connect to the database. We can see this by outputting environments of the container.

```
1  docker exec -it books-ms env
```

The output of the command is as follows.

```
1  PATH=/usr/local/sbin:/usr/local/bin:/usr/sbin:/usr/bin:/sbin:/bin
2  HOSTNAME=eb3443a66355
3  DB_HOST=books-ms-db
4  DB_DBNAME=books
5  DB_COLLECTION=books
6  HOME=/root
```

As you can see, one of the environment variables is *DB_HOST* with the value *books-ms-db*.

What we have right now is Docker networking that created hosts alias *books-ms-db* pointing to the IP of the network Docker created. We also have an environment variable *DB_HOST* with value *books-ms-db*. The code of the service uses that variable to connect to the database.

As expected, we can specify *network* as part of our Docker Compose specification. Before we try it out, let's remove those two containers and the network.

```
1  docker rm -f books-ms books-ms-db
2
3  docker network rm my-network
```

This time, we'll run containers through Docker Compose. We'll use the *net* argument inside *docker-compose-swarm-v2.yml* and, in that way, do the same process as we did earlier. The alternative would be to use new Docker Compose argument *–x-networking* that would create the network for us but, at this moment, it is in the experimental stage and not entirely reliable. Before we proceed, let us take a quick look at the relevant targets inside the docker-compose-swarm-v2.yml[250] file.

```
1   app:
2     image: 10.100.198.200:5000/books-ms
3     ports:
4       - 8080
5     net: books-ms
6     environment:
7       - SERVICE_NAME=books-ms
8       - DB_HOST=books-ms-db
9
10  db:
11    container_name: books-ms-db
```

---

[250]https://github.com/vfarcic/books-ms/blob/master/docker-compose-swarm-v2.yml

```
12    image: mongo
13    net: books-ms
14    environment:
15      - SERVICE_NAME=books-ms-db
```

The only important difference is the addition of the *net* argument. Everything else is, more or less, the same as in many other targets we explored by now.

Let us create the network and run our containers through Docker Compose.

```
1  docker network create \
2      --driver overlay books-ms
3
4  docker-compose -f docker-compose-swarm-v2.yml \
5      up -d db app
```

The output of the command we just run is as follows.

```
1  Creating booksms_app_1
2  Creating books-ms-db
```

Before creating the services *app* and *db*, we created a new network called *books-ms*. The name of the network is the same as the value of the *net* argument specified in the *docker-compose-swarm-v2.yml* file.

We can confirm that the network was created by running the `docker network ls` command.

```
1  docker network ls
```

The output is as follows.

```
1   NETWORK ID      NAME                            DRIVER
2   6e5f816d4800    swarm-node-1/host               host
3   aa1ccdaefd70    swarm-node-2/docker_gwbridge    bridge
4   cd8b1c3d9be5    swarm-node-2/none               null
5   ebcc040e5c0c    swarm-node-1/bridge             bridge
6   6768bad8b390    swarm-node-1/docker_gwbridge    bridge
7   8ebdbd3de5a6    swarm-node-1/none               null
8   58a585d09bbc    books-ms                        overlay
9   de4925ea50d1    swarm-node-2/bridge             bridge
10  2b003ff6e5da    swarm-node-2/host               host
```

As you can see, the *overlay* network *books-ms* has been created.

We can also double check that the *hosts* file inside containers has been updated.

```
1  docker exec -it booksms_app_1 bash
2
3  cat /etc/hosts
4
5  exit
```

The output is as follows.

```
1  10.0.0.2           3166318f0f9c
2  127.0.0.1           localhost
3  ::1             localhost ip6-localhost ip6-loopback
4  fe00::0          ip6-localnet
5  ff00::0          ip6-mcastprefix
6  ff02::1          ip6-allnodes
7  ff02::2          ip6-allrouters
8  10.0.0.3          books-ms-db
9  10.0.0.3          books-ms-db.my-network
```

Finally, let's see how did Swarm distribute our containers.

```
1  docker ps --filter name=books --format "table {{.Names}}"
```

The output is as follows.

```
1  NAMES
2  swarm-node-2/books-ms-db
3  swarm-node-1/booksms_app_1
```

Swarm deployed the *app* container to the *swarm-node-1* and the *db* container to the *swarm-node-2*.

Finally, let's test whether the *book-ms* service is working properly. We do not know where did Swarm deploy the container nor which port is exposed. Since we do not (yet) have a proxy, we'll retrieve the IP and the port of the service from Consul, send a PUT request to store some data in the database residing in a different container and, finally, send a GET request to check whether we can retrieve the record. Since we do not have a proxy service that would make sure that requests are redirected to the correct server and port, we'll have to retrieve the IP and the port from Consul.

```
1  ADDRESS=`curl \
2      10.100.192.200:8500/v1/catalog/service/books-ms \
3      | jq -r '.[0].ServiceAddress + ":" + (.[0].ServicePort | tostring)'`
4
5  curl -H 'Content-Type: application/json' -X PUT -d \
6    '{"_id": 2,
7    "title": "My Second Book",
8    "author": "John Doe",
9    "description": "A bit better book"}' \
10   $ADDRESS/api/v1/books | jq '.'
11
12 curl $ADDRESS/api/v1/books | jq '.'
```

The output of the last command is as follows.

```
1  [
2    {
3      "author": "John Doe",
4      "title": "My Second Book",
5      "_id": 2
6    }
7  ]
```

If the service could not communicate with the database located on a different node, we would not be able to put, nor to get data. Networking between containers deployed to separate servers worked! All we had to do is use an additional argument with Docker Compose (*net*) and make sure that the service code utilizes information from the hosts file.

Another advantage of Docker networking is that, if one container stops working, we can redeploy it (potentially to a separate server) and, assuming that the service can handle the temporary connection loss, continue using it as if nothing happened.

Scaling Services with Docker Swarm

As you've already seen, scaling with Docker Compose is easy. While examples we run by now were limited to a single server, with Docker Swarm we can extend scaling to the whole cluster. Now that we have one instance of *books-ms* running, we can scale it to, let's say, three.

```
1  docker-compose -f docker-compose-swarm-v2.yml \
2      scale app=3
3
4  docker ps --filter name=books \
5      --format "table {{.Names}}"
```

The output of the *ps* command is as follows.

```
1  NAMES
2  swarm-node-2/booksms_app_3
3  swarm-node-1/booksms_app_2
4  swarm-node-2/books-ms-db
5  swarm-node-1/booksms_app_1
```

We can see that Swarm continues distributing containers evenly. Each node is currently running two containers. Since we asked Docker Swarm to scale the *books-ms* containers to three, two of them are now running alone and the third one is deployed together with the database. Later on, when we start working on the automation of the deployment to the Docker Swarm cluster, we'll also make sure that all the instances of the service are properly set in the proxy.

For the future reference, we might want to store the number of instances in Consul. Later on, it might come in handy if, for example, we want to increase or decrease that number.

```
1  curl -X PUT -d 3 \
2      10.100.192.200:8500/v1/kv/books-ms/instances
```

Services can be as easily descaled. For example, the traffic might drop, later during the day, and we might want to free resources for other services.

```
1  docker-compose -f docker-compose-swarm-v2.yml \
2      scale app=1
3
4  curl -X PUT -d 1 \
5      10.100.192.200:8500/v1/kv/books-ms/instances
6
7  docker ps --filter name=books \
8      --format "table {{.Names}}"
```

Since we told Swarm to scale (down) to one instance and, at that moment, there were three of them running, Swarm removed instances two and three leaving the system with only one running. That can be observed from the output of the *docker ps* command that is as follows.

```
1  NAMES
2  swarm-node-2/books-ms-db
3  swarm-node-1/booksms_app_1
```

We descaled and went back to the beginning, with one instance of each target running.

We are about to explore few more Swarm options. Before we proceed, let us stop and remove running containers, and start over.

```
1  docker-compose stop
2
3  docker-compose rm -f
```

Scheduling Containers Depending on Reserved CPUs and Memory

Up until now, Swarm was scheduling deployments to servers that have the least number of them running. That is the default strategy applied when there is no other constraint specified. It is often not realistic to expect that all containers require equal access to resources. We can further refine Swarm deployments by giving hints of what we expect from containers. For example, we can specify how many CPUs we need for a particular container. Let's give it a spin.

```
1  docker info
```

The relevant parts of the output of the command are as follows.

```
1  ...
2  Nodes: 2
3   swarm-node-1: 10.100.192.201:2375
4    └ Containers: 2
5    └ Reserved CPUs: 0 / 1
6    └ Reserved Memory: 0 B / 1.535 GiB
7  ...
8   swarm-node-2: 10.100.192.202:2375
9    └ Containers: 2
10   └ Reserved CPUs: 0 / 1
11   └ Reserved Memory: 0 B / 1.535 GiB
12 ...
```

Even though we are already running two containers on each node (*Registrator* and *Swarm*), there are no reserved CPUs, nor reserved memory. When we run those containers, we did not specify that CPU or memory should be reserved.

Let's try running Mongo DB with one CPU reserved for the process. Keep in mind that this is only a hint and will not prevent other containers already deployed on those servers from using that CPU.

```
1  docker run -d --cpu-shares 1 --name db1 mongo
2
3  docker info
```

Since each node has only one CPU assigned, we could not assign more than one. The relevant parts of the output of the docker info command are as follows.

```
1   ...
2   Nodes: 2
3    swarm-node-1: 10.100.192.201:2375
4     └ Status: Healthy
5     └ Containers: 3
6     └ Reserved CPUs: 1 / 1
7     └ Reserved Memory: 0 B / 1.535 GiB
8    ...
9    swarm-node-2: 10.100.192.202:2375
10    └ Status: Healthy
11    └ Containers: 2
12    └ Reserved CPUs: 0 / 1
13    └ Reserved Memory: 0 B / 1.535 GiB
14   ...
```

This time, *swarm-node-1* has one (out of one) CPU reserved. Since there are no more available CPUs on that node, if we repeat the process and bring up one more Mongo DB with the same constraint, Swarm will have no option but to deploy it to the second node. Let's try it out.

```
1  docker run -d --cpu-shares 1 --name db2 mongo
2
3  docker info
```

The relevant parts of the output of the *ps* command are as follows.

```
1   ...
2   Nodes: 2
3    swarm-node-1: 10.100.192.201:2375
4     └ Status: Healthy
5     └ Containers: 3
6     └ Reserved CPUs: 1 / 1
7     └ Reserved Memory: 0 B / 1.535 GiB
8    ...
9    swarm-node-2: 10.100.192.202:2375
```

```
10      └ Status: Healthy
11      └ Containers: 3
12      └ Reserved CPUs: 1 / 1
13      └ Reserved Memory: 0 B / 1.535 GiB
14      ...
```

This time, both nodes have all the CPUs reserved.

We can take a look at the processes and confirm that both DBs are indeed running.

```
1   docker ps --filter name=db --format "table {{.Names}}"
```

The output is as follows.

```
1   NAMES
2   swarm-node-2/db2
3   swarm-node-1/db1
```

Indeed, both containers are running, one on each node.

Let's see what happens if we try to bring up one more container that requires one CPU.

```
1   docker run -d --cpu-shares 1 --name db3 mongo
```

This time, Swarm returned the following error message.

```
1   Error response from daemon: no resources available to schedule container
```

We requested deployment of a container that requires one CPU, and Swarm got back to us saying that there are no available nodes that fulfill that requirement. Before we proceed to explore other constraints, please bear in mind that *CPU Shares* do not work in the same way with Swarm as when applied to a Docker running on a single server. For more information regarding such a case, please consult CPU share constraint[251] page for more information.

Let's remove our containers and start over.

```
1   docker rm -f db1 db2
```

We can also use memory as a constraint. For example, we can direct Swarm to deploy a container reserving one CPU and one GB of memory.

---

[251]http://docs.docker.com/engine/reference/run/#cpu-share-constraint

```
1  docker run -d --cpu-shares 1 -m 1g --name db1 mongo
2
3  docker info
```

The output of the `docker info` command is as follows (limited to relevant parts).

```
1   ...
2   Nodes: 2
3    swarm-node-1: 10.100.192.201:2375
4      └ Status: Healthy
5      └ Containers: 3
6      └ Reserved CPUs: 1 / 1
7      └ Reserved Memory: 1 GiB / 1.535 GiB
8    ...
9    swarm-node-2: 10.100.192.202:2375
10     └ Status: Healthy
11     └ Containers: 2
12     └ Reserved CPUs: 0 / 1
13     └ Reserved Memory: 0 B / 1.535 GiB
14   ...
```

This time not only that one CPU is reserved, but almost all of the memory as well. While we could not demonstrate much when using CPU constraints, since our nodes have only one each, with memory we have a bit bigger margin to experiment. For example, we can bring up three instances of Mongo DB with 100 MB reserved for each.

```
1  docker run -d -m 100m --name db2 mongo
2
3  docker run -d -m 100m --name db3 mongo
4
5  docker run -d -m 100m --name db4 mongo
6
7  docker info
```

The output of the `docker info` command is as follows (limited to relevant parts).

```
1  ...
2  Nodes: 2
3   swarm-node-1: 10.100.192.201:2375
4     └ Status: Healthy
5     └ Containers: 3
6     └ Reserved CPUs: 1 / 1
7     └ Reserved Memory: 1 GiB / 1.535 GiB
8  ...
9   swarm-node-2: 10.100.192.202:2375
10    └ Status: Healthy
11    └ Containers: 5
12    └ Reserved CPUs: 0 / 1
13    └ Reserved Memory: 300 MiB / 1.535 GiB
14 ...
```

It is obvious that all of those three containers were deployed to the *swarm-node-2*. Swarm realized that the second node had less available memory on the *swarm-node-1* and decided to deploy the new container to the *swarm-node-2*. That decision was repeated two more times since the same constraints were used. As a result, the *swarm-node-2* now has all those three containers running and 300 MB of memory reserved. We can confirm that by checking the running processes.

```
1  docker ps --filter name=db --format "table {{.Names}}"
```

The output is as follows.

```
1  NAMES
2  swarm-node-2/db4
3  swarm-node-2/db3
4  swarm-node-2/db2
5  swarm-node-1/db1
```

There are many other ways we can give hints to Swarm where to deploy containers. We won't explore all of them. I invite you to check Docker documentation for Strategies[252] and Filters[253].

At this moment, we have more than enough knowledge to attempt deployment automation to the Docker Swarm cluster.

Before we proceed, let's remove the containers we run until now.

---

[252]https://docs.docker.com/swarm/scheduler/strategy/

[253]https://docs.docker.com/swarm/scheduler/filter/

```
1  docker rm -f db1 db2 db3 db4
```

Automating Deployment With Docker Swarm and Ansible

We are already familiar with Jenkins Workflow, and it should be relatively easy to extend this knowledge to Docker Swarm deployments.

First things first. We need to provision our *cd* node with Jenkins.

```
1  ansible-playbook /vagrant/ansible/jenkins-node-swarm.yml \
2      -i /vagrant/ansible/hosts/prod
3
4  ansible-playbook /vagrant/ansible/jenkins.yml \
5      -c local
```

The two playbooks deployed the familiar Jenkins instance with two nodes. This time, the slaves we are running are *cd* and *swarm-master*. Among other jobs, the playbook created the *books-ms-swarm* job based on the *Multibranch Workflow*. The only difference between this and the other multibranch jobs we used earlier is in the *Include branches* filter that, this time, is set to *swarm*.

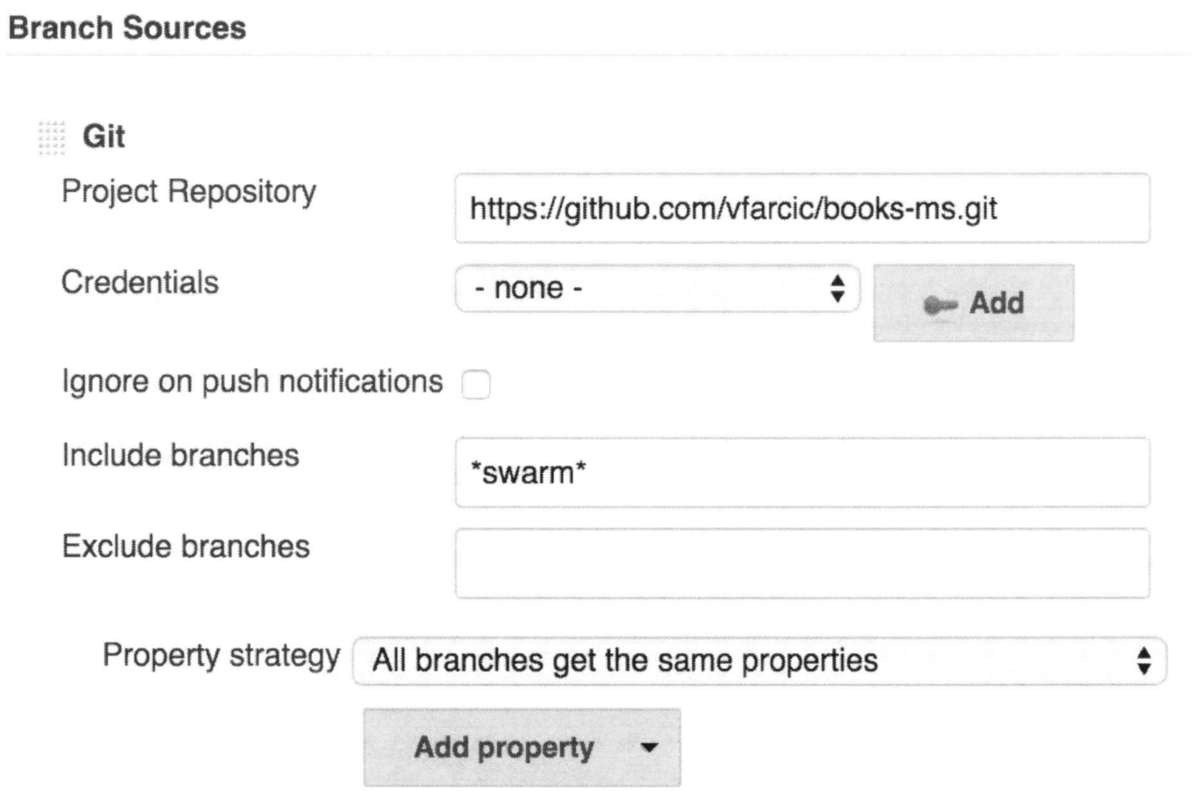

Branch Sources

Figure 14-13: Configuration screen of the *books-ms-swarm* Jenkins job

Let's index the branches and let the job run while we explore the Jenkinsfile[254] located in the books-ms swarm branch[255].

Please open the books-ms-swarm[256] job and click *Branch Indexing* followed by *Run Now*. Since there is only one branch matching the specified filter, Jenkins will create one subproject called *swarm* and start building it. If you are curious about the progress of the build, you can monitor the progress by opening the build console[257].

Examining the Swarm Deployment Playbook

The content of the Jenkins workflow defined in the Jenkinsfile[258] is as follows.

---

[254]https://github.com/vfarcic/books-ms/blob/swarm/Jenkinsfile

[255]https://github.com/vfarcic/books-ms/tree/swarm

[256]http://10.100.198.200:8080/job/books-ms-swarm/

[257]http://10.100.198.200:8080/job/books-ms-swarm/branch/swarm/lastBuild/console

[258]https://github.com/vfarcic/books-ms/blob/swarm/Jenkinsfile

```
1   node("cd") {
2       def serviceName = "books-ms"
3       def prodIp = "10.100.192.200" // Modified
4       def proxyIp = "10.100.192.200" // Modified
5       def proxyNode = "swarm-master"
6       def registryIpPort = "10.100.198.200:5000"
7       def swarmPlaybook = "swarm.yml" // Modified
8       def proxyPlaybook = "swarm-proxy.yml" // Added
9       def instances = 1 // Added
10
11      def flow = load "/data/scripts/workflow-util.groovy"
12
13      git url: "https://github.com/vfarcic/${serviceName}.git"
14      flow.provision(swarmPlaybook) // Modified
15      flow.provision(proxyPlaybook) // Added
16      flow.buildTests(serviceName, registryIpPort)
17      flow.runTests(serviceName, "tests", "")
18      flow.buildService(serviceName, registryIpPort)
19
20      def currentColor = flow.getCurrentColor(serviceName, prodIp)
21      def nextColor = flow.getNextColor(currentColor)
22
23      flow.deploySwarm(serviceName, prodIp, nextColor, instances) // Modified
24      flow.runBGPreIntegrationTests(serviceName, prodIp, nextColor)
25      flow.updateBGProxy(serviceName, proxyNode, nextColor)
26      flow.runBGPostIntegrationTests(serviceName, prodIp, proxyIp, proxyNode, curr\
27  entColor, nextColor)
28  }
```

I added comments to the modified and added lines (when compared with Jenkinsfile from the previous chapter) so that we can explore the differences from the Jenkinsfile defined in the blue-green branch[259].

The variables *prodIp* and *proxyIp* have been changed to point to the *swarm-master* node. This time, we are using two Ansible playbooks to provision the cluster. The *swarmPlaybook* variable holds the name of the playbook that configures the whole *Swarm* cluster while the *proxyPlaybook* variable references the playbook in charge of setting up the *nginx* proxy on the *swarm-master* node. In "real world" situations, Swarm master and the proxy service should be separated but, in this case, I opted against an additional VM to save a bit of resources on your laptop. Finally, the *instances* variable with the default value of *1* is added to the script. We'll explore its usage shortly.

The only truly notable difference is the usage of the *deploySwarm* function that replaces *deployBG*. It

---

[259]https://github.com/vfarcic/books-ms/tree/blue-green

is one more utility function defined in the workflow-util.groovy[260] script. Its contents are as follows.

```
1  def deploySwarm(serviceName, swarmIp, color, instances) {
2      stage "Deploy"
3      withEnv(["DOCKER_HOST=tcp://${swarmIp}:2375"]) {
4          sh "docker-compose pull app-${color}"
5          try {
6              sh "docker network create ${serviceName}"
7          } catch (e) {}
8          sh "docker-compose -f docker-compose-swarm-v2.yml \
9              -p ${serviceName} up -d db"
10         sh "docker-compose -f docker-compose-swarm-v2.yml \
11             -p ${serviceName} rm -f app-${color}"
12         sh "docker-compose -f docker-compose-swarm-v2.yml \
13             -p ${serviceName} scale app-${color}=${instances}"
14     }
15     putInstances(serviceName, swarmIp, instances)
16 }
```

As before, we start by pulling the latest container from the registry. The new addition is the creation of a Docker network. Since it can be created only once, and all subsequent attempts will result in an error, the *sh* command is enclosed inside a *try/catch* block that will prevent the script from failing.

The creation of the network is followed by deployment of the *db* and *app* targets. Unlike DB that, in this scenario, is always deployed as a single instance, the *app* target might need to be scaled. For that reason, the first one is deployed through the *up* and the other through the *scale* command available through Docker Compose. The *scale* command utilizes the *instances* variable to determine how many copies of the release should be deployed. We can increase or decrease their number simply by changing the *instances* variable in the Jenkinsfile[261]. Once such a change is committed to the repository, Jenkins will run a new build and deploy as many instances as we specified.

Finally, we are putting the number of instances to Consul by invoking the helper function *putInstances* which, in turn. executed a simple Shell command. Even though we won't be using the information right now, it will come in handy in the next chapter when we start building a self-healing system.

That's it. There were only a few changes we had to apply to the Jenkinsfile to have the *blue-green* deployment extended from a single server to the whole Swarm cluster. Both Docker Swarm and Jenkins Workflow proved to be very easy to work with, even easier to maintain, and, yet, very powerful.

---

[260]https://github.com/vfarcic/ms-lifecycle/blob/master/ansible/roles/jenkins/files/scripts/workflow-util.groovy

[261]https://github.com/vfarcic/books-ms/blob/swarm/Jenkinsfile

By this time, the build of the *swarm* sub-project probably finished. We can validate that from the build console[262] screen or, directly, by opening the books-ms-swarm[263] job and confirming that the status of the last build is represented with the *blue* ball. If you are curious why the success is represented with blue instead of green color, please read the Why does Jenkins have blue balls?[264] article.

 **books-ms-swarm**

✏add description

| All | + | | | | | |

S	W	Name ↓	Last Success	Last Failure	Last Duration	
⬤	☁	swarm	1 hr 15 min - #5	1 hr 22 min - #4	8 min 34 sec	⟳

Icon: S M L

Legend   🔊 RSS for all   🔊 RSS for failures   🔊 RSS for just latest builds

Figure 14-14: The *books-ms-swarm* Jenkins job screen

Now that we understand what is behind the *Jenkinsfile* script and the build is finished, we can manually validate that everything seems to be working correctly.

Running the Swarm Jenkins Workflow

The first run of the swarm[265] subproject was initiated by Jenkins automatically once it finished indexing branches. All that's left for us is to double check that the whole process was indeed executed correctly.

This was the first deployment so the *blue* release should be running somewhere inside the cluster. Let's take a look where did Swarm decide to deploy our containers.

```
1  export DOCKER_HOST=tcp://10.100.192.200:2375
2
3  docker ps --filter name=books --format "table {{.Names}}"
```

The output of the *ps* command is as follows.

---

[262]http://10.100.198.200:8080/job/books-ms-swarm/branch/swarm/lastBuild/console

[263]http://10.100.198.200:8080/job/books-ms-swarm/

[264]https://jenkins-ci.org/blog/2012/03/13/why-does-jenkins-have-blue-balls/

[265]http://10.100.198.200:8080/job/books-ms-swarm/branch/swarm/

```
1  NAMES
2  swarm-node-2/booksms_app-blue_1
3  swarm-node-1/books-ms-db
```

In this case, Swarm deployed the *books-ms* container to the *swarm-node-2* and the Mongo DB to the *swarm-node-1*. We can also verify whether the service was correctly stored in Consul.

```
1  curl swarm-master:8500/v1/catalog/service/books-ms-blue \
2      | jq '.'
3
4  curl swarm-master:8500/v1/kv/books-ms/color?raw
5
6  curl swarm-master:8500/v1/kv/books-ms/instances?raw
```

The output of all three commands is as follows.

```
1  [
2    {
3      "ServicePort": 32768,
4      "ServiceAddress": "10.100.192.202",
5      "ServiceTags": null,
6      "ServiceName": "books-ms-blue",
7      "ServiceID": "swarm-node-2:booksms_app-blue_1:8080",
8      "Address": "10.100.192.202",
9      "Node": "swarm-node-2"
10   }
11 ]
12 ...
13 blue
14 ...
15 1
```

According to Consul, the release was deployed to *swarm-node-2* (*10.100.192.202*) and has the port *32768*. We are currently running the *blue* release, and have only one instance running.

Finally, we can double check that the service is indeed working by sending a few requests to it.

```
1  curl -H 'Content-Type: application/json' -X PUT -d \
2    '{"_id": 1,
3    "title": "My First Book",
4    "author": "John Doe",
5    "description": "Not a very good book"}' \
6    swarm-master/api/v1/books | jq '.'
7
8  curl swarm-master/api/v1/books | jq '.'
```

The first request was PUT, sending a signal to the service that we want to store the book. The second retrieved the list of all books.

The automated process seems to be working correctly when run for the first time. We'll execute the build again and deploy the green release.

The Second Run of the Swarm Deployment Playbook

Let's deploy the next release.

Please open the swarm subproject[266] and click the *Build Now* link. The build will start, and we can monitor it from the Console screen[267]. After a few minutes, the build will finish executing, and we'll be able to check the result.

```
1  docker ps -a --filter name=books --format "table {{.Names}}\t{{.Status}}"
```

The output of the *ps* command is as follows.

```
1  NAMES                            STATUS
2  swarm-node-2/booksms_app-green_1  Up 7 minutes
3  swarm-node-2/booksms_app-blue_1   Exited (137) 15 seconds ago
4  swarm-node-1/books-ms-db          Up 10 hours
```

Since we run the *green* release, the *blue* release is in the *Exited* status. We can observe the information about the currently running release from Consul.

```
1  curl swarm-master:8500/v1/catalog/service/books-ms-green \
2      | jq '.'
```

The response from the Consul request is as follows.

---

[266]http://10.100.198.200:8080/job/books-ms-swarm/branch/swarm/
[267]http://10.100.198.200:8080/job/books-ms-swarm/branch/swarm/lastBuild/console

```
 1  [
 2    {
 3      "ModifyIndex": 3314,
 4      "CreateIndex": 3314,
 5      "Node": "swarm-node-2",
 6      "Address": "10.100.192.202",
 7      "ServiceID": "swarm-node-2:booksms_app-green_1:8080",
 8      "ServiceName": "books-ms-green",
 9      "ServiceTags": [],
10      "ServiceAddress": "10.100.192.202",
11      "ServicePort": 32770,
12      "ServiceEnableTagOverride": false
13    }
14  ]
```

Now we can test the service itself.

```
 1  curl swarm-master/api/v1/books | jq '.'
```

Since we already have the Consul UI running, please open the http://10.100.192.200:8500/ui[268] address in your favorite browser to get a visual representation of services we deployed.

As an exercise, fork the books-ms[269] repository and modify the job to use you repository. Open the *Jenkinsfile* inside the *swarm* branch, change it to deploy three instances of the service, and push the changes. Run the build again and, once it's finished, confirm that three instances were deployed to the cluster.

Cleaning Up

This concludes our tour of Docker Swarm. We'll use it more throughout the next chapters. Before moving to the next subject, lets destroy the VMs. We'll create them again when we need them.

```
 1  exit
 2
 3  vagrant destroy -f
```

The solution we developed still has quite a few problems. The system is not fault tolerant, and is difficult to monitor. The next chapter will address the first of those problems through creation of a self-healing system.

[268]http://10.100.192.200:8500/ui
[269]https://github.com/vfarcic/books-ms

Self-Healing Systems

Healing takes courage, and we all have courage, even if we have to dig a little to find it.

– Tori Amos

Let's face it. The systems we are creating are not perfect. Sooner or later, one of our applications will fail, one of our services will not be able to handle the increased load, one of our commits will introduce a fatal bug, a piece of hardware will break, or something entirely unexpected will happen.

How do we fight the unexpected? Most of us are trying to develop a bullet proof system. We are attempting to create what no one did before. We strive for the ultimate perfection, hoping that the result will be a system that does not have any bugs, is running on hardware that never fails, and can handle any load. Here's a tip. There is no such thing as perfection. No one is perfect, and nothing is without fault. That does not mean that we should not strive for perfection. We should, when time and resources are provided. However, we should also embrace the inevitable, and design our systems not to be perfect, but able to recuperate from failures, and able to predict likely future. We should hope for the best but prepare for the worst.

There are plenty of examples of resilient systems outside software engineering, none of them better than life itself. We can take ourselves, humanity, as an example. We're the result of a very long experiment based on small and incremental evolutionary improvements, performed over millions of years. We can learn a lot from a human body, and apply that knowledge to our software and hardware. One of the fascinating abilities we (humans) possess is the capacity to self-heal.

Human body has an amazing capacity to heal itself. The most fundamental unit of human body is cell. Throughout our life, cells inside our body are working to bring us back to a state of equilibrium. Each cell is a dynamic, living unit that is continuously monitoring and adjusting its own processes, working to restore itself according to the original DNA code it was created with, and to maintain balance within the body. Cells have the ability to heal themselves, as well as to make new cells that replace those that have been permanently damaged or destroyed. Even when a large number of cells are destroyed, the surrounding cells replicate to make new cells, thereby quickly replacing the cells that were destroyed. This ability does not make us, individuals, immune to death, but it does make us very resilient. We are continuously attacked by viruses. We succumb to diseases and yet, in most cases, we come out victorious. However, looking at us as individuals would mean that we are missing the big picture. Even when our own lives end, the life itself not only survives, but thrives, ever growing, and ever adapting.

We can think of a computer system as a human body that consists of cells of various types. They can be hardware or software. When they are software units, the smaller they are, the easier it is for them to self-heal, recuperate from failures, multiply, or even get destroyed when that is needed. We call those small units microservices, and they can, indeed, have behaviors similar to those observed in a human body. The microservices-based system we are building can be made in a way that is can self-heal. That is not to say that self-healing we are about to explore is applicable only to microservices. It is not. However, like most other techniques we explored, self-healing can be applied to almost any type of architecture, but provides best results when combined with microservices. Just like life that consists of individuals that form a whole ecosystem, each computer system is part of something bigger. It communicates, cooperates, and adapts to other systems forming a much larger whole.

Self-Healing Levels and Types

In software systems, the self-healing term describes any application, service, or a system that can discover that it is not working correctly and, without any human intervention, make the necessary changes to restore itself to the normal or designed state. Self-healing is about making the system capable of making its decisions by continually checking and optimizing its state and automatically adapting to changing conditions. The goal is to make fault tolerant and responsive system capable of responding to changes in demand and recuperation from failures.

Self-healing systems can be divided into three levels, depending on size and type of resources we are monitoring, and acting upon. Those levels are as follows.

- Application level
- System level
- Hardware level

We'll explore each of those three types separately.

Self-Healing on the Application Level

Application level healing is the ability of an application, or a service, to heal itself internally. Traditionally, we're used to capturing problems through exceptions and, in most cases, logging them for further examination. When such an exception occurs, we tend to ignore it and move on (after logging), as if nothing happened, hoping for the best in the future. In other cases, we tend to stop the application if an exception of certain type occurs. An example would be a connection to a database. If the connection is not established when the application starts, we often stop the whole process. If we are a bit more experienced, we might try to repeat the attempt to connect to the database. Hopefully, those attempts are limited, or we might easily enter a never ending loop, unless database connection failure was temporary and the DB gets back online soon afterwards. With time, we got better ways to deal with problems inside applications. One of them is Akka[270]. It's usage of supervisor, and design patterns it promotes, allow us to create internally self-healing applications and services. Akka is not the only one. Many other libraries and frameworks enable us to create fault tolerant applications capable of recuperation from potentially disastrous circumstances. Since we

---

[270]http://akka.io/

are trying to be agnostic to programming languages, I'll leave it to you, dear reader, investigation of ways to self-heal your applications internally. Bear in mind that self-healing in this context refers to internal processes and does not provide, for example, recuperation from failed processes. Moreover, if we adopt microservices architecture, we can quickly end up with services written in different languages, using different frameworks, and so on. It is truly up to developers of each service to design it in a way that it can heal itself and recuperate from failures.

Let's jump into the second level.

Self-Healing on the System Level

Unlike the application level healing that depends on a programming language and design patterns that we apply internally, system level self-healing can be generalized and be applied to all services and applications, independently from their internals. This is the type of self-healing that we can design on the level of the whole system. While there are many things that can happen at the system level, the two most commonly monitored aspects are failures of processes and response time. If a process fails, we need to redeploy the service, or restart the process. On the other hand, if the response time is not adequate, we need to scale, or descale, depending whether we reached upper or lower response time limits. Recuperating from process failures is often not enough. While such actions might restore our system to the desired state, human intervention is often still needed. We need to investigate the cause of the failure, correct the design of the service, or fix a bug. That is, self-healing often goes hand in hand with investigation of the causes of that failure. The system automatically recuperates and we (humans) try to learn from those failures, and improve the system as a whole. For that reason, some kind of a notification is required as well. In both cases (failures and increased traffic), the system needs to monitor itself and take some actions.

How does the system monitor itself? How does it check the status of its components? There are many ways, but two most commonly used are TTLs and pings.

Time-To-Live (TTL)

Time-to-live (TTL) checks expect a service, or an application, to periodically confirm that it is operational. The system that receives TTL signals keeps track of the last known reported state for a given TTL. If that state is not updated within a predefined period, the monitoring system assumes that the service failed and needs to be restored to its designed state. For example, a healthy service could send an HTTP request announcing that it is alive. If the process the service is running in fails, it will be incapable to send the request, TTL will expire, and reactive measures will be executed.

The main problem with TTL is coupling. Applications and services need to be tied to the monitoring system. Implementing TTL would be one of the microservices anti-patterns since we are trying to design them in a way that they are as autonomous as possible. Moreover, microservices should have a clear function and a single purpose. Implementing TTL requests inside them would add additional functionality and complicate the development.

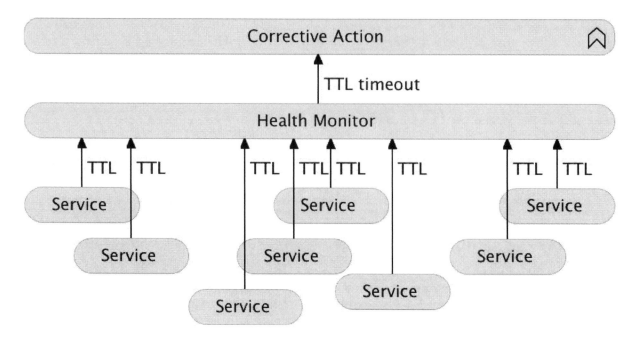

Figure 15-01: System level self-healing with time-to-live (TTL)

Pinging

The idea behind pinging is to check the state of an application, or a service, externally. The monitoring system should ping each service periodically and, if no response is received, or the content of the response is not adequate, execute healing measures. Pinging can come in many forms. If a service exposes HTTP API, it is often a simple request, where desired response should be HTTP status in 2XX range. In other cases, when HTTP API is not exposed, pinging can be done with a script, or any other method that can validate the state of the service.

Pinging is opposite from TTL, and, when possible, is a preferable way of checking the status of individual parts of the system. It removes repetition, coupling, and complications that could occur when implementing TTL inside each service.

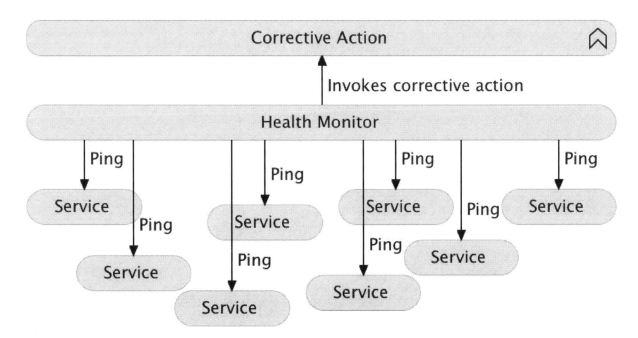

Figure 15-02: System level self-healing with pings

Self-Healing on the Hardware Level

Truth be told, there is no such a thing as hardware self-healing. We cannot have a process that will automatically heal failed memory, repare broken hard disk, fix malfunctioning CPU, and so on. What healing on this level truly means is redeployment of services from an unhealthy to one of the healthy nodes. As with the system level, we need to periodically check the status of different hardware components, and act accordingly. Actually, most healing caused due to hardware level will happen at the system level. If hardware is not working correctly, chances are that the service will fail, and thus be fixed by system level healing. Hardware level healing is more related to preventive types of checks that we'll discuss shortly.

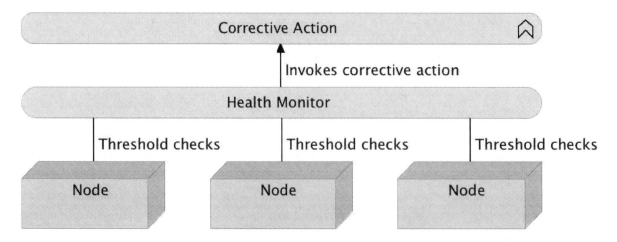

Figure 15-03: Hardware level self-healing

Besides the division based on the check levels, we can also divide it based on the moment actions are taken. We can react to a failure, or we can try to prevent it.

Reactive healing

Most of the organizations that implemented some kind of self-healing systems focused on reactive healing. After a failure is detected, the system reacts and restores itself to the designed state. A service process is dead, ping returns the code 404 (not found), corrective actions are taken, and the service is operational again. This works no matter whether service failed because its process failed, or the whole node stopped being operational (assuming that we have a system that can redeploy to a healthy node). This is the most important type of healing and, at the same time, the easiest one to implement. As long as we have all the checks in place, as well as actions that should be performed in case of a failure, and we have each service scaled to at least two instances distributed on separate physical nodes, we should (almost) never have downtime. I said almost never because, for example, the whole datacenter might loose power, thus stopping all nodes. It's all about evaluating risks against costs of preventing those risks. Sometimes, it is worthwhile to have two datacenters in different locations, and in other cases it's not. The objective is to strive towards zero-downtime, while accepting that some cases are not worthwhile trying to prevent.

No matter whether we are striving for zero-downtime, or almost zero-downtime, reactive self-healing should be a must for any but smallest settings, especially since it does not require big investment. You might invest in spare hardware, or you might invest in separate datacenters. Those decisions are not directly related with self-healing, but with the level of risks that are acceptable for a given use case. Reactive self-healing investment is primarily in knowledge how to do it, and time to implement it. While time is an investment in itself, we can spend it wisely, and create a general solution that would work for (almost) all cases, thus reducing the time we need to spend implementing such a system.

Preventive healing

The idea behind preventive healing is to predict the problems we might have in the future, and act in a way that those problems are avoided. How do we predict the future? To be more precise, what data do we use to predict the future?

Relatively easy, but less reliable way of predicting the future, is to base assumptions on (near) real-time data. For example, if one of the HTTP requests we're using to check the health of a service responded in more than 500 milliseconds, we might want to scale that service. We can even do the opposite. Following the same example, if it took less than 100 milliseconds to receive the response, we might want to descale the service, and reassign those resources to another one that might need it more. The problem with taking into account the current status when predicting the future is variability. If it took a long time between the request and the response, it might indeed be the sign that scaling is needed, but it might also be a temporary increase in traffic, and the next check (after the traffic spike is gone) will deduce that there is a need to descale. If microservices architecture is applied, this can be a minor issue, since they are small and easy to move around. They are easy to scale, and descale. Monolithic applications are often much more problematic if this strategy is chosen.

If historical data is taken into account, preventive healing becomes much more reliable but, at the same time, much more complicated to implement. Information (response times, CPU, memory, and so on) needs to be stored somewhere and, often complex, algorithms need to be employed to evaluate tendencies, and make conclusions. For example, we might observe that, during the last hour, memory usage has been steadily increasing, and that it reached a critical point of, let's say, 90%. That would be a clear indication that the service that is causing that increase needs to be scaled. The system could also take into account longer period of time, and deduce that every Monday there is a sudden increase in traffic, and scale services well in advance to prevent long responses. What would be, for example, the meaning of a steady increase in memory usage from the moment a service is deployed, and sudden decrease when a new version is released? Probably memory leaks and, in such a case, the system would need to restart the application when certain threshold is reached, and hope that developers would fix the issue (hence the need for notifications).

Let us change the focus, and discuss architecture.

Self-Healing Architecture

No matter the internal processes and tools, every self-healing system will have some common elements.

In the very beginning, there is a cluster. A single server cannot be made fault tolerant. If a piece of its hardware fails, there is nothing we can do to heal that. There is no readily available replacement. Therefore, the system must start with a cluster. It can be composed out of two or two hundred servers. The size is not of the essence, but the ability to move from one hardware to another in the case of a failure. Bear in mind that we always need to evaluate benefits versus costs. If financially viable, we would have at least two physically and geographically separated datacenters. In such a case, if there is a power outage in one, the other one would be fully operational. However, in many instances that is not a financially viable option.

Figure 15-04: Self-healing system architecture: Everything starts with a cluster

Once we have the cluster up and running, we can begin deploying our services. However, managing services inside a cluster without some orchestrator is tedious, at best. It requires time and often ends up with a very unbalanced usage of resources.

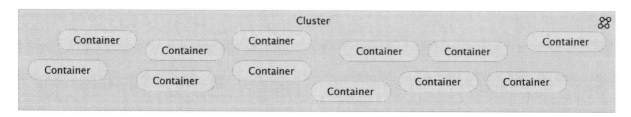

Figure 15-05: Self-healing system architecture: Services are deployed to the cluster, but with a very unbalanced usage of resources

In most cases, people treat a cluster as a set of individual servers, which is wrong, knowing that today we have tools at our disposal that can help us do the orchestration in a much better way. With Docker Swarm[271], Kubernetes[272], or Apache Mesos[273], we can solve the orchestration within a cluster. Cluster orchestration is important, not only to ease the deployment of our services, but also as a way to provide fast re-deployments to healthy nodes in case of a failure (be it of software or hardware nature). Bear in mind that we need at least two instances of every service running behind a proxy. Given such a situation, if one instance fails, the others can take over its load, thus avoiding any downtime while the system re-deploys the failed instance.

---

[271]https://docs.docker.com/swarm/

[272]http://kubernetes.io/

[273]http://mesos.apache.org/

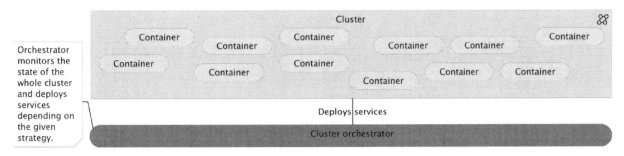

Figure 15-06: Self-healing system architecture: Some deployment orchestrator is required to distribute services across the cluster

The basis of any self-healing system is monitoring of the state of deployed services, or applications, as well as the underlying hardware. The only way we can monitor them is to have information about their existence. That information can be available in many different forms, ranging from manually maintained configuration files, through traditional databases, all the way until highly available distributed service registries like Consul[274], etcd[275], or Zookeeper[276]. In some cases, the service registry can be chosen by us, while in others it comes as part of the cluster orchestrator. For example, Docker Swarm has the flexibility that allows it to work with a couple of registries, while Kubernetes is tied to etcd.

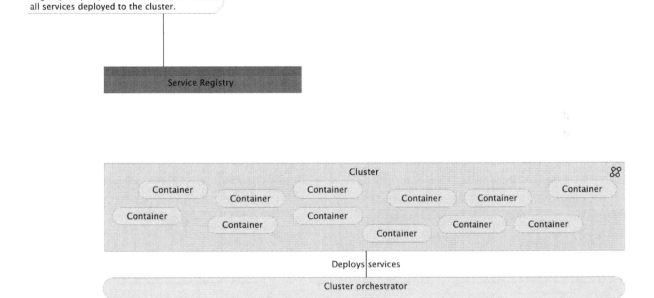

Figure 15-07: Self-healing system architecture: Primary requirement for monitoring the state of the system is to have the information of the system stored service registry

No matter the tool we choose to act as a service registry, the next obstacle is to put the information

---

[274]https://www.consul.io/

[275]https://github.com/coreos/etcd

[276]https://zookeeper.apache.org/

into the service registry of choice. The principle is a simple one. Something needs to monitor hardware and services and update the registry whenever a new one is added, or an existing one is removed. There are plenty of tools that can do that. We are already familiar with Registrator[277], which fulfills this role pretty well. As with service registries, some cluster orchestrators already come with their own ways to register and de-register services. No matter which tool we choose, the primary requirement is to be able to monitor the cluster and send information to service registry in near-realtime.

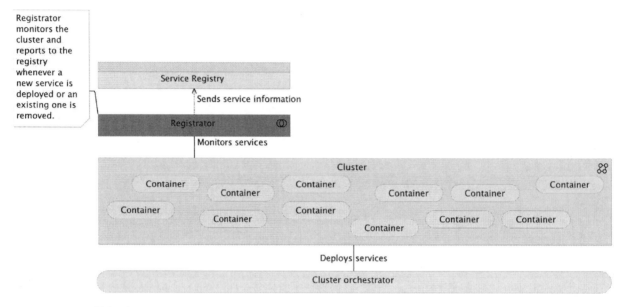

Figure 15-08: Self-healing system architecture: Service registry is useless if no mechanism will monitor the system and store new information

Now that we have the cluster with services up and running, and we have the information about the system in the service registry, we can employ some health monitoring that will detect anomalies. Such a tool needs to know not only what the desired state is, but, also, what the actual situation is at any moment. Consul Watches[278] can fulfill this role while Kubernetes and Mesos come with their own tools for this type of tasks. In a more traditional environment, Nagios[279] or Icinga[280] (only to name a few), can fulfill this role as well.

---

[277]https://github.com/gliderlabs/registrator

[278]https://www.consul.io/docs/agent/watches.html

[279]https://www.nagios.org/

[280]https://www.icinga.org/

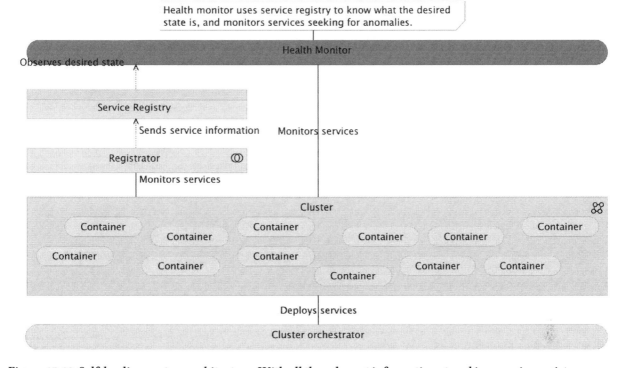

Figure 15-09: Self-healing system architecture: With all the relevant information stored in a service registry, some health monitoring tools can utilize it to verify whether the desired state is maintained

The next piece of the puzzle is a tool that would be able to execute corrective actions. When the health monitor detects an anomaly, it would send a message to perform a corrective measure. As a minimum, that corrective action should send a signal to the cluster orchestrator, which, in turn, would redeploy the failed service. Even if a failure was caused by a hardware problem, cluster orchestrator would (temporarily) fix that by redeploying the service to a healthy node. In most cases, corrective actions are not that simple. There could be a mechanism to notify interested parties, record what happened, revert to an older version of the service, and so on. We already adopted Jenkins, and it is a perfect fit to act as the tool that can receive a message from the health monitor and, as a result, initiate corrective actions.

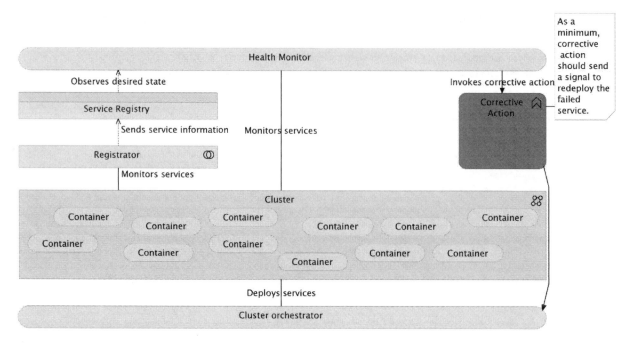

Figure 15-10: Self-healing system architecture: As a minimum, corrective action should send a signal to the cluster orchestrator to redeploy the service that failed

The process, as it is for now, is dealing only with reactive healing. The system is continuously monitored and, if a failure is detected, corrective actions are taken, which, in turn, will restore the system to the desired state. Can we take it a step further and try to accomplish preventive healing? Can we predict the future and act accordingly? In many cases we can, in some we can't. We cannot know that a hard disk will fail tomorrow. We cannot predict that there will be an outage today at noon. However, in some cases, we can see that the traffic is increasing, and will soon reach a point that will require some of our services to be scaled. We can predict that a marketing campaign we are about to launch will increase the load. We can learn from our mistakes, and teach the system how to behave in certain situations. The essential elements of such a set of processes are similar to those we should employ for reactive healing. We need a place to store data and a process that collects them. Unlike service registry that deals with a relatively small amount of data and benefits from being distributed, preventive healing requires quite bigger storage and capabilities that would allow us to perform some analytic operations.

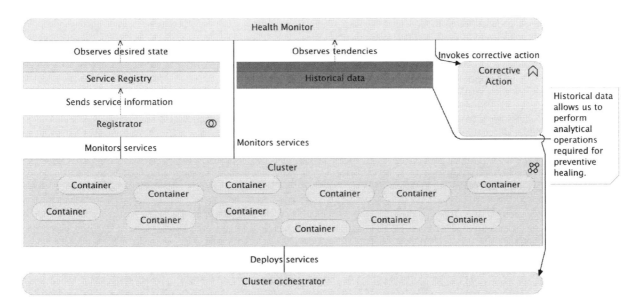

Figure 15-11: Self-healing system architecture: Preventive healing requires historical data to be analyzed

Similarly to the registrator service, we'll also need some data collector that will be sending historical data. That data can be quite massive and include, but not be limited by, CPU, HD, network traffic, system and service logs, and so on. Unlike the registrator that listens to events, mostly generated by the cluster orchestrator, data collector should be continuously collecting data, digesting the input, and producing an output that should be stored as historical data.

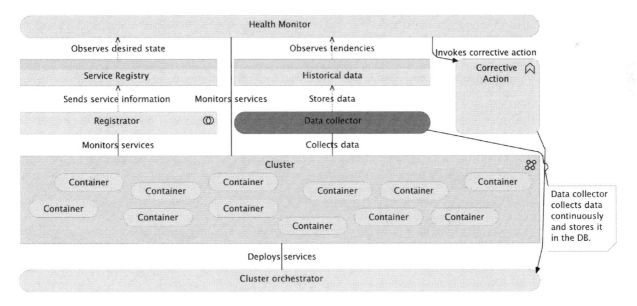

Figure 15-12: Self-healing system architecture: Preventive healing requires vast quantities of data to be collected continuously

We already used some of the tools needed for reactive self-healing. Docker Swarm can be used as the cluster orchestrator, Registrator and Consul for service discovery, and Jenkins for performing, among other duties, corrective actions. The only tool that we haven't used are two subsets of Consul; checks and watches. Preventive healing will require exploration of some new processes and tools, so we'll leave it for later on.

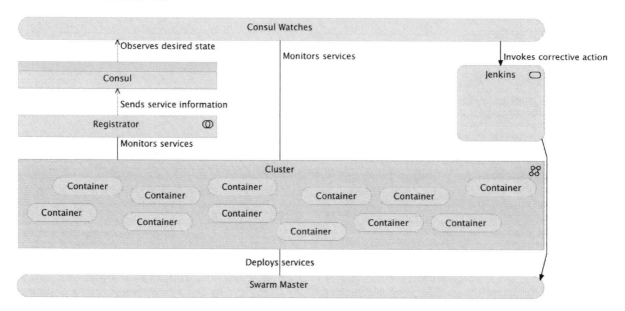

Figure 15-13: Self-healing system architecture: One of the combinations of tools

Let's see if we can set up a sample reactive self-healing system.

Self-Healing with Docker, Consul Watches, and Jenkins

The good news is that we already used all the tools that we require to make a reactive self-healing system. We have Swarm that will make sure that containers will be deployed to healthy nodes (or at least nodes that are operational). We have Jenkins that can be used to execute the healing process and, potentially, send notifications. Finally, we can use Consul not only to store service information, but also to perform health checks and send requests to Jenkins. The only piece we haven't used until now are Consul watches that can be programmed to perform health checks.

 One thing to note about how Consul does health checks is that it differs from traditional way Nagios[281] and other similar tools are operating. Consul avoids the thundering herd problem by using gossip, and only alerts on state changes.

As always, we'll start by creating VMs we'll use throughout the rest of the chapter. We'll create the familiar combination of one *cd* and three *swarm* servers (one master and two nodes).

---

[281]https://www.nagios.org/

Setting Up the Environments

The following command will create the four VMs we'll use in this chapter. We'll create the *cd* node and use it to provision the other nodes with Ansible. This VM will also host Jenkins, that will be an important part of the self-healing process. The other three VMs will form the Swarm cluster.

```
1  vagrant up cd swarm-master swarm-node-1 swarm-node-2
```

With all the VMs operational, we can proceed and set up the Swarm cluster. We'll start by provisioning the cluster in the same way as we did before, and then discuss changes we need to make it self-heal.

```
1  vagrant ssh cd
2
3  ansible-playbook /vagrant/ansible/swarm.yml \
4      -i /vagrant/ansible/hosts/prod
```

Finally, the time has come to provision the *cd* server with Jenkins.

```
1  ansible-playbook /vagrant/ansible/jenkins-node-swarm.yml \
2      -i /vagrant/ansible/hosts/prod
3
4  ansible-playbook /vagrant/ansible/jenkins.yml \
5      --extra-vars "main_job_src=service-healing-config.xml" \
6      -c local
```

We reached the point where the whole cluster is operational, and Jenkins server will be up and running soon. We set one Swarm master (*swarm-master*), two Swarm nodes (*swarm-node-1* and *swarm-node-2*), and one server with Ansible and, soon to be running, Jenkins (*cd*). Feel free to continue reading while Jenkins provisioning is running. We won't need it right away.

Setting Up Consul Health Checks and Watches for Monitoring Hardware

We can send instructions to Consul to perform periodic checks of services or entire nodes. It does not come with predefined checks. Instead, it runs scripts, performs HTTP requests, or wait for TTL signals defined by us. While the lack of predefined checks might seem like a disadvantage, it gives us the freedom to design the process as we see fit. In case we're using scripts to perform checks, Consul will expect them to exit with certain codes. If we exit from the check script with the *code 0*, Consul will assume that everything works correctly. Exit *code 1* is expected to be a warning, and the exit *code 2* is an error.

We'll start by creating a few scripts that will perform hardware checks. Getting information of, let's say, hard disk utilization is relatively easy with the df command.

```
1  df -h
```

We used the *-h* argument to output *human-readable* information, and the output is as follows.

```
1   Filesystem      Size  Used Avail Use% Mounted on
2   udev            997M   12K  997M   1% /dev
3   tmpfs           201M  440K  200M   1% /run
4   /dev/sda1        40G  4.6G   34G  13% /
5   none            4.0K     0  4.0K   0% /sys/fs/cgroup
6   none            5.0M     0  5.0M   0% /run/lock
7   none           1001M     0 1001M   0% /run/shm
8   none            100M     0  100M   0% /run/user
9   none            465G  118G  347G  26% /vagrant
10  none            465G  118G  347G  26% /tmp/vagrant-cache
```

Bear in mind that in your case the output might be slightly different.

What we truly need are numbers from the root directory (the third row in the output). We can filter the output of the df command so that only the row with the value / of the last column is displayed. After the filter, we should extract the percentage of used disk space (column 5). While we are extracting data, we might just as well get the disk size (column 2), and the amount of used space (column 3). Data that we extract should be stored as variables that we could use later on. The commands we can use to accomplish all that is as follows.

```
1  set -- $(df -h | awk '$NF=="/"{print $2" "$3" "$5}')
2
3  total=$1
4
5  used=$2
6
7  used_percent=${3::-1}
```

Since the value that represents the used space percentage contains the % sign, we removed the last character before assigning the value to the *used_percent* variable.

We can double-check whether the variables we created contain correct values with a simple printf command.

```
1  printf "Disk Usage: %s/%s (%s%%)\n" $used $total $used_percent
```

The output of the last command is as follows.

```
1  Disk Usage: 4.6G/40G (13%)
```

The only thing left is to exit with 1 (warning) or 2 (error) when a threshold is reached. We'll define the error threshold as 95% and warning as 80%. The only thing missing is a simple *if/elif/else* statement.

```
1  if [ $used_percent -gt 95 ]; then
2    echo "Should exit with 2"
3  elif [ $used_percent -gt 80 ]; then
4    echo "Should exit with 1"
5  else
6    echo "Should exit with 0"
7  fi
```

For testing purposes, we put echos. The script that we are about to make should exit with *2, 1* or *0*.

Let's move into the *swarm-master* node, create the script, and test it.

```
1  exit
2
3  vagrant ssh swarm-master
```

We'll start by creating a directory where Consul scripts will reside.

```
1  sudo mkdir -p /data/consul/scripts
```

Now we can create the script with the commands we practiced.

```
1  echo '#!/usr/bin/env bash
2
3  set -- $(df -h | awk '"'"'$NF=="/"{print $2" "$3" "$5}'"'"')
4  total=$1
5  used=$2
6  used_percent=${3::-1}
7  printf "Disk Usage: %s/%s (%s%%)\n" $used $total $used_percent
8  if [ $used_percent -gt 95 ]; then
9    exit 2
10 elif [ $used_percent -gt 80 ]; then
11   exit 1
12 else
13   exit 0
14 fi
15 ' | sudo tee /data/consul/scripts/disk.sh
16
17 sudo chmod +x /data/consul/scripts/disk.sh
```

Let's try it out. Since there's quite a lot of free disk space, the script should echo the disk usage and return zero.

```
1  /data/consul/scripts/disk.sh
```

The command provided an output similar to the following.

```
1  Disk Usage: 3.3G/39G (9%)
```

We can easily display the exit code of the last command with $?.

```
1  echo $?
```

The echo returned zero, and the script seems to be working. You can test the rest of exit codes by modifying the threshold to be below the current disk usage. I'll leave that to you, as a simple exercise.

 Consul check threshold exercise

Modify the disk.sh script in a way that warning and error thresholds are lower than the current HD usage. Test the changes by running the script and outputting the exit code. Once the exercise is done, revert the script to its original values.

Now that we have the script that checks the disk usage, we should tell Consul about its existence. Consul uses JSON format for specifying checks. The definition that utilizes the script we just created is as follows.

```
 1  {
 2    "checks": [
 3      {
 4        "id": "disk",
 5        "name": "Disk utilization",
 6        "notes": "Critical 95% util, warning 80% util",
 7        "script": "/data/consul/scripts/disk.sh",
 8        "interval": "10s"
 9      }
10    ]
11  }
```

That JSON would tell Consul that there is a check with the ID *disk*, name *Disk utilization* and notes *Critical 95% util, warning 80% util*. The *name* and *notes* are purely for visualization purposes (as you'll see soon). Next, we are specifying the path to the script to be */data/consul/scripts/disk.sh*. Finally, we are telling Consul to run the script every *10* seconds.

Let's create the JSON file.

```
1   echo '{
2     "checks": [
3       {
4         "id": "disk",
5         "name": "Disk utilization",
6         "notes": "Critical 95% util, warning 80% util",
7         "script": "/data/consul/scripts/disk.sh",
8         "interval": "10s"
9       }
10    ]
11  }' | sudo tee /data/consul/config/consul_check.json
```

When we started Consul (through the Ansible playbook), we specified that configuration files are located in the */data/consul/config/* directory. We still need to reload it, so that it picks up the new file we just created. The easiest way to reload Consul is by sending it the *HUP* signal.

```
1   sudo killall -HUP consul
```

We managed to create hard disk checks in Consul. It will run the script every ten seconds and, depending on its exit code, determine the health of the node it runs on (in this case *swarm-master*).

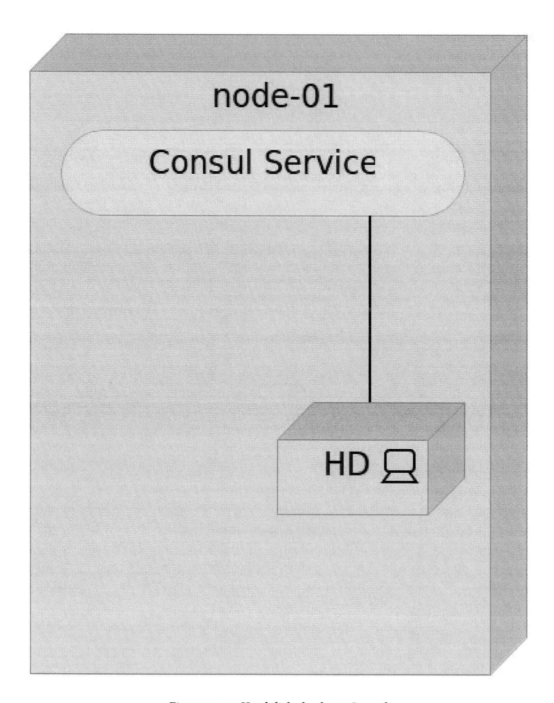

Figure 15-14: Hard disk checks in Consul

Let's take a look at the Consul UI by opening http://10.100.192.200:8500/ui/[282] from a browser. Once the UI is opened, please click the *Nodes* button, and then the *swarm-master* node. Among other information, you'll see two checks. One of them is *Serf Health Status*. It's Consul's internal check based on TTL. If one of the Consul nodes is down, that information will be propagated throughout

---

[282]http://10.100.192.200:8500/ui/

the cluster. The check check, called *Disk utilization*, is the one we just created, and, hopefully, the status is *passing*.

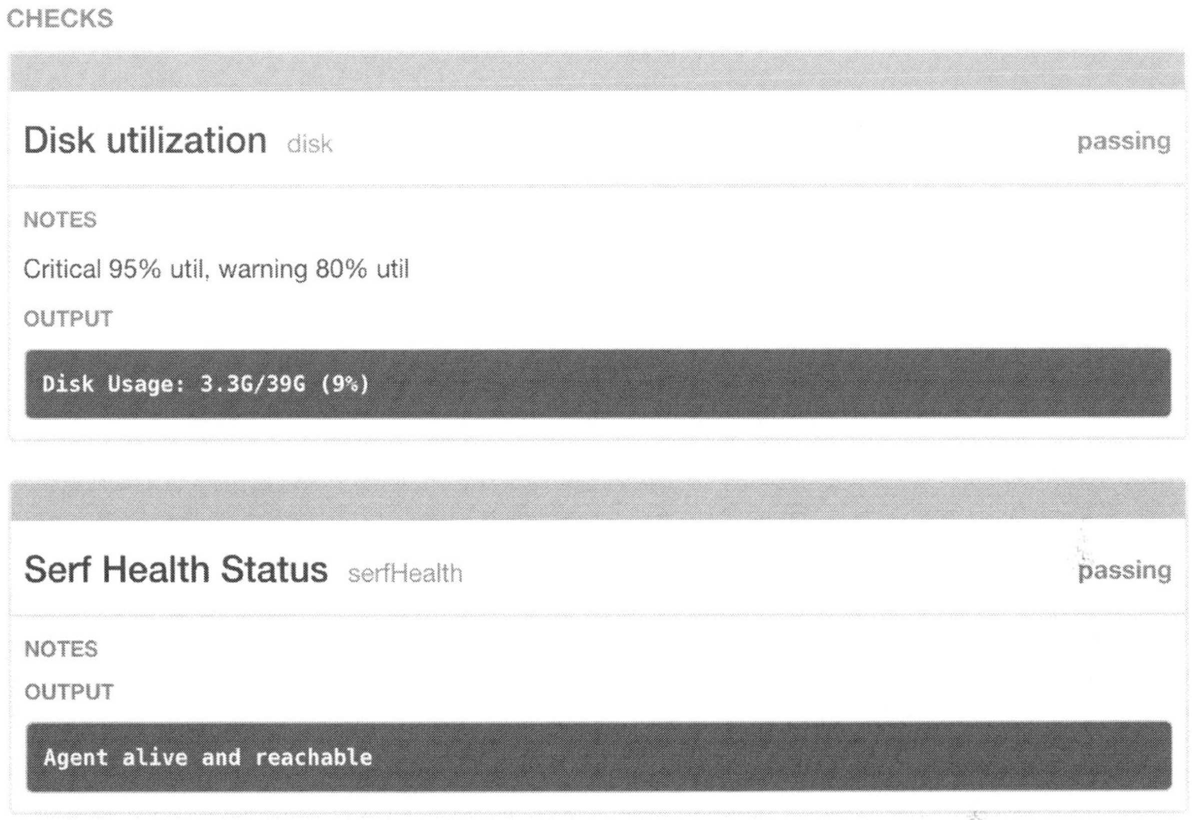

CHECKS

Disk utilization disk   passing

NOTES

Critical 95% util, warning 80% util

OUTPUT

`Disk Usage: 3.3G/39G (9%)`

Serf Health Status serfHealth   passing

NOTES

OUTPUT

`Agent alive and reachable`

Figure 15-15: Hard disk checks in Consul UI

Now that we know how easy it is to add a check in Consul, we should define what action should be performed when a check fails. We do that through Consul watches. As with checks, Consul does not offer an out-of-the-box final solution. It provides a mechanism for us to create the solution that fits our needs.

Consul supports seven different types of watches.

- key - Watch a specific KV pair
- keyprefix - Watch a prefix in the KV store
- services - Watch the list of available services
- nodes - Watch the list of nodes
- service - Watch the instances of a service
- checks - Watch the value of health checks
- event - Watch for custom user events

Each of the types is useful in certain situations and, together, they provide a very comprehensive framework for building your self-healing, fault tolerant, system. We'll concentrate on the *checks* type, since it will allow us to utilize the hard disk check we created earlier. Please consult the watches[283] documentation for more info.

We'll start by creating the script that will be run by Consul watcher. The *manage_watches.sh* script is as follows (please don't run it).

```bash
1  #!/usr/bin/env bash
2
3  RED="\033[0;31m"
4  NC="\033[0;0m"
5
6  read -r JSON
7  echo "Consul watch request:"
8  echo "$JSON"
9
10 STATUS_ARRAY=($(echo "$JSON" | jq -r ".[].Status"))
11 CHECK_ID_ARRAY=($(echo "$JSON" | jq -r ".[].CheckID"))
12 LENGTH=${#STATUS_ARRAY[*]}
13
14 for (( i=0; i<=$(( $LENGTH -1 )); i++ ))
15 do
16     CHECK_ID=${CHECK_ID_ARRAY[$i]}
17     STATUS=${STATUS_ARRAY[$i]}
18     echo -e "${RED}Triggering Jenkins job http://10.100.198.200:8080/job/hardwar\
19 e-notification/build${NC}"
20     curl -X POST http://10.100.198.200:8080/job/hardware-notification/build \
21         --data-urlencode json="{\"parameter\": [{\"name\":\"checkId\", \"value\"\
22 :\"$CHECK_ID\"}, {\"name\":\"status\", \"value\":\"$STATUS\"}]}"
23 done
```

We started by defining *RED* and *NC* variables that will help us paint critical parts of the output in red. Then, we are reading the Consul input and storing it into the *JSON* variable. That is followed by the creation of *STATUS_ARRAY* and *CHECK_ID_ARRAY* arrays that will hold *Status* and *CheckID* values for each element from the JSON. Finally, those arrays allow us to iterate through each item, and send a POST request to Jenkins to build the *hardware-notification* job (we'll take a look at it later). The request uses "Jenkins friendly" format for passing the *CHECK_ID* and *STATUS* variables. Please consult Jenkins remote access API[284] for more information.

Let's create the script.

---

[283]https://www.consul.io/docs/agent/watches.html
[284]https://wiki.jenkins-ci.org/display/JENKINS/Remote+access+API

```
1   echo '#!/usr/bin/env bash
2
3   RED="\033[0;31m"
4   NC="\033[0;0m"
5
6   read -r JSON
7   echo "Consul watch request:"
8   echo "$JSON"
9
10  STATUS_ARRAY=($(echo "$JSON" | jq -r ".[].Status"))
11  CHECK_ID_ARRAY=($(echo "$JSON" | jq -r ".[].CheckID"))
12  LENGTH=${#STATUS_ARRAY[*]}
13
14  for (( i=0; i<=$(( $LENGTH -1 )); i++ ))
15  do
16      CHECK_ID=${CHECK_ID_ARRAY[$i]}
17      STATUS=${STATUS_ARRAY[$i]}
18      echo -e "${RED}Triggering Jenkins job http://10.100.198.200:8080/job/hardwar\
19  e-notification/build${NC}"
20      curl -X POST http://10.100.198.200:8080/job/hardware-notification/build \
21          --data-urlencode json="{\"parameter\": [{\"name\":\"checkId\", \"value\"\
22  :\"$CHECK_ID\"}, {\"name\":\"status\", \"value\":\"$STATUS\"}]}"
23  done
24  ' | sudo tee /data/consul/scripts/manage_watches.sh
25
26  sudo chmod +x /data/consul/scripts/manage_watches.sh
```

Now that we have the script that will be executed whenever there is a check with the *warning* or *critical* status, we'll inform Consul about its existence. The Consul watches definition is as follows.

```
1   {
2     "watches": [
3       {
4         "type": "checks",
5         "state": "warning",
6         "handler": "/data/consul/scripts/manage_watches.sh >>/data/consul/logs/wat\
7   ches.log"
8       }, {
9         "type": "checks",
10        "state": "critical",
11        "handler": "/data/consul/scripts/manage_watches.sh >>/data/consul/logs/wat\
12  ches.log"
```

```
13      }
14    ]
15  }
```

This definition should be self-explanatory. We defined two watches, both of type *checks*. The first one will be run in case of a *warning*, and the second when a check is in the *critical* state. We're trying to keep things simple by specifying, in both instances, the same handler *manage_watches.sh*. In a "real world" setting, you should differentiate those two states and run different actions.

Let's create the watches file.

```
1   echo '{
2     "watches": [
3       {
4         "type": "checks",
5         "state": "warning",
6         "handler": "/data/consul/scripts/manage_watches.sh >>/data/consul/logs/wat\
7   ches.log"
8       }, {
9         "type": "checks",
10        "state": "critical",
11        "handler": "/data/consul/scripts/manage_watches.sh >>/data/consul/logs/wat\
12  ches.log"
13      }
14    ]
15  }' | sudo tee /data/consul/config/watches.json
```

Before we proceed, and reload Consul, we should have a quick discussion about the Jenkins job *hardware-notification*. It was already created when we provisioned Jenkins. Its configuration can be seen by opening http://10.100.198.200:8080/job/hardware-notification/configure[285]. It contains two parameters, *checkId* and *status*. We're using those two parameters as a way to avoid creating separate jobs for each hardware check. Whenever Consul watcher sends the POST request to build this job, it passes values to those two variables. In the build phase, we are simply running an echo command that sends values of those two variables to standard output (*STDOUT*). In a "real world" situation, this job would do some actions. For example, if disk space is low, it could remove unused logs and temporary files. Another example would be creation of additional nodes, if we're using one of the cloud services like Amazon AWS. In some other situations, no automated reaction is possible. In any case, besides concrete actions like those, this job should also send some kind of a notification (email, instant messaging, and so on) so that operators are informed about the potential problem. Since those situations would be difficult to reproduce locally, the initial definition of this job does nothing of the sort. I'll leave it up to you to extend it for your own needs.

---

[285]http://10.100.198.200:8080/job/hardware-notification/configure

The *hardware-notification* Jenkins job exercise

Modify the *hardware-notification* Jenkins job so that logs are deleted in case the *checkId* value is *disk*. Create mock logs (feel free to use the touch command to create files) on the server and run the job manually. Once the job build is finished, confirm that the logs were indeed removed.

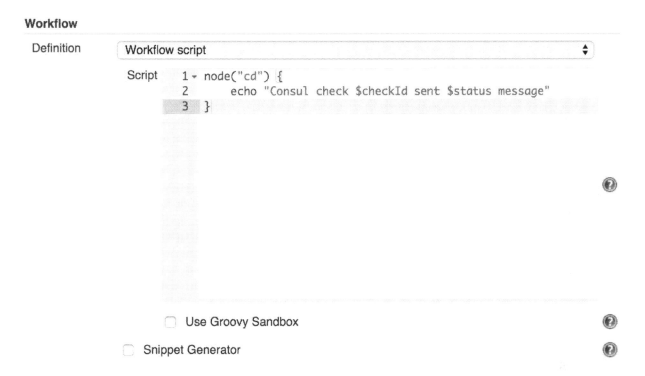

Figure 15-16: Settings screen of the Jenkins job hardware-notification

The problem we have right now is that the hard disk on the *swarm-master* node is mostly empty, thus preventing us from testing the system we just set up. We'll have to change the thresholds defined in the *disk.sh*. Let's modify the 80% warning threshold to 2%. Current HD usage is surely more than that.

```
1  sudo sed -i "s/80/2/" /data/consul/scripts/disk.sh
```

Finally, let's reload Consul and see what happens.

```
1  sudo killall -HUP consul
```

The first thing we should check is the watches log.

```
1  cat /data/consul/logs/watches.log
```

The relevant part of the output is as follows.

```
1  Consul watch request:
2  [{"Node":"swarm-master","CheckID":"disk","Name":"Disk utilization","Status":"war\
3  ning","Notes":"Critical 95% util, warning 80% util","Output":"Disk Usage: 3.3G/3\
4  9G (9%)\n","ServiceID":"","ServiceName":""}]
5  Triggering Jenkins job http://10.100.198.200:8080/job/hardware-notification/build
```

Please note that it might take a few seconds until Consul's check is run. If you did not receive the similar output from logs, repeat the cat command.

We can see the JSON that consul sent to the script and that the request to build the Jenkins job *hardware-notification* has been dispatched. We can also take a look at the Jenkins Console Output of this job by opening http://10.100.198.200:8080/job/hardware-notification/lastBuild/console[286] URL in a browser.

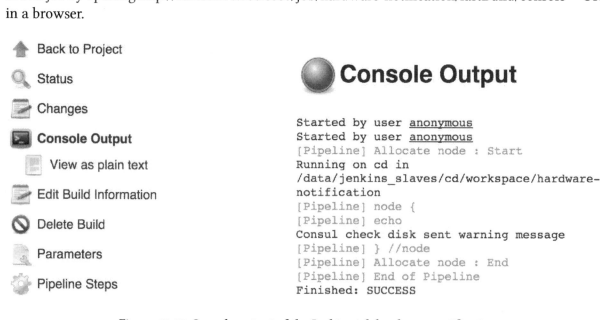

Figure 15-17: Console output of the Jenkins job hardware-notification

Since, at this moment, we have only one Consul check used for hard disk utilization, we should implement at least one more. The suitable candidate is memory. Even if we do not do any corrective action when some hardware check fails, having the information in Consul is already very useful in itself.

Now that we understand the process, we can do better, and use Ansible to set up everything. Besides, different checks should be set up not only in the *swarm-master* node but also in the rest of the cluster, and we don't want to do that manually unless it's for learning purposes.

Before we proceed, let's exit the *swarm-master* node.

---

[286]http://10.100.198.200:8080/job/hardware-notification/lastBuild/console

```
1  exit
```

Automatically Setting Up Consul Health Checks and Watches for Monitoring Hardware

At this moment, we have one hardware watcher configured only in the *swarm-master* node. Now that we are familiar with the way Consul watches work, we can use Ansible to deploy hardware monitoring to all the nodes of the Swarm cluster.

We'll run the Ansible playbook first, and then explore the roles that were used to setup the checks.

```
1  vagrant ssh cd
2
3  ansible-playbook /vagrant/ansible/swarm-healing.yml \
4      -i /vagrant/ansible/hosts/prod
```

The swarm-healing.yml[287] playbook is as follows.

```
1  - hosts: swarm
2    remote_user: vagrant
3    serial: 1
4    sudo: yes
5    vars:
6      - debian_version: vivid
7      - docker_cfg_dest: /lib/systemd/system/docker.service
8      - is_systemd: true
9    roles:
10     - common
11     - docker
12     - consul-healing
13     - swarm
14     - registrator
```

The only difference, when compared with the *swarm.yml* playbook, is the usage of the *consul-healing* role. Those two roles (*consul* and *consul-healing*) are very similar. The major difference is that the latter copies few more files to destination servers (roles/consul-healing/files/consul_check.json[288], roles/consul-healing/files/disk.sh[289], and roles/consul-healing/files/mem.sh[290]). We already created all those files manually, except the *mem.sh* that is used to check memory, and follows the

[287]https://github.com/vfarcic/ms-lifecycle/blob/master/ansible/swarm-healing.yml

[288]https://github.com/vfarcic/ms-lifecycle/blob/master/ansible/roles/consul-healing/files/consul_check.json

[289]https://github.com/vfarcic/ms-lifecycle/blob/master/ansible/roles/consul-healing/files/disk.sh

[290]https://github.com/vfarcic/ms-lifecycle/blob/master/ansible/roles/consul-healing/files/mem.sh

similar logic as the *disk.sh* script. The roles/consul-healing/templates/manage_watches.sh[291] and roles/consul-healing/templates/watches.json[292] files are defined as templates so that a few things can be customized through Ansible variables. All in all, we are mostly replicating manual steps through Ansible, so that provisioning and configuration of the whole cluster can be done automatically.

Please open the http://10.100.192.200:8500/ui/#/dc1/nodes[293] URL, and click on any of the nodes. You'll notice that each has *Disk utilization* and *Memory utilization* watches that, in the case of a failure, will start the build of the Jenkins job hardware-notification/[294].

While watching hardware resources, and performing predefined actions in case a threshold is reached, is interesting and useful, there is often a limitation to corrective actions that can be taken. If, for example, a whole node is down, the only thing we can do, in most cases, is to send a notification to someone who will manually investigate the problem. The real benefits are obtained by monitoring services.

Setting Up Consul Health Checks and Watches for Monitoring Services

Before we dive into service checks and watches, let's initiate deployment of our *books-ms* container. That way we'll use our time wisely, and discuss the subject while Jenkins is working hard to have the service up and running.

We'll start by indexing the branches defined in the Jenkins job books-ms[295]. Please open it in a browser, click the *Branch Indexing* link located in the left-hand menu, and follow it with *Run Now*. Once the indexing is done, Jenkins will detect that the *swarm* branch matches the filter, create the subproject, and run the first build. When finished, we'll have the *books-ms* service deployed to the cluster, and we'll be able to experiment with more self-healing techniques. You can monitor the build progress from the console screen[296].

The first step in self-healing is identifying that something is wrong. On the system level, we can observe services we're deploying and, if one of them does not respond, perform some corrective actions. We can continue using Consul checks in a similar manner as with did with memory and disk verifications. The major difference is that this time we'll be better of by using *http* instead *script* checks. Consul will perform periodic requests to our services, and send failures to the watches we already set up.

Before we proceed, we should discuss what should be checked. Should we check each service container? Should we check auxiliary containers like databases? Should we care about containers at all? Each of those checks can be useful depending on specific scenarios. In our case, we'll use a more general approach and monitor the service as a whole. Are we losing control if we are not

---

[291]https://github.com/vfarcic/ms-lifecycle/blob/master/ansible/roles/consul-healing/templates/manage_watches.sh

[292]https://github.com/vfarcic/ms-lifecycle/blob/master/ansible/roles/consul-healing/templates/watches.json

[293]http://10.100.192.200:8500/ui/#/dc1/nodes

[294]http://10.100.198.200:8080/job/hardware-notification/

[295]http://10.100.198.200:8080/job/books-ms/

[296]http://10.100.198.200:8080/job/books-ms/branch/master/lastBuild/console

monitoring each container separately? The answer to that question depends on the goals we're trying to accomplish. What do we care about? Do we care if all containers are running, or whether our services are working and performing as expected? If we'd need to choose, I'd say that the latter is more important. If our service is scaled to five instances and it continues performing well even after two of them stop working, there is probably nothing we should do. Only if service as a whole stops working, or if it doesn't perform as expected, some corrective actions should be taken.

Unlike hardware checks that benefit from uniformity, and should be located in one place, system checks can vary from one service to another. In order to avoid dependencies between a team that maintains a service and a team in charge of the overall CD processes, we'll keep check definitions inside the service code repository. That way, service team has full freedom to define checks they think are appropriate for the service they're developing. Since parts of the checks are variables, we'll define them through the Consul Template format. We'll, also, employ naming convention and always use the same name for the file. The consul_check.ctmpl[297] describes checks for the *books-ms* service, and is as follows.

```
1  {
2    "service": {
3      "name": "books-ms",
4      "tags": ["service"],
5      "port": 80,
6      "address": "{{key "proxy/ip"}}",
7      "checks": [{
8        "id": "api",
9        "name": "HTTP on port 80",
10       "http": "http://{{key "proxy/ip"}}/api/v1/books",
11       "interval": "10s",
12       "timeout": "1s"
13     }]
14   }
15 }
```

We defined not only checks but also the service named *books-ms*, the tag *service*, port it is running on and the address. Please note that, since this is the definition of the service as a whole, the port is *80*. In our case, the service as a whole is accessible through the proxy, no matter how many containers we deploy, nor ports they are running on. The address is obtained from Consul, through the *proxy/ip* key. This service should behave the same, no matter which color is currently deployed.

Once the service is defined, we proceed with the checks (in this case only one). Each check has an ID and a name, which are used for informational purposes only. The key entry is *http* that defines the address Consul will use to ping this service. Finally, we specified that ping should be performed every ten seconds and that the timeout should be one second. How do we use this template? To answer

---

[297]https://github.com/vfarcic/books-ms/blob/master/consul_check.ctmpl

that question, we should explore the Jenkinsfile[298], located in the *master* branch of the *books-ms* repository.

```
1   node("cd") {
2       def serviceName = "books-ms"
3       def prodIp = "10.100.192.200"
4       def proxyIp = "10.100.192.200"
5       def swarmNode = "swarm-master"
6       def proxyNode = "swarm-master"
7       def registryIpPort = "10.100.198.200:5000"
8       def swarmPlaybook = "swarm-healing.yml"
9       def proxyPlaybook = "swarm-proxy.yml"
10      def instances = 1
11
12      def flow = load "/data/scripts/workflow-util.groovy"
13
14      git url: "https://github.com/vfarcic/${serviceName}.git"
15      flow.provision(swarmPlaybook)
16      flow.provision(proxyPlaybook)
17      flow.buildTests(serviceName, registryIpPort)
18      flow.runTests(serviceName, "tests", "")
19      flow.buildService(serviceName, registryIpPort)
20
21      def currentColor = flow.getCurrentColor(serviceName, prodIp)
22      def nextColor = flow.getNextColor(currentColor)
23
24      flow.deploySwarm(serviceName, prodIp, nextColor, instances)
25      flow.runBGPreIntegrationTests(serviceName, prodIp, nextColor)
26      flow.updateBGProxy(serviceName, proxyNode, nextColor)
27      flow.runBGPostIntegrationTests(serviceName, prodIp, proxyIp, proxyNode, curr\
28  entColor, nextColor)
29      flow.updateChecks(serviceName, swarmNode)
30  }
```

The only significant difference, when compared with Jenkinsfiles we used in previous chapters, is the last line that invokes the *updateChecks* function from the roles/jenkins/files/scripts/workflow-util.groovy[299] utility script. The function is as follows.

---

[298]https://github.com/vfarcic/books-ms/blob/master/Jenkinsfile

[299]https://github.com/vfarcic/ms-lifecycle/blob/master/ansible/roles/jenkins/files/scripts/workflow-util.groovy

```
1  def updateChecks(serviceName, swarmNode) {
2      stage "Update checks"
3      stash includes: 'consul_check.ctmpl', name: 'consul-check'
4      node(swarmNode) {
5          unstash 'consul-check'
6          sh "sudo consul-template -consul localhost:8500 \
7              -template 'consul_check.ctmpl:/data/consul/config/${serviceName}.jso\
8  n:killall -HUP consul' \
9              -once"
10     }
11 }
```

In a nutshell, the function copies the file *consul_check.ctmpl* to the *swarm-master* node, and runs Consul Template. The result is the creation of, yet another, Consul configuration file that will perform service checks.

With the checks defined, we should take a closer look at the roles/consul-healing/templates/manage_watches.sh[300] script. The relevant part is as follows.

```
1      if [[ "$CHECK_ID" == "mem" || "$CHECK_ID" == "disk" ]]; then
2          echo -e "${RED}Triggering Jenkins job http://{{ jenkins_ip }}:8080/job/h\
3  ardware-notification/build${NC}"
4          curl -X POST http://{{ jenkins_ip }}:8080/job/hardware-notification/buil\
5  d \
6              --data-urlencode json="{\"parameter\": [{\"name\":\"checkId\", \"val\
7  ue\":\"$CHECK_ID\"}, {\"name\":\"status\", \"value\":\"$STATUS\"}]}"
8      else
9          echo -e "${RED}Triggering Jenkins job http://{{ jenkins_ip }}:8080/job/s\
10 ervice-redeploy/buildWithParameters?serviceName=${SERVICE_ID}${NC}"
11         curl -X POST http://{{ jenkins_ip }}:8080/job/service-redeploy/buildWith\
12 Parameters?serviceName=${SERVICE_ID}
13     fi
```

Since we aim at performing two types of checks (hardware and services), we had to introduce an *if/else* statement. When hardware failure is discovered (*mem* or *disk*), build request is sent to the Jenkins job *hardware-notification*. This part is the same as the definition we created earlier. On the other hand, we're assuming that any other type of checks is related to services, and a request is sent to the *service-redeploy* job. In our case, when *books-ms* service fails, Consul will send a request to build the *service-redeploy* job, and pass *books-ms* as the *serviceName* parameter. We're creating this job in Jenkins in the same way as we created others. The main difference is the usage of the roles/jenkins/templates/service-redeploy.groovy[301] script. The content is as follows.

---

[300]https://github.com/vfarcic/ms-lifecycle/blob/master/ansible/roles/consul-healing/templates/manage_watches.sh
[301]https://github.com/vfarcic/ms-lifecycle/blob/master/ansible/roles/jenkins/templates/service-redeploy.groovy

```
1   node("cd") {
2       def prodIp = "10.100.192.200"
3       def swarmIp = "10.100.192.200"
4       def proxyNode = "swarm-master"
5       def swarmPlaybook = "swarm-healing.yml"
6       def proxyPlaybook = "swarm-proxy.yml"
7
8       def flow = load "/data/scripts/workflow-util.groovy"
9       def currentColor = flow.getCurrentColor(serviceName, prodIp)
10      def instances = flow.getInstances(serviceName, swarmIp)
11
12      deleteDir()
13      git url: "https://github.com/vfarcic/${serviceName}.git"
14      try {
15          flow.provision(swarmPlaybook)
16          flow.provision(proxyPlaybook)
17      } catch (e) {}
18
19      flow.deploySwarm(serviceName, prodIp, currentColor, instances)
20      flow.updateBGProxy(serviceName, proxyNode, currentColor)
21  }
```

You probably noticed that the script is much shorter than the Jenkinsfile[302] we used before. We could easily use the same script to redeploy as the one we're using for deployment, and the end result would be (almost) the same. However, the objectives differ. One of the crucial requirements is speed. If our service failed, we want to redeploy is as fast as possible, while having into account as many different scenarios as possible. One of the important differences is that we are not running tests during redeployment. All tests already passed during deployment, or the service would not be running in the first place and there would be nothing to fail. Besides, the same set of tests running against the same release will always produce the same result, or our tests are flaky and unreliable, indicating grave mistakes in the testing process. You'll also notice that building and pushing to the registry is missing. We do not want to build and deploy a new release, that's what deployment is for. We want to get the latest release back to production as soon as possible. Our need is to restore the system to the same state as it was before the service failed. Now that we covered what is, intentionally, missing from the redeployment script, let's go through it.

The first change is in the way how we obtain the number of instances that should be running. Up until now, Jenkinsfile, residing in the service repository, was deciding how many instances to deploy. We had the statement def instances = 1 in the Jenkinsfile. However, since this redeployment job should be used for all services, we had to create a new function called *getInstances* that will retrieve the number stored in Consul. It represents the *desired* number of instances, and corresponds with the value specified in the Jenkinsfile. Without it, we would risk deploying a fixed number of containers

---

[302]https://github.com/vfarcic/books-ms/blob/swarm/Jenkinsfile

and, potentially, destroying someone else's intention. Maybe developers decided to run two instances of the service, or maybe they scaled it to five after realizing that the load is too big. For that reason, we have to discover how many instances to deploy, and put that information to good use. The *getInstances* function defined in the roles/jenkins/files/scripts/workflow-util.groovy[303] script is as follows.

```
1  def getInstances(serviceName, swarmIp) {
2      return sendHttpRequest("http://${swarmIp}:8500/v1/kv/${serviceName}/instance\
3  s?raw")
4  }
```

The function sends a simple request to Consul and returns the number of instances of the specified service.

Next, we are deleting the job workspace directory before cloning the code from GitHub. This removal of the files is necessary since the Git repository is different from one service to another, and Git repository cannot be cloned on top of the other. We don't need all the code, but rather few configuration files, specifically, those for Docker Compose and Consul. Never the less, it's easier if we clone everything. If the repository is big, you might consider getting only the files you need.

```
1      deleteDir()
2      git url: "https://github.com/vfarcic/${serviceName}.git"
```

Now that all the files we'll need (and many more that we won't) are in the workspace, we can initiate the redeployment. Before we proceed, let's discuss what might have caused the failure in the first place. We can identify three main culprits. One of the nodes stopped working, one of the infrastructure services is down (Swarm, Consul, and so on), or our own service failed. We'll skip the first possibility and leave it for later. If one of the infrastructure services stopped working, we could fix that by running Ansible playbooks. On the other hand, if the cluster is operating as expected, all we have to do is redeploy the container with our service.

Let's explore provisioning with Ansible. The part of the script that runs Ansible playbooks is as follows.

```
1      try {
2          flow.provision(swarmPlaybook)
3          flow.provision(proxyPlaybook)
4      } catch (e) {}
```

The major difference, when compared with the previous Jenkins Workflow scripts, is that, this time, provisioning is inside the *try/catch* block. The reason is a possible node failure. If the culprit for this

---

[303]https://github.com/vfarcic/ms-lifecycle/blob/master/ansible/roles/jenkins/files/scripts/workflow-util.groovy

redeployment is one malfunctioning node, provisioning will fail. That's not a problem in itself if the rest of the script is run. For that reason, we have this script block under *try/catch*, thus ensuring that the script continues running no matter the provisioning result. After all, if a node is not working, Swarm will redeploy the service somewhere else (explained in more detail later on). Let's move onto the next use case.

```
1    flow.deploySwarm(serviceName, prodIp, currentColor, instances)
2    flow.updateBGProxy(serviceName, proxyNode, currentColor)
```

Those two lines are the same as in the deployment script in the Jenkinsfile. The only, subtle, difference is that the number of instances is not hardcoded, but, as we saw earlier, discovered.

That's it for now. With the script we explored, we have two out of three scenarios covered. Our system will recover if one of infrastructure or one of our services fails. Let's try it out.

We'll stop one of the infrastructure services and see whether the system will get restored to the original state. There is probably no better candidate than *nginx*. It is part of our services infrastructure and, without it, none of our services work.

Without nginx, our service is not accessible through the port 80. At no point, Consul will know that *nginx* failed. Instead, Consul checker will detect that the *books-ms* service is not operational, and initiate a new build of the Jenkins job *service-redeploy*. As a result, provisioning and redeployment will be executed. Part of Ansible provisioning is in charge of ensuring that, among others, nginx is running.

Let's enter the *swarm-master* node and stop the *nginx* container.

```
1    exit
2
3    vagrant ssh swarm-master
4
5    docker stop nginx
6
7    exit
8
9    vagrant ssh cd
```

With nginx process dead, the *books-ms* service is not accessible (at least not through the port 80). We can confirm that by sending an HTTP request to it. Please bear in mind that Consul will initiate redeployment through Jenkins, so hurry up before it becomes operational again.

```
1    curl swarm-master/api/v1/books
```

As expected, *curl* returned the *Connection refused* error.

```
1  curl: (7) Failed to connect to swarm-master port 80: Connection refused
```

We can also take a look at the Consul UI. The Service books-ms check[304] should be in the critical state. You can click on the *swarm-master* link to get more details about all the service running on that node and their statuses. As a side note, *books-ms* is registered as running on the *swarm-master* server because that's where the proxy is. There is also *books-ms-blue* or *books-ms-green* service that contains data specific to deployed containers.

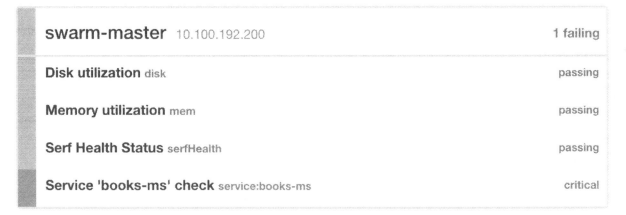

books-ms

TAGS

service

NODES

swarm-master 10.100.192.200	1 failing
Disk utilization disk	passing
Memory utilization mem	passing
Serf Health Status serfHealth	passing
Service 'books-ms' check service:books-ms	critical

Figure 15-18: Consul status screen with one check in the critical status

Finally, We can take a look at the service-redeploy console screen[305]. The redeployment process should be on the way, or, more likely, finished by now.

Once the build of the *service-redeploy* job is finished, everything should be restored to the original status, and we can use our service.

```
1  curl -I swarm-master/api/v1/books
```

The output of the response is as follows.

---

[304]http://10.100.192.200:8500/ui/#/dc1/services/books-ms

[305]http://10.100.198.200:8080/job/service-redeploy/lastBuild/console

```
1  HTTP/1.1 200 OK
2  Server: nginx/1.9.9
3  Date: Tue, 19 Jan 2016 21:53:00 GMT
4  Content-Type: application/json; charset=UTF-8
5  Content-Length: 2
6  Connection: keep-alive
7  Access-Control-Allow-Origin: *
```

The proxy service has been, indeed, redeployed, and everything is working as expected.

What would happen if, instead stopping one of the infrastructure services, we remove the *book-ms* instance entirely? Let's remove the service container, and see what happens.

```
1  export DOCKER_HOST=tcp://swarm-master:2375
2
3  docker rm -f $(docker ps --filter name=booksms --format "{{.ID}}")
```

Go ahead and open the service-redeploy Jenkins console screen[306]. It might take a couple of seconds until Consul initiates a new build. Once started, all we need to do is wait a bit longer, until the build finishes running. Once you see the *Finished: Success* message, we can double check whether the service is indeed operational.

---

[306]http://10.100.198.200:8080/job/service-redeploy/lastBuild/console

```
true[Workflow] stage: Update proxy
Entering stage Update proxy
Proceeding
[Workflow] stash
Stashed 4 file(s)
[Workflow] Allocate node : Start
Running on swarm-master in /data/jenkins_slaves/swarm-master/workspace/service-
redeploy
[Workflow] node {
[Workflow] unstash
[Workflow] sh
[service-redeploy] Running shell script
+ sudo cp nginx-includes.conf /data/nginx/includes/books-ms.conf
[Workflow] sh
[service-redeploy] Running shell script
+ sudo consul-template -consul localhost:8500 -template nginx-upstreams-
blue.ctmpl:/data/nginx/upstreams/books-ms.conf:docker kill -s HUP nginx -once
[Workflow] sh
[service-redeploy] Running shell script
+ curl -X PUT -d blue http://localhost:8500/v1/kv/books-ms/color
  % Total    % Received % Xferd  Average Speed   Time    Time     Time  Current
                                 Dload  Upload   Total   Spent    Left  Speed

    0     0    0     0    0     0      0      0 --:--:-- --:--:-- --:--:--     0
  100     8  100     4  100     4    782    782 --:--:-- --:--:-- --:--:--   800
true[Workflow] } //node
[Workflow] Allocate node : End
[Workflow] } //node
[Workflow] Allocate node : End
[Workflow] End of Workflow
Finished: SUCCESS
```

Figure 15-19: Output of the service-redeploy build

```
1  docker ps --filter name=books --format "table {{.Names}}"
2
3  curl -I swarm-master/api/v1/books
```

The combined output of both commands is as follows.

```
1  NAMES
2  swarm-node-2/booksms_app-blue_1
3  swarm-node-1/books-ms-db
4
5  ...
6
7  HTTP/1.1 200 OK
8  Server: nginx/1.9.9
9  Date: Tue, 19 Jan 2016 22:05:50 GMT
```

```
10  Content-Type: application/json; charset=UTF-8
11  Content-Length: 2
12  Connection: keep-alive
13  Access-Control-Allow-Origin: *
```

Our service is, indeed, running and accessible through the proxy. The system healed itself. We can stop almost any process, on any of the Swarm nodes, and, with a few seconds delay, system will restore itself to the previous state. The only thing we haven't tried is to stop the whole node. Such an action would require a few more changes to our scripts. We'll explore those changes later on. Please be aware that this is a demo setting and it does not mean that the system, as it is now, is ready for production. On the other hand, it's not far either. With a bit of tweaking, you could consider applying this to you system. You might want to add some notifications (email, Slack, and so on) and adapt the process to your needs. The important part is the process. Once we understand what we want, and how to get there, the rest is usually only a question of time.

The process we have, at this moment, is as follows.

- Consul performs periodic HTTP requests, runs custom scripts or waits for time-to-live (TTL) messages from services.
- In case Consul's request does not return status code 200, the script returns a non-zero exit code, or TTL message was not received, Consul sends a request to Jenkins.
- Upon receiving a request from Consul, Jenkins initiates redeployment process, sends notification messages, and so on.

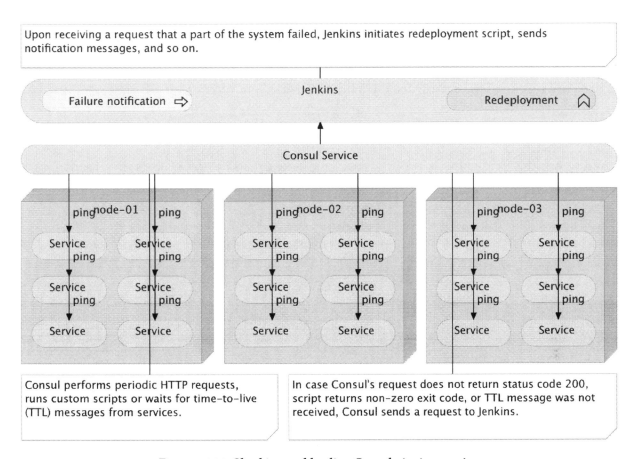

Figure 15-20: Checking and healing Consul pinging services

We explored a few examples of reactive healing. Those were, by no means, exhaustive enough to provide you with everything you need to set up your own system, but, hopefully, provided you with a path that you should explore in more depth, and adapt to your own needs. Right now, we'll move our attention to preventive measure we can take. We'll examine scheduled scaling and descaling. It is a good candidate as an introduction to preventive healing since it is probably the easiest one to implement.

Preventive Healing Through Scheduled Scaling and Descaling

Preventive healing is a huge topic in itself and, in all but the simplest scenarios, requires historical data that can be used to analyze the system and predict the future. Since, at this moment, we neither have the data, nor the tools to generate them, we'll start with a very simple example that does not require any of those.

The scenario we'll explore is as follows. We are working on an online book store. Marketing department decided that, starting from the new years eve, all readers will be able to purchase books with a discount. The campaign will last for a day, and we expect it to generate a huge interest. In technical terms, that means that during 24 hours, starting from midnight, January the first, our system will be under heavy load. What should we do? We already have processes and tools that allow us to scale our system (or parts that will be most affected). What we need to do is scale selected services before the campaign starts and, once it's finished, restore it to the original state. The problem is that no one wants to celebrate new years eve in the office. We can fix that easily with Jenkins. We can create a scheduled job that will scale, and, later on, descale our services. With this problem solved, another one emerges. To how many instances should we scale? We can define a number in advance but, in that way, we risk making a mistake. For example, we might decide to scale to three instances (at this moment we have only one). Between today and the start of the campaign, due to some other reason, the number of instances might increase to five. In such a scenario, not only that we would not increase the capacity of our system, but would accomplish quite contrary. Our scheduled job would descale the service from five to three. The solution might be to use relative values. Instead of specifying that the system should be scaled to three instances, we should set it up in a way that the number of instances should be increased by two. If there is one instance running, such a process would launch two more and increase the overall number to three. On the other hand, if someone already scaled the service to five, the end result would be seven containers running inside our cluster. The similar logic can be employed after the campaign is finished. We can create the second scheduled job that would decrease the number of running instances by two. From three, to one. From five, to three. It does not matter how many will be running at that moment since we would decrease that number by two.

This process of preventive healing is similar to the usage of vaccinations. Their primary use is not to heal an existing infection, but to develop immunity that will prevent them from spreading in the first place. In the same way, we'll schedule scaling (and later on descaling), in order to prevent the increased load affecting our system in unexpected ways. Instead of healing an infected system, we'll prevent it from getting into bad shape.

Let's see such the process in action.

Please open the Jenkins books-ms-scale configuration[307] screen. The job configuration is very straightforward. It has one parameter called *scale* with the default value of *2*. It can be adjusted when starting a build. *Build Triggers* is set to *build periodically* with the value "45 23 31 12 ". *If you already used *cron scheduling, this should look familiar. The format is *MINUTE HOUR DOM MONTH DOW*. The first number represents minutes, the second hours, the third is the day of a month, followed by month and the day of the week. Asterisk, can be translated to any. So, the value we are using is fourty fifth minute of the twenty third hour, on thirty first day of the twelfth month. In other words, fifteen minutes before new years eve. That is more than enough time for us to increase the number of instances before the campaign starts. For more information about the scheduling format, please click the icon with a question mark located right of the *Schedule* field.

The third, at last, part of the job configuration is the following Workflow script.

---

[307]http://10.100.198.200:8080/job/books-ms-scale/configure

```
1  node("cd") {
2      def serviceName = "books-ms"
3      def swarmIp = "10.100.192.200"
4
5      def flow = load "/data/scripts/workflow-util.groovy"
6      def instances = flow.getInstances(serviceName, swarmIp).toInteger() + scale.\
7  toInteger()
8      flow.putInstances(serviceName, swarmIp, instances)
9      build job: "service-redeploy", parameters: [[$class: "StringParameterValue",\
10  name: "serviceName", value: serviceName]]
11  }
```

Since there is no real reason to duplicate the code, we are using the helper functions from the roles/jenkins/files/scripts/workflow-util.groovy[308] script.

We start by defining the number of instances we want to run. We do that by adding the value of the *scale* parameter (defaults to two) to the number of instances our service is currently using. We get the latter by invoking the *getInstances* function we already utilized in a couple of cases throughout the book. That new value is put to Consul through the *putInstances* function. Finally, we run a build of the *service-redeploy* job which does the redeployment that we need. To summarize, since the *service-redeploy* job reads the number of instances from Consul, all we had to do in this script, before invoking the *service-redeploy* build, was to change the *scale* value in Consul. From there on, *service-redeploy* job will do what's needed to scale the number of containers. By invoking the *service-redeploy* job, we avoided replicating the code that is already used elsewhere.

---

[308]https://github.com/vfarcic/ms-lifecycle/blob/master/ansible/roles/jenkins/files/scripts/workflow-util.groovy

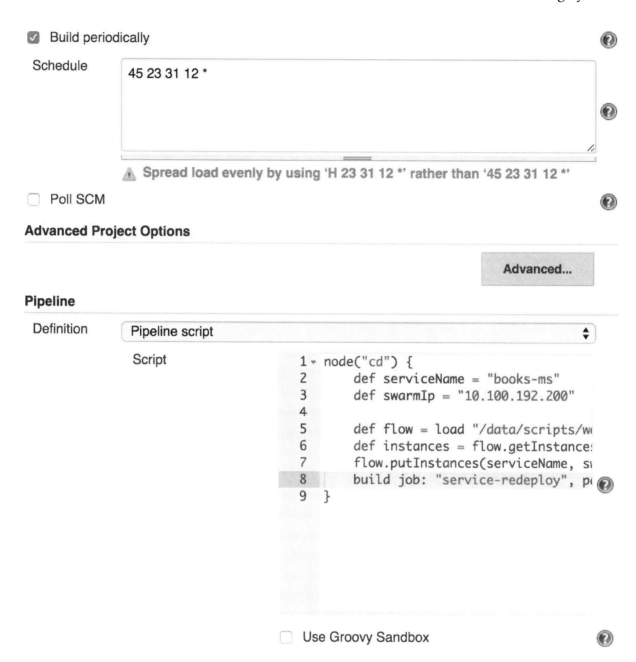

Figure 15-21: Configuration of the books-ms-scale job representing scheduled scaling

Now we have two paths we can take. One is to wait until new years eve and confirm that the job works. I will take liberty and assume that you do not have so much patience, and proceed with the alternative. We'll run the job manually. Before we do that, let's take a quick look at the current situation inside our Swarm cluster.

```
1  export DOCKER_HOST=tcp://swarm-master:2375
2
3  docker ps --filter name=books --format "table {{.Names}}"
4
5  curl swarm-master:8500/v1/kv/books-ms/instances?raw
```

The combined output of the commands is as follows.

```
1  NAMES
2  swarm-node-1/booksms_app-blue_1
3  swarm-node-2/books-ms-db
4  ...
5  1
```

We can see that only one instance of the books-ms service is running (*booksms_app-blue_1*) and that Consul has the value of *1* stored as the *books-ms/instances* key.

Let's run the *books-ms-scale* Jenkins job. If everything works as expected, it should increase the number of *books-ms* instances by two, resulting in three in total. Please open the books-ms-scale build screen[309] and click the *Build* button. You can monitor the progress by opening the books-ms-scale console screen[310]. You'll see that, after storing the new number of instances in Consul, it will invoke a build of the service-redeploy[311] job. After a few seconds, the build will finish, and we'll be able to verify the result.

```
1  docker ps --filter name=books --format "table {{.Names}}"
2
3  curl swarm-master:8500/v1/kv/books-ms/instances?raw
```

The combined output of the commands is as follows.

```
1  NAMES
2  swarm-node-2/booksms_app-blue_3
3  swarm-node-1/booksms_app-blue_2
4  swarm-node-1/booksms_app-blue_1
5  swarm-node-2/books-ms-db
6  ...
7  3
```

---

[309]http://10.100.198.200:8080/job/books-ms-scale/build?delay=0sec
[310]http://10.100.198.200:8080/job/books-ms-scale/lastBuild/console
[311]http://10.100.198.200:8080/job/service-redeploy/lastBuild/console

As we can see, this time, three instances of the service are running. We can observe the same result from the Consul UI, by navigating to the key/value books-ms/instances screen[312].

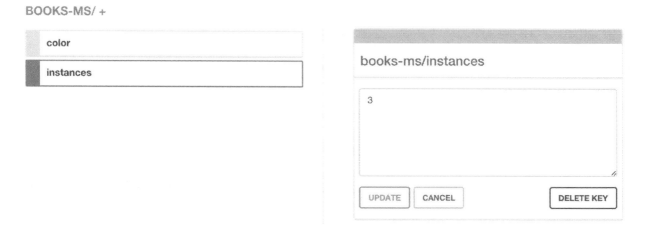

Figure 15-22: Consul UI Key/Value books-ms/instances screen

Our system is now ready to take the increased load during those 24 hours. As you saw, we were very generous by scheduling it to run 15 minutes before the due date. The execution of the build lasted only a couple of seconds. We could speed it even more by skipping the provisioning part of the *service-redeploy* job. I'll leave that to you as an exercise.

 ### Add conditional to the *service-redeploy* job

Modify the *service-redeploy* Jenkins job so that provisioning is optional. You'll have to add a new parameter that accepts boolean value and add an *if/else* statement to the workflow script. Make sure that the parameter has the default value set to true so that provisioning is always performed unless specified otherwise. Once finished, switch to the configuration of the *books-ms-scale* job and modify it so that the call to the *service-redeploy* job passes the signal to skip provisioning.

What happens after 24 hours passes, and the campaign is over? The Jenkins job books-ms-descale[313] will be run. It is the same as the *books-ms-scale* job with two notable differences. The *scale* parameter is set to -2 and it is scheduled to run on the second of January, fifteen minutes after midnight (15 0 2 1 *). We gave our system fifteen minutes of cool-down time. The Workflow script is the same.

Let's run it by opening the books-ms-descale build screen[314], and clicking the *Build* button. It will reduce the number of instances by two, and run a build of the *service-redeploy* job. Once finished, we can have another look at our cluster.

---

[312]http://10.100.192.200:8500/ui/#/dc1/kv/books-ms/instances/edit

[313]http://10.100.198.200:8080/job/books-ms-descale/configure

[314]http://10.100.198.200:8080/job/books-ms-descale/build?delay=0sec

```
1  docker ps --filter name=books --format "table {{.Names}}"
2
3  curl swarm-master:8500/v1/kv/books-ms/instances?raw
```

The combined output of the commands is as follows.

```
1  NAMES
2  swarm-node-1/booksms_app-blue_1
3  swarm-node-2/books-ms-db
4  ...
5  1
```

We are back where we started. The campaign is finished, and the service is reduced from three instances to one. The value in Consul is restored as well. The system survived horde of visitors desperately trying to benefit from our new years eve discount, business is happy that we were able to serve them all, and life continues as it was.

We could have created different formulas to accomplish our goals. It could be as simple as multiplying the number of existing instances. That would give us a bit more realistic scenario. Instead of adding two new containers, we could have multiplied them by two. If three were running before, six would be running afterwards. As you can imagine, those formulas can often be much more complicated. More importantly, they would require much more consideration. If, instead of running one, we were running fifty different services, we would not apply the same formula to all of them. Some would need to be scaled a lot, some not so much, while other not at all. The best way to proceed would be to employ some kind of stress tests that would tell us which pieces of the system require scaling, and how much that scaling should be. There's plethora of tools that can run those tests, with JMeter[315] and Gatling[316] (my favorite) being only a few.

I mentioned, at the beginning of this chapter, that preventive healing is based on historical data. This was a very poor, yet very efficient and simple way of demonstrating that. In this case, historical data was in our heads. We knew that a marketing campaign will increase the load on our service, and acted in a way that potential problems are avoided. The real, and much more complicated, way to create preventive healing require more than our memory. It requires a system capable of storing and analyzing data. We'll discuss requirements for such a system in the next chapter.

Reactive Healing with Docker Restart Policies

Those more familiar with Docker might be asking why I did not mention Docker restart policies. On a first look, they seem to be a very effective way to recuperate failed containers. They are, indeed, the easiest way to define when to restart containers. We can use the `--restart` flag on `docker run` (or the equivalent Docker Compose definition), and the container will be restarted on exit. The following table summarizes the currently supported restart policies.

---

[315]http://jmeter.apache.org/

[316]http://gatling.io/

Policy	Result
no	Do not automatically restart the container when it exits. This is the default.
on-failure[:max-retries]	Restart only if the container exits with a non-zero exit status. Optionally, limit the number of restart retries the Docker daemon attempts.
always	Always restart the container regardless of the exit status. When you specify always, the Docker daemon will try to restart the container indefinitely. The container will also always start on daemon startup, regardless of the current state of the container.
unless-stopped	Always restart the container regardless of the exit status, but do not start it on daemon startup if the container has been put to a stopped state before.

An example of the usage of restart policy is as follows (please do not run it).

```
1   docker run --restart=on-failure:3 mongo
```

In that case, mongo would be restarted up to three times. The restart would occur only if the process running inside the mongo container exits with a non-zero status. If we stop that container, the restart policy would not be applied.

The problem with restart policies is that there are too many corner cases not contemplated. The process running inside a container might fail due problems not directly related to the container that failed. For example, a service inside the container might be trying to connect to a database through a proxy. It might have been designed to stop if the connection could not be established. If, for some reason, the node with the proxy is not operational, it doesn't matter how many times we restart the container, the result will always be the same. There is nothing wrong in trying, but, sooner or later, someone needs to be notified about the problem. Maybe provisioning scripts need to be run to restore the system to the desired state. Maybe more nodes need to be added to the cluster. Maybe even the whole data center is not operational. No matter the cause, there are many more possible paths that could be taken than what restart policy permits. For those reasons, we do need a more robust system to deal with all those circumstances, and we are already on the way of creating it. The flow we have established is much more robust than simple restart policies, and it already covers the same problems as those that can be solved with the Docker restart policy. Actually, as it is now, we have many more paths covered. We perform containers orchestration with Docker Swarm that will make sure that our services are deployed to the most suited nodes inside the cluster. We use Ansible that is continuously (with each deploy) provisioning the cluster, thus ensuring that the whole infrastructure is in the correct state. We are using Consul in combination with Registrator and Consul Template for service discovery, making sure that the registry of all our services is always up to date. Finally, Consul health checks are continuously monitoring the state of our cluster and, in case of a failure, sends requests to Jenkins that will initiate appropriate corrective actions.

We are utilizing the Docker's slogan *batteries included but removable* to our benefit by extending the system to suit our needs.

Combining On-Premise with Cloud Nodes

I won't start a discussion whether to use on-premise servers or cloud hosting. Both have their advantages and disadvantages. The decision what to use depends on individual needs. Besides, such an attempt would be better suited inside the clustering and scaling chapter. However, there is a clear use case in favour of cloud hosting that would suit very well the needs of, at least, one of the scenarios from this chapter.

Cloud hosting shines when we need a temporary increase in the cluster capacity. A good example would be our fictional scenario with the new years eve campaign. We needed to boost our capacity for a day. If you are already hosting all your servers in the cloud, this scenario would require a few more nodes to be created and, later on, destroyed, once the load is reduced to its former size. On the other hand, if you use on-premise hosting, that would be an opportunity to contract cloud hosting only for those additional nodes. Buying a new set of servers that will be used only during a short period is very costly, especially if we take into account that the cost consists not only of hardware price, but also maintenance. If, in such cases, we use cloud nodes, the invoice would be paid only for the time we use them (assuming that we destroy them afterwards). Since we have all the scripts for provisioning and deploying services, the setup of those nodes would be almost effortless.

Personally, I prefer the combination of on-premise and cloud hosting. My on-premise servers are fulfilling the need for the minimum capacity, while cloud hosting nodes are being created (and destroyed) whenever that capacity needs to be temporarily increased. Please note that such a combination is only my personal preference, and might not apply to your use cases.

The important part is that everything you learned from this book is equally applicable to both situations (on-premise or cloud). The only significant difference is that you should not be using Vagrant on production servers. We are using it only to create quickly virtual machines on your laptop. If you are looking for a way to create production VMs in a similar way as with Vagrant, I suggest you explore another HashiCorp product called Packer[317].

Self-Healing Summary (So Far)

What we built so far is, in some cases, close to what Kubernetes and Mesos offer out of the box, while in others exceeds their functionality. The real advantage of the system we are working on is its the ability to fine-tune it to your needs. That is not to say that Kubernetes and Mesos should not be used. You should, at least, be familiar with them. Do not take anyone's word for granted (not even mine). Try them out and make your own conclusions. There are as many use cases as there are projects, and each is different from the other. While in some cases the system we built would provides a good base to build upon, there are others where, for example, Kubernetes or Mesos might be more appropriate. I could not fit all the possible combinations in detail inside a single book. That would increase it to an unmanageable size. Instead, I choose to explore ways we can build systems that are highly extensible. Almost any piece we used by now can be extended, or replaced with

---

[317]https://www.packer.io/

another. I feel that this approach gives you more possibilities to adapt examples to your own needs and, at the same time, learn not only how something works, but why we chose it.

We went far from the humble beginnings of this book, and we are not yet done. The exploration of self-healing systems will continue. However, first we need turn our attention to different ways of collecting data generated inside our cluster.

As the first part of the self-healing subject is closing to an end, let us destroy our VMs, and start the new chapter fresh.

You know what follows next. We'll destroy everything we did, and begin the next chapter fresh.

```
1  exit
2
3  vagrant halt
```

Centralized Logging and Monitoring

I have so much chaos in my life, it's become normal. You become used to it. You have just to relax, calm down, take a deep breath and try to see how you can make things work rather than complain about how they're wrong.

– Tom Welling

Our exploration of DevOps practices and tools led us towards clustering and scaling. As a result, we developed a system that allows us to deploy services to a cluster, in an easy and efficient way. The result is an ever increasing number of containers running on a cluster consisting of, potentially, many servers. Monitoring one server is easy. Monitoring many services on a single server poses some difficulties. Monitoring many services on many servers requires a whole new way of thinking and a new set of tools. As you start embracing microservices, containers, and clusters, the number of deployed containers will begin increasing rapidly. The same holds true for servers that form the cluster. We cannot, anymore, log into a node and look at logs. There are too many logs to look at. On top of that, they are distributed among many servers. While yesterday we had two instances of a service deployed on a single server, tomorrow we might have eight instances deployed to six servers. The same holds true for monitoring. Old tools, like Nagios, are not designed to handle constant changes in running servers and services. We already used Consul that provides a different, not to say new, approach to managing near real-time monitoring and reaction when thresholds are reached. However, that is not enough. Real-time information is valuable to detect that something is wrong, but it does not give us information why the failure happened. We can know that a service is not responding, but we cannot know why.

We need historical information about our system. That information can be in the form of logs, hardware utilization, health checking, and many other things. The need to store historical data is not new and has been in use for a long time. However, the direction that information travels changed over time. While, in the past, most solutions were based on a centralized data collectors, today, due to very dynamic nature of services and servers, we tend to have data collectors decentralized.

What we need for cluster logging and monitoring is a combination of decentralized data collectors that are sending information to a centralized parsing service and data storage. There are plenty of products specially designed to fulfill this requirement, ranging from on-premise to cloud solutions, and everything in between. FluentD[318], Loggly[319], GrayLog[320], Splunk[321], and DataDog[322] are only a few of the solutions we can employ. I chose to show you the concepts through the ELK stack

---

[318]http://www.fluentd.org/

[319]https://www.loggly.com/

[320]https://www.graylog.org/

[321]http://www.splunk.com/

[322]https://www.datadoghq.com/

(ElasticSearch[323], LogStash[324], and Kibana[325]). The stack has the advantage of being free, well documented, efficient, and widely used. ElasticSearch[326] established itself as one of the best databases for real-time search and analytics. It is distributed, scalable, highly available, and provides a sophisticated API. LogStash[327] allows us to centralize data processing. It can be easily extended to custom data formats and offers a lot of plugins that can suit almost any need. Finally, Kibana[328] is an analytics and visualization platform with intuitive interface sitting on top of ElasticSearch. The fact that we'll use the ELK stack does not mean that it is better than the other solutions. It all depends on specific use cases and particular needs. I'll walk you through the principles of centralized logging and monitoring using the ELK stack. Once those principles are understood, you should have no problem applying them to a different stack if you choose to do so.

We switched the order of things and chose the tools before discussing the need for centralized logging. Let's remedy that.

The Need for Centralized Logging

In most cases, log messages are written to files. That is not to say that files are the only, nor the most efficient way of storing logs. However, since most teams are using file-based logs in one form or another, for the time being, I'll assume that is your case as well.

If we are lucky, there is one log file per a service or application. However, more often than not, there are multiple files into which our services are outputting information. Most of the time, we do not care much what is written in logs. When things are working well, there is not much need to spend valuable time browsing through logs. A log is not a novel we read to pass the time, nor it is a technical book we spend time with as a way to improve our knowledge. Logs are there to provide valuable info when something, somewhere, went wrong.

The situation seems to be simple. We write information to logs that we ignore most of the time, and when something goes wrong, we consult them and find the cause of the problem in no time. At least, that's what many are hoping for. The reality is far more complicated than that. In all but most trivial systems, the debugging process is much more complex. Applications and services are, almost always, interconnected, and it is often not easy to know which one caused the problem. While it might manifest in one application, investigation often shows that the cause is in another. For example, a service might have failed to instantiate. After some time spent browsing its logs, we might discover that the cause is in the database. The service could not connect to it and failed to launch. We got the symptom, but not the cause. We need to switch to the database log to find it out. With this simple example, we already got to the point where looking at one log is not enough.

---

[323]https://www.elastic.co/products/elasticsearch

[324]https://www.elastic.co/products/logstash

[325]https://www.elastic.co/products/kibana

[326]https://www.elastic.co/products/elasticsearch

[327]https://www.elastic.co/products/logstash

[328]https://www.elastic.co/products/kibana

With distributed services running on a cluster, the situation complicates exponentially. Which instance of the service is failing? Which server is it running on? What are the upstream services that initiated the request? What is the memory and hard disk usage in the node where the culprit resides? As you might have guessed, finding, gathering, and filtering the information needed for the successful discovery of the cause is often very complicated. The bigger the system, the harder it gets. Even with monolithic applications, things can easily get out of hand. If (micro)services approach is adopted, those problems are multiplied. Centralized logging is a must for all but simplest and smallest systems. Instead, many of us, when things go wrong, start running from one server to another, jumping from one file to the other. Like a chicken with its head cut off - running around with no direction. We tend to accept the chaos logging creates, and consider it part of our profession.

What do we look for in centralized logging? As it happens, many things, but the most important are as follows.

- A way to parse data and send them to a central database in near real-time.
- The capacity of the database to handle near real-time data querying and analytics.
- A visual representation of the data through filtered tables, dashboards, and so on.

We already choose the tools that will be able to fulfill all those requirements (and more). The ELK stack (LogStash, ElasticSearch, and Kibana) can do all that. As in the case of all other tools we explored, this stack can easily be extended to satisfy the particular needs we'll set in front of us.

Now that we have a vague idea what we want to accomplish, and have the tools to do that, let us explore a few of the logging strategies we can use. We'll start with the most commonly used scenario and, slowly, move towards more complicated and more efficient ways to define our logging strategy.

Without further ado, let's create the environments we'll use to experiment with centralized logging and, later on, monitoring. We'll create three nodes. You should already be familiar with the *cd* and *prod* VMs. The first one will be used mainly for provisioning while the second will act as a production server. We'll introduce a new one called *logging*. It will be an imitation of a production server aimed at running all the logging and monitoring tools. Ideally, instead of a single production server (*prod*), we would run examples against the, let's say, Swarm cluster. That would allow us to see the benefits in a more production-like setting. However, since the previous few chapters already stretched limits of what could be run on a single laptop, I did not want to risk it and opted for a single VM. That being said, all the examples are equally applicable to one, ten, hundred, or thousand servers. You should have no problem extending them to you entire cluster.

```
1  vagrant up cd prod logging
2
3  vagrant ssh cd
```

Sending Log Entries to ElasticSearch

We'll start by provisioning the *logging* server with the ELK stack (ElasticSearch, LogStash, and Kibana). We'll continue using Ansible for provisioning since it converted itself into our favorite configuration management tool.

Let's run the elk.yml[329] playbook and explore it while it's executing.

```
1  ansible-playbook /vagrant/ansible/elk.yml \
2      -i /vagrant/ansible/hosts/prod \
3      --extra-vars "logstash_config=file.conf"
```

The definition of the playbook is as follows.

```
1  - hosts: logging
2    remote_user: vagrant
3    serial: 1
4    roles:
5      - common
6      - docker
7      - elasticsearch
8      - logstash
9      - kibana
```

We used the *common* and the *docker* roles many times before, so we'll skip them, and jump straight into *elasticsearch* tasks defined in the roles/elasticsearch/tasks/main.yml[330] file.

```
1  - name: Container is running
2    docker:
3      name: elasticsearch
4      image: elasticsearch
5      state: running
6      ports:
7        - 9200:9200
8      volumes:
9        /data/elasticsearch:/usr/share/elasticsearch/data
10   tags: [elasticsearch]
```

---

[329]https://github.com/vfarcic/ms-lifecycle/blob/master/ansible/elk.yml

[330]https://github.com/vfarcic/ms-lifecycle/blob/master/ansible/roles/elasticsearch/tasks/main.yml

Thanks to Docker, all we have to do is run the official elasticsearch image[331]. It exposes its API through the port *9200* and defines a single volume we'll use to persist data in the host.

The next in line is the logstash[332] role. The tasks set in the roles/logstash/tasks/main.yml[333] file are as follows.

```
 1  - name: Directory is present
 2    file:
 3      path: "{{ item.path }}"
 4      recurse: yes
 5      state: directory
 6      mode: "{{ item.mode }}"
 7    with_items: directories
 8    tags: [logstash]
 9
10  - name: File is copied
11    copy:
12      src: "{{ item.src }}"
13      dest: "{{ item.dest }}"
14    with_items: files
15    tags: [logstash]
16
17  - name: Container is running
18    docker:
19      name: logstash
20      image: logstash
21      state: running
22      expose:
23        - 5044
24        - 25826
25        - 25826/udp
26        - 25827
27        - 25827/udp
28      ports:
29        - 5044:5044
30        - 5044:5044/udp
31        - 25826:25826
32        - 25826:25826/udp
33        - 25827:25827
34        - 25827:25827/udp
```

---

[331]https://hub.docker.com/_/elasticsearch/

[332]https://github.com/vfarcic/ms-lifecycle/tree/master/ansible/roles/logstash

[333]https://github.com/vfarcic/ms-lifecycle/blob/master/ansible/roles/logstash/tasks/main.yml

```
35        volumes:
36          - /data/logstash/conf:/conf
37          - /data/logstash/logs:/logs
38        links:
39          - elasticsearch:db
40        command: logstash -f /conf/{{ logstash_config }}
41      tags: [logstash]
```

While a big more numerous than the *elasticsearch* tasks, these are still pretty straightforward. The tasks create a directory, copy few configuration files we'll use throughout this chapter, and run the official logstash image[334]. Since we'll experiment with quite a few scenarios, different ports need to be exposed and defined. The role exposes two volumes. The first one will hold configuration files while we'll use the second as a directory to place some logs. Finally, the task creates the link to the *elasticsearch* container and specifies that the *command* should start *logstash* with the configuration file defined as the variable. The command we used to run the playbook contained the *logstash_config* variable set to file.conf[335]. Let us take a quick look at it.

```
1   input {
2     file {
3       path => "/logs/**/*"
4     }
5   }
6
7   output {
8     stdout {
9       codec => rubydebug
10    }
11    elasticsearch {
12      hosts => db
13    }
14  }
```

LogStash configurations consist of three main sections: *input*, *output*, and *filters*. We'll skip *filter*, for now, and focus on the other two.

The *input* section defines one or more log sources. In this case, we defined that input should be handled through the file plugin[336], with the *path* set to */logs/**/**. One asterisk means any file or directory while two consecutive ones mean any file in any directory or subdirectory. The */logs/**/** value can be described as any file in the */logs/* directory or any of its subdirectories. Bear in mind

---

[334]https://hub.docker.com/_/logstash/

[335]https://github.com/vfarcic/ms-lifecycle/blob/master/ansible/roles/logstash/files/file.conf

[336]https://www.elastic.co/guide/en/logstash/current/plugins-inputs-file.html

that, even though we specified only one input, there can, and often are, multiple inputs. For more information on all the supported input plugins, please consult the official input plugins page[337].

The *output* section defines the destination of log entries collected through the input. In this case, we set two. The first one is using the stdout output plugin[338] that will print everything to standard output using *rubydebug* codec. Please note that we are using *stdout* only for demonstration purposes so that we can quickly see the result. In a production setting, you should probably remove it for performance reasons. The second output is more interesting. It uses the ElasticSearch output plugin[339] to send all the log entries to the database. Please note that the *hosts* variable is set to *db*. Since we linked the *logstash* and *elasticsearch* containers, Docker created the *db* entry in the */etc/hosts* file. For more information on all supported output plugins, please consult the official output plugins page[340].

This configuration file is probably one of the simplest we could start with. Before we see it in action, let us go through the last element in the stack. Kibana will provide user interface we can use to interact with ElasticSearch. The tasks of the kibana role[341] are defined in the roles/kibana/tasks/main.yml[342] file. It contains backup restoration tasks that we'll skip, for now, and concentrate only on the part that runs the container.

```
1  - name: Container is running
2    docker:
3      image: kibana
4      name: kibana
5      links:
6        - elasticsearch:elasticsearch
7      ports:
8        - 5601:5601
9    tags: [kibana]
```

Just like the rest of the ELK stack, Kibana[343] has the official Docker image. All we have to do is link the container to *elasticsearch*, and expose the port *6501* that we'll use to access the UI. We'll see Kibana in action soon.

Before we simulate some log entries, we'll need to enter the *logging* node where the ELK stack is running.

[337]https://www.elastic.co/guide/en/logstash/current/input-plugins.html

[338]https://www.elastic.co/guide/en/logstash/current/plugins-outputs-stdout.html

[339]https://www.elastic.co/guide/en/logstash/current/plugins-outputs-elasticsearch.html

[340]https://www.elastic.co/guide/en/logstash/current/output-plugins.html

[341]https://github.com/vfarcic/ms-lifecycle/tree/master/ansible/roles/kibana/

[342]https://github.com/vfarcic/ms-lifecycle/blob/master/ansible/roles/kibana/tasks/main.yml

[343]https://hub.docker.com/_/kibana/

```
1  exit
2
3  vagrant ssh logging
```

Since the *data/logstash/logs* volume is shared with the container, and LogStash is monitoring any file inside it, we can create a log with a single entry.

```
1  echo "my first log entry" \
2      >/data/logstash/logs/my.log
```

Let us take a look at LogStash output and see what happened.

```
1  docker logs logstash
```

Please note that it might take a few seconds until the first log entry is processed, so, if the docker logs command did not return anything, please re-execute it. All new entries to the same file will be processed much faster.

The output is as follows.

```
1  {
2          "message" => "my first log entry",
3         "@version" => "1",
4       "@timestamp" => "2016-02-01T18:01:04.044Z",
5             "host" => "logging",
6             "path" => "/logs/my.log"
7  }
```

As you can see, LogStash processed our *my first log entry* and added a few additional pieces of information. We got the timestamp, host name, and the path of the log file.

Let's add a few more entries.

```
1  echo "my second log entry" \
2      >>/data/logstash/logs/my.log
3
4  echo "my third log entry" \
5      >>/data/logstash/logs/my.log
6
7  docker logs logstash
```

The output of the docker logs command is as follows.

```
 1  {
 2            "message" => "my first log entry",
 3           "@version" => "1",
 4         "@timestamp" => "2016-02-01T18:01:04.044Z",
 5               "host" => "logging",
 6               "path" => "/logs/my.log"
 7  }
 8  {
 9            "message" => "my second log entry",
10           "@version" => "1",
11         "@timestamp" => "2016-02-01T18:02:06.141Z",
12               "host" => "logging",
13               "path" => "/logs/my.log"
14  }
15  {
16            "message" => "my third log entry",
17           "@version" => "1",
18         "@timestamp" => "2016-02-01T18:02:06.150Z",
19               "host" => "logging",
20               "path" => "/logs/my.log"
21  }
```

As expected, all three log entries were processed by LogStash, and the time has come to visualize them through Kibana. Please open http://10.100.198.202:5601/[344] from a browser. Since this is the first time we run Kibana, it will ask us to configure an index pattern. Luckily, it already figured out what the index format is (*logstash-**), as well as which field contains timestamps (*@timestamp*). Please click the *Create* button, followed with *Discover* located in the top menu.

---

[344]http://10.100.198.202:5601/

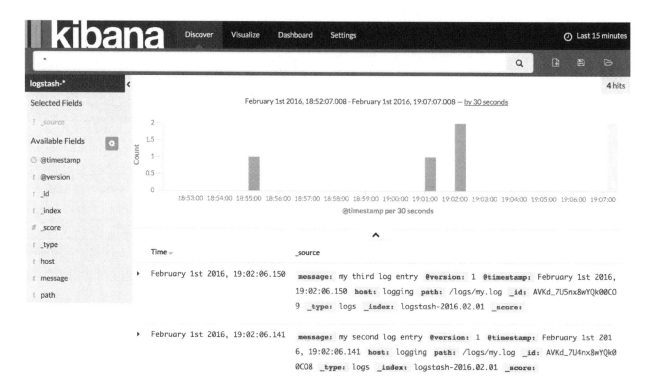

Figure 16-01: Kibana Discover screen with a few log entries

By default, the *Discover* screen displays all the entries generated in ElasticSearch during the last fifteen minutes. We'll explore functions this screen offers later on when we produce more logs. For now, please click the arrow on the left-most column of one of the log entries. You'll see all the fields LogStash generated and sent to ElasticSearch. At the moment, since we are not using any filters, those fields are limited to the *message* representing the whole log entry, and a few generic fields LogStash generated.

The example we used was trivial, and it did not even look like a log entry. Let us increase the complexity of our logs. We'll use a few entries I prepared. The sample log is located in the */tmp/apache.log* file, and it contains a few log entries following the Apache format. Its content is as follows.

```
1  127.0.0.1 - - [11/Dec/2015:00:01:45 -0800] "GET /2016/01/11/the-devops-2-0-toolk\
2  it/ HTTP/1.1" 200 3891 "http://technologyconversations.com" "Mozilla/5.0 (Macint\
3  osh; Intel Mac OS X 10.9; rv:25.0) Gecko/20100101 Firefox/25.0"
4  127.0.0.1 - - [11/Dec/2015:00:01:57 -0800] "GET /2016/01/18/clustering-and-scali\
5  ng-services/ HTTP/1.1" 200 3891 "http://technologyconversations.com" "Mozilla/5.\
6  0 (Macintosh; Intel Mac OS X 10.9; rv:25.0) Gecko/20100101 Firefox/25.0"
7  127.0.0.1 - - [11/Dec/2015:00:01:59 -0800] "GET /2016/01/26/self-healing-systems\
8  / HTTP/1.1" 200 3891 "http://technologyconversations.com" "Mozilla/5.0 (Macintos\
9  h; Intel Mac OS X 10.9; rv:25.0) Gecko/20100101 Firefox/25.0"
```

Since LogStash is expecting log files in the */data/logstash/logs/* directory, let us copy the sample.

```
1  cat /tmp/apache.log \
2      >>/data/logstash/logs/apache.log
```

Let us take a look the output LogStash generated.

```
1  docker logs logstash
```

LogStash might need a few seconds to detect that there is a new file to monitor. If the docker logs output does not display anything new, please repeat the command. The output should be similar to the following.

```
1  {
2          "message" => "127.0.0.1 - - [11/Dec/2015:00:01:45 -0800] \"GET /2016/01/1\
3  1/the-devops-2-0-toolkit/ HTTP/1.1\" 200 3891 \"http://technologyconversations.c\
4  om\" \"Mozilla/5.0 (Macintosh; Intel Mac OS X 10.9; rv:25.0) Gecko/20100101 Fire\
5  fox/25.0\"",
6         "@version" => "1",
7       "@timestamp" => "2016-02-01T19:06:21.940Z",
8             "host" => "logging",
9             "path" => "/logs/apache.log"
10  }
11  {
12          "message" => "127.0.0.1 - - [11/Dec/2015:00:01:57 -0800] \"GET /2016/01/1\
13  8/clustering-and-scaling-services/ HTTP/1.1\" 200 3891 \"http://technologyconver\
14  sations.com\" \"Mozilla/5.0 (Macintosh; Intel Mac OS X 10.9; rv:25.0) Gecko/2010\
15  0101 Firefox/25.0\"",
16         "@version" => "1",
17       "@timestamp" => "2016-02-01T19:06:21.949Z",
18             "host" => "logging",
19             "path" => "/logs/apache.log"
20  }
21  {
22          "message" => "127.0.0.1 - - [11/Dec/2015:00:01:59 -0800] \"GET /2016/01/2\
23  6/self-healing-systems/ HTTP/1.1\" 200 3891 \"http://technologyconversations.com\
24  \" \"Mozilla/5.0 (Macintosh; Intel Mac OS X 10.9; rv:25.0) Gecko/20100101 Firefo\
25  x/25.0\"",
26         "@version" => "1",
27       "@timestamp" => "2016-02-01T19:06:21.949Z",
28             "host" => "logging",
29             "path" => "/logs/apache.log"
30  }
```

The same data can be observed from Kibana running on http://10.100.198.202:5601/[345].

---

[345]http://10.100.198.202:5601/

We just started, and we already accomplished a vast improvement. When something fails on a server, we do not need to know which service failed, nor where its logs are. We can get all the log entries from that server from a single place. Anyone, be it a developer, tester, operator, or any other role, can open Kibana running on that node, and inspect all the logs from all services and applications.

The last examples of the Apache log were more production-like than the first one we used. However, the entries are still stored as one big message. While ElasticSearch is capable of searching almost anything, in almost any format, we should help it a bit and try to split this log into multiple fields.

Parsing Log Entries

We mentioned earlier that LogStash configurations consist of three main sections: *input*, *output*, and *filters*. The previous examples used only *input* and *output*, and the time has come to get introduced to the third section. I already prepared an example configuration that can be found in the roles/logstash/files/file-with-filters.conf[346] file. Its content is as follows.

```
1  input {
2    file {
3      path => "/logs/**/*"
4    }
5  }
6
7  filter {
8    grok {
9      match => { "message" => "%{COMBINEDAPACHELOG}" }
10   }
11   date {
12     match => [ "timestamp" , "dd/MMM/yyyy:HH:mm:ss Z" ]
13   }
14 }
15
16 output {
17   stdout {
18     codec => rubydebug
19   }
20   elasticsearch {
21     hosts => db
22   }
23 }
```

---

[346]https://github.com/vfarcic/ms-lifecycle/blob/master/ansible/roles/logstash/files/file-with-filters.conf

The *input* and *output* sections are the same as before. The difference is the addition of the *filter*. Just like the other two, we can use one or more of the plugins. In this case, we specified that the grok filter plugin[347] should be used. If for no other reason, the official description of the plugin should compel you to at least try it out.

Grok is currently the best way in logstash to parse **crappy unstructured log data** into something structured and queryable.

Grok sits on top of regular expressions, and LogStash already comes with quite a few patterns. They can be found in the logstash-plugins/logstash-patterns-core[348] repository. In our case, since the log we used matches Apache format that is already included, all the had to do is tell LogStash to parse the *message* using the *COMBINEDAPACHELOG* pattern. Later on, we'll see how we can combine different patterns but, for now, *COMBINEDAPACHELOG* should do.

The second filter we'll be using is defined through the date plugin[349]. It will transform the timestamp from log entries into LogStash format.

Please explore filter plugins[350] in more details. Chances are you'll find one, or more, that suit your needs.

Let's replace the *file.conf* with the *file-with-filters.conf* file, restart LogStash, and see how it behaves.

```
1  sudo cp /data/logstash/conf/file-with-filters.conf \
2      /data/logstash/conf/file.conf
3
4  docker restart logstash
```

With the new LogStash configuration, we can add a few more Apache log entries.

```
1  cat /tmp/apache2.log \
2      >>/data/logstash/logs/apache.log
3
4  docker logs logstash
```

The docker logs output of the last entry is as follows.

---

[347]https://www.elastic.co/guide/en/logstash/current/plugins-filters-grok.html

[348]https://github.com/logstash-plugins/logstash-patterns-core/blob/master/patterns/grok-patterns

[349]https://www.elastic.co/guide/en/logstash/current/plugins-filters-date.html

[350]https://www.elastic.co/guide/en/logstash/current/filter-plugins.html

```
 1  {
 2          "message" => "127.0.0.1 - - [12/Dec/2015:00:01:59 -0800] \"GET /api/v1/b\
 3  ooks/_id/5 HTTP/1.1\" 200 3891 \"http://cadenza/xampp/navi.php\" \"Mozilla/5.0 (\
 4  Macintosh; Intel Mac OS X 10.9; rv:25.0) Gecko/20100101 Firefox/25.0\"",
 5          "@version" => "1",
 6        "@timestamp" => "2015-12-12T08:01:59.000Z",
 7             "host" => "logging",
 8             "path" => "/logs/apache.log",
 9         "clientip" => "127.0.0.1",
10            "ident" => "-",
11             "auth" => "-",
12        "timestamp" => "12/Dec/2015:00:01:59 -0800",
13             "verb" => "GET",
14          "request" => "/api/v1/books/_id/5",
15      "httpversion" => "1.1",
16         "response" => "200",
17            "bytes" => "3891",
18         "referrer" => "\"http://cadenza/xampp/navi.php\"",
19            "agent" => "\"Mozilla/5.0 (Macintosh; Intel Mac OS X 10.9; rv:25.0) Ge\
20  cko/20100101 Firefox/25.0\""
21  }
```

As you can see, the message is still there in its entirety. In addition, this time we got quite a few additional fields. The *clientip, verb, referrer, agent*, and other data, are all properly separated. This will allow us to filter logs much more efficiently.

Let's open Kibana running on the address http://10.100.198.202:5601/[351]. One of the things you'll notice is that Kibana claims that no results are found even though we just parsed three log entries. The reason behind that is in the second filter that transformed the log timestamp to the LogStash format. Since, by default, Kibana displays last 15 minutes of logs, and log entries were made during December 2015, they are indeed older than 15 minutes. Click on the *Last 15 minutes* button located in the top-right corner of the screen, select *Absolute* and pick the range starting from December 1st to December 31th, 2015. That should give us all logs made during December 2015. Click the *Go* button and observe that the three logs we just sent to ElasticSearch, through LogStash, are displayed on the screen. You'll notice that many new fields are available in the right-hand menu. We'll use them later when we explore Kibana filters. For now, the important thing to note is that this time we parsed the log entries before sending them to ElasticSearch.

By employing LogStash filters, we improved the data that is stored in ElasticSearch. The solution relies on the whole ELK stack being installed on the same server where logs are, and we can see all the logs we decided to tail from a single interface (Kibana). The problem is that the solution is limited to a single server. If, for example, we'd have ten servers, we'd need to install ten ELK stacks.

---

[351]http://10.100.198.202:5601/

That would introduce quite a significant overhead on resources. ElasticSearch is memory hungry, and LogStash can grab more CPU than what we would be willing to part from. Of equal importance is that, while what we have by now is an improvement, it is far from ideal. We would still need to know which server produced a problem and, potentially, go from one Kibana to another, when trying to cross-reference different services and applications involved.

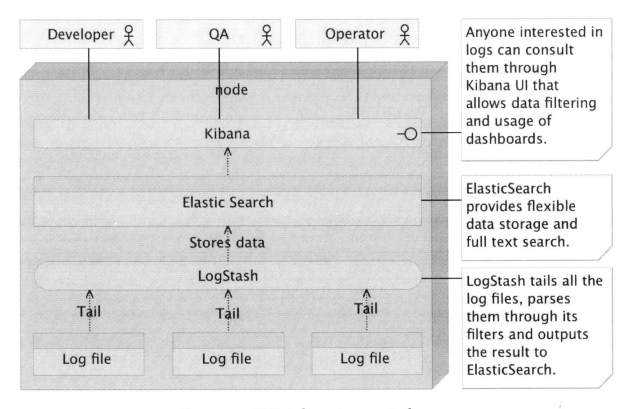

Figure 16-02: ELK stack running on a single server

Before I introduce you to the concept of decentralized logs and centralized logs parsing, let us remove the LogStash instance and go back to the *cd* node.

```
1  docker rm -f logstash
2
3  exit
4
5  vagrant ssh cd
```

Sending Log Entries to a Central LogStash Instance

What we did by now is helpful, but it still does not solve the problem of having all logs in one place. At the moment, we have all logs from a single server in a single location. How can we change that?

One simple solution would be to install LogStash on each server, and configure it to send entries to a remote ElasticSearch. At least, that's how most companies I worked with solved it. Should we do the same? The answer is no; we shouldn't. The problem lies in LogStash itself. While it is an excellent solution for collecting, parsing, and outputting logs, it uses too many resources. Having LogStash installed on each and every server would result in a huge waste. Instead, we'll use Filebeat.

Filebeat[352] is a lightweight shipper for log files and represents the next-generation of LogStash Forwarder[353]. Just like LogStash, it tails log files. The difference is that it is optimized for just tailing and sending logs. It will not do any parsing. Another difference is that it is written in Go. Those two things alone make it much more resource efficient with such a small footprint that we can safely run it on all servers without noticing a significant increase in memory and CPU consumption.

Before we see Filebeat in action, we need to change the *input* section of our LogStash configuration. The new configuration is located in the roles/logstash/files/beats.conf[354] file and its content is as follows.

Filebeat on each server with logs,

ELK on one server.

```
 1  input {
 2    beats {
 3      port => 5044
 4    }
 5  }
 6
 7  output {
 8    stdout {
 9      codec => rubydebug
10    }
11    elasticsearch {
12      hosts => db
13    }
14  }
```

As you can see, the only difference is in the input section. It uses the beats plugin[355] that is set to listen to the port *5044*. With this configuration, we can run a single LogStash instance, and have all the other servers send their logs to this port.

Let's deploy LogStash with these settings.

---

[352]https://www.elastic.co/products/beats/filebeat

[353]https://github.com/elastic/logstash-forwarder

[354]https://github.com/vfarcic/ms-lifecycle/blob/master/ansible/roles/logstash/files/beats.conf

[355]https://www.elastic.co/guide/en/logstash/current/plugins-inputs-beats.html

```
1  ansible-playbook /vagrant/ansible/elk.yml \
2      -i /vagrant/ansible/hosts/prod \
3      --extra-vars "logstash_config=beats.conf"
```

LogStash is now running inside the *logging* server and listening for beats packets on port *5044*. Before we proceed and deploy Filebeat on, let's say, the *prod* node, let us take a quick look at the prod3.yml[356] playbook.

```
1  - hosts: prod
2    remote_user: vagrant
3    serial: 1
4    roles:
5      - common
6      - docker
7      - docker-compose
8      - consul
9      - registrator
10     - consul-template
11     - nginx
12     - filebeat
```

The only new addition is the roles/filebeat[357] role. Its tasks, defined in the roles/filebeat/tasks/-main.yml[358] file, are as follows.

```
1  - name: Download the package
2    get_url:
3      url: https://download.elastic.co/beats/filebeat/filebeat_1.0.1_amd64.deb
4      dest: /tmp/filebeat.deb
5    tags: [filebeat]
6
7  - name: Install the package
8    apt:
9      deb: /tmp/filebeat.deb
10   tags: [filebeat]
11
12 - name: Configuration is present
13   template:
14     src: filebeat.yml
15     dest: /etc/filebeat/filebeat.yml
```

[356]https://github.com/vfarcic/ms-lifecycle/blob/master/ansible/prod3.yml

[357]https://github.com/vfarcic/ms-lifecycle/blob/master/ansible/roles/filebeat/

[358]https://github.com/vfarcic/ms-lifecycle/blob/master/ansible/roles/filebeat/tasks/main.yml

```
16    tags: [filebeat]
17
18  - name: Service is started
19    service:
20      name: filebeat
21      state: started
22    tags: [filebeat]
```

The tasks will download the package, install it, copy the configuration, and, finally, run the service. The only thing worth looking at is the roles/filebeat/templates/filebeat.yml[359] configuration file.

```
1  filebeat:
2    prospectors:
3      -
4        paths:
5          - "/var/log/**/*.log"
6
7  output:
8    logstash:
9        hosts: ["{{ elk_ip }}:5044"]
```

The *filebeat* section specifies a list of prospectors which are used to locate and process log files. Each prospector item begins with a dash (-) and specifies prospector-specific configuration options, including the list of paths that are crawled to locate log files. In our case, we're having only one path set to */var/log/**/*.log*. When started, Filebeat will look for all files ending in *.log located in the */var/log/* directory, or any of its subdirectories. Since that happens to be the location where most of Ubuntu logs are located, we'll have quite a lot of log entries to process.

The *output* section is used to send log entries to various destinations. In our case, we specified LogStash as the only output. Since the current LogStash configuration does not have any filtering, we could have set ElasticSearch as output, and the result would be the same, but with less overhead. However, since it is very likely that we'll add some filters in the future, the output is set to logstash.

Please note that filters are a blessing and a curse at the same time. They allow us to split log entries into easier-to-manage fields. On the other hand, if log formats differ too much, you might spend an eternity writing parsers. Whether you should use filters, or depend on ElasticSearch filtering capabilities without specialized fields, is entirely up to you. I tend to go both ways. If log contains an important piece of information (as you will see in one of the following examples), filtering logs is a must. If log entries are generic messages without analytical value, I skip filtering altogether. With a bit of practice, you'll establish your rules.

---

[359]https://github.com/vfarcic/ms-lifecycle/blob/master/ansible/roles/filebeat/templates/filebeat.yml

For more information about configuration options, please consult the Filebeat configuration details[360] page.

Let's run the playbook and see Filebeat in action.

```
1   ansible-playbook /vagrant/ansible/prod3.yml \
2       -i /vagrant/ansible/hosts/prod
```

Now that Filebeat is running in the *prod* node, we can take a look at logs generated by LogStash running on the *logging* server.

```
1   docker -H tcp://logging:2375 \
2       logs logstash
```

The last few lines of the docker logs command are as follows.

```
1    ...
2    {
3            "message" => "ttyS0 stop/pre-start, process 1301",
4           "@version" => "1",
5         "@timestamp" => "2016-02-02T14:50:45.557Z",
6               "beat" => {
7           "hostname" => "prod",
8               "name" => "prod"
9        },
10             "count" => 1,
11            "fields" => nil,
12        "input_type" => "log",
13            "offset" => 0,
14            "source" => "/var/log/upstart/ttyS0.log",
15              "type" => "log",
16              "host" => "prod"
17   }
```

FileBeats sent all the log entries from the */var/log/* directory in the *prod* node to LogStash running in the *logging* server. It did that without breaking a sweat and, as a result, we got over 350 log entries stored in ElasticSearch. OK, 350 log entries is not something to brag about, but, it there were 350000, it would still do it effortlessly.

Let's confirm that logs reached Kibana. Please open http://10.100.198.202:5601/[361]. If you see no entries, it means that more than fifteen minutes passed, and you should increase the time by clicking the *time selector* button in the top-right corner of the screen.

---

[360]https://www.elastic.co/guide/en/beats/filebeat/current/filebeat-configuration-details.html
[361]http://10.100.198.202:5601/

Please note that every time a new field type is added to ElasticSearch index, we should recreate the pattern. We can do that by navigating to the *Settings* screen and clicking the *Create* button.

We, again, improved the solution quite a bit. There is a central place where logs are parsed (LogStash), stored (ElasticSearch), and explored (Kibana). We can plug in any number of servers with Filebeat running on each of them. It will tail logs and send them to LogStash.

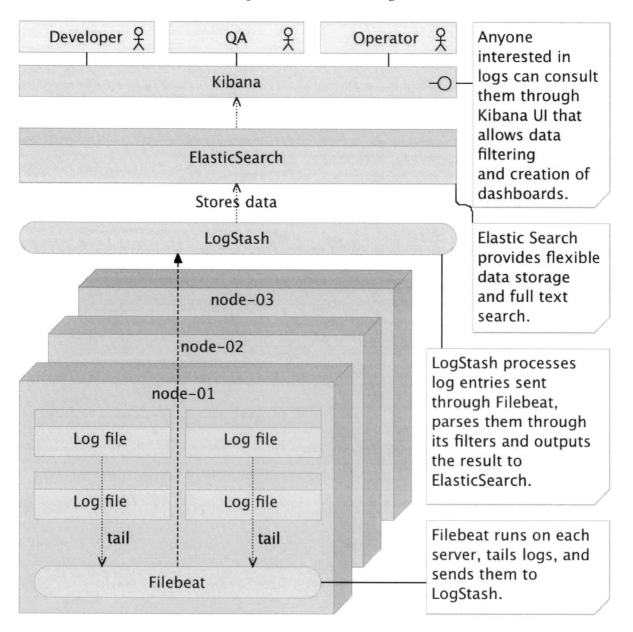

Figure 16-03: ELK stack running on a single server with Filebeat distributed to the whole cluster

Let's up the ante a bit and apply what we learned to Docker containers. Since we'll change the LogStash configuration, let us end this section by removing the running instance.

```
1  docker -H tcp://logging:2375 \
2      rm -f logstash
```

Sending Docker Log Entries to a Central LogStash Instance

Since we are using containers, we can run them with volume sharing the directory where the service is writing its logs. Shall we do that? The answer is no and, at this time, you probably think that I am continuously leading you from one wrong solution to another. What I'm really trying to do is to build the solution step by step and, at the same time, show you different paths that you might choose to take. My preferred solution does not necessarily have to be adopted by you. The more choices you have, the more informed decisions you'll make.

Let's go back to the subject of writing logs to a file and shipping them to LogStash. My, strongly subjective, opinion is that all logs, no matter the way we package our services, should be sent to standard output or error (*stdout* or *stderr*). There are many practical reasons for this opinion which, be it as it may, I won't elaborate. I already received quite a few emails from people stating that my views and practices are too radical (most of them got a response saying that the century changed more than fifteen years ago). I'll just try to avoid another war on the logging subject in general terms, and skip to reasons for not writing logs to files when services are deployed inside containers. Two of them stick from the crowd. First of all, the less we use volumes, the less are containers dependent on the host they're running on, and easier it is to move them around (either in the case of a failure or for scaling purposes). The second reason is that Docker's logging drivers[362] expect logs to be sent to *stdout* and *stderr*. By not writing logs to files, we avoid coupling with a server or particular logging technology.

> If you are about to send me a hate email stating that log files are a grace from heaven, please note that I am referring to their output destination when generated inside containers (even though I was applying the rule before I started using them).

What is the alternative to exposing container directory with logs as a volume? Docker introduced logging driver feature in its version 1.6. While it passed mostly unnoticed, it is a very cool capability and was a huge step toward creating a comprehensive approach to logging in Docker environments. Since then, besides the default *json-file* driver, we got *syslog*, *journald*, *gelf*, *fluentd*, *splunk*, and *awslogs*. By the time you read this book, new ones might have arrived as well.

Now that we decided to use Docker's logging drivers[363], the question arises which one to choose. The GELF driver writes messages in *Greylog Extended Log Format* supported by LogStash. If all we need is to store logs generated by our containers, this is a good option. On the other hand, if we want not only logs generated by services running inside containers but also from the rest of the system, we

---

[362]https://docs.docker.com/engine/reference/logging/overview/

[363]https://docs.docker.com/engine/reference/logging/overview/

might opt for *JournalD* or *syslog*. In such a case, we'd get truly (almost) complete information about everything that happens, not only inside containers but on the whole OS level. The latter option (*JournalD* or *syslog*) is preferable when there is a substantial available memory for ElasticSearch (more logs equals more memory consumption), and that is the one we'll explore deeper. Do not get scared by ElasticSearch's need for a lot of memory. With clever cleanups of old data, this can be easily mitigated. We'll skip the debate whether *JournalD* is a better or worse solution than *syslog*, and use the latter. It does not matter which one is your preference since the same set of principles applies to both.

This time, we'll use the roles/logstash/files/syslog.conf[364] file as LogStash configuration. Let's go through its sections one by one.

```
1  input {
2    syslog {
3      type => syslog
4      port => 25826
5    }
6  }
```

The *input* section should be self-explanatory. We're using the syslog plugin[365] with two settings. The first one adds a type field to all events handled by this input. It will help us distinguish logs coming from *syslog*, from those we're generating through other methods. The *port* setting states that LogStash should listen on *25826* for syslog events.

The filter section of the config file is a bit more complicated. I decided to use it mostly as a way to showcase a fraction of what can be done through filters.

```
1  filter {
2    if "docker/" in [program] {
3      mutate {
4        add_field => {
5          "container_id" => "%{program}"
6        }
7      }
8      mutate {
9        gsub => [
10         "container_id", "docker/", ""
11        ]
12     }
13     mutate {
14       update => [
```

---

[364]https://github.com/vfarcic/ms-lifecycle/blob/master/ansible/roles/logstash/files/syslog.conf
[365]https://www.elastic.co/guide/en/logstash/current/plugins-inputs-syslog.html

```
15          "program", "docker"
16        ]
17      }
18    }
19    if [container_id] == "nginx" {
20      grok {
21        match => [ "message" , "%{COMBINEDAPACHELOG} %{HOSTPORT:upstream_address} \
22  %{NOTSPACE:upstream_response_time}"]
23      }
24      mutate {
25        convert => ["upstream_response_time", "float"]
26      }
27    }
28  }
```

It starts with an *if* statement. Docker will send logs to syslog with a value of the *program* field set in the *docker/[CONTAINER_ID]* format. We are leveraging that fact to distinguish log entries coming from Docker, from those generated through some other means. Inside the *if* statement, we are performing a few mutations. The first one is the addition of a new field called *container_id* that, for now, has the same value as the *program* field. The second mutation is the removal of the *docker/* part of that value so that we are left with only container ID. Finally, we change the value of the *program* field to *docker*.

Variables, and their values, before and after mutations, are as follows.

Variable name	Value before	Value after
program	docker/[CONTAINER_ID]	docker
container_id	/	[CONTAINER_ID]

The second conditional starts by checking whether the *container_id* is set to *nginx*. If it is, it parses the message using the *COMBINEDAPACHELOG* pattern that we already saw in action and adds to it two new fields called *upstream_address* and *upstream_response_time*. Both of those fields also use predefined grok patterns *HOSTPORT* and *NOTSPACE*. If you'd like to dive deeper, and take a closer look at those patterns, please consult the logstash-plugins/logstash-patterns-core[366] repository. If you are familiar with regular expressions, this should be easy to understand (if there is such a thing as easy with RegEx). Otherwise, you might want to rely on declared names to find the expression you need (at least until you learn regular expressions). The truth is that RegEx is a very powerful language for parsing text but, at the same time, very hard to master.

> My wife claimed that my hair went gray at approximately the same time I worked on a project that required quite a lot of regular expressions. That is one of the few things we agreed on.

---

[366]https://github.com/logstash-plugins/logstash-patterns-core/blob/master/patterns/grok-patterns

Finally, the mutation inside *nginx* conditional transforms *upstream_response_time* field from *string* (default) to *float*. We'll use this information later on, and will need it to be a number.

The third and the last section of the configuration file is *output*.

```
1  output {
2    stdout {
3      codec => rubydebug
4    }
5    elasticsearch {
6      hosts => db
7    }
8  }
```

It is the same as the previous ones. We're sending filtered log entries to standard output and ElasticSearch.

Now that we understand the configuration file, or, at least, pretend that we do, we can deploy LogStash one more time through the Ansible playbook elk.yml[367].

```
1  ansible-playbook /vagrant/ansible/elk.yml \
2      -i /vagrant/ansible/hosts/prod \
3      --extra-vars "logstash_config=syslog.conf"
```

Now we have LogStash up and running, and configured to use *syslog* as input. Let's remove the currently running *nginx* instance and run it again with Docker log driver set to *syslog*. While at it, we'll also provision the *prod* node with *syslog*. The prod4.yml[368] playbook that we'll use is as follows.

```
1  - hosts: prod
2    remote_user: vagrant
3    serial: 1
4    vars:
5      - log_to_syslog: yes
6    roles:
7      - common
8      - docker
9      - docker-compose
10     - consul
11     - registrator
12     - consul-template
13     - nginx
14     - rsyslog
```

---

[367]https://github.com/vfarcic/ms-lifecycle/blob/master/ansible/elk.yml

[368]https://github.com/vfarcic/ms-lifecycle/blob/master/ansible/prod4.yml

As you can see, this playbook is similar to the others we used for provisioning the *prod* server. The difference is in the *log_to_syslog* variable, and the addition of the *rsyslog* role.

The relevant part of the *nginx* tasks defined in the roles/nginx/tasks/main.yml[369] file is as follows.

```
 1  - name: Container is running
 2    docker:
 3      image: nginx
 4      name: nginx
 5      state: running
 6      ports: "{{ ports }}"
 7      volumes: "{{ volumes }}"
 8      log_driver: syslog
 9      log_opt:
10        syslog-tag: nginx
11    when: log_to_syslog is defined
12    tags: [nginx]
```

The difference is in the addition of *log_driver* and *log_opt* declarations. The first one sets Docker log driver to *syslog*. The *log_opt* can be used to specify additional logging options, which depend on a driver. In this case, we are specifying the *tag*. Without it, Docker would use container ID to identify logs sent to syslog.That was, when we query ElasticSearch, it will be much easier to find *nginx* entries.

The *rsyslog* tasks defined in the roles/rsyslog/tasks/main.yml[370] file are as follows.

```
 1  - name: Packages are present
 2    apt:
 3      name: "{{ item }}"
 4      state: latest
 5      install_recommends: no
 6    with_items:
 7      - rsyslog
 8      - logrotate
 9    tags: [rsyslog]
10
11  - name: Config file is present
12    template:
13      src: 10-logstash.conf
14      dest: /etc/rsyslog.d/10-logstash.conf
15    register: config_result
```

[369]https://github.com/vfarcic/ms-lifecycle/blob/master/ansible/roles/nginx/tasks/main.yml
[370]https://github.com/vfarcic/ms-lifecycle/blob/master/ansible/roles/rsyslog/tasks/main.yml

```
16    tags: [rsyslog]
17
18  - name: Service is restarted
19    shell: service rsyslog restart
20    when: config_result.changed
21    tags: [rsyslog]
```

It will make sure that *rsyslog* and *logrotate* packages are installed, copy the *10-logstash.conf* configuration file, and restart the service. The roles/rsyslog/templates/10-logstash.conf[371] template is as follows.

```
1  *.* @@{{ elk_ip }}:25826
```

Please note that the file is an Ansible's template and that *{{ elk_ip }}* will be replaced with the IP. The configuration is dead simple. Everything sent to syslog will be re-sent to the LogStash running on the specified IP and port.

Now we're ready to remove the currently running *nginx* container and run the playbook.

```
1  docker -H tcp://prod:2375 \
2      rm -f nginx
3
4  ansible-playbook /vagrant/ansible/prod4.yml \
5      -i /vagrant/ansible/hosts/prod
```

Let's see what was sent to LogStash.

```
1  docker -H tcp://logging:2375 \
2      logs logstash
```

You should see the syslog entries generated by the system. One of them might look as follows.

---

[371]https://github.com/vfarcic/ms-lifecycle/blob/master/ansible/roles/rsyslog/templates/10-logstash.conf

```
 1  {
 2             "message" => "[55784.504413] docker0: port 3(veth4024c56) entered for\
 3  warding state\n",
 4            "@version" => "1",
 5          "@timestamp" => "2016-02-02T21:58:23.000Z",
 6                "type" => "syslog",
 7                "host" => "10.100.198.201",
 8            "priority" => 6,
 9           "timestamp" => "Feb  2 21:58:23",
10           "logsource" => "prod",
11             "program" => "kernel",
12            "severity" => 6,
13            "facility" => 0,
14      "facility_label" => "kernel",
15      "severity_label" => "Informational"
16  }
```

We can also explore the same data through Kibana running on http://10.100.198.202:5601/[372].

Let's see what happens when we deploy our services packed into containers. First we'll enter the *prod* node from which we'll run the *books-ms* service.

```
 1  exit
 2
 3  vagrant ssh prod
 4
 5  git clone https://github.com/vfarcic/books-ms.git
 6
 7  cd books-ms
```

Before we deploy the *books-ms* service, let us take a quick look at the docker-compose-logging.yml[373] file.

---

[372]http://10.100.198.202:5601/

[373]https://github.com/vfarcic/books-ms/blob/master/docker-compose-logging.yml

```
1  app:
2    image: 10.100.198.200:5000/books-ms
3    ports:
4      - 8080
5    links:
6      - db:db
7    environment:
8      - SERVICE_NAME=books-ms
9    log_driver: syslog
10   log_opt:
11     syslog-tag: books-ms
12
13 db:
14   image: mongo
15   log_driver: syslog
16   log_opt:
17     syslog-tag: books-ms
```

As you can see, it follows the same logic as the one we used to provision *nginx* with Ansible. The only difference is that, in this case, it is Docker Compose configuration. It contains the same *log_driver* and *log_opt* keys.

Now that we understand the changes we had to add to the Docker Compose configuration, we can deploy the service.

```
1  docker-compose -p books-ms \
2      -f docker-compose-logging.yml \
3      up -d app
```

Let's double check that it is indeed running by listing and filtering Docker processes.

```
1  docker ps --filter name=booksms
```

Now that the service is up and running, with the *syslog* logging driver, we should verify that log entries were indeed sent to LogStash.

```
1  docker -H tcp://logging:2375 \
2      logs logstash
```

Part of the output is as follows.

```
1  {
2              "message" => "[INFO] [02/03/2016 13:28:35.869] [routingSystem-akka.ac\
3  tor.default-dispatcher-5] [akka://routingSystem/user/IO-HTTP/listener-0] Bound t\
4  o /0.0.0.0:8080\n",
5            "@version" => "1",
6          "@timestamp" => "2016-02-03T13:28:35.000Z",
7                "type" => "syslog",
8                "host" => "10.100.198.201",
9            "priority" => 30,
10          "timestamp" => "Feb  3 13:28:35",
11          "logsource" => "prod",
12            "program" => "docker",
13                "pid" => "11677",
14           "severity" => 6,
15           "facility" => 3,
16     "facility_label" => "system",
17     "severity_label" => "Informational",
18       "container_id" => "books-ms"
19  }
```

Service logs are indeed sent to LogStash. Please notice that LogStash filters did what we told them to do. The *program* field was transformed from *docker/books-ms* to *docker*, and a new field called *container_id* was created. Since we defined *message* parsing only when *container_id* is *nginx*, it stayed intact.

Let us confirm that *message* parsing is indeed working correctly for log entries coming from *nginx*. We'll need to make a few requests to the proxy, so we'll start by configuring it properly.

```
1  cp nginx-includes.conf \
2      /data/nginx/includes/books-ms.conf
3
4  consul-template \
5      -consul localhost:8500 \
6      -template "nginx-upstreams.ctmpl:\
7  /data/nginx/upstreams/books-ms.conf:\
8  docker kill -s HUP nginx" \
9      -once
```

You already used *nginx* configurations and Consul Template, so there is no need for an explanation of those commands.

Now that the service is running, is integrated, and is sending logs to LogStash, let us generate a few *nginx* log entries by making a few requests.

```
1   curl -I localhost/api/v1/books
2
3   curl -H 'Content-Type: application/json' -X PUT -d \
4       "{\"_id\": 1,
5       \"title\": \"My First Book\",
6       \"author\": \"John Doe\",
7       \"description\": \"Not a very good book\"}" \
8       localhost/api/v1/books | jq '.'
9
10  curl http://prod/api/v1/books | jq '.'
```

Let's see what did LogStash receives this time.

```
1   docker -H tcp://logging:2375 \
2       logs logstash
```

Part of the output of the docker logs command is as follows.

```
1   {
2                       "message" => "172.17.0.1 - - [03/Feb/2016:13:37:12 +0000] \"G\
3   ET /api/v1/books HTTP/1.1\" 200 269 \"-\" \"curl/7.35.0\" 10.100.198.201:32768 0\
4   .091 \n",
5                       "@version" => "1",
6                     "@timestamp" => "2016-02-03T13:37:12.000Z",
7                         "type" => "syslog",
8                         "host" => "10.100.198.201",
9                     "priority" => 30,
10                    "timestamp" => [
11      [0] "Feb  3 13:37:12",
12      [1] "03/Feb/2016:13:37:12 +0000"
13  ],
14                    "logsource" => "prod",
15                      "program" => "docker",
16                          "pid" => "11677",
17                     "severity" => 6,
18                     "facility" => 3,
19              "facility_label" => "system",
20              "severity_label" => "Informational",
21                "container_id" => "nginx",
22                     "clientip" => "172.17.0.1",
23                        "ident" => "-",
24                         "auth" => "-",
```

```
25                        "verb" => "GET",
26                     "request" => "/api/v1/books",
27                 "httpversion" => "1.1",
28                    "response" => "200",
29                       "bytes" => "269",
30                    "referrer" => "\"-\"",
31                       "agent" => "\"curl/7.35.0\"",
32            "upstream_address" => "10.100.198.201:32768",
33      "upstream_response_time" => 0.091
34  }
```

This time, not only that we stored logs coming from containers, but we also parsed them. The main reason for parsing *nginx* logs lies in the *upstream_response_time* field. Can you guess why? While you think about possible usages of that field, let us take a closer look at a few of the features of the *Discover* screen in Kibana.

We generated quite enough logs, so we might, just as well, want to start using Kibana filters. Please open http://10.100.198.202:5601/[374]. Please change the time to, let's say, 24 hours, by clicking the top-right button. That will give us plenty of time to "play" with the few logs we created. Before we jump into filtering, please go to the *Settings* screen, and click *Create*. That will refresh our index pattern with new fields. When finished, please return to the *Discover* screen.

Let us begin with the left-hand menu. It contains all the available fields, found in all logs that match given period. Clicking on any of those fields provides us with the list of values it holds. For example, *container_id* contains *books-ms* and *nginx*. Next to those values are icons with the magnifying glass. The one with the plus sign can be used to filter only entries that contain that value. Similarly, the icon with the minus sign can be used to exclude records. Click the icon with the plus sign next to *nginx*. As you can see, only log entries coming from *nginx* are displayed. The result of applied filters is located in the horizontal bar above. Hovering over one of the filters (in this case *container_id: "nginx"*), allows us to use additional options to enable, disable, pin, unpin, invert, toggle, and remove that filter.

---

[374]http://10.100.198.202:5601/

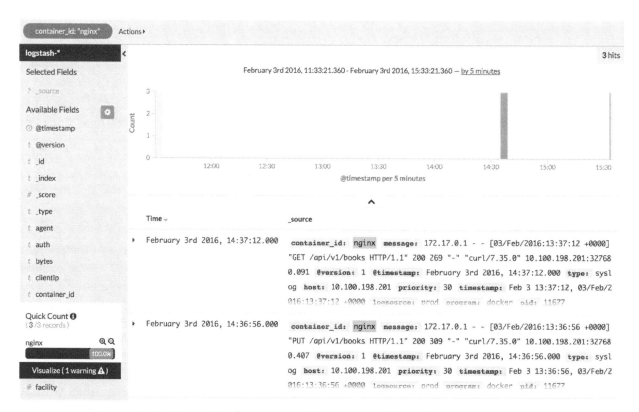

Figure 16-04: Kibana Discover screen with log entries filtered by container_id nginx

At the top of the main frame is a graph with the number of logs distributed over the specified period. Below it is a table with log entries. By default, it shows the *Time* and the *_source* columns. Please click the arrow icon on the left side of one of the rows. It expands the row to display all the fields available in that log entry. They are a combination of data generated by LogStash and those we parsed through its configuration. Each field has the same icons as those we found in the left-hand menu. Through them, we can *filter for value* or *filter out value*. The third button, represented by an icon that looks like a single row table with two columns, can be used to *toggle that column in table*. Since default columns are not very useful, not to say boring, please toggle *logsource*, *request*, *verb*, *upstream_address*, and *upstream_response_time*. Click, again, the arrow, to hide the fields. We just got ourselves a nice table that shows some of the most important pieces of information coming from *nginx*. We can see that the server where requests are made (*logsource*), the address of requests (*request*), the type of requests (*verb*), how much it took to receive responses (*upstream_response_time*), and where were the requests proxied to (*upstream_address*). If you think the *search* you created is useful, you can save it by clicking the *Save Search* button located in the top-right part of the screen. Next to it is the *Load Saved Search* button.

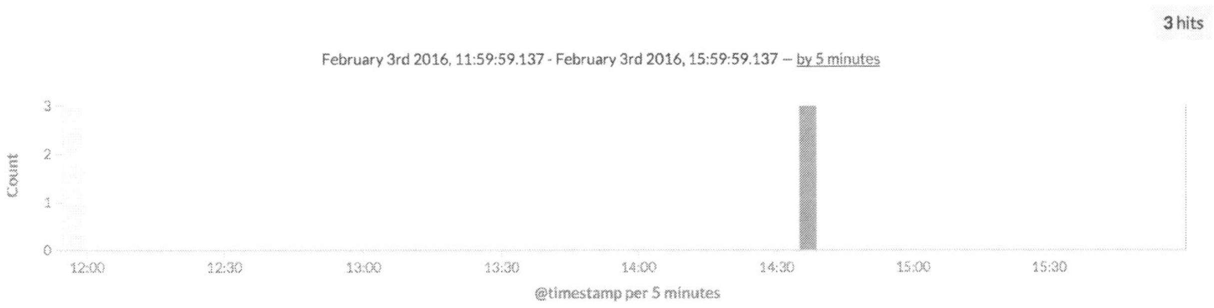

February 3rd 2016, 11:59:59.137 - February 3rd 2016, 15:59:59.137 — by 5 minutes

Time ▾	logsource	request	verb	upstream_address	upstream_response_time
▸ February 3rd 2016, 14:37:12.000	prod	/api/v1/books	GET	10.100.198.201:32768	0.091
▸ February 3rd 2016, 14:36:56.000	prod	/api/v1/books	PUT	10.100.198.201:32768	0.407
▸ February 3rd 2016, 14:35:56.000	prod	/api/v1/books	HEAD	10.100.198.201:32768	0.105

Figure 16-05: Kibana Discover screen with log entries filtered by container_id nginx and custom columns

We'll explore *Visualize* and *Dashboard* screens a bit later.

Let's us summarize the flow we have at this moment.

- Containers are deployed with Docker's logging driver set to *syslog*. With such a configuration, Docker redirects everything that is sent to standard output, or error (stdout/stderr), to syslog.
- All the log entries, be it from containers or processes deployed through other methods, are redirected from syslog to LogStash.
- LogStash receives syslog events, applies filters and transformations, and re-sends them to ElasticSearch.
- Everybody is happy, because finding specific log entries is a breeze, and life, during office hours, is a bit easier to cope with.

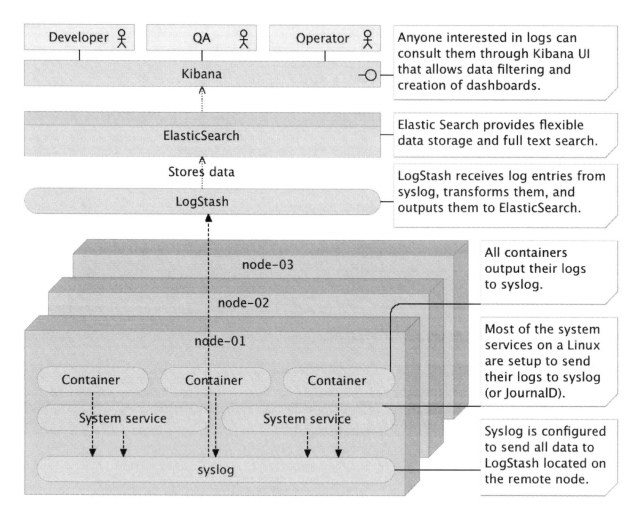

Figure 16-06: ELK stack running on a single server with containers logging to syslog

Self-Healing Based on Software Data

Let us put the response time we are logging through *nginx* to a good use. Since data is stored in ElasticSearch, we might do a few quick examples of using its API. We can, for instance, retrieve all entries stored inside the *logstash* index.

```
1  curl 'http://logging:9200/logstash-*/_search' \
2    | jq '.'
```

Elastic search returned the first ten entries (default page size), together with some additional information, like the total number of records. There's not much use in retrieving all the entries, so let us try to narrow it down. We can, for example, request all records that have *nginx* as *container_id* value.

```
1  curl 'http://logging:9200/logstash-*/_search?q=container_id:nginx' \
2      | jq '.'
```

The results are the same three entries we observed from LogStash logs. Again, there's not much use of them. If this were a production system, we would get thousands upon thousands of results (distributed among multiple pages).

This time, let us try something truly useful. We'll analyze data and, for example, retrieve the average response time from *nginx* logs.

```
1  curl 'http://logging:9200/logstash-*/_search?q=container_id:nginx' \
2      -d '{
3    "size": 0,
4    "aggs": {
5      "average_response_time": {
6        "avg": {
7          "field": "upstream_response_time"
8        }
9      }
10   }
11 }' | jq '.'
```

The output of the last command is as follows.

```
1  {
2    "aggregations": {
3      "average_response_time": {
4        "value": 0.20166666666666666
5      }
6    },
7    "hits": {
8      "hits": [],
9      "max_score": 0,
10     "total": 3
11   },
12   "_shards": {
13     "failed": 0,
14     "successful": 10,
15     "total": 10
16   },
17   "timed_out": false,
18   "took": 26
19 }
```

With something like that request, we can extend our self-healing system and, for example, retrieve average response time of a service during last hour. If responses were, on average, slow, we could scale the service. Similarly, if responses were fast, we can descale it.

Let's filter the results so that only those made by *nginx*, with a request to */api/v1/books* (the address of our service), and created during the last hour, are retrieved. Once data is filtered, we'll aggregate all the results and get the average value of the *upstream_response_time* field.

The chances are that more than one hour passed since you sent a request to the service through *nginx*. If that's the case, the resulting value would be *null* since there are no records that would match the filter we are about to make. We can easily fix that, by making, let's say, a hundred new requests.

```
1  for i in {1..100}; do
2    curl http://prod/api/v1/books | jq '.'
3  done
```

Now that we have recent data, we can ask ElasticSearch to give us the average response time.

```
1  curl 'http://logging:9200/logstash-*/_search' \
2      -d '{
3    "size": 0,
4    "aggs": { "last_hour": {
5      "filter": {
6        "bool": { "must": [ {
7          "query": { "match": {
8            "container_id": {
9              "query": "nginx",
10             "type": "phrase"
11           }
12         } }
13       }, {
14         "query": { "match": {
15           "request": {
16             "query": "/api/v1/books",
17             "type": "phrase"
18           }
19         } }
20       }, {
21         "range": { "@timestamp": {
22           "gte": "now-1h",
23           "lte": "now"
24         } }
```

```
25        } ] }
26      },
27      "aggs": {
28        "average_response_time": {
29          "avg": {
30            "field": "upstream_response_time"
31          }
32        }
33      }
34    } }
35  }' | jq '.'
```

The ElasticSearch API and the Lucene engine[375] used in the background are so vast that it would require a whole book to describe it, so the explanation is out of the scope of this book. You can find detailed information in the Document APIs[376] page.

The output of the request will vary from one case to another. My result was as follows.

```
1   {
2     "aggregations": {
3       "last_hour": {
4         "average_response_time": {
5           "value": 0.005744897959183675
6         },
7         "doc_count": 98
8       }
9     },
10    "hits": {
11      "hits": [],
12      "max_score": 0,
13      "total": 413
14    },
15    "_shards": {
16      "failed": 0,
17      "successful": 10,
18      "total": 10
19    },
20    "timed_out": false,
21    "took": 11
22  }
```

---

[375]https://lucene.apache.org/core/
[376]https://www.elastic.co/guide/en/elasticsearch/reference/current/docs.html

We can now take this response time and, depending on the rules we set, scale, descale, or do nothing. Right now we have all the elements to extend our self-healing system. We have the process that stores response times in ElasticSearch and the API to analyze data. We can create one more Consul watch that will, periodically, query the API and, if an action is needed, send a request to Jenkins to prevent the disease from spreading. I'll leave that to you, as a few exercises.

Exercise: scaling the service if response time is too long

Create a new Consul watch that will use the ElasticSearch request we created, and invoke a Jenkins job that will scale the service if the average response time is too long. Similarly, descale the service if the response time is too short, and more than two instances are running (less than two poses a downtime risk).

Without introducing more complexity, we can try other types of future predictions. We can, for example, predict the future by observing the previous day.

Exercise: predict the future by observing the past

Repeat the process from the previous exercise with the different analysis.

Variables:

- T: The current time
- $AVG1$: Average traffic between T and T+1h of the previous day.
- $AVG2$: Average traffic between T+1h and T+2h of the previous day.

The task:

- Calculate the increase (or the decrease) of the traffic between $AVG1$ and $AVG2$.
- Decide whether to scale, de-scale, or do nothing.

We do not need to base our analysis only on the previous day. We can also evaluate the same day of the preceding week, of the past month, or even of the last year. Do we have an increase in traffic every first day of the month? What happened on Christmas day last year? Do people visit our store less after summer vacations? The beauty is not only that we have the data to answer those questions, but we can incorporate the analysis into the system and run it periodically.

Bear in mind that some of the analysis are better of running as Consul watches, while the others belong to Jenkins. Tasks that should be run periodically with the same frequency are good use cases for Consul. While they can run as easily from Jenkins, Consul is more lightweight, and will use fewer resources. Examples would be every hour or every 5 minutes. On the other hand, Consul does not have a proper scheduler. If you'd like to run analysis at specific moments in time, Jenkins with its cron-like scheduler is a better fit. Examples would be each day at midnight, each first day of a month, two weeks before Christmas, and so on. You should evaluate both tools for each given case, and choose the one that fits better. An alternative would be to run all such analysis from Jenkins and benefit from having everything in one place. Then again, you might opt for an entirely different set of tools. I'll leave the choice to you. The importance lies in understanding the process and the goals we want to accomplish.

Please note that I provided one example that can be used as a self-healing process. Response times analysis does not have to be the only thing we do. Look at the data you can collect, decide what is useful, and what isn't, and make other types of data crunching. Collect everything you need, but not more. Do not fall into the trap of storing all you can think of, without using it. That is a waste of memory, CPU, and hard disk space. Do not forget to set up a process that periodically cleans data. You won't need all the logs from a year ago. Heck, you probably won't need most of the logs older than a month. If a problem is not found within thirty days, the chances are that there is no problem and, even if there is, it relates to an old release not running anymore. If, after reading this book, your release cycle lasts for months, and you are not planning to shorten it, I failed miserably. Please do not send me an email confirming this. It would only make me feel depressed.

That was a short detour from the main subject of the chapter (logging and monitoring). Since the book is mostly based on hands-on examples, I could not explain *self-healing based on historical response times* without having data to work with. Therefore, this discussion was added here. Throughout the rest of this chapter, there will be at one more excursion into a subject that might just as well belong to the Self-Healing Systems chapter. Now, let's get back to logging and monitoring.

Since we have **all the information representing the past and the present status of the cluster**, we can... This is the moment I imagine you, dear reader, rolling your eyes and mumbling to yourself that software logs do not constitute the full information about the cluster. Only software (logs), together with hardware data (metrics), can be close to a complete information about the cluster. Then again, my imagination might not (and often doesn't) represent reality. You might not have rolled your eyes, or even noticed that hardware is missing. If that's the case, you are not paying close attention to what I wrote, and should have a good night sleep, or, at least, grab a coffee. Truth be told, we do have hardware information in Consul, but that is only the current status. We cannot analyze that data, see tendencies, find out why something happened, nor predict the future. If you are still awake, let's look at how we can log hardware status.

Before we move on, we'll remove the currently running LogStash instance, and exit the *prod* node.

```
1  docker -H tcp://logging:2375 \
2      rm -f logstash
3
4  exit
```

Logging Hardware Status

One of the first things they teach you when starting to learn to work on computers is that software runs on hardware. A software cannot run without hardware and hardware is useless without software. Since they are dependent on each other, any attempt to collects the information about the system needs to include both. We explored some of the ways to gather software data, so the next step is to try to accomplish a similar result with hardware.

We need a tool that will collect statistics about the system it is running on and has the flexibility to send that information to LogStash. Once we find and deploy such a tool, we can start using statistics it provides to find past and current performance bottlenecks and predict future system requirements. Since LogStash will send the information received from that tool to ElasticSearch, we can create formulas that will allow us to perform performance analysis and capacity planning.

One such tool is CollectD[377]. It is free open source project written in C, making it high performant and very portable. It can easily handle hundreds of thousands of data sets, and it comes with over ninety plugins.

Luckily for us, LogStash has the CollectD input plugin[378] that we can use to receive its events through a UDP port. We'll use (roles/logstash/files/syslog-collectd.conf)[https://github.com/vfarcic/ms-life-cycle/blob/master/ansible/roles/logstash/files/syslog-collectd.conf] file to configure LogStash to accept *CollectD* input. It is a copy of the (roles/logstash/files/syslog.conf)[https://github.com/vfarcic/ms-lifecycle/blob/master/ansible/roles/logstash/files/syslog.conf] with an additional input definition. Let's take a look at its *input* section.

```
1   input {
2     syslog {
3       type => syslog
4       port => 25826
5     }
6     udp {
7       port => 25827
8       buffer_size => 1452
9       codec => collectd { }
10      type => collectd
11    }
12  }
```

As you can see, all we did was add a new input that listens on the UDP port 25827, set buffer size, define that *collectd* codec should be used, and added a new field called type. With the value from the type field, we can distinguish *syslog* logs from those coming from *collectd*.

---

[377]https://collectd.org/

[378]https://www.elastic.co/guide/en/logstash/current/plugins-codecs-collectd.html

Let's run the playbook that will provision the *logging* server with LogStash and configure it to accept both *syslog* and *collectd* input.

```
1  vagrant ssh cd
2
3  ansible-playbook /vagrant/ansible/elk.yml \
4      -i /vagrant/ansible/hosts/prod \
5      --extra-vars "logstash_config=syslog-collectd.conf restore_backup=true"
```

You might have noticed the usage of the *restore_backup* variable. One of *kibana* tasks is to restore an ElasticSearch backup with the definitions of Kibana Dashboards that will be discussed soon. Backup is restored through the vfarcic/elastic-dump[379] container containing a nifty tool called elasticsearch-dump[380] by taskrabbit[381]. It can be used to create and restore ElasticSearch backups.

Now that LogStash is configured to accept *CollectD* input, let's turn our attention to the *prod* server, and install *CollectD*. We'll use the prod5.yml[382] playbook that, in addition to the tools we used before, contains the collectd[383] role. The tasks are defined in the (roles/collectd/tasks/-main.yml)[https://github.com/vfarcic/ms-lifecycle/tree/master/ansible/roles/collectd/tasks/main.yml] file. Its content is as follows.

```
1  - name: Packages are installed
2    apt:
3      name: "{{ item }}"
4    with_items: packages
5    tags: ["collectd"]
6
7  - name: Configuration is copied
8    template:
9      src: collectd.conf
10     dest: /etc/collectd/collectd.conf
11   register: config_result
12   tags: ["collectd"]
13
14 - name: Service is restarted
15   service:
16     name: collectd
17     state: restarted
18   when: config_result|changed
19   tags: ["collectd"]
```

---

[379]https://hub.docker.com/r/vfarcic/elastic-dump/

[380]https://github.com/taskrabbit/elasticsearch-dump

[381]https://github.com/taskrabbit

[382]https://github.com/vfarcic/ms-lifecycle/blob/master/ansible/prod5.yml

[383]https://github.com/vfarcic/ms-lifecycle/tree/master/ansible/roles/collectd

By this time, you should probably consider yourself an expert in Ansible, and do not need an explanation of the role. The only thing worth commenting is the roles/collectd/files/collectd.conf[384] template that represents the *CollectD* configuration. Let's take a quick look at it.

```
 1  Hostname "{{ ansible_hostname }}"
 2  FQDNLookup false
 3
 4  LoadPlugin cpu
 5  LoadPlugin df
 6  LoadPlugin interface
 7  LoadPlugin network
 8  LoadPlugin memory
 9  LoadPlugin swap
10
11  <Plugin df>
12          Device "/dev/sda1"
13          MountPoint "/"
14          FSType "ext4"
15          ReportReserved "true"
16  </Plugin>
17
18  <Plugin interface>
19          Interface "eth1"
20          IgnoreSelected false
21  </Plugin>
22
23  <Plugin network>
24          Server "{{ elk_ip }}" "25827"
25  </Plugin>
26
27  <Include "/etc/collectd/collectd.conf.d">
28          Filter ".conf"
29  </Include>
```

It starts by defining the hostname through the Ansible variable *ansible_hostname*, followed by the load of the plugins we'll use. Their names should be self-explanatory. Finally, few of the plugins have additional configurations. Please consult CollectD documentation[385] for more information about configuration format, all the plugins you can use, and their settings.

Let's run the playbook.

---

[384]https://github.com/vfarcic/ms-lifecycle/tree/master/ansible/roles/collectd/templates/collectd.conf

[385]https://collectd.org/documentation.shtml

```
1  ansible-playbook /vagrant/ansible/prod5.yml \
2      -i /vagrant/ansible/hosts/prod
```

Now that CollectD is running, we can give it a few seconds to kick in and take a look at LogStash logs.

```
1  docker -H tcp://logging:2375 \
2      logs logstash
```

A few of the entries are as follows.

```
1  {
2                   "host" => "prod",
3             "@timestamp" => "2016-02-04T18:06:48.843Z",
4                 "plugin" => "memory",
5          "collectd_type" => "memory",
6          "type_instance" => "used",
7                  "value" => 356433920.0,
8               "@version" => "1",
9                   "type" => "collectd"
10 }
11 {
12                  "host" => "prod",
13            "@timestamp" => "2016-02-04T18:06:48.843Z",
14                "plugin" => "memory",
15         "collectd_type" => "memory",
16         "type_instance" => "buffered",
17                 "value" => 31326208.0,
18              "@version" => "1",
19                  "type" => "collectd"
20 }
21 {
22                  "host" => "prod",
23            "@timestamp" => "2016-02-04T18:06:48.843Z",
24                "plugin" => "memory",
25         "collectd_type" => "memory",
26         "type_instance" => "cached",
27                 "value" => 524840960.0,
28              "@version" => "1",
29                  "type" => "collectd"
30 }
31 {
```

```
32                "host" => "prod",
33          "@timestamp" => "2016-02-04T18:06:48.843Z",
34              "plugin" => "memory",
35       "collectd_type" => "memory",
36       "type_instance" => "free",
37               "value" => 129638400.0,
38            "@version" => "1",
39                "type" => "collectd"
40  }
```

From that output, we can see that CollectD sent information about memory. The first entry contains *used*, the second *buffered*, the third *cached*, and, finally, the fourth represents *free* memory. Similar entries can be seen from the other plugins. CollectD will periodically repeat the process, thus allowing us to analyze both historical and near real-time tendencies and problems.

Since CollectD generated the new fields, let us recreate index pattern by opening http://10.100.198.202:5601/[386], navigating to the *Settings* screen, and clicking the *Create* button.

While there are many reasons to visit Kibana's *Discover* screen for software logs, there are only a few, if any, to use it for CollectD metrics, so we'll concentrate on Dashboards. That being said, even if we are not going to look at hardware data from this screen, we still need to create searches required for visualization. An example search that would retrieve all records from *collectd*, made in the *prod* host, through the *memory* plugin, would be as follows.

```
1  type: "collectd" AND host: "prod" AND plugin: "memory"
```

That line can be written (or pasted) to the *search* field in the *Discover* screen, and it will return all data matching that filter and the time set in the top-right corner of the screen. The backup we restored already contained a few saved searches that can be opened through the *Open Saved Search* button in the top-right corner of the screen. With those searches, we can proceed to visualizations. As an example, please open the *prod-df* saved search.

Kibana Dashboards consist of one or more visualizations. They can be accessed by clicking the *Visualize* button. When you open the *Visualize* screen, you'll see different types of graphs you can choose to create a new visualization. Since we restored a backup with a few visualizations I prepared, you can load one by clicking it from the *open a saved visualization* section located at the bottom of the screen. Please note that this screen appears only the first time and, from there on, the same action can be accomplished by the *Load Saved Visualization* button located on the top-right side of the screen. Go ahead and "play" a bit with Kibana visualizations. Once you're done, we'll move to dashboards.

---

[386]http://10.100.198.202:5601/

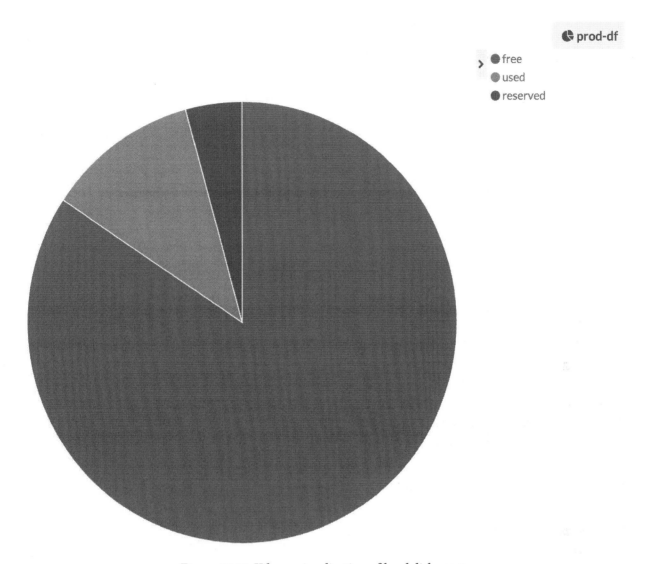

Figure 16-07: Kibana visualization of hard disk usage

Dashboard can be opened from the top menu. The backup we restored contains one so let's use it to see CollectD in action. Please click the *Dashboard* button, followed by the *Load Saved Dashboard* icon, and select the *prod* dashboard. It will display visualizations with one (and the only) *CPU* (*prod-cpu-0*), *hard disk* (*prod-df*), and *memory* (*prod-memory*) usage inside the *prod* VM. CollectD offers many more plugins than those we used. With more information coming in, this dashboard can be made much more "colorful", not to say useful. However, even though the dashboard we created does not have much activity, you can probably imagine how it could be transformed into an indispensable tool for monitoring the cluster status. There could be a separate dashboard for each server, one for the whole cluster, and so on.

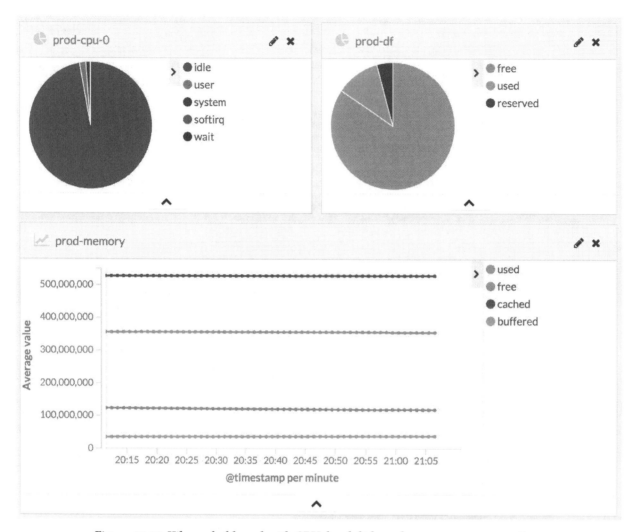

Figure 16-08: Kibana dashboard with CPU, hard disk, and memory usage over time

That was the basis of your future hardware monitoring dashboard. What else can with do with hardware information (besides looking at dashboards)?

Self-Healing Based on Hardware Data

Using hardware data for self-healing is as important as software information. Now that we have both, we can extend our system. Since we already went through all the tools and practices required for such a system, there is no real need for us to go through them in the hardware context. Instead, I'll just give you a few ideas.

Consul is already monitoring hardware utilization. With historical data in ElasticSearch, we can predict not only that the warning threshold is reached (for example 80%), but when it will get critical (for example 90%). We can analyze the data and see that, for instance, during last 30 days, disk utilization was increasing by an average rate of 0.5%, meaning that we have twenty days until it reaches the critical state. We could also draw a conclusion that even through the warning threshold is reached, it was a one time deal, and the available space is not shrinking anymore.

We could combine software and hardware metrics. With only software data, we might conclude that at peak hours, when traffic increases, we need to scale our services, by adding hardware we might change that opinion after realizing that the problem was actually in the network that cannot support such a load.

Analysis combinations we can create are limitless, and the number of formulas we'll create will grow with time and experience. Every time we pass through one door, another one opens.

Final Thoughts

This is my favorite chapter. It combines most of the practices we learned throughout the book into a grand finale. Almost everything happening on a server, be it software or hardware, system programs or those we deployed, is sent to LogStash and, from there, to ElasticSearch. And it's not only one server. With a simple *rsyslog* and *collectd* configurations applied to all your nodes, the whole cluster will be sending (almost) all the logs and events. You'll know who did what, which processes started, and which were stopped. You'll be aware what was added, and what was removed. You be alerted when a server is low on CPU, which one is about to get its hard disk full, and so on. You'll have the information about every service you deploy or remove. You'll know when were containers scaled, and when descaled.

We created a logging and monitoring system that can be described through the *Figure 16-09*.

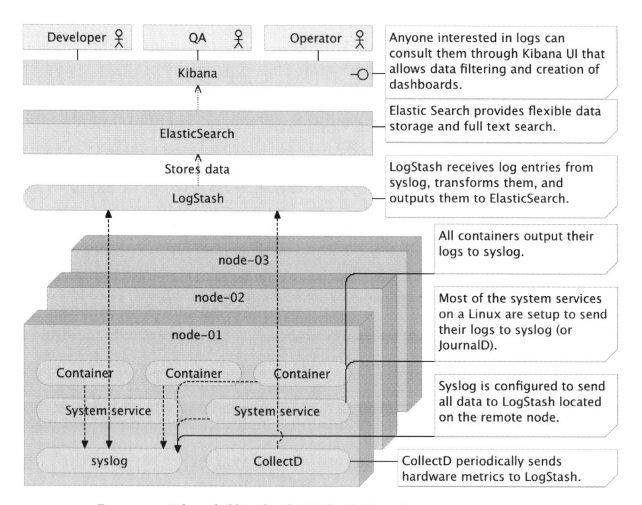

Figure 16-09: Kibana dashboard with CPU, hard disk, and memory usage over time

Knowing everything is a worthy goal and, with a system we designed, you are one step closer to fulfilling it. On top of knowing everything about the past and the present, you made the first step towards knowing the future. If you combine the practices from this chapter with those we learned in the Self-Healing Systems, your systems will be able to recuperate from failures and, in many cases, prevent a disease from happening in the first place.

Let us finish with some cleaning.

```
1  exit
2
3  vagrant destroy -f
```

Farewell

You don't learn to walk by following rules. You learn by doing, and by falling over.

– Richard Branson

The custom is to summarize the book at its end. I'll break that tradition by not writing a summary. We went through so many practices and tools that summarizing them would require quite a big chapter. After all, if, at this point, you need a summary of what you learned, it would only mean that you didn't learn as much as I hoped. Consequently, I would feel that I failed, get depressed, and never write another book.

The book was never meant to be a comprehensive cookbook. I haven't explained everything you can do with Docker. Nor I showed you all the power behind Ansible. As a matter a fact, I haven't gone into great details with any of the tools. Such an approach would require dedication of a single book for each of them. The world is full of cookbooks. I wanted to write something different. I wanted to write a book that connects the dots between different practices and tools. I wanted to show you the logic behind some of the processes we applied. However, since I am a very hands-on type of person, my way of learning logic and processes involves a lot of practice and a lot of dedication. For that reason, the book is full of many hands-on examples. I thought that the best approach is to learn by doing. I hope I accomplished my goal. I hope I opened some doors that you might not have known existed, or you didn't know how to step through.

Let us not end the journey here. Let's continue in a more direct manner. Please use the Disqus channel The DevOps 2.0 Toolkit[387] if you'd like to discuss any aspect of the book. If you got stuck somewhere, if you failed to grasp something, or if you disagree with one of my views (or even all of them), just post it on the channel. I created it today while writing the final words. The problem is that nobody wants to be the first to post something in an empty place. I encourage you to be that first person. Others will benefit from our discussion and join in. If, on the other hand, you prefer a more one-on-one conversation, please send me an email to viktor@farcic.com, contact me through HangOuts or Skype (my user is vfarcic), or come to Barcelona and invite me for a beer.

If you would like to get notifications about book updates, please subscribe to the mailing list[388].

I will continue writing posts in my blog TechnologyConversations.com[389] until, one day, I gather the courage to start writing a new book. Maybe it will be *The DevOps 3.0 Toolkit*. Or, more likely, it will be something entirely different. Time will tell.

Keep learning, keep exploring, and keep improving the way you work. That is the only way to move forward in our line of business.

---

[387]https://disqus.com/home/channel/thedevops20toolkit/
[388]http://eepurl.com/bXonVj
[389]http://technologyconversations.com/

Good night, and good luck.

Viktor Farcic

5th of February 2016, Barcelona

Made in the USA
Middletown, DE
03 November 2016